STOLEN PRIDE

ALSO BY ARLIE RUSSELL HOCHSCHILD

Strangers in Their Own Land: Anger and Mourning on the American Right

So How's the Family? And Other Essays

The Outsourced Self: Intimate Life in Market Times

Global Woman: Nannies, Maids, and Sex Workers in the New Economy (co-editor)

The Commercialization of Intimate Life: Notes from Home and Work

The Time Bind: When Work Becomes Home and Home Becomes Work

The Second Shift: Working Families and the Revolution at Home

The Managed Heart: Commercialization of Human Feeling

The Unexpected Community: Portrait of an Old Age Subculture

Coleen the Question Girl

STOLEN PRIDE

LOSS, SHAME, AND THE RISE OF THE RIGHT

Arlie Russell Hochschild

THE
NEW
PRESS

NEW YORK
LONDON

Published in the United States by The New Press, New York, 2024

Distributed by Two Rivers Distribution

ISBN 978-1-62097-646-3 (hc)
ISBN 978-1-62097-647-0 (ebook)

Library of Congress Cataloging-in-Publication Data

Names: Hochschild, Arlie Russell, 1940- author.
Title: Stolen pride: loss, shame, and the rise of the right/by Arlie Russell Hochschild.
Description: New York : The New Press, 2024. | Includes bibliographical
references and index. | Summary: "An exploration of the "pride paradox" that
has given the right's appeals such resonance"—Provided by publisher.
Identifiers: LCCN 2024005179 | ISBN 9781620976463
(hardcover) | ISBN 9781620976470 (ebook)
Subjects: LCSH: Political culture—Kentucky—Pikeville. | Conservatism—Kentucky—
Pikeville. | Right and left (Political science)—Kentucky—Pikeville. | Public opinion—
Kentucky—Pikeville. | Social change—Political aspects—Kentucky—Pikeville. |
Group identity—Political aspects—Kentucky—Pikeville. | Pikeville (Ky.)—Social
conditions—21st century. | United States—Politics and government—Public opinion.
Classification: LCC F459.P55 H63 2024 | DDC 320.520973--dc23/eng/20240403
LC record available at https://lccn.loc.gov/2024005179

The New Press publishes books that promote and enrich public discussion and understanding of
the issues vital to our democracy and to a more equitable world. These books are made possible
by the enthusiasm of our readers; the support of a committed group of donors, large and small;
the collaboration of our many partners in the independent media and the not-for-profit sector;
booksellers, who often hand-sell New Press books; librarians; and above all by our authors.

www.thenewpress.com

Composition by Dix Digital Prepress and Design

This book was set in Fairfield LT Std

Printed in the United States of America

2 4 6 8 10 9 7 5 3 1

For Joan Cole

Telling a story is like reaching into a granary
full of wheat and drawing out a handful.
There is always more to tell than can be told.

—Wendell Berry, *Jayber Crow*

Contents

CONTENTS

STOLEN PRIDE

PART ONE

The March

1

A Polite Voice

The voice was polite. The tone was measured. The accent, that of an outsider to Appalachia. The call came on an early April morning in 2017, as red and white buds on mountainside redwood and dogwood trees were slowly opening a window to spring around Pikeville, Kentucky.

The phone had rung at the office of Donovan Blackburn, Pikeville's city manager. "My assistant poked her head into my office and asked me what we should do about a request for a permit to hold a march here down Main Street. The name was Matthew Heimbach." A tall, lean, fortyish man with keen blue eyes, graying blond hair, and an unflappable manner, Blackburn would later tell me, "So we Googled Heimbach and found out that he was a neo-Nazi." Donovan often used the word *we* to refer to his expanding team, which was later widely praised for its resilience in handling all that was to happen.

"Wherever Heimbach goes, he leaves a trail of violence behind him," Donovan would tell me. Indeed, only nine months earlier, the man with the polite voice had co-led a white nationalist march in Sacramento, California, where people were beaten, kicked, and dragged, and ten were hospitalized with stab wounds.

Pikeville is nestled below a mountain in a struggling county within Kentucky's 5th Congressional District (KY-5), the second-poorest of the nation's 435 congressional districts as well as the whitest. The city had once been the hub of a thriving coal region. "We kept the nation's lights on!" I would hear. "We fueled World War II!" Indeed, busy trains once hissed and screeched along a railroad that passed through the middle of town transporting heaps of black gold dug from the surrounding mountains into the open mouth of industrial America. But nowadays coal was leaving, drugs had come in, and the region was struggling. "People don't really know about hard times here," one person explained, "or else they blame us for them." In recent years, Pike County voters had once been Roosevelt, Kennedy, and Bill Clinton Democrats. But the county had now become one of five counties in the nation most rapidly shifting Republican.

White nationalist protests had been erupting elsewhere across the nation. In the previous three months before that 2017 phone call, such groups had marched in Seattle, Washington, and Lake Oswego, Oregon. In Minneapolis, a white man shot five Black Lives Matter protesters. The white supremacist Knights Party held a Love Your Heritage flag rally in Harrison, Arkansas. In Berkeley, California, over a thousand opponents clashed with supporters of the flamboyant alt-right speaker Milo Yiannopoulos. Although California bans permitless guns in public spaces, the public university could not ban non-student California citizens from its campus, and videos would reveal masked and black-clad participants smashing glass windows and setting fires, causing the university $800,000 in damages.

In 2000, the Southern Poverty Law Center counted 599 hate groups, but by the time of Heimbach's phone call in 2017, that number had risen to 954. Kentucky alone was headquarters for eleven. Extremist media outlets such as Alt-Right TV, White Pride Radio, and White Resistance News were also on the rise, reporting on their public events and searching for supporters.

Meanwhile, Pike County, like nearly all of Kentucky's 120 counties, had declared itself a Second Amendment sanctuary, in which gun restrictions did not apply. Heimbach's white nationalist marchers and their opponents, if over age twenty-one, were eligible to openly carry fully loaded guns, without background checks or permits, including assault weapons, with no restrictions on their magazine capacity. As a "stand your ground" state, Kentucky also authorizes gun carriers to shoot back in self-defense and in what they consider the defense of others. And since 2010, gun deaths in Kentucky had been on the rise.

As Donovan Blackburn would tell me, "I don't believe in white nationalism. I grew up close by here in Greasy Creek. My ancestors lived here. My family lives here now. I went through school here. The people I come from believe in right to life, Second Amendment, and human decency. When someone comes into your community, you offer them love, dignity, and respect. We have minorities—Blacks, Jews, Muslims—and they deserve to feel as safe as anyone else. We'll do all we can to protect them. But we're a free country. We honor free speech. We're good people here."

Journey into the Divide

I had come to Pikeville with a growing concern about the nation's growing political divide, a keen interest in an unfamiliar place, and an idea about emotion in politics that I thought could illuminate the storm I felt brewing. In my last book, *Strangers in Their Own Land: Anger and Mourning on the American Right*, I had ventured into the bayous and neighborhoods around the petrochemical plants of southern Louisiana and spent time getting to know people on the conservative side of the divide. There I uncovered a half-buried story—what I came to call a "deep story." In it, many felt as if they were standing in line waiting to move forward toward the American Dream, I found. But the line was stalled, because—as it seemed to them—women, African Americans, immigrants, and refugees were "line-cutters." The people in line were turning to right-wing politics to stop this perceived injustice.

At the time, though, I did not foresee the continuing escalation of anger at "the other side" to hate and talk of "revenge." A Pike County businessman and ardent Trump supporter predicted that "the 2024 election is going to be violent. We've been polarized before, but now conversation between us has stopped. It's like 1861. We're leading up to a civil war." In her research on preppers—Americans preparing for disaster—sociologist Kirstin Krusell observes that interest in prepping has surged in the aftermath of recent presidential elections, both when Barack Obama won in 2008 and again when Donald Trump won in 2016. I wanted to "go upstream" from anger to the experiences and circumstances that fueled it.

An idea had gripped the American right with electrical force and cleaved the nation: the idea that the 2020 election had been "stolen." Sixty percent of all Americans—90 percent of Democrats and 23 percent of Republicans—believed the election was won fairly. But Trump declared it "stolen" and promised retribution.

I wanted to move my focus from the Deep South to Appalachia, with a focus on eastern Kentucky. Each of the nation's regions has its own political tradition, history, economy, and lore. For Louisiana, it was that of the great plantations; for Appalachia, it was one of isolated settlements in a rugged mountainous landscape. Each lent a different tone to the reception of this "electric" idea.

Louisiana had long been Republican—a stationary heart, it seemed, of the right. Kentucky had been moderate but had recently moved right. According to a 2023 analysis by the Cook Political Report, in 1996 KY-5 sat almost at the nation's political center, with nearly 235 congressional districts rated as more liberal and 200 as more conservative. But by 2023, compared to all other of the nation's 435 congressional districts, Kentucky's 5th Congressional District had become the second-most-conservative congressional district of all. Together with Oklahoma's 2nd Congressional District, KY-5 "gave Donald Trump two of his five biggest local margins of victory in both 2016 and 2020." Indeed, 80 percent of KY-5—and Pike County—voted for Trump first in 2016 and again in 2020. I wanted to learn why.

For much of American history, the Republican Party attracted anti-tax, well-to-do opponents to government welfare programs and this remains true to this day. But today it also attracts many poor whites. In 2014, Kentucky's 5th Congressional District came in last of all the nation's districts on a "Well-Being Index" constructed by Gallup and Healthways. In life evaluation, work environment, emotional health, physical health, healthy behaviors, and access to health care, the region ranked at the bottom. At the same time, 36 percent of KY-5 residents were covered by Medicaid, which the Republican Party had traditionally disapproved of and wish to limit. During COVID, nearly half of the residents of Pike County—one of thirty-one counties in Kentucky's 5th Congressional District—were on Medicaid. As for the right-leaning state of Kentucky itself, 38 percent of its budget came from the federal government. My picture of the Republican Party didn't fit the people I was getting to know, and I wondered what I was missing.

Much of my past work has focused on women, but the study of right-wing politics brought me to men. For, in 2020, 58 percent of the nation's white voters favored Donald Trump—including 61 percent of white men, and 70 percent of white men without a bachelor's degree.

Behind this trend seemed to me to lie a certain crisis for men. As Helena Norberg-Hodge noted in her study of Asian rural cultures under pressure to modernize, it is young males who most exhibit the strains of this trend. In the United States, marches like the one Matthew Heimbach was planning for Pikeville and militant right-wing groups as a whole were virtually all male. Blue-collar men have proved most vulnerable to so-called diseases of despair—addiction, alcoholism, and suicide—a scourge for which Appalachia has sadly become ground zero.

To some on the left, those same four words—*rural, white, blue-collar, male*—evoke a stereotype, one that I wished to explore from the inside rather than judge from afar. For it occurred to me that a close look at this vulnerable patch of red America—Kentucky's 5th Congressional District—might offer clues to red America as a whole, and indeed to the winds of white nationalism blowing around the world. More than anything, I wanted to talk in depth with men who called this place home and to understand how they saw the trends impacting them, and to talk in the same way with the white nationalist who hoped to recruit them.

So my focus became a small city in Appalachia and, within it, primarily men. As it happened, it was in this very region, within this population, that I discovered a perfect storm—something that Pike County shared with much of red-state America. Since the 1970s, red states have taken the brunt of globalization: offshoring, automation, and union decline have left red states poorer and in worse health than blue states, with less well-financed schools, an increased susceptibility to accidents, and a lower life expectancy. Adding to these strains were other, newer ones—sickness and deaths from COVID-19 and climate-change-related storms.

But compared to the rest of red-state America, Pike County took an even bigger hit. Its traditional economy was in decline. Coal camps were long closed but their remains stood as reminders. Rumbling tipples that once sorted and cleaned coal now stood silent, like giant long-legged crickets. But as jobs were leaving, a drug crisis was coming in. A rogue drug company, Purdue Pharma, had targeted eastern Kentucky and West Virginia with false claims about its painkiller OxyContin, leading to widespread addiction, overdose deaths, and great personal distress. As if to take advantage of these two blows, a white nationalist march was now coming to Pikeville offering a "solution" to the community's woes. Pikeville seemed like an epicenter of a larger crisis.

How, I wondered, were the residents Donovan Blackburn so lovingly described managing this storm? Were they turning with trust to the federal government? Only with ambivalence.[30] In 1964, 77 percent of Americans declared their trust in the federal government "to do the right thing always" or "most of the time." But by 2023, this had shrunk to 16 percent. Central to Ronald Reagan's message in the 1980s had been a mocking critique of government services and regulations, a critique echoed by Republican president George H. W. Bush and Democratic president Bill Clinton, inspiring a general distrust of the federal government. Over half of Republicans want more power to devolve to the states, compared to only 18 percent of Democrats who do, but trust in government has declined in both parties.

Some voters favor a "strong leader," even one who feels "above" voting. When asked by the Democracy Fund Voter Study Group whether they want a "strong leader who does not have to bother with Congress and elections," 24 percent of Americans answered yes. Desire for such a strong leader can rise on either the right or left, of course, but in a 2017 global Pew survey of ten advanced democracies, those people favoring such a "strong leader" were two or three times more common on the right. In the United States today, 27 percent of those on the right call for such a leader, as do 14 percent of those on the left. Two years into his presidency, in 2018, Donald Trump praised Chinese president Xi Jinping: "He's now president for life. . . . I think it's great. Maybe we'll give that a shot someday."

"President for life"—was this said in jest, I wondered, or in a spirit of exploratory seriousness? If serious, what questions could this raise for Donovan Blackburn's fellow townspeople and for us all? The question has resonance outside the United States, too: since 2000, the political scientist Cas Mudde observed, the world's democracies have experienced a post–World War II wave in the radical right. By 2020 some quarter of the world population had come to live under authoritarian leadership, a vision of which Matthew Heimbach was to offer Pikeville: a "strong man" above the rule of law, the Constitution, or checks and balances. Many of the preconditions for such a wave have come to exist in the United States and elsewhere in the West—distrust of government, dismay about immigration, economic uncertainty and discontent among those outside the industrial-financial centers of power and organized labor. I wondered if America would join or resist this wave. And I wondered how this all felt to the Appalachians who kindly allowed me into their lives.

Pride and Shame

I took with me to Pikeville a deep interest in the emotions underlying politics—and in particular the emotions of pride and shame. If a leader appeals to a follower, it is usually emotion to which he or she appeals. Emotion is not a casual add-on to the cognitive talk of policies we think of as politics. On the contrary, politics can be the platter on which emotions are delivered. And to understand politicized emotion, we need to understand what people have gone through and care about.

Many Appalachians I came to know were caught in a "pride paradox." On one hand, rural KY-5 Republicans felt fierce pride in hard work and personal responsibility. If you succeeded, you felt proud. If you failed, you felt shame. On the other hand, their beleaguered economy greatly lowered their chance of success and vulnerability to shame. This presented its victims with a dilemma: how to respond to unwarranted shame. People devised various ways to respond: turn shame inward, project shame outward, or find a creative solution to the paradox.

As I sat down to interview eastern Kentuckians, I always set my voice recorder on the table between us. Before pushing record, I explained my purpose and asked permission to record their words. "If for any reason you wish something you tell me to be off the record, please let me know. I'll turn the recorder off," I would say. I noticed the times when a person pointed or nodded toward the tape recorder, telling me to turn it off. Almost never was the nod to protect the speaker him- or herself; it was nearly always to protect the pride of loved ones.

Often such stories centered on drugs. One person sorrowfully described a brother who impregnated a seventeen-year-old girl and moved away to take a high-paying factory job in order to be able to pay child support. Meanwhile, the young mother became depressed, then addicted to drugs, and was forced to give up the baby to foster care. Another man described his beloved dad, a laid-off coal miner who hitchhiked rides to other mines seeking work but later fell into drugs and overdosed. This was a poignant reminder that we don't simply feel our own sadness or shame; we also carry the sadness and shame of others.

It began to occur to me that just as Americans live in a material economy, we also live in an equally important pride economy. For while pride and shame always *feel* personal, the roots of these feelings lie in larger social circumstances. Among the people I met, I discovered many bases of pride—regional pride, work ethic pride, bad-boy pride, recovery pride. But what happens when a community's primary source of pride—well-paid jobs—leaves, or when old skills or folkways become useless and devalued? What happens when—in the absence of real solutions to real problems—feelings of loss and shame become the "ore" for which politicians prospect?

Top to Bottom, Side to Side

I wanted to understand the "perfect storm" from as many vantage points as I could, top to bottom and side to side. In taking this pulse, I talked to the city's protectors—those such as Donovan Blackburn—and also to the town's provocateur, Matthew Heimbach. I talked with potential victims of the march—an African American resident, a Jewish refugee from Nazi Germany, and a Muslim immigrant doctor who oversaw a mosque. I talked to city leaders—a former governor of Kentucky, a mayor, assistant mayor, a judge, a car dealer, business owner, teacher, a lawn cutter, road crew leader and medical researcher, artist, pastor and others, to felons and recovering drug addicts. I talked with Democrats, independents, Republicans, and political opt-outs. All faces in an imagined typical crowd, I wanted to learn how they felt about the march, about their lives, about politics, and about pride. Indeed, for each person I came to know, I wanted to understand his story of pride and shame, his pride biography, as it were.

I also hoped to learn how the people I came to know felt about reaching out to people on the other side of our deepening political divide. At the moment, Americans seemed to be doing poorly at talking across it—especially, as it turns out, white liberals. According to a revealing 2019 Pew poll, 45 percent of Americans have stopped talking about politics with someone because of something the other person said. This included 45 percent of conservative Republicans but 60 percent of liberal Democrats. White people were also more likely to cut off conversation than Black people: 50 percent versus 37 percent. What can we learn, I wondered, from those who were keeping the gates of communication open?

As a "flatlander" from a West Coast blue state who wanted to get to know "mountain people," as some called themselves, I planned to take my time. I've lived nearly all my life in coastal cities and had previously traveled to Kentucky only once, on an academic invitation. But I was not a stranger to rural life, for I had spent childhood summers on my grandmother's dairy farm in rural Maine. By the time I was born, the cows were gone, but the barn, the milk shed, the scent, the lore, the work ethic, and a large, weedy garden remained. And with this in my mix of memories, I set off for Pike County, Kentucky, in 2017.

Pikeville carries with it many traditions from America's past; it is 140 miles from Lexington, a station on a major route of the Underground Railroad. It is 260 miles from Fort Knox, the world's most secure vault of concrete and steel, storing over half of the Treasury's gold. It is 66 miles from Blair Mountain, the site of the nation's largest post–Civil War insurrection, in which coal companies dropped bombs from World War I–era planes on striking coal miners—Black, white, and foreign-born, many of them veterans. It is 51 miles from Inez, Kentucky, where in 1964 President Lyndon Johnson famously inaugurated the War on Poverty—which was often recalled, I found, with downcast eyes or shaking heads. Johnson had vowed to "set the people of this region out on a highway of hope." But decades after Johnson's visit, many I talked to felt the promise unfulfilled. Many I came to know in the region felt impatient for progress and also the need to ward off a cluck-clucking outside world that seemed to either ignore or shame them. Pikeville was also 225 miles from Sinking Spring Farm, Kentucky, the birthplace of Abraham Lincoln, whose call for national and racial unity seemed a message for our time.

Then, in April 2017, flyers began appearing on Pikeville doorsteps with an image of a tall, strong dad fondly tossing a smiling child in the air, an adoring mother at his side. The flyer was addressed to "white working families" and notified residents of the upcoming white nationalist march.

Donovan Blackburn had already gotten to work. "After we got the call from Heimbach, I called the city attorney to find out the marchers' rights and our city's rights. Then I called our chief of police, the sheriff's department, and the state police." Just as he did, even worse news came in. "I got a call from the Department of Homeland Security. They'd been monitoring Facebook sites for certain buzzwords—KKK, the NSM [the National Socialist Movement, a neo-Nazi organization], the League of the South, the *n*-word. Counting the white nationalists and Antifa and other protesters from Louisville, Homeland Security told me they think we should prepare for two thousand, three thousand, even six thousand marchers and protesters. Here in Pikeville we're only about seven thousand residents. I won't say I panicked."

Word spread and offers of help poured in. "When I heard about the march," the mayor of the nearby town of Coal Run told me, "I called Donovan and asked, 'How can I help? Do you need extra police coverage?'" Donovan had other offers of help too: "The governor called us and offered to put the National Guard on standby. State troopers were ready to be bused in. The FBI called. Even Fish and Wildlife offered to lend us a hand."

Donovan Blackburn also received a more worrisome offer of help. "A guy from the Proud Boys called. 'We've seen all the trouble Antifa caused in Berkeley,' they told me. 'We carry guns and we're coming in to support you.' I told the man, 'We appreciate your offer, but we're not asking for you to do that.'"

Then, weighing it all—the violence trailing Heimbach, the national rise of right-wing extremism, Kentucky gun laws, Pike County's hospitable culture, his personal commitment to its culture and freedom of speech—Donovan Blackburn made a decision.

"I took a breath. Then I issued the permit."

2

"We're Good People Here"

A gem-like city of about seven thousand, Pikeville is set in a horseshoe-shaped valley gracefully looped around a small mountain, and sits at a fork of the Big Sandy River in the rolling coal-studded mountains of eastern Kentucky. Coal jobs had gone out. Drugs had come in. White nationalists were preparing to march into town.

But on the surface, this "perfect storm" was hard to see. In fact, Pikeville seemed to be quietly thriving. In June, baskets of white and purple petunias hung from streetlamp posts down a tidy, shop-lined Main Street, as did poster-sized photographs of the beaming faces of high school graduates. Anchored by a regional hospital and small university, Pikeville was described as "rich" by a number of people from the surrounding hollers, which were "poor." Tours showcased the dramas of the once deadly backwoods feud between the McCoys and Hatfields—over the claim of a stolen pig. You could buy a Butcher Holler key chain or *Coal Miner's Daughter* DVD honoring local country-and-western singer turned national star Loretta Lynn.

Pikeville seemed to be a way station between bigger cities—Louisville, Cincinnati, and Detroit, to which workers migrated in lean times—and the hollers, where clustered homes of kin and friends lined narrow roads that wound down hillsides to the valley floor. Well-kept homes were down the road from rusted-out abandoned trailers. A pastor described Pikeville as "politely Republican." An African American administrator who had moved to Pikeville from New York described it as "safer than my neighborhood in Queens."

As well-paid jobs were leaving the region, so were some residents. It was estimated that the population of Pike County, currently 59,000, would decline to 48,000 by 2040. Still, the town's shop displays seemed to appeal to a desire to stay. Next to Bridgett's Quilting on Second Street, a local shop featured a fireplace, a large sign saying HOME, a Christmas wreath, and a sign that read WHERE I WANT TO BE. A featured female artist wrote, as part of her encased display, "Inspired by my great grannies . . . from stringing garden beans for canning to baking scratch-made cornbread, these east Kentucky ladies done it all without a single complaint." Was this, I wondered, an appeal to restless leavers, to defiant stayers, or to nostalgic tourists? For as the Kentucky-born author and activist Wendell Berry mused during a visit, "After Americans leave the land, we keep on moving and become permanent migrants." *But maybe*, the Pikeville shop displays seemed to say, *one day you'll come back and stay*.

City leaders were trying hard to bring good jobs to the county. The president of the University of Pikeville—or UPike, as it is affectionately called—had publicized a series of interviews with entrepreneurs who were planning to bring industry to the area. Two prominent retired coal mine owners determined to reskill and upskill laid-off coal miners started a training center in programming and digital design called Bit Source, housed in a renovated Coca-Cola bottling plant. "A coal miner truly is a tech worker that gets dirty," one of them, Rusty Justice, explained to me brightly. "Motivation through starvation," one of Bit Source's developers quipped. Bit Source was helping some, but the town was on a constant lookout for more and better jobs.

Dart on a Board or Sitting Duck?

Meanwhile, residents had begun debating: why would a neo-Nazi choose to bring trouble *here*, to peaceful Pikeville? Two explanations began to circulate. The first was pure chance. "That guy tacked up a map of the U.S. on a dartboard and threw a dart," a businessman surmised. A Hampton Inn hotel clerk agreed: "That guy went through the alphabet and came to the *P*'s." A powderman, who sets dynamite sticks into mountainsides to widen roadways, said, "If extremists are marching in Minneapolis, Minnesota, and Berkeley, California, and now eastern Kentucky, they're trying to unite the right and they figure the right is located in bits and pieces all over the country."

The second explanation was that eastern Kentucky was an easy target, "a sitting duck." It was just the sort of place—poor, white, rural, forgotten—where the white nationalists thought they could get a hearing. "Oh, the neo-Nazis want a race war, so they're coming to the whitest place they can find, imagining we're racists—which we're not," one man told me solemnly. A middle school math teacher surmised, "The neo-Nazis are looking for a place that's down-and-out, where good jobs have gone out, drugs poured in, and no one is noticing or helping. That's us!"

The marchers were to bring with them two ideas—one about race, the other about the undemocratic exercise of power. Had Matthew Heimbach pored over recent national surveys, he would have discovered a link between Pike County's demographic portrait (again, nearly all white, older, rural, high-school-educated, victims of economic downturns, native-born, poor) and views about white identity. The American National Election Studies asked some six thousand white respondents, "How important is being white to your identity?" Answers ranged from "extremely" to "not at all." Of whites with a bachelor's or higher degree and in the highest income bracket, only 15 percent said that their race was "extremely" or "very important." Among those with a high school degree or less and whose households fell in the lowest income bracket, 30 percent answered that being white was "extremely" or "very important." So, the study suggested, even in what Matthew Heimbach would imagine a "promising demographic," two-thirds of the poorest and least-educated whites did *not* feel their race was "extremely" or "very important" to their identity.

Even in KY-5, the nation's whitest congressional district, "white" was also not a simple category. As the historian David Hackett Fischer writes in *Albion's Seed*, in the eighteenth century many Appalachian whites considered themselves "mixed," and some as nonwhite. Early on, the term *mixed* referred to the mix of Irish, Scottish, Italian, German, English, and Scandinavian, in varying proportions. Later *mixed* also referred to those with Native American and African ancestry. When I first explained my project to Mayor Andrew H. Scott of Coal Run, he kindly offered to guide my inquiry, telling me proudly, "Actually, I'm Melungeon." This refers to a mixture of white, Native American, and African American heritage. "Here in Appalachia, a number of us are."

But economic downturns can also alter people's feelings about race— at least for a time. In their paper "Tides and Prejudice: Racial Attitudes During Downturns in the United States, 1979–2014," economists Arjun Jayadev and Robert Johnson trace racial attitudes between 1979 and 2014—before and after the 2008 downturn. White racial hostility rose, the researchers discovered, during periods of high white unemployment. At the same time, in a finding that is both hopeful and intriguing, this hostility fell when employment rose. This, in turn, suggests the idea that anxiety caused by one thing, in this case lost jobs, can fuel hostility regarding another, race. In the same way, anxiety about mass shootings, COVID, or climate change may fuel preexisting feelings about race or democracy. Red states generally and Appalachia in particular have suffered a bigger hit from many forms of adversity than the rest of the country. To what degree, I wondered, can skilled political leaders divert vast pipelines of emotional fuel? That might figure into an educated guess as to where white nationalist extremists might find open ears.

In the past, the federal government had given a hand to hard-hit regions of the nation, though it had now increasingly become an object of complaint—as too big, too profligate, too suspiciously "deep." Yet in the upcoming march, Matthew Heimbach's men would march past the federal courthouse—built in 1940 by the Works Progress Administration (WPA)—once associated with good government and still in service.

Curiously, the area's biggest example of federal aid was the extraordinary Cut-Through, constructed by the U.S. Army Corps of Engineers between 1973 and 1987. Time and again, I was asked, "Do you know about the Cut-Through?" or "Have you seen the overlook?" (which offers a view of it). Learning I was new in town, a civic-minded retired coal mine owner kindly drove me to see it. A bronze plaque there described the Cut-Through as "the largest engineering feat in the US and second in the world only to the Panama Canal. . . . It eliminated the disastrous flooding of the Big Sandy River by moving a 4-lane highway, a railroad and a river through the mountain." A tourism website described Pikeville as a town that "dared to dream big" and the "tiny town that moved a mountain." Pikeville is now a clean, dry, charming regional center, and the Cut-Through itself stands as a proud tourist site. Buried in tourist bureau write-ups, and missing from my conversations with residents, however, was a memory that the federal government had funded it.

Local Touch, Distant Dream

As Donovan Blackburn expanded his team of helpers, it came to include the dapper, bespectacled eighty-one-year-old former Democratic governor of Kentucky and emeritus chancellor of the University of Pikeville, Paul Patton. A native of the county, Patton had skyrocketed from a modest life into the governorship, from which he successfully pressed for better schools and jobs. Now retired, he was seated in his leather chair in a grand office at the University of Pikeville, images of his social ascent surrounding him in dozens of framed photos—smiling male faces, handshakes with other governors, senators, and presidents. Rising spryly from behind his desk, he moved around his chair and pointed to a great mural-sized oil painting of an expansive green lawn and pathway guiding the eye to a majestic, white-pillared home: the governor's mansion.

Patton is memorialized again in a nine-foot bronze statue at the bottom of a flight of ninety-nine steps leading up to the entrance to the university and to the office where we sat talking. The statue's ringed right hand crosses his chest, holding a large tablet, a replica of the state of Kentucky. He wears an academic robe over a business suit, a large volume in his other hand. Patton's bronze gaze is directed out at his beloved Appalachia.

Born in a retrofitted corn silo in Fallsburg, Kentucky, eighty miles north of Pikeville, Patton recounted, "We ate from the garden and hunted rabbit, squirrels, hogs. We got a refrigerator when I was eleven, and a car when I was twelve. I went to a four-room elementary school built by the WPA. We didn't use a telephone until after I graduated from high school." Patton's father was an itinerant schoolteacher whose own education at a local Baptist school he had reluctantly ended in the eighth grade. "Our family followed my dad, job to job. Later to earn more money, he was a construction worker on the railroad.

"My mother quit school in the eighth grade too, but she was an avid reader of *Woman's Home Companion* and *Good Housekeeping* and got the idea to set flowers on the dining room table of our tiny house." The father of the woman Patton met in college and married owned a coal mine and paid for the last two years of Patton's engineering degree, later taking him into the business. In the 1970s, Patton himself became a coal mine owner, a millionaire, and a politician on the rise—from Pike County judge-executive to deputy secretary of state, leader of the Kentucky Democratic Party, and then governor of Kentucky.

"I'm known as Kentucky's jobs-and-education-governor," Patton told me, beaming. "When I first served in 1995, Kentucky was near the bottom in education. Thank God for Mississippi," he chuckled, "otherwise we'd have been dead last. But in my second term, in 2003, we rose to mid-rank."

Kentucky now ranks thirty-first out of the fifty states in education. Patton had suffered setbacks: a sex scandal, a divorce, a drug-addicted son. But in one of the nation's hardest-hit regions, Patton, like Kentucky-born Abraham Lincoln, had climbed his own ninety-nine steps to the American Dream.

Like nearly everyone I spoke with, Patton deplored the neo-Nazis, upheld their right to march, but feared the stain of extremism on his proud town. The Kentucky legislature likewise feared that shame would be cast on the entire state. Weeks before the march was due to happen in Pikeville, it passed a resolution by voice vote, condemning the Traditionalist Workers Party, the group headed by the permit requester, Matthew Heimbach. "While they have a First Amendment right to espouse their hatred," the resolution said, "we have a First Amendment right to stand up and say we're not going to accept this in our community." Sentiment from the top was clear.

Nevertheless, the march would serve as a preview of what white nationalism might look like when and if it appeared in other local towns. Rough-looking, heavily armed men in boots, with short-cropped hair, dark glasses, sullen, determined, fierce—that would be the look. The men would march rigidly, conjuring a vision of an infamous German who rose to power with the support of 30 percent of German voters in 1933. A weak and isolated left had been blamed for Germany's shameful defeat in World War I, and the Nazi Party rose on its promises to win back the pride that had been lost with that defeat. Matthew Heimbach's march would evoke this man and time—and so, seem strange, faraway, un-American, and to the vast majority, unwelcome. After all, the local hillside cemeteries were dotted with small American flags and Veterans of Foreign Wars grave markers and floral bouquets. "A lot of our grandfathers and great-grandfathers fought the Nazis," a retired nurse told me as I watched her wash an ancestor's gravestone, "and we haven't forgotten."

Meanwhile, the current president of the University of Pikeville, having refused to allow white nationalist protesters on campus, had just received a death threat. Who issued it? No one knew. The Pikeville city manager also faced risks. "The FBI warned me that my own name was being used on Twitter," Donovan said, adding calmly, "in a negative way."

Donovan prepared for the use of massive force while minimizing public alarm. "We planned for anti-riot armored vehicles to be on hand, along with National Guard personnel, but we decided to keep them in the town's Expo Center, out of sight," he said. Then came a last-minute inspiration. "In other cities, the extremists often hid their identity," Donovan explained, "so the Pikeville City Commission passed an emergency order: 'no masks or hoods to be worn in public places.' This way we can see their faces and know who they are. We also added a misdemeanor penalty and fine of up to $250 and maximum stay of fifty days in jail."

Meanwhile, the University of Pikeville's energetic chaplain, Rob Musick, had an idea. A forty-one-year-old man with a luminous smile, in rimless glasses and clerical collar, bearded, balding, Musick paid a visit to retired Chancellor Patton in his spacious office.

"Pike County's hit tough times. The last thing we need is outside extremists coming here," the chaplain told Patton. "In the news, that's going to give us a black eye. We'll look as bad as Berkeley, the last thing we need." But, Musick continued, "we need to teach our students how to deal with extremists. Otherwise, they won't know how to. So shouldn't we engage Matthew Heimbach in an on-campus dialogue?"

Drawing on the full authority of his many high offices—as Kentucky's two-time governor, CEO of a coal company, university president, and chancellor—Paul Patton stood before the young chaplain, arms folded. "He got very quiet and red in the face," the chaplain later recalled.

Then Patton declared:

"Free speech? Yes.

"Humanizing exchange? Of course.

"But *hate* speech from a neo-Nazi thug on our *own* University of Pikeville campus?

"Absolutely not!"

3

The Pride Paradox

That's all right,
That's okay,
You're goin' to work for us
One day!

"In my freshman year at Pikeville Independent High School, I remember Lexington High football team came down to play us. They thought they were better than us. They were city. We were hicks. They were rich. We were poor. They were sure they were going to butcher us. But that was our hick chant against them, because in the 1980s, we were in the middle of a coal boom. Many of my classmates were overnight rich—you could say nouveau riche. There were Mercedeses in our school parking lot.

"Coal!" Andrew Scott was restraining his Great Dane, who was wrestling with the family's rambunctious Australian shepherd, named Chief (short for "police chief," bought and named in honor of law enforcement after he saw police being denigrated by Antifa protestors in Portland, Oregon). A beloved, two-term mayor of Coal Run, Scott was sitting in the wood-paneled study of his spacious mountaintop home, surrounded by a wide skirt of green lawn. On one wall were mounted heads of elk and deer. To the side of the stone fireplace stood a decorative foot-and-a-half square rock of shiny coal—near its place of use but on display. On the mantel was a collection of brass elephants, which Andrew's paternal grandmother had collected over the years, representing the family's political leaning even back through the 1880s, when Democrats had a three-to-one advantage in the Kentucky state legislature. Scott was from an old Pike County family that had purchased vast tracts of mineral rights to sell to coal companies in the mid-1880s—a source of grief to farmers who were sold rights to the surface of that same land and who sometimes found coal companies digging up their gardens and even grave-yards. In the 1980s, as a Pike County circuit court judge, Scott's father ruled in favor of a local landowner against a subsidiary of Bethlehem Steel—a case that was appealed and finally won in the Supreme Court.

A tall, brown-haired man in his early forties, Andrew Scott wore rimmed glasses and displayed a boyish, studious expression. A firm low-tax low-spend Republican, Andrew largely came to his dedication to former President Trump through hereditary tradition. He was deeply devoted to Coal Run, which bordered Pikeville. "We're pretty much two shopping malls on each side of Route 23, but we boast the lowest property taxes rate in the state, not a dollar wasted," he added proudly. Andrew's Twitter account showed an appreciative video of a snowplow's headlights beaming through pelting nighttime snow as it cleared narrow mountainside roads on Christmas Eve. "Rising prices for gas, eggs, and other things are tough on us," Scott said. "In August, we gave out free school backpacks and supplies to Coal Run children, and they need them." On Halloween, he passed out candy to children, and on Christmas, toys. "I think we're a great little town here. We love America, but the county's been hit hard and I'm doing what I can to help and voting for the Republican party helps us here."

Pride and Shame: A Lens

My talks with Andrew Scott, like those with Donovan Blackburn, former governor Paul Patton, and others, were helping me grasp how such town leaders saw the town's needs. But how did the people living farther out in Pike County see their place in the world, and how might they react to the various political appeals that were being made to them?

Prompting my questions was a set of hunches I'd brought with me from my prior research on right-leaning residents of Louisiana in the years leading up to the 2016 election of Donald Trump. I began with the idea that emotion almost always underlies the appeal of any political candidate. As a potential experience, many emotions exist within any voter. As one man told me, "The first thing a political leader appeals to is fear, then to grief, then pride and shame." But I focus here on pride and shame, especially unwarranted shame.

Let me briefly lay out a few premises before continuing, because these premises form this story's backdrop. Pride and shame signal the juncture between the identity we hold out to the world, and how the world responds to our identity. Pride functions as an emotional "skin of the self," so to speak; it signals when our identity is safe, accepted, and admired, and when we are in danger of rejection. It is our inner response to our outer appearance. Shame also feels like a "skin"—one we wish to shed. We all feel a desire for pride and fear of shame. This is insightfully explored in David Keen's 2023 book *Shame: The Politics and Power of an Emotion*, whose thinking dovetails with this book's (and which also draws on my last book *Strangers*, even as I now draw on insights in his). As such, other emotions also enter in response to pride and shame, of course; for example, we may feel eager for pride, and angry at being shamed.

Aristotle describes pride as the "crown of virtues"—an emotion we feel when achieving something great. (In the thirteenth century, pride was often associated with arrogance, "inordinate self-esteem," or "conceit," a connotation I set aside here.) Instead, I focus on pride as a feeling of "being of use." Indeed, the word *pride* is derived from the Late Latin *prode*, which means "being of use"—implicitly, to a person, a group, or a communally-held goal. When I asked Andrew what made him feel proud, he answered that, next to being a family man, it was "helping Coal Run."

I use the word *pride* as a master term, with honor, respect, and status being distinct subtypes of it. Shame is the mirror opposite of pride, and is likewise a master term referring to a range of feelings such as humiliation, mortification, or embarrassment. Shame is felt as an unpleasant sense of self-deflation. It is often associated with remorse, self-mortification, or fear of punishment. Shame, as I see it, is the feeling that we have done wrong in the eyes of others. Guilt is the feeling that we have done wrong in our own eyes. We can, of course, experience the two independently or together. What makes shame especially important is that it can stir preexisting feelings of inadequacy from which we seek rescue, and it can also serve as the basis of political appeal.

Along with pride and shame, we experience secondary attitudes toward these feelings. If I am shamed, do I deserve to feel shamed? Or deserve to feel proud? On the basis of what? While such bases of pride are in some contention, we find ourselves—if society holds together—in a national pride economy. I had discovered some sense of challenged pride in my study of the petrochemical belt around Lake Charles, Louisiana, and so I could hazard guesses about a wider, similarly voting region of the right-swinging South. But how, I wondered, might the very building blocks of pride come together in such a way as to predispose a people to one or another political viewpoint?

As children, we are assigned a place in a material economy, within which we earn our way. So too with our placement in the pride economy. We are born into a region, a social class, a race, a gender, and these increase or decrease our value in the wider pride economy. Each of these characteristics comes with the highly contested notion of privilege. For example, the coal region of Appalachia, once the nation's major source of electrical power, has suffered decline. Pride in the job of coal miner and in the moral fortitude and know-how the job requires, pride in being in a region so central to the nation—all these have shifted.

As a result, many I came to know felt under social attack, for they had suffered a certain loss of "structural" or "carried" pride. That is, to varying extents, most people "carry" the pride or shame of a larger entity—a region, a nation, a football team, a family—whose standing in the pride economy is beyond their control (i.e., structural). Many people, like Mayor Andrew Scott and college chaplain Rob Musick, spoke as if they had to defend "being a hillbilly" in a national, urban court of opinion where "hillbillies" were excluded from the concept of diversity. "If you go to a bigger city," a graduate student named Ashley told me, "They think you talk wrong and your views are out of date. People ask you to repeat what you just said because they can't understand."

Or they joke. Ashley visited Boston on a school trip with Upward Bound, a federally funded pre-college preparation program, and recalled visiting a bookstore. "After I spoke with the man behind the counter, he asked where I was raised, and when I said eastern Kentucky, he leaned over the counter to see if I was barefoot. It was a joke, but it made me aware there was a joke to be made about me that I couldn't make about him." Being the butt of stereotyping could even give strangers a potential point in common. For example, when I told one man that my father had a strong New England accent that turned "yard" into "yaaad" and my name, Arlie, into "Ahlee," the man smiled in sympathy and said, "Blessings on him."

It reminds me of a scene in Barbara Kingsolver's superb novel *Demon Copperhead*, in which the titular character, in a public bathroom, says, "This is what I would say if I could, to all smart people of the world with their dumb hillbilly jokes: We are right here in the stall. We can actually hear you."

Without thinking much about it, we draw on different bases of pride—national, regional, professional, intellectual, and moral—as well as pride related to cultural values assigned to our ethnicity, gender, sexual orientation, and body type. Clearly, some of these bases of pride are beyond our personal control. But we nonetheless pool these separate bases of pride to form a generalized sense of personal pride, normally without giving it much thought. The more highly placed a person is, the less they tend to think about it.

We live in both a material economy and a pride economy, and while we pay close attention to shifts in the material economy, we often neglect or underestimate the importance of the pride economy, parallel to its station within the nation's material economy. Just as the fortunes of Appalachian Kentucky have risen and fallen with the fate of coal, so has its standing in the pride economy. Our standings in the material and pride economies are often connected in ways we hardly notice. In our pride bank account we may have enough, and so we can spend it on extras, or we may have not a penny to spare.

And our place in the material economy is often linked to that in the pride economy. If we become poor, we have two problems. First, we are poor (a material matter), and second, we are made to feel ashamed of being poor (a matter of pride). If we lose our job, we are jobless (a material loss) and then ashamed of being jobless (an emotional loss). Many also feel shame at receiving government help to compensate that loss. If we live in a once-proud region that has fallen on hard times, we first suffer loss, then shame at the loss—and, as we shall see, often anger at the real or imagined shamers.

But the pride economy is also linked to our placement in cultural hierarchies that shift independent of the economy. Just as the material economy vacillates according to the impact of world trade or regional booms and busts, so our position in the pride economy varies with shifts in culture. In Appalachia, the pride stories I heard often hinged not simply on earning wealth—despite the early Pikeville football chant—but on the fortitude and ingenuity it took to be poor.

But in doing so, we become only dimly aware of how much each basis of our personal sense of pride is subject to influences far removed from our personal intention or wishes. For example, pride in a closeness to nature or rural life is subject to rise or decline in a shared cultural view of rural life itself—which shifts depending on broad cultural trends. While romanticized on holiday cards, rural life has also become linked in the public mind with things dull, backward, behind the times, while the city is associated with the new and exciting. For example, in the "rural purge" of 1971, television networks canceled many shows centered on rural life, like *Green Acres*, *Hee Haw*, *Lassie*, *Petticoat Junction*, and *The Beverly Hillbillies*, replacing them with programming aimed at urban audiences. Pride is embedded in public narrative.

At one point, places of coal and oil extraction were heralded as key national assets—high in the pride economy—and later as places of contaminated streams and flattened mountains, low in the pride economy. A young man drove me up a mountain near his home to look out at the jagged horizon. "See that mountain there? And that one over there? They should not be flat. Their tops were blasted off, the land scarred up, topsoil dumped in the creek. To me, there's nothing more beautiful than our mountains. But mountain-blasting is a damn shame. People ask how we let it happen."

People take personal pride in many other aspects of life also subject to change. Even in body type, certain features go in and out of fashion as desirable, and so as objects of pride. Large breasts and hips were points of pride in the 1940s and 1950s, while smaller breasts and longer legs were admired in the 1960s. At one point in time, thin and blond may be in, and at another time curvy and dark-haired may be. A beauty ideal may be white for a time, or Asian or Black at another time. In this way, many if not all bases of personal pride are, in unnoticed ways, wired to cultural shifts in the wider society. In just such ways we may suffer from carried shame, rooted in the fate of a region—due to such things as company closures or corporate drug sales—along with all that is within our personal control.

The Pride Paradox

Looming largest as a basis of pride is our closeness to the American Dream. A term first coined by author and historian James Truslow Adams in 1931, the American Dream evoked the idea of life in the middle-class—a secure job, a home, a car—and the idea of earning one's way up, a man outearning his father.

But attached to this dream is a hidden paradox, which creates different cultural worlds—a red-state world of lower opportunity and strict expectations, and a blue-state world of higher opportunity and less-strict expectations. Within the red-state world, as we shall see, those who can't reach the American Dream are vulnerable to shame. Those caught in this predicament can make one of three "moves" in response to shame.

But first, the paradox itself. It is made up of two parts—the presence in one's region of economic opportunity and one's cultural belief about responsibility for accessing it. From roughly 1970 on, the United States gradually divided into two economies—the winners and losers of globalization. Rising in opportunity have been cities and regions with diversified economies, often the site of newer, less vulnerable industries, which typically hired college-educated workers in service and tech fields. Declining in opportunity have been rural and semi-rural areas, offering blue-collar jobs in older manufacturing industries more vulnerable to offshoring and automation. These also include regions where jobs are based on extracting oil, coal, and other minerals, the demand for which fluctuates with world demand. The urban middle class, which leans Democratic, has become a so-called mobility incubator, while many rural blue-collar areas, now leaning Republican, have become mobility traps. Between 2008 and 2017, one study found, the nation's Democratic congressional districts saw median household income rise from $54,000 to $61,000, while incomes in Republican districts fell from $55,000 to $53,000. In recent years, residents in Republican districts have suffered higher rates of COVID than residents in Democratic districts. Studies of optimism reflect a person's closeness to or distance from the opportunity to achieve the American Dream— the least optimistic being poor rural whites, who are more pessimistic than poor urban Blacks. Also, those living in Republican counties—and especially the white males in them—have suffered higher death rates than those living in Democratic counties. Over time, death rates have decreased in Democratic counties more than in Republican ones; the gap between those two rates increased more than sixfold from 2001 to 2019. Just as a flagging economy has led to lost pride in Kentucky's 5th Congressional District, so it has for others in the nation's red counties as well.

The second part of the paradox lies in core ideas about hard work and individual responsibility for one's economic fate. Most of us have attached some idea about individualism to our view of the American Dream. This is the core belief in what the sociologist Max Weber called the Protestant ethic and credited as the motivational engine driving capitalism. Hard work is twinned with the idea of individual responsibility. If you find yourself a success, take full credit for it yourself. If you find yourself a failure, that too is on you. We don't have to be Protestant, of course, to feel the influence of the Protestant ethic, but as a basis for pride, its influence is deep and wide.

More Republicans than Democrats hold to the old-time Protestant ethic, however hardworking members of each party are. When asked in a national survey why it is that a person ends up being poor, 31 percent of Republicans (party members or those who lean that way) say it is due to "circumstances beyond their control," in contrast to 69 percent of Democrats (party members or those who lean that way). Similarly, 71 percent of Republicans but only 22 percent of Democrats think "people are rich because they work hard." For Appalachians—many of whose ancestors came from Scotland and Ireland, the population Weber took as prime examples of this ethic-crediting or blaming yourself for success or failure is based on a centuries-long tradition. "We're more old-fashioned in a lot of ways," Andrew Scott told me, and taking responsibility for your own success is probably one of them." Thus, people growing up in the two kinds of economy experience different degrees of moral pinch between the cultural terms set for earning pride and the economic opportunity to do so.

Regardless of political party, in the United States, the poor are nearly as likely as the rich to believe that one is individually responsible for one's economic fate. In a 2020 poll conducted by NPR, the Robert Wood Johnson

Foundation, and Harvard's T. H. Chan School of Public Health, a random sample of Americans across class lines were asked: "For each of the following, please tell me how important you think it is for being economically successful in America today." The various factors included hard work, coming from an upper-income family, growing up in an upper-income neighborhood, and a person's racial or ethnic background. Among those in the top 1 percent (family income of $500,000 or more), 93 percent felt hard work got them there. Only about a third or less thought growing up in an upper-income family or neighborhood or race made any difference. But even among the very poorest—those with a family income of $35,000 or less—a full 87 percent answered "hard work." No more than a third felt that a boost from social class, race, or ethnicity made it easier to rise. Rich or poor, the idea is that whether you rise or fall depends on *you*.

As mentioned earlier, the American Dream tacitly refers to a young man who not only is doing well for himself but also is doing better than his father, achieving father-to-son upward mobility. A man we shall meet later described his father's feelings about hard work as the ticket to success: "My dad had a very hard life and had to try his hardest at the things he did. He was not one to accept excuses for not trying hard enough. He would tell me, 'Try your very best.' But at the end of it, he could say to himself and to me, 'Your best *isn't good enough*. You're not trying *hard enough*.' That's because he had to try so hard, so young." Reflecting on his own life, the son told me, "So sometimes I wonder if I have the right to feel proud of myself, since I haven't pushed myself as hard as I think he did."

On the issue of individual responsibility, in recent years, Republicans and Democrats have become increasingly divided. In 2014, 47 percent of Republicans agreed that a person is poor generally "because of a lack of effort on their part." But by 2017, that rose to 56 percent. In 2014, 29 percent of Democrats agreed, but by 2017 that had sunk to 19 percent—creating a yawning gap between the two parties of 37 percentage points.

Thus Republicans unwittingly impose harsher conditions for deserving pride even as they struggle with making a living in the hardest-hit regions—those more prone to factory closures and lowered wages. Democrats are more likely to credit "larger circumstances" for their more fortunate fates.

So across the nation, a poignant, unnamed pride paradox has taken shape. And it is this: We have divided into two economies and two cultures, one red, one blue. Red states faced both tougher economic times and the more demanding, old-school brand of individualism in which no government help, no class or racial advantage—only one's *own* hard work—could account for one's fate. Those in blue states experience better economic times through a less shame-inducing cultural lens.

Interestingly, Republicans also have stronger faith than do Democrats in capitalism without government help or regulation—that is, raw capitalism. In the states they control, unregulated capitalism has given them a rougher ride. Whatever its ups and downs, the unhampered free market works best, according to Adam Smith in *The Wealth of Nations*, guided only by its own trustworthy "invisible hand." But that hand has been hardest on the populations who most believe in that hand, and easier on populations that call for activist welfare policies as part of the mix. Again, if the supply of premium coal becomes exhausted or natural gas undersells coal, many Republicans believe this is the invisible hand of capitalism at work, and the individual's job is to adapt to it by working harder.

Particularly for Republicans, the individual American Dream has been hooked to a corporate American Dream—one of greater shareholder profit. During much of the twentieth century the two dreams linked together well. But from the 1970s on, increasingly the two dreams have clashed. Through offshoring, many corporations hired cheaper labor in places such as Mexico, China, and Vietnam, raising profits by lowering the cost of labor. That is the corporate American Dream, as William Greider argues in *One World Ready or Not*, one which broke free from the former restraints imposed on one hand by labor unions and on the other hand by the federal government.

Eastern Kentucky coal companies reduced crew size by introducing machines to do the work and by shifting their operations elsewhere. Revelation Energy, Blackjewel, and Peabody, for example, moved their operations from Kentucky to Wyoming, currently the main source of U.S. coal.

Both political parties accepted the clash between the American Dream and the corporate American Dream. But to manage the painful fallout, the Democrats turned to the federal government and the Republicans redoubled faith in—and participation in—the corporate American Dream. In fact, Republicans generally oppose interfering with the practices of corporate giants, even those which hurt small business.

So what happens, I wondered, when workers are exhorted to believe that capitalism needs no government hand and that each individual working in it bears personal responsibility for how well or poorly he or she fares—and then companies pull out? Those left behind find themselves trapped inside a pride paradox.

Most hurt are those who live in regions depleted of good jobs and who also lack training for other good jobs, wherever they are. Doubly blocked, they become vulnerable to structural shame.

From Structural Shame to Personal Shame

But how does a man go from getting laid off the job—through no fault of his own—to blaming himself for an absence of personal responsibility and feeling shame? Over lunch, one forty-year-old grandson of a coal miner offered an answer. "Shame comes gradually. Let me give you an example of guys around where I live. First thing, a guy gets his layoff slip and he blames the inspector. Then the supervisor. Then he shakes his fist at the Obama administration for putting in the Clean Air Act and adds in Biden and the Democratic Party and the deep state.

"Then when his unemployment runs low and his wife asks for money for groceries for the kids, he faces a hard choice—if you need money and

34

don't have a degree, you've got to leave. But his family's here and he doesn't want to leave.

"That's when he starts to feel bad about himself. He looks around at the jobs on offer at $9.00 or $10.50 an hour, and he turns his nose up at what he thinks of as girly service jobs because he can't support his family on that kind of money. But then his partner says, 'We need to feed the kids.' So he takes the crap job, and she says, 'There's still not enough money for food, gas, and fixing the roof.'

"It's then that his shame begins to get stronger, because now he feels the problem is on *him*. And if he leaves on Route 23 looking for work and comes back empty-handed, that's shame waiting for him at home.

"Then if he gets into drugs—take it from me—he's ashamed. That can lead to divorce and separation from his kids, and now he's on the dole. He always felt superior to others he saw on the dole. And now he's on it too. So he's ashamed about that and mad that he's made to feel ashamed.

"Then he may read some op-ed in the *Appalachian News-Express* calling people like him a deadbeat for not supporting his family and paying taxes the town needs for its sewer repair. He's not a contributor.

"On top of all that, he sees on the internet people outside the region firing insults at him as ignorant, racist, sexist, or homophobic. Now he's mad at the shamers. And by this point he's forgotten about the shame. He's just plain pissing mad."

The Precarity of Pride

For eastern Kentuckians, economic life had long been up and down, beginning with down. "Before coal, we were living a tough pioneer life here," Andrew Scott explained. "We had been poor and made to feel ashamed for being poor. Coal pulled us out of poverty." Ever since the Chesapeake and Ohio Railway first came to Pikeville in 1905 to haul away the immense local coal deposits, production rose and rose. By 1977 Pike County led the entire state of Kentucky in cumulative production—a record that it still holds, and one that is a point of great pride. It was around then that Andrew Scott recalls seeing Mercedeses in the parking lot of his school.

In a neighborhood of some fifty homes in Pikeville called Bowles Addition—where former Governor Patton now lives—sit formal, white-pillared mansions, once homes of those at the top of the pride economy: coal barons. "Within a ten-mile radius of the town there are more than a hundred people with a net worth of a million dollars or more, making the area one of the largest concentrations of millionaires in Kentucky," according to a 1983 article in *National Geographic*. Nor was it only coal company owners who flourished. Independent truck miners—men with a truck, a pick, and an idea where surface coal could be found—as well as miners who worked deep underground, many lifted from poverty. Thanks to their new salaries, the great Kentucky journalist Harry M. Caudill wrote, "lace curtains fluttered" from the miner's wife's windows, and "flashy carpets covered her pine floors." Miners might also wear "silk underwear and shirts and expensive Stetson hats."

At the same time, coal didn't pull everyone out of poverty, or not permanently. For Scott also grew up to see Appalachia viewed as one of the nation's main examples of abject poverty. He recalled a 1964 CBS News special called *Christmas in Appalachia* (available on YouTube) of life in Beaver Creek, a half hour's drive northwest of Pikeville. "A lot of people around here felt offended by reports like that. We're shown as dirt poor, uncombed hair, ragged clothes, objects of pity." In a concerned voice, CBS journalist Charles Kuralt asked one father, a man who looked older than his years, why he didn't send his children to school. "Because classmates would make fun of their clothes," came the answer. A child would "feel so embarrassed to go in front of other kids in the condition they're in, so they wouldn't learn anything." This embarrassment left a parent with "no cause to send them." Poignantly, the show itself, like others to follow, revealed to Appalachians how poor they seemed to outsiders. To many I spoke with, these well-intentioned films portraying hard times in Appalachia evoked shame and resentment at being shamed. The message they gave was "the world feels sorry for us, but it hasn't bothered to get to know us—especially all we've done and are proud of."

"I've felt personally proud to live in the energy capital of the world," Scott continued, "and proud of my neighbors who were miners." For most, jobs were handed down through families, father to son to grandson. "My granddad and father both worked in the mines," one man in his thirties told me. Like a family recipe or heirloom, he spoke of it as a shared trade bound by generations. Even when a miner warned his sons away from mining, because it was too dangerous and caused black lung disease, a man might say he wasn't in mining because "my dad told me not to." Men I spoke to seemed proud of the father-to-son tradition even if they had stepped out of it.

Miners were appreciated for their knowledge, their competence, and the qualities of character their jobs called for, including bravery, tenacity, and patience, as well as their capacity to manage boredom, discomfort, and, most of all, fear—of a collapsing mine wall, dangerous trapped fumes, equipment failures, and shortened lives. One appreciative daughter relayed the life of her coal-mining father in this way: "Dad would take off his lamp, put his lunch pail down, and sit at the kitchen table. My mom brought him coffee and my sister and I picked off pieces of coal from my father's shins. In the mine, he had to walk stooping over in a low-ceilinged shaft to get to his spot, then lie flat and pick coal. He ate lunch lying on his side. He did that every day but Sunday for my mom and us seven girls.

"See that?" she continued, pointing to a framed picture on her living room wall. "I cut that out from the front page of the *Mineworkers' Journal* and framed it because it reminds me of my dad." The image was of a lean man in a headlamp, a battery pack at his belt, his face looking out, his expression worried. Below the image were the words "NO WORK

TOMORROW." "That happened to my dad; he got laid off," she said. "We grew our own beans—corn, turnips, potatoes—and raised hogs. But during strikes, we needed food stamps. We didn't think we were poor or would ever need government help. Around here, that's shameful. But we needed government help. So we took the welfare check to shop at a store away from town, where they didn't know us. We didn't want to be seen. Dad endured a lot."

Lost Jobs

Just as the demand for coal had risen in this one-industry county— especially through the 1990s—it fell. In 2000 coal had provided 52 percent of the nation's electricity, but by early 2024 that had dropped to 16 percent. The coal industry also automated. By 1948, the continuous mining machine—a sort of conveyor belt with teeth—was already re- ducing the average mine work crew from "thirteen or fourteen miners to just six or seven, while producing more coal," according to historian Max Fraser. Next came the rise of fracking to increase the supply of natural gas. Then in the 1990s demand for coal fell, taking with it jobs as coal truckers, machine repair technicians, and restaurant workers. "Since the 1990s, we've been losing coal jobs and now we're in free fall," Andrew explained. In 1990, Kentucky had 30,498 coal jobs; in 2000 it had 14,508 jobs, and by 2020 only 3,874 jobs. I could see faded I LOVE COAL stickers on the backs of more than a few trucks and cars. When jobs went out, labor unions—which once connected workers to the Democratic party— largely went out with them.

"I live at the top of our holler," Andrew explained, "and up here we have about thirty nice homes, all spaced out. Ten years ago, my neighbors were wealthy coal company executives and miners. But those men have been laid off. One ex-miner went to barber school. One retrained to be- come a nurse. We have former coal miners who are homeless, living under bridges, because they don't want to live in a shelter. Neighbors and friends lend a hand. There is a miner's discount day—20 percent off—in local stores. When I was city commissioner there was Coal Miner Appreciation Day that offered free haircuts. Today up here, our neighbors are doctors working at the Pikeville Medical Center."

There was another terrible loss Andrew wasn't counting. In search of coal, companies had begun using monster machines to blast off the tops of mountains—five hundred across Appalachia, three hundred of those in Kentucky alone, some in Pike County just off the "hillbilly highway," Route 23. Tons of soil had been dumped into streambeds, contaminating water and harming wildlife. Some companies, such as Blackjewel in Harlan County, promised to remediate the damage they caused but declared bankruptcy before doing so. The nation's most eloquent defender of rural life, Kentucky-based writer Wendell Berry, sat in at the governor's office in a protest against mountaintop removal. "Coal you burn once and it's gone. But the mountaintops you blast off, the water you contaminate, the wildlife you disrupt—those injuries last forever," Berry was to remark later, when I and others were to meet him.

In addition to the losses of jobs, ex-miners felt hurt by another loss, just as important as that of jobs—a depreciation in the value of their competence and knowledge. A miner knew how to read the seams in a mine wall, to time blasts, to repair broken equipment, to sense danger. A miner possessed a vast store of knowledge specific to a particular time, place, and trade, but it was little use outside those particular circumstances. As some residents began to leave, a miner could also lose parts of the very community that appreciated his knowledge and the work he'd done.

Many saw their lives described by the musical legend John Prine, whose parents were born in Muhlenberg County, Kentucky:

Well, the coal company came with the world's largest shovel,
They tortured the timber and stripped all the land

Well, they dug for their coal till the land was forsaken
And wrote it all down as the progress of man.

And Pikeville-born country-and-western musician Dwight Yoakam warned of bad news, whether the miner stayed in the mines or quit and left:

Have you ever heard
A mountain man cough his life away
From diggin' that black coal
In those dark mines, those dark mines,
If you had you might just understand
The reason that they left it all behind.

Of those migrating out of the Kentucky hills in search of industrial jobs in Cincinnati, Toledo, Chicago, and elsewhere, Yoakam wrote:

They thought readin', writin', Route 23
Would take them to the good life that they had never seen
They didn't know that old highway
Could lead them to a world of misery.

"After being one of the fastest growing parts of the region during the first decades of the twentieth century," Max Fraser writes, "the coalfields of eastern Kentucky and West Virginia—where per capita incomes stood at half the national average—saw their overall post-war population drop by as much as 10 or 15 percent between 1945 and 1960." Such migrants were part of the roughly 8 million whites who between 1900 and 1975 made their way to the booming factory towns of the industrial Midwest. There they tended to congregate in such neighborhoods as Uptown, Chicago (known as "Hillbilly Heaven"), the East End in Dayton or in the town of South Lebanon, Ohio, and Shedtown in Muncie or Stringtown in

Indianapolis, Indiana. In their new homes, the migrant was often looked down on by northern-born whites, just as migrating Black southerners found themselves looked down on by northern Blacks. As one man who had moved from eastern Kentucky to Cincinnati and returned told me, "Hillbillies are a minority there too, you know, second-class." Some jobless men were recruited from their Appalachian homes for jobs that did not exist. In the 1910s and 1920s, for example, Goodyear Tire and Rubber Company in Akron, Ohio, sent recruiters into Appalachia in order to urge poor white farmers to move north to Akron. But as one such migrant reported, "They were laying off men instead of hiring them." With a labor surplus, the company could lower wages and undercut union activism, at least for a time, sparking distrust between new migrants and white old-timers, who accused incoming hillbillies of stealing jobs and undermining wages.

Crucially, whether they stayed or left, Appalachians were exposed to life in the more prosperous blue states, where the haves of globalization lived. It would have been reasonable to wonder: *Why are they better off than we are? If we're supposed to be personally responsible for our economic fate, what have we been doing wrong?*

Almost everyone I spoke to in eastern Kentucky quickly nodded when I asked whether they'd ever been put down for being hillbillies. Mayor Andrew Scott commented, "When I travel, I see how a lot of people outside our area see us in eastern Kentucky. It's not just those photos of barefoot kids in ragged clothes and mussed hair that President Lyndon Johnson showed the world. We know how we're seen and they barely know us. Then we've got the put-downs by liberal comedians and commentators making fun of us for being fat, drugged out, talking funny, being poor and prejudiced. Tell me, should I have to defend myself against outside critics like that?"

For those in the region, the American Dream had flickered on the horizon, had come to center stage for some, then receded, leaving many to chase after it into the cities of the Midwest and beyond.

Many in Pike County were suffering economic loss, but that wasn't all. They were suffering devaluation of their culture and challenges to their status, but that wasn't all either. They were noticing that others outside their region were better off than they were, but that still wasn't all. Loss had led many to bear the burden of a pride paradox.

Andrew Scott rubbed the ears of his dog Chief. "Urban liberals don't even think about it but they're the pride news. To them, coal miners with dirty faces, off and on poverty, lung disease, we're the shame news. And we don't like it. Some in my [Republican] party talk about seceding from the Union." A Kentucky Republican member of the House of Representatives has indeed called for his state's secession from the nation. "I think he's wrong about seceding," Andrew said, "but I get why he's mad."

4

"Come to Help Y'all Out"

As city manager Donovan Blackburn was finalizing plans to avoid violence during Saturday's march, a caravan of white nationalists was heading for Whitesburg, Kentucky, some forty miles southwest of Pikeville. There, Heimbach had secured access to private land, which would serve as a staging area for socializing, speeches, and military-style drills beginning on Friday evening. Pickups, vans, and cars drove up a winding narrow road through hillside hollers dotted with wooden homes. They passed trailers, parked vehicles, roadside billboards (for personal injury attorneys, army recruitment, organ donation, and foster care), and leftover campaign signs, such as TRUMP DIGS COAL!

In the caravan were, among others, members of:

The Global Crusaders
The Order of the Ku Klux Klan
The League of the South
Knights of the Ku Klux Klan
National Socialist Movement
The Right Stuff
The Dirty White Boys
The Masons
The Council of Conservative Citizens
White Lives Matter

Identity Evropa

Vanguard America

Traditionalist Workers Party (Matthew Heimbach's Indiana-based
    group)

The men parked along the edge of a large vacant field near the vans
of the organizers, who had arrived earlier to set up tents and food tables.
Dismounting from their vehicles, the men—no women invited—received
hearty handshakes from the tall, heavyset twenty-six-year-old Heimbach.

"Welcome!" Pointing newcomers to a long table laid out with coffee
and donuts, Matthew told them cheerfully, "A good wholesome *American*
breakfast! No *bagels*."

They were assembling the day before the march in Pikeville, preparing their appeal to white pride. Heimbach was dressed in black pants,
shirt, and boots, later reporting excitedly to me that they "were manu-
factured by Hugo Boss, the same company that made boots for Hitler
and the SS." His jet-black hair was cropped short and bristly, and his
beard was trimmed close, creating an appearance of order and control.
Matthew was adept at moving the conversational ball forward in lively,
fact-studded paragraph-sized strips of talk. This was probably why many
followers imagined him as "the next David Duke"—a reference to the
Louisiana-based former Ku Klux Klan Grand Wizard and America's most
widely known spokesperson for the KKK.

The crowd grew and mingled. Cigarettes were lit, shared, smoked, in-
haled, stamped out, and new ones lit. With the exception of a few older
veterans, nearly every one of the 150 or so men at the gathering seemed
to be in their twenties, thirties, or forties. Clothed in black or tan, a few
with stomachs protruding, some with shaved heads and carefully disciplined beards, many of the men wore sunglasses slung to brow. Tattoos
crept up arms, crossed chests, announced messages along necks, cheeks,
and foreheads. Some men hung out by their pickups, smoking with their
own group. One Kentucky neo-Nazi, a sallow musician named Jason

who was a member of a black-metal punk band, "had left New York City to move to a mostly white community in Indiana." Another man, Scott, "had recently been kicked out of an Irish pub in Kentucky for celebrating Hitler's birthday." Rifles were slung over shoulders, handguns strapped to waists or legs. Some men toted walkie-talkies. The black T-shirt of one bald man bore the words DONALD PUMPS with an image of Donald Trump's imagined strong, bare arms lifting a heavy iron weight. One thin, beardless young man seemed out of place in a blue-and-white checked shirt.

To Matthew Heimbach's delight, vans and trucks from ABC, *The Guardian*, and a television crew from France had established themselves at the edge of the field. The marchers and media seemed to hold each other in an intense reciprocal gaze.

Matthew Heimbach's Message

How, I wondered, would Heimbach's message appeal to the townspeople and those beyond in congressional district KY-5? On the surface, Matthew's message seemed to boil down to this: *We hear your distress. There's much you do not have. We're here to raise the value of what you do have—your whiteness.*

Translated into the language of pride, his message was this: *You've lost your regional pride, your well-paid jobs, suffered devaluation of what you do have, and you've had enough. We on the violent right will erase shame from you and seamlessly divert your shame to blame—blame of Jews, Muslims, Blacks, immigrants, liberals, and Democrats. Your access to the American Dream? They took it! Everything that ever hurt you is their fault. Our guns are cocked and loaded.*

Heimbach's main friend and ally was Jeff Schoep, the former head of the National Socialist Movement (NSM)—the largest, most active neo-Nazi group in America. The two stood as armed defenders, as it were, of pride against shame. Those liberals and leftists who dwelled on sources of shame—the toll of slavery, Jim Crow, the Holocaust, the effects of coal on climate—were wrongly engaged in *shaming America.*

There were rules about how proud to feel about America, and liberals and Democrats were violating them. In his defense of Christian white pride, Matthew felt new political winds at his back. Republican Presidents Ronald Reagan and George H. W. Bush had both denounced KKK leader David Duke as a racist. But Donald Trump had not. "It wasn't easy for Trump to refuse to denounce Duke. We understood that," Heimbach explained to me later. "So, we figured, Trump's with us. And Appalachia might be too. The people here feel like the coal companies don't care. The federal government doesn't care. Neither party cares. Pike County voted for Donald Trump and that made us think we might get a good hearing."

Matthew Aids Trump at Rally

Fifteen months earlier, adding a MAGA hat to his signature black shirt, pants, and boots, Matthew had joined thousands of excited fans in the International Convention Center in Louisville, Kentucky, for a March 2016 presidential campaign rally for Donald Trump. Matthew had watched on the news as Trump told fans at an earlier pre-election rally in Iowa, "If you see somebody getting ready to throw a tomato, knock the crap out of them. . . . I will pay the legal fees." Trump also promised he was "looking into" paying the legal fees for a white man who sucker-punched a Black protester at a widely videoed campaign rally in Fayetteville, North Carolina. When Trump again spotted Black Lives Matter protesters, this time in Louisville, he called on fans to "get them out of here!"

Video caught Matthew's answer to Trump's call, his face in a grimace, shouting "Get *out!*" and repeatedly shoving a young Black woman, Kashiya Nwanguma, a University of Louisville student, toward the exit. Along with other protesters, Nwanguma later filed charges against Heimbach and Trump for inciting violence.

Matthew was arrested. "At the police station I pled guilty to disorderly conduct and acted as my own attorney," he later recalled. "I told them Donald Trump is a world-famous businessman and candidate for president. For authority, how much higher can you get?" In his decision, federal judge David J. Hale wrote, "It is plausible that Trump's direction to 'get 'em out of here' could be seen as advocating the use of force." The judge then gave Heimbach a suspended ninety-day jail sentence on the condition that he stay out of legal trouble for the next two years. This Matthew was not to do.

Matthew's local efforts expressed part of a grander vision, as he imagined it, of an international white nationalist movement that would eliminate the great weakness of democracy. He loved Russia. He admired the extremist Golden Dawn Party in Greece and had traveled there three times to visit its officials. Now the third-largest party in Greece, Golden Dawn was calling for a purely white Christian "Greater Greece," modeled on Hitler's greater Germany. Heimbach had also met with white nationalists in the Czech Republic and had spoken at an annual conference of Germany's neo-Nazi National Democratic Party. He maintained friendly relations with the neo-Nazi party National Action in England and honeymooned in Bucharest, Romania, where, he later told me, "I know some great nationalists." He read approvingly of the National Front (soon to be renamed the National Rally) led by Marine Le Pen in France, the Vlaams Belang and Nieuwe-Vlaamse Alliantie in Belgium, Lega Nord in Italy, the Freedom Party of Austria, and One Nation in Australia. Once Matthew had gathered the extreme right from the four corners of America, he hoped to forge ties with his "international brothers" to restore what the Polish journalist Ryszard Kapuscinski aptly described as an imagined "Great Yesterday."

Conflicting Goals

For now, Heimbach was focusing on his "grassroots brothers" from Appalachia, which had led him to hand out flyers on Pikeville doorsteps addressed to "white working families" with that image of the tall dad fondly tossing up the smiling child, and to hand out donuts to the men now gathering on a field to practice a military drill.

In truth, Matthew Heimbach had set himself two conflicting goals. One goal was to mainstream an extremist message in the peaceful town of Pikeville. To do this, he planned to go slowly, soft-pedal white nationalism, and avoid sounding harsh, mean, or inhumane. He could appeal to their anguish and anger at the unfairness of their loss and offer pride to native-born whites, claiming, *Whites built America, so it's all ours.*

He could then casually add the idea of racial separation. "Don't some Blacks—like the Black Muslims—*want* separation?" he would later ask me. "I'm not against Blacks. I'm with Black separatists who want their own place to live." To mainstream such a message, Heimbach felt, the marchers shouldn't look too weird or extreme: no sheets, no hoods, no burning crosses. He could push the Nazi ideals without once mentioning the name of that stiff-walking uniformed man with slicked-over hair, nose-wide mustache, and notorious straight-arm salute.

But it wasn't clear how his men would respond to this idea of "soft-pedaling it." "A lot of the guys hadn't gotten much chance to get out before the public," Matthew noted. Members of the Ku Klux Klan wanted to display their fearsome robes and wave their Confederate flags. The neo-Nazis wanted to show off their swastikas. Identity Evropa members wanted to display their Celtic cross. Others were bringing homemade shields saying NOG ÄR NOG, a slogan used by anti-immigrant groups in Sweden, meaning "enough is enough."[113] But as Vegas Tenold, a journalist who was on the scene, vividly describes in *Everything You Love Shall Burn*, the main reason most of the marchers had come was to express their extremism—not to mainstream it.

Matthew wanted to give his marchers the chance to show off, but he also wanted to lure regular people to his cause. And he added to this a third aim: he wanted the groups he had brought with him to learn to get along with each other. This proved a further fly in the ointment. "Uniting these guys was like herding cats," Heimbach later confessed. Each group had its own identity, which it yearned to display, but no group wanted to risk being confused with others. The Aryan Brotherhood and Dirty White Boys weren't sure what they had in common with those proclaiming Nog Är Nog. The KKK rejected the Masons, and Identity Evropa didn't care about them one way or another. It was not in the charter of the KKK to deny the reality of the Holocaust, but to the neo-Nazis that denial was center stage. While some groups didn't differ from other extremist groups in headlined beliefs, they privately disliked each other personally. Heimbach privately criticized members of the KKK as "old guys who had trouble mastering the internet." He disparaged skinheads as illiterate street fighters, in contrast to Islamic extremists, whom Heimbach admired because they were "real readers."

Curiously, while the assembled groups sometimes privately disparaged each other, Heimbach had reconciled their differences in a private realm. "I have a lot of political symbols on my body," Heimbach later confided. "Above my heart, I have a large swastika inside a cogwheel. And on this arm"—he held up the left one—"I have a Confederate flag. And I've got tattoos of a Celtic cross and rune." His body was a virtual United Nations of the extreme right.

The march was scheduled for Saturday at 2:00 p.m. That morning, out on the secluded flat green field above Whitesburg, Kentucky, Heimbach's men assembled in rows for military drills.

"Atten-*tion!* Face *for*-ward! Arms *down!* Forward, *march!*"

Leading this drill were older men, veterans of U.S. wars in Iraq, Afghanistan, and the Gulf. On display to all on the field that day was unity of purpose, preparation for combat, and fatherly leadership. As the men received instruction on how to wield a gun and adjust a gas mask, the gathering seemed to offer community to the isolated, attention to the fatherless, masculine pride to the uncertain, and pride of race to those trapped in a pride deficit—the answer to a dream.

Stranger in Town

How, I wondered, had a young outsider come to stir such a great commotion in a peaceful Appalachian town in which many blue-collar white Americans were stoically adapting to hard times? What, I wondered, was Matthew Heimbach's personal story? Was he even from Appalachia? In a series of meetings over four years, in bits and pieces, Matthew Heimbach shared his story.

"I had a very normal, middle-class childhood. I grew up in a McMansion on Cheswell Street in Poolesville, Maryland." After we'd ordered meals at a restaurant in Pikeville, Matthew began to deftly locate his family on a larger social map. "It's a 95 percent white town in Montgomery County, Maryland, the eleventh-richest county in the U.S. Poolesville is in the agricultural reserve of this county, so I got all the perks of good schools, good roads, good everything, but grew up in a town of five thousand which to this day doesn't have a traffic light.

"My parents were middle-class, Catholic, Mitt Romney moderate Republicans, and they wholeheartedly embrace racial diversity. My dad has German heritage, and my mom is Irish. My dad was brought up in an orphanage, poor. He works as a high school teacher and basketball coach. My mom stayed home when I was small. Then when I was about eight, she worked as a high school teacher and coached girls' basketball."

If anything, as a child, Matthew had also been better off than ex-governor Paul Patton, whose family lacked a telephone until after he'd graduated from high school. Matthew had also been born far closer to the American Dream than the university's pastor, Reverend Rob Musick, whose idea of an on-campus debate with Heimbach Patton had so resolutely been refused.

But there were other things to know. In Matthew's normally even-toned voice, I noted an occasional raw, angry catch when he said: "I almost never saw my dad. He was always working. When I was a kid, he took on second jobs he didn't have to take on. My dad took me with him to see Civil War reenactments, but I felt like he would have rather gone by himself.

"I'm the oldest of three," Matthew told me, "and my parents gave me the biggest bedroom, the room I wanted, in the basement. I put up a Confederate flag and Waffen SS flags. But my dad never came down to my room, so he never saw them. When my parents divorced"—Matthew was about seventeen—"it didn't make any difference in how much I saw him." After the divorce, Matthew's father remained present as an object of resentment.

Many boys across America grow up with come-and-go fathers, or no fathers, and turn to mothers, uncles, older brothers, cousins, friends. Matthew seemed to remain disappointingly—and angrily—fixed on his father, and the German culture to which Matthew linked him. "After my parents divorced and he retired, my dad traveled to Germany dozens of times, because that was his ancestry and he was interested. As a kid, I got really interested in Germany and World War II," he said. "I watched a lot of the History Channel on TV. I saw pictures of ten German POWs from the Battle of the Bulge, all worn out. I couldn't imagine how these men could be evil. I had a copy of *Mein Kämpf* and *The Turner Diaries*." The latter is a white supremacist novel, written in the 1970s by William Luther Pierce, describing a scenario in which guns are banned and African Americans force their way into the homes of whites to rob and rape; it ends with the eradication of all Jews.

Like many other children, Matthew also watched the 1970s blockbuster film *Star Wars*. But he didn't cheer in the same way others in the theater did. "Everyone else in the theater cheered for Princess Leia and Luke Skywalker," Matthew recalled. "But I thought the Imperial stormtroopers were way cooler." Faceless, armed with guns, wearing white and chrome, disciplined, implacable, the stormtroopers defended the story's villain, the leader of the Galactic Empire, Darth Vader. Fearsome in their uniformity, the stormtroopers were deployed to exterminate the virtuous Jedi. "I knew all the kinds of stormtroopers—the Purge troopers, Death troopers, Dark troopers, Incinerator stormtroopers," Matthew recalled. Stormtroopers had armor where faces might be. They had no feeling, it seemed, or independent agency. They moved in unison, obedient to their leader, which is what Matthew seemed to think made them cool.

"I always thought the German SS looked like *Star Wars* stormtroopers," he added. Indeed, perhaps George Lucas had Nazi soldiers in mind when he designed the film's stormtroopers. Years later, with their cool invulnerability, they appeared to Matthew a fitting model for his ragtag followers about to roll into the peaceful town of Pikeville.

Millions of children have identified with the characters in *Star Wars*, of course. But Matthew brought to his fascination with stormtroopers a mental focus on brutal leaders he admired— the Assads of Syria, Rodrigo Duterte of the Philippines, Pol Pot of Cambodia, Kim Jong Un of North Korea, Augusto Pinochet of Chile, and Adolf Hitler, those leading the stormtroopers of actual history.

But how, I wondered, did Matthew's story veer into what, in the eyes of most, seems wildly aberrant? He understood my line of questioning, and his own explanation started with playground teasing he'd experienced as a child. "In elementary school," Matthew recalled, "kids teased me because I was tubby and had a funny last name. I got called 'Kraut' and 'Jerry.'" But many children who are bullied on the playground never become neo-Nazis. Was there more to it than the name-calling?

Over the course of many interviews, Matthew offered an almost clinical judgment about himself: "I think I'm on the spectrum, high-functioning. I try not to let it get in the way." Matthew was referring to autism, a disability in which high intelligence can be paired with an inability to feel empathy for others. Needless to say, there are many degrees and expressions of autism, and purposes to which the minds of people on the spectrum can be turned. The world-famous Swedish climate change activist Greta Thunberg is on the autistic spectrum, for example. Still, this might help account for Matthew's fixity of thought and absence of empathy for the many victims implied in his neo-Nazi line of thinking.

Like the history of his negligent father and his autism, one further incident might have shaped the young Matthew Heimbach. Describing his childhood, Matthew mentioned an extraordinary episode that occurred when his mother was a schoolteacher in Rockville, Maryland. "When my mother was pregnant with me, she was teaching school. Rockville was diverse, and the classes my mother taught were diverse. She had given a failing grade to a Black male student because he hadn't shown up for class. So, at the end of one school day, as she walked to her car, that Black student followed her with a gun and threatened to kill her if she didn't pass him. After that," Matthew recounted, "my parents decided to move to Poolesville, the 95 percent white town where I was born. I don't know if it was done consciously or unconsciously, but I think my parents decided we needed to flee to a majority-white area because it was safer." Then Matthew added, "My mother is not a racist. She has no implicit biases of any kind. I know her. She's a multiculturalist. She toes the party line. But when her kid was threatened, she acted. So that's always bothered me." His mother, as he saw her, was a prisoner of a liberal worldview that nearly prevented her from protecting herself—or him—from "Black violence." But rather than exploring this incident, Matthew seemed to weld it to the well-armored category of a white victim of a Black perpetrator, a victim in need of stormtrooper-type defense.

In *Healing from Hate*, the sociologist Michael Kimmel describes the lives of male extremists in the United States, Germany, and England who later abandon their fearsome beliefs to become "ex-extremists." Most of the men Kimmel studied had been severely abused, abandoned, or traumatized by their fathers. Most of those who hadn't been so treated by their fathers had been abused physically or sexually by stepfathers. Those fathers or stepfathers who were not absent or openly abusive were "emotionally shut down, opaque, phantom presences in their own homes." Such boys grow up to feel, Kimmel argues, like "failed men." They can then fill in the blank space where "good man" or "successful man" might be with the idea of "killer." As the historian George Mosse observed of German male extremists in the 1930s: "Battle was part of their very being. They carried war in their blood."

Women, while not as scapegoated as were Jews, Blacks, and immigrants in Matthew's worldview, were confined to a secondary role, as was right and proper in the Russian Orthodox Church to which—breaking with his family's Catholic tradition—he now belonged. He didn't resent women, as did many members of the Proud Boys, according to one study. Still, white nationalism was a man's game.

But was something else also going on?

A Shame Shield

Through the many interviews Matthew and I were to have over four years, during which he would undergo astonishing changes, I noticed a great sensitivity to what Matthew felt to be falsely imposed, ethnically based shame placed upon himself. Liberals, he declared, were preventing him from taking pride in his German heritage, his Irish heritage, his whiteness.

"I've felt like I've been accused of crimes committed by ancestors on both my mother's and father's sides, and that makes me *furious*. I'm sure my dad's relatives back in Germany fought against the U.S. in World War II. I'm sure my mom's ancestors in Virginia fought against the Union. I'm told Germans and Confederates are evil. But"—and here his voice hardened—"I am not going to take on that guilt, to apologize for their heritage. I think liberals are putting America on an apology overload. And I won't stand for it."

Even as a nine-year-old boy, Matthew recalled, "my school basketball team had always been called the Poolesville Indians. To be politically correct, some liberals want to change the team's name to the Poolesville Falcons. I fought that." In high school, he became determined to exonerate his ancestors and himself from an imagined shame. "I checked into my maternal grandmother's history until I found Confederate ancestors. In high school, I joined the Descendants of Confederate Veterans. I started doing Virginia 8th Infantry Confederate reenactments."

One way to blot out real or imagined shame is to enhance what feels like a depleted fund of racial pride. This seemed to be what Matthew was trying to do. He was white. He wanted to be allowed to be proud of being white. But from this point, he made a number of additional moves. "I was told the Confederate side was evil and my mom's mother's ancestors were evil Confederates." Given this, Matthew wanted to restore what he imagined as a lost—even stolen—pride in them, and in himself. So his project was to show what his ancestors did was noble and what they thought was right, and to declare as adversaries those in the way of his project. Shame had become attached to categories—whites, Southerners, Germans— and as he felt, indelibly. His project was to wage a war against the unjust shaming of the social categories that held his people. He seemed to think that liberals wanted him to feel carried shame for the past sins of his people, and he stood ready to beat up anyone asking him to do that.

"When I got older," he continued, "I proposed to the Poolesville town council that we build a monument to the Confederate soldiers of Poolesville. The town council came back to me: 'What about *both* sides . . . ?' But Poolesville was an entirely Confederate sympathizer town. There are Union soldiers buried there, but they died of disease or in battles in north Virginia. There weren't *two* sides." To Matthew, the idea behind building a Confederate monument was not simply to commemorate history but to restore pride to his people.

Matthew had been shamed as a child for being tubby, for having a consonant-full last name—and, it would seem, he was not protected from that shame. He was furious at being unjustly shamed, even now as an adult. He saw himself as a victim and set out to gather like-minded others to wage his own war against shame.

One way to counter shame, of course, is to deny what the shame was attached to. Although deeply interested in history, Matthew had the ability to gloss over or deny great mountains of historical fact when he felt such facts personally belittled him and his ancestors. So, as he saw it, the American Civil War concerned not slavery but states' rights. As for slavery itself? "Most Black slaves were treated well," he thought. About the Holocaust, Matthew remarked, "I don't accept that there were death camps or that 6 million people died." If nothing wrong happened, he seemed to reason, there was no reason for shame. For Matthew, it was not possible to imagine redress for past wrongdoing without soaking all living white Americans and German gentiles in permanent, abject shame. As he declared with great certainty, "I'll be absolutely damned if anyone's going to blame me. I don't have to take it."

The Shame Erasure Police

So inspired, Matthew Heimbach took his anti-shame crusade with him as he entered Towson University in Baltimore. "In my junior year, I joined Youth for Western Civilization.

"I discovered that Towson had a Black Student Union. It had a Women's Union. It had a Gay and Lesbian Union. But it didn't have a white union. So I tried to start a White Student Union." Imagining himself a stout protector of white pride and a victim of political correctness, Heimbach also created a quasi-vigilante group of "guards" who roamed around the Towson campus at night with flashlights and pepper spray. Previously, he had organized a Towson chapter of Youth for Western Civilization, which had provoked controversy by chalking the sidewalk with phrases like "White Pride" and "White Guilt ends now." As one Black undergraduate later recalled to a journalist, "it was scary."

To shame prevention, Matthew had gradually added the threat of violence. Armed with a BA in history from Towson, he applied for a teaching credential—a ticket to his American Dream. But, he said, "I was told I had to give up white nationalism if I wanted to teach. And I chose white nationalism. I gave up health care, pension, and starting salary of some $50,000 a year. Now, with my BA, I'll be eternally working for $10 or $11 an hour in factories because I think it's the right thing to do. I can't afford to look at my grandchildren and not have fought and given everything for their sake," he said. So Matthew's pride now had two bases. One basis was as a brave guardian of the American Dream for white Christians. The other was as the sacrificial renouncer of his own chance to achieve that dream.

BA in hand, Matthew entered blue-collar life. In 2015, in a Paoli, Indiana, trailer encampment, he co-founded the Traditionalist Workers Party, which by 2017 already had—or so he claimed—some three hundred adherents in Kentucky alone.

Matthew moved smoothly from his account of his life into a rant against his real and imagined critics. "The left are eternal victims. They worship victimhood, and the flip side is they are big guilt-trippers. But they rely on the farm boys from Tennessee to uphold a system that lets them run their mouths. Who are these bourgeois folks coming to tell us in Poolesville who our mascot should be?" (As noted above, the teams had formerly been known as the Indians.) "You have the secrets of the universe figured out because you have your BA?" Matthew went on. "You're some barista at Starbucks, repackaging talking points from Jon Stewart and Bill Maher. Those guilt-trippers are *weak* and *pathetic*. If they didn't have the power of the state behind them, they would get run over in a day."

In his mind, whites were victims, and liberals were victimizers. The Confederacy and Nazis were also victims of liberal shamers. Perhaps Appalachians felt like victims as well, and the groups could bond, not simply on better times for hard-hit families but on joint anger at being shamed. I came to believe that it was this that had brought Matthew Heimbach to Pikeville.

In the material economy, Matthew's father had worked hard to attain the American Dream while Matthew had bravely given it up, as he saw it, for his beliefs. In fact, his pride in renouncing the Dream was mixed with his disdain for those who wanted it: "I know a guy who worked his ass off, came home to a loveless marriage and affluence and smoked weed: what a *waste*." As for himself, Matthew aspired to proudly rise through the ranks of a hate movement and lead the nation's stormtroopers to the victory of white nationalism.

Matthew confessed that from time to time, "I look at the entry they have for me at the Southern Poverty Law Center website." His notoriety among liberals fascinated him. "There's already a book about me by a Norwegian. Pretty good for age twenty-six!" he said, smiling. He was referring to Vegas Tenold's fine *Everything You Love Will Burn*.

Although his notoriety pleased him, Matthew's family was mortified. "When I told my family I was a neo-Nazi," he recalled in a flat voice, "my parents disowned me." His newfound pride was their shame. "I haven't talked to them since my grandfather's funeral [when he was sixteen] and don't know if any of them are alive or dead. I heard my father's adoptive mother got dementia, and I thought to visit her, but I don't know where she is. I emailed him but I never heard back. My sister changed her last name before she married, so as not to be associated with me. The white nationalist movement is my real family."

So what was going on? Perhaps this: Rejected by his father, as he felt, Matthew came to feel like the "son" of his ancestors—German on one side and southern on the other. Liberals were shaming them for the Holocaust (his father's side) and slavery (his mother's side). So, bright and historically informed as he was, Matthew stormtrooped his way through historical fact, erasing the entirety of the Holocaust and imagining slavery as benign. Lost memory and denied truth were part of the stormtrooper's protective armor. Millions of deaths, lynchings, desperate efforts to escape—all this he saw as lies in an effort to recover what he felt was stolen pride.

Matthew Heimbach had come to a region facing a pride paradox. This region combined declining opportunity and strong ideas about individual responsibility: if you succeed, you take credit; if you fail, you take blame.

Where it was tough to succeed and easy to hit bottom, many felt stuck with an undeserved burden of shame. He was coming to offer them a move out of it. Now, leading up to the Pikeville march, he sought to merge two sources of loss and shame. One was the loss and shame of a whole category of people hurt by globalization, coal depletion, layoff slips, the declining value of hard-won skills—victims of carried shaming. The second was his own imagined racial humiliation. They were victims. He was a victim. Together they could be brother victims.

The move that Matthew was to offer the town was from shame to blame, and from blame to revenge. As he saw things then, the election of Barack Obama, the rise of Black Lives Matter, the Martin Luther King Jr. national holiday, the renaming of buildings, the removed Confederate statues, new courses about race history—these were the work of pride thieves.

Matthew Heimbach felt like a prospector in search of a cultural version of that get-rich-quick seam of coal. He would dig out aggrieved pride, ignite it into a furious flame, and lead an expanding band of troops on to white glory.

5

Insiders, Outsiders

"That march? I'm locking my door."

Ruth Mullins, a gentle, retired African American civil servant who had worked in the Social Service Administration, was a faithful member of the Mt. Zion Baptist Church and an avid reader of the *Washington Post*. A youthful seventy-three, Ruth had light brown eyes and a softly etched face encircled by graying hair. An arthritic hip gave her some trouble as we made our way to a quiet table in a nearby restaurant in Pikeville. I had picked her up in front of her house, which was ensconced in a grove of pines near the homes of her mother and two sisters. As we lingered over dinner, she speculated matter-of-factly about why the marchers were coming to town: "I was born and grew up in Pikeville like my parents, grandparents, and great-grandparents. But we're 1 percent of the population in Pike County. So maybe they think we're not here."

Whether the marchers were unaware of Blacks, Jews, and immigrants in eastern Kentucky or openly targeting them in the whitest congressional district in the United States, there were signs of their presence as points of pride. For one thing, a bronze plaque in the historic center of Pikeville featured Effie Waller Smith, a Pikeville-born African American poet, the daughter of slaves, and author of three praised books of poetry, her first published in 1904 at the age of twenty-five. For another thing, Pikeville's Dils Cemetery, established by a colonel in the Union Army, is reputed to be the first integrated cemetery in eastern Kentucky.

Immigrants had a local presence too. Most residents got their annual checkups and specialized care at the Pikeville Medical Center, which listed on its staff such names as Dr. Al Addasi, Dr. Muhammad Ahmad, and Dr. Ramya Akella. "It's very hard to get good medical care here in the mountains," Mayor Andrew Scott told me. "Thank God we've got them here." And many Pikeville residents ate at restaurants with names such as El Azul Grande, Mi Hacienda, El Picante, El Burrito Loco—run by workers of Mexican heritage who also formed part of a quietly welcomed minority.

While Matthew Heimbach, born in Maryland, resident of Indiana, and a newcomer to Appalachia, was praising Nazi Germany, he was bringing his message to a town that had, in effect, welcomed those his marchers reviled. As Ruth explained to me, "The KKK is not the norm around Pikeville and never was. A hundred years ago, maybe, but not in recent times." The KKK had indeed appeared in Pikeville about a hundred years ago—1924—and also once again in 1990.[126] Echoing Donovan Blackburn's refrain, she added with a tired sigh, "Racists have the same rights to free speech as the rest of us, but I know this place, and people around here aren't going for the bait."

This was also the view of other local African Americans, both older and younger. Ruth's ninety-two-year-old great-aunt, Thelma Mullins, a diminutive woman who when I met her was seated by a table surrounded by family photos in her living room, tended to by a loving daughter and grandson, hadn't heard of the march. When told about it, she replied, "I don't pay it any mind." The daughter of sharecroppers, a retired custodian for the First National Bank of Pikeville, and the mother of ten, Thelma recalled her own childhood: "The nine of us lived on Dr. Wallis's farm, and Daddy paid the rent in corn and built the log cabin we lived in. He broke the soil with our mule, Big John, and my mother canned our vegetables. It was a lot of work."

Thelma had graduated from what was then called the Perry A. Cline School, established by a lawyer who was part of the McCoy clan and an active participant in the feud between the McCoys and Hatfields. In 1930, when Thelma attended it, the school taught some eighty-seven Black students and had a Spanish club and a choir that regularly sang at the First National Bank. (Pikeville High began admitting Black students in 1956, but the county's schools were not fully integrated until a decade later in 1966, when the Perry A. Cline School closed.) Thelma dismissed the marchers coming to town with a light laugh and shake of her head. "Ask them if they ever worked as hard as I have."

A neighboring African American minister in her forties who conducted services in a small church and stocked a three-shelf "Prayer Box" outside it with canned food for those in need echoed Ruth's account. Her Sunday service drew some dozen worshippers, mostly Black with a few whites, her nephew playing the guitar. "When my husband [a minister] died, the choirmaster and choir left," she said philosophically, "but the rest of us make joyful noise." As for the march, she said, "That's not worth messing with at church."

An earnest, twenty-nine-year-old Black administrator at UPike who oversaw its student affairs described the racial scene at college. "At the college, we're 7 percent Black. We had Black History Day a while back, but the kids are young, have their exams, sports, dating, and weren't that interested. I'm planning to get up a mobile Black history van with photos of various figures in Black history, maybe go around to the dorms, rouse a little more interest. But on the dance floor." He paused. "It's funny about the *n*-word. It's fine for Blacks to use the *n*-word on themselves. But I noticed at a recent dance, a few kids would whirl around to see if a white was using it. They feel proprietary—like Pike County whites feel about the word *hillbilly*." As for the forthcoming march, he shook his head. "Who likes this stuff? But you get to say what you think so long as you're peaceful, right? This is America."

Most of Ruth Mullins's family had come to Pike County long ago, about as far back as the ancestors of Donovan Blackburn, the city manager, Burton Webb, the president of the university, and many others. Ruth's ancestors came to Kentucky long before the Great Migration of Blacks out of the deep South between about 1910 and 1970, a few of whom turned a stop-over into a permanent stay.

Ruth's father had been a coal miner in the last of the boom times when football fans were chanting "That's all right, that's okay . . ." As in much of America, Pikeville residents were highly attuned to company investments and divestments, which sucked workers in or flushed them out, creating a culture of boom and bust. In boom times coal jobs attracted Black workers to the area. Between 1912 and 1927, five hundred companies had set up coal camps throughout southern Appalachia, providing a third of the region's jobs. Pike County alone had at least fifty-four company-owned coal camps built between 1907 and 1958 to house miners and their families. These ranged in size from ten workers at the Elkhorn City Coal Company's camp in Praise to 1,500 workers at the Ford Motor Company's camp in Stone. By the onset of World War II, Pike County was among the most populous in the state.

The largest camp in the entire state had been built by U.S. Steel in 1917 in the town of Lynch, sixty-five miles south of Pikeville, to house two thousand workers needed at the company's coal mines. It contained over a thousand houses, a four-story department store, and a bowling alley. By the end of World War II, Lynch was home to twelve thousand residents hailing from thirty-eight nations.

The camps were a story of diversity in rural America. As the public intellectual, lawyer, and writer Harry Caudill writes: "Up from the worn-out cotton fields of the Deep South came the sons and daughters of dirt-poor tenant-farmers to seek a new start." Added to these were workers from Italy, Hungary, Poland, Romania, Albania, and Greece. "The 900 new houses in Jenkins sheltered more than 8,000 people on land which a few years ago had . . . been [one man's] corn and pasture fields." New towns sprang up with names such as Happy, Sassafras, and Hi-Hat. In "the Golden Age of the coal industry in the Cumberland Plateau[, coal] was eagerly sought for the nation's fireplaces, furnaces and mills, and the black diamonds poured in endless torrents out of hundreds of great and small tipples . . . The principal tools of the miner's trade were a manually operated breast auger, a pick, a No. 9 shovel, a carbide lamp, a miner's cap of soft canvas and leather, and a round tin dinner pail," Caudill writes. Up through the layoffs, this was the life of Ruth Mullins's dad. "After Dad lost his job mining coal in the 1990s," she recalled, "he found work here in Pikeville at a local sand-dredging company, raising us kids."

Seated at the restaurant, having ordered our meals, Ruth began recalling her girlhood in Pikeville. "I went to a small all-Black elementary school near here, which integrated after I left. In 1959, I was one of four Black students, all girls, who integrated Pikeville High. There was no problem with integration, really not," she reflected. Records show that Pikeville High admitted 140 Black students as early as 1956, two years after the Supreme Court's decision in *Brown v. Board of Education* ruled separate schools "inherently unequal." "Jenkins [a nearby town] didn't integrate until the late 1960s," Ruth noted.

As a teenager, Ruth also encountered parts of town that were segregated. "In those days, Pikeville's Liberty Theater had two sections, downstairs for whites and the balcony for people of color. A second theater had eight rows of seats set apart for Blacks in the back. Across from school was the Bobby Sox Grill. White teenagers, like Ruth's white friend Margaret, could play the jukebox and dance, maybe have a Coke and a hot dog," Ruth recounted.

"Margaret asked me, 'Why didn't you ever go?'

"'You didn't know? I wasn't allowed; it was segregated.'

"Margaret was *shocked*. Whites lived in a cocoon," Ruth noted matter-of-factly. It was not just segregation itself that was painful, but the solitude in her experience of it, given Margaret's stance as a bystander. It was this that stuck with Ruth years later. I was reminded of a comment by the late Dr. Paul Farmer, founder of Partners in Health, an organization that brought quality health care to rural Haiti and Rwanda, among many other places. When once speaking about interracial friendship, he reflected that a knowledge of history is the price of admission to intimacy.

Ruth also recalled a more searing experience, casually ignored by a high school teacher she once loved. "We had an excellent English teacher who took our class to the Barter Theater in Abingdon, Virginia, in 1963 to see *The Taming of the Shrew.* It was a great treat. But it was followed by dinner at the Martha Washington Inn. When the class got there, we discovered that me and three other Black girls were asked to eat in the restaurant's kitchen while the white kids could eat in the restaurant." The teacher did nothing to alter the plan. "So we Black girls refused to eat separately in the kitchen and went back to sit in the bus and return home hungry." The Supreme Court had already desegregated schools in 1954, but it wasn't until 1964 that the Civil Rights Act forbade such discrimination. Recalling the sting of sitting isolated and hungry in the bus while the white students ate at the restaurant, her classmates' and teacher's inaction, weak apology and heavy silence, the shame she felt, Ruth mused, "I hold it against that teacher to this day."

Conversation on Two Tracks

While sharing these childhood memories over dinner, Ruth was continually flipping through many dozens of family photos stored on her cellphone, her eye acutely attuned, as it turned out, to pigment. To the side of her plate, Ruth's fingers swept up the screen in search of certain faces. Indeed, our dinner conversation proceeded along two tracks, one through words, the other through the images she slowly combed through. Image by image, solemn face by solemn face—with Ruth stopping to share one or another—some dark, many light, she traced her lineage back through 160 years of life in Kentucky.

Her mother, with light brown skin tone, captured in middle age, born in Pike County in 1931, with a gracious yet solemn expression.

Her mother's mother, born in Pike County in 1911, looked similar.

Ruth paused at an image. "He looks sort of white, don't you think? . . . My whole family is very white; some have blue eyes and blond hair."

Scrolling to another ancestor, Ruth paused, then said, "She was half white." She went on to tell me, "A white co-worker in Washington, DC, once told me, 'I don't know what race you are. You're not white and you're not not-white.' I didn't like her saying that. I am what I am."

By the time the entrees had arrived, Ruth was still slowly scrolling through images. Her paternal great-grandfather had been fathered, she surmised, by a slaveholder, the oldest son of the white owner of a medium-sized farm in Harold, in neighboring Floyd County, Kentucky, a twenty-six-minute drive northwest of Pikeville. Her paternal great-grandmother's white owner, Ruth discovered, had been born in Virginia but moved to Kentucky and bought a farm—not a plantation, and without a pillared mansion. "My maternal great-grandfather had also arrived from Virginia before 1840, also in shackles." As for her ancestors' light color, Ruth added matter-of-factly, "You know how the sons of the plantation owners did with the women. There's a history to that a lot of us aren't looking at."

Until 1865, "the census designated Blacks by using numbers," Ruth noted. "After 1865, they were recorded by name." In 1860, Blacks made up about 20 percent of the state's population, and 4.5 percent of them were free. In mountainous eastern Kentucky, which was unsuitable for large-scale agriculture, the Black population was far smaller than other parts of the state. In 1860, Pike County listed a population of 7,325 whites, 29 slave owners, 37 enslaved Blacks, 60 enslaved mulattoes, 5 free Blacks, and 35 free mulattoes. After the Civil War, the 1870 census listed as born in Pike County 64 Blacks, 32 mulattoes, and 7 U.S. Colored Troops. Ruth told me, "One of my ancestors actually owned a coal mine in West Virginia."

A century on, Ruth's cellphone images revealed other relatives who had arrived in Kentucky between 1910 and 1970 as part of the Great

Migration. "My Alabama relatives moved to Kentucky to work in the coal mines," she explained. But with the downturn in coal, "my uncles and aunts and neighbors moved north for jobs at Inland Steel in Illinois and Chevrolet in Michigan." For them, Kentucky was a stopover in the migration out of the Deep South. As sociologist Karida Brown writes in her book *Gone Home: Race and Roots Through Appalachia*, part of the Great Migration came through eastern Appalachia. "The first generation migrated out of the bowels of the Deep South to the mountains of eastern Kentucky in search of liberty and citizenship," she writes, and then moved on for jobs in Cincinnati, Cleveland, Columbus, Dayton, Middletown, Pontiac, Flint, and other cities before the auto plants themselves moved to Mexico and China.

But during their years and sometimes decades in eastern Kentucky, Blacks worked in the mines, living in towns with names like Black Joe, Harlan, Hazard, Red Fox, and Wheelwright. Even today, Black reunions in Kentucky gather cars with license plates from New Jersey, Ohio, and Virginia, historian Bill Turner writes in *The Harlan Renaissance*. Lynch County (named for a man, not a crime) had four thousand Blacks during World War I. In 1946, Harlan alone counted 8,500 Black coal miners and members of their families—a population that has now dwindled to just over 500 residents in the county as a whole.

Still, Ruth's father, like other Black residents at the time, was likely to have kept an eye out for signs of danger. Across America in the twentieth century some ten thousand so-called sundown towns emerged. Such towns required Blacks to leave before sundown, under threat of violence. Pikeville was not one of them.

The most notorious incident Ruth knew about had taken place in Corbin, an hour's drive west of Pikeville, in 1919, when Ruth's father would have been about eight years old. White male townspeople drafted into the U.S. Army to fight in World War I returned home, war-weary, to search for work in a shrinking economy. Arriving home, these white vets discovered that the Louisville and Nashville Railroad (L&N) had hired

Black workers to lay new tracks. A mob of 125 white men then drove some 200 to 400 Black workers and their families out of Corbin at gunpoint. No one was killed, but Corbin's Black residents had been traumatized, dispossessed, and wrongly shamed, nearly all of them never to return.

The Corbin expulsion happened an hour away from her home in Pikeville, but she knew and remembered the history of Corbin, and her white friend Margaret did not. Indeed, many white people I spoke to did not recall the Corbin expulsion, and it did not come up in conversations with the history-minded Matthew Heimbach. "I didn't grow up knowing about the Bobby Sox Grill or any segregated Pikeville movie theater, or Corbin," another man told me. "It wasn't till I got to college in my forties that I began to open my eyes to the idea that it's not just stores and jobs that get segregated but our memories themselves."

Ruth's own journey to the American Dream began in the Pikeville mayor's office and took her to Maryland, near the nation's capital. "After I graduated from Pikeville High, I took a course in bookkeeping and I found a job keeping the books in a ladies' dress shop," she recalled. In 1960, Pikeville's mayor, William Hambley, began orchestrating the historic Pikeville Cut-Through, the immense engineering project that many compared to the dredging of the Panama Canal. Hambley sought bright applicants to conduct a survey. "I was hired, and I loved the work," Ruth recalled.

Later, "a civil service test was going around, and people urged me to take it. I took it and earned a top score. So, I got a job offer as a clerk typist in the benefits office of the Social Security Administration in Washington, D.C. I was twenty-one! I found an apartment in Silver Spring, Maryland, and started work. Back then, the office rated you on the state of your carbon copies and your phone skills." But Ruth's world broadened. "After a while, I did intakes of Japanese internees, Holocaust survivors, Chinese custom marriage requestees, young legless Vietnam vets. You weren't supposed to look shocked."

Thirty years later, Ruth got word from her sisters back in Pikeville. "My mom was developing dementia. So I came back to help." Once home, Ruth said, "I got a job in the Mine Safety and Health Administration handling claims for black lung here." When she retired, she stayed in Pikeville.

Dessert had arrived, and Ruth set aside her phone, which remained open to the image of a stern, gray-bearded Black man staring into the camera from a hard life. She picked it up again and scrolled to a grainy image she had been searching for—her paternal great-grandmother. She had been born into slavery in the early 1800s in Virginia. She had been the first in the Mullins family to arrive in Kentucky, roughly two hundred years ago.

Between the inhales and exhales of capitalism, including federal investment in the Cut-Through, through shifts in federally directed desegregation and the post–Civil War movements of Blacks, Ruth Mullins had made her way to and back from the nation's capital. Meanwhile, Matthew Heimbach was coming to reverse the progress Ruth had lived through and reintroduce the shame of exclusion.

From the Holocaust to East Kentucky

"We'd had the KKK come around Prestonsburg in the 1990s. So, when I heard about the Pikeville march"—John Rosenberg raised his eyes to heaven—"I thought, 'God, not *again*.'" A man who lived a half hour's drive from Ruth's home, John was a retired civil rights lawyer who in his earlier years had helped with the full integration of such places as the Bobby Sox Grill and Pikeville High School and who, as a Jew, had his own place on Matthew Heimbach's white nationalist list of enemies.

John was a short, balding, bespectacled, curious, and friendly man of eighty-eight, with twinkly eyes. He and his Quaker wife, Jean, greeted me at the front door of their home, tucked along a row of other modest, well-kept homes with front gardens on the outskirts of Prestonsburg, a short drive north of Pikeville. As we walked down the front hall beside a wall crowded with small framed photos, Jean, a pleasant silver-haired woman, pointed out to me one after another of John's German Jewish family members. "In our immediate family"—the *our* and *we* in her speech born of a long, devoted marriage—"fourteen didn't make it," she told me, referring to family members who perished in the Holocaust.

John offered me a seat at their cozy kitchen table, set with coffee cups and a dish of nuts and cookies. A warm man who exuded a faith in the possibility of goodness, he related the traumatic events of his childhood without hesitation. While some survivors bear witness to the Holocaust with mournful reticence, in John's open-hearted telling, I felt an invitation to know personal events that he had relived many times before in a spirit of moral remembrance.

To Matthew Heimbach, reminders of the Holocaust, like those of racism, had the power to evoke shame and blame, so one needed to suppress them. But to John the purpose of memory was to remind and warn. In the face of marchers' denial, John said: "We don't want to forget these things. They could happen again."

He began, "I was born in 1931 in the small town of Magdeburg, Germany, and we lived next door to a synagogue where my dad was an assistant rabbi. My name was Hans then, and I was studying at home because the Nazis had already barred Jewish students from public schools. One night when I was seven, we woke up to the sound of breaking glass and pounding at our front door. It was 1938: Kristallnacht. We opened the door and saw armed soldiers ordering my parents, my two-year-old sister, and me to the courtyard, where we found our Jewish neighbors too. It was November and cold. The soldiers hauled out Jewish scrolls from the synagogue to the courtyard and burned them in a big fire. Then they blew up the synagogue. We returned after midnight and found our home wrecked."

Throughout Germany, homes, stores, and synagogues were vandalized on Kristallnacht, and in the days immediately following, Jewish men in Magdeburg were rounded up, herded onto trains, and transported to death camps. "My father was forced by gunpoint into a line, and the next morning taken to Buchenwald. Thank God the local mayor intervened, and my father was released seventeen days later and given thirty days to leave Germany. We were among the last to stand in line for a visa," John said.

"We arrived without a penny in New York. My father was a teacher, and after some time set out for the South to take a job sweeping floors in a textile mill in Gastonia, North Carolina. My mother and us children followed, and she took a job as a maid. I entered school, learned English, joined the Eagle Scouts, got called John, and wore red, white, and blue on Thursdays." Later John joined the American army, earned a law degree on the GI Bill, and determined to dedicate his law training to civil rights. He was to end up as a trial attorney in the civil rights division of the U.S. Department of Justice, focusing on the South.

Rosenberg went on to establish the Appalachian Citizens' Law Center, a nonprofit law firm that helps ensure the medical rights of coal miners like Ruth Mullins's father. These included the rights for ex-miners with black lung, such as those addressed on the claim forms Ruth helped process. Rosenberg also represented small farmers whose unknowing ancestors had signed ruinous broad-form deed rights to farmland, not realizing the deed had sold them rights to the surface of the land, while selling to others the right to mine coal beneath its surface.

John joined a slow-moving but successful effort to amend the Kentucky state constitution in 1987 to outlaw such deeds. An ancestor of Andrew Scott, the mayor of Coal Run, had sold such rights, Scott would tell me ruefully; but his father, then Kentucky's attorney general, later facilitated the ban on them. Rosenberg also established the Appalachian Research and Defense Fund of Kentucky, which serves low-income clients in thirty-seven counties in eastern Kentucky, including Pike County.

John gave talks on the Holocaust at local schools, joined charitable boards, and socialized easily with his Prestonsburg neighbors. At any gathering, he could be found deeply engaged in conversation, and over the years his wife, Jean, developed a slow, measured walk to the car, to signal John it was time to go.

Now, having called Appalachia home for most of his life, and long retired from his law practice, he kept an anti-extremist speech in his desk drawer which he'd given to townspeople the last time the KKK and neo-Nazis came to Prestonsburg, in 1990, and he had it ready again if he was asked to speak at the upcoming march. In it he wrote, "The Klan . . . brings suffering to Blacks and other minorities, to Jews and to Catholics." He recalled the civil rights workers murdered by the KKK in 1964 in Mississippi, naming each slain man: "James Chaney, African American, and Michael Schwerner and Andrew Goodman, both white Jews."

Meanwhile, mindful of potential violence, the UPike president had asked organizers to postpone the counter-rally at which John would have spoken, so John had tucked his speech in his desk drawer and remained on call.

Now retired from law, John and Jean Rosenberg sat on the board of the local homeless shelter. "We pack food for the homeless together with other volunteers who are our neighbors and friends. We're helping the homeless because we feel so lucky to have a home here. Most of our friends are either 'dipped' or 'sprinkled,'" John said, fondly referring to two forms of Christian baptism.

"Before they met us, many had never heard of a Jew or Quaker. But we all prepare lunches and dinners at the shelter and have very dear friends from Baptist Free Will. One of my evangelical friends told me, 'Jews are the chosen people.'

"But I told her, 'I'm Jewish but I don't think I'm chosen just because I'm a Jew. I think we're *all* chosen living here in America.'

"My evangelical neighbors love me dearly. The way I talk, they worry I won't go to heaven and they really want me to go there. I'm touched they worry for me." But John Rosenberg felt that in his lifetime, he had already been saved by the Allied victory in World War II, which was in part the legacy of the Appalachian soldiers who gave their lives for it.

As he walked me to his front door, John asked, "Who else are you visiting?" I answered that I would be seeing the acting imam at the local mosque, Dr. Syed Badrudduja. "Oh!" John exclaimed. "Dr. Budgy—we call him that—he's a good friend. Before Budgy retired, he was my doctor. He invites me to visit his mosque during Ramadan and Diwali," John added, "and we drive together to Williamson in West Virginia, where he goes for religious services to a mosque and I go to the nearest synagogue. Give him my best!"

Masjid Al-Farooq and 9/11

Inside the Masjid Al-Farooq Islamic Center of East Kentucky, on Masjid Avenue off Big Branch of Abbott Creek outside Prestonsburg, Dr. Syed Badrudduja's assistant answered the phone. He asked me the purpose of my proprosed interview, and when I mentioned the march and my interest in the shifting politics in the area, he said, "We're good people! What these extremists say, what Donald Trump says about us Muslims after the September 11 attack in New York in 2001—*no, no, no!* That was terrible! We here, we didn't do it. Please excuse me for shouting. I'm only the assistant here. We're *good* people!"

When shortly thereafter I met Dr. Badrudduja, he lit up at the name John Rosenberg. "A very good man!" A mannerly, slender man of seventy-seven, with a carefully trimmed gray beard, wearing large glasses, Dr. Budgy walked out of the mosque to meet me at my car where he bowed his head with prayerful hands in greeting.

Like Rosenberg, Dr. Budgy had made a home in white Christian Appalachia. He lived a ten-minute drive from the Rosenbergs and oversaw the only building of its kind in this Bible Belt for miles around—the Islamic Center of East Kentucky. A large white plaque read WELCOME TO MASJID AL-FAROOQ in English and Arabic. Dr. Budgy conducted me inside to two chairs and a table on the far side of a large, carpeted prayer room. He had set out a bottle of juice and sweets.

On Fridays, he explained, the large prayer room was partitioned to separate male from female worshippers kneeling on the room-length blue carpet. "Some women prefer to worship on the floor below," he said. The walls gave over to large arched windows on all sides. On the floor to the side of the entrance was a rectangular basin and faucet for worshippers to wash their feet and hands before worship.

"I came to Prestonsburg in 1976 from Hyderabad, India, as a general surgeon. The hills were so high, the roads narrow, travel slow, and I felt cut off," Syed began. "And at that time, I was the only person in this area from India. By the 1990s we had two or three, then twelve Indian families. Now, forty-two years later, in Prestonsburg we have fifteen or thirty Muslims from India, Pakistan, Lebanon, Bangladesh, Syria. Most of them are medical specialists, and Kentucky needs us. One of our worshippers is a Syrian-born pediatrician who serves five thousand patients from a seven-county area," Syed said with a touch of pride. At the University of Pikeville, there are enough Muslim medical students to form a Muslim Doctors' Association. "If someone should suffer an injury while praying," the imam said, "we have cardiologists, surgeons, pediatricians. Someone here could help.

"I've just returned from a visit to Hyderabad," he said. The son of a state employee, he'd grown up as one of nine children, two brothers of whom had also emigrated. After attending medical school in India, Dr. Budgy entered the United States in 1971 and repeated a five-year surgical residency at the University of Louisville before he was offered a special visa to set up practice in the government-designated "underserved area" of eastern Kentucky.

"Generally, it's a very safe place for foreigners—'foreigners' meaning anyone from outside eastern Kentucky," Dr. Budgy added slyly. "If you talk about someone from Lexington, well, that's not *eastern* Kentucky; that's *central* Kentucky."

Did he feel that people stereotyped him? I asked. "No," he mused. "Here it's the other way around: the people of eastern Kentucky are stereotyped by the rest of America."

Still, he added, "by the color of your skin, you're an outsider, because people here aren't exposed to those of us from other nations. Brown skin means non-native-born." A sociology professor at a local community college later told me, "I bring in my students to the mosque and ask them to write reports. Some wrote that they were sweating, nervous, scared to walk in. It felt so foreign."

Of the orientation of early Appalachian settlers to those considered outsiders, historian David Hackett Fischer has written wryly, "The people of the southern highlands have been remarkably even-handed in their antipathies—which they have applied to all strangers without regard to race, religion or nationality." But for immigrants like John Rosenberg and Syed Badrudduja, the story seemed like one of gradual affectionate adoption, perhaps helped by the fact that they were highly educated and brought badly needed skills.

Only after 9/11 did Syed Badrudduja feel targeted as a Muslim. "I got some harassing drunk phone calls at 2:00 a.m. We traced the call, and it came in from Ohio." A few months later, however, BB gun holes appeared in two mosque windows and a street sign in front of the mosque was thrown in a ditch. "We installed an alarm system and combination lock."

For Ruth Mullins, race had been a preoccupying fact of life at school, at the movies, at the Bobby Sox Grill, on the trip to Virginia, and in moments of missed intimacy with her color-blind friend Margaret. Ironically, having been born in India, Dr. Badrudduja had grown up in a culture with three thousand years of the Hindu caste system, ranging from Brahmins at the top to Dalits (formerly known as "untouchables") at the bottom, and Muslims such as he were now suffering increasing discrimination under the Hindu nationalist government in India.

But whatever social position he'd been assigned in India, in eastern Kentucky as a foreigner on a J-1 visa as an urgently needed doctor, Dr. Badrudduja found himself defined these days as "a person of color." John Rosenberg, a victim of Hitler in Germany, was now a non-Protestant in Protestant Kentucky. And, though earlier discriminated against as an

African American, Ruth Mullins and her family were among the most time-honored residents of Pike County.

Those like Ruth, John, and Dr. Budgy—who in different ways counted as "minorities"—seemed to adopt a unique stance: to be on guard for thrown-off shame-turned-blame. KKK and neo-Nazi marches through town. BB gun marks in the window.

Ruth Mullins was a longtime resident whose most painful memories were linked to pigment. For John Rosenberg, such moments were bound to being a Jewish refugee, and for Dr. Budgy, it was his color, religion, accent, and immigration status. In different ways, all three had taken a hit in pride.

In her book *Caste: The Origins of Our Discontent,* the historian Isabel Wilkerson compares their three countries of origin—the United States, India, and Germany—and finds in all three the beliefs and practices that express caste. Comparing practices of separation and subordination in the three countries, Wilkerson argues that all are based on the fixed underlying concept of purity and pollution, and each borrows legitimacy from religion.

Every form of caste has been historically based on shame. In India, caste crystallized over thousands of years of history as a cosmology alongside Hinduism as a religion, arranging people into rank and occupation by tradition. A Brahmin might have the same skin tone as a Dalit, since there it is not color itself that determines a person's place in the caste hierarchy. In its ultimate form, the Indian caste system relies on the idea of untouchability. In Germany, the ghettoization of Jews preceded the most dreadful measures taken by the Nazis. In the United States, the "color line" established separation, first through slavery, then through Jim Crow.

But through different routes, all three had encountered and overcome caste barriers to achieve their American Dream and in different ways enjoyed welcome and pride in doing so.

Most of the neighbors and friends of these three in the region were working their way out of a pride paradox—low opportunity coupled with the belief that the blame is on you if you fail. To cope with unwarranted shame, they were making moves—to turn it inward, turn it outward, or find a third way to understand and cope with it. But the main concern for Ruth, John, and Dr. Budgy was to get out of the way of other people's thrown-off shame. For that thrown-off shame looked like, hit like, and hurt like blame.

But now new danger was afoot. In the United States, as in India and parts of Germany, the winds of majoritarian nationalism were blowing— Hindu nationalism in India, white Christianism in Germany, and white nationalism in America, each legitimated by its own version of pride. The message was the same: *Stop. Go back. What you want—including pride— is ours.*

On the eve of the march, John Rosenberg reminded himself which desk drawer held his anti-KKK speech, in case he got a last-minute call. The imam double-checked the lock on the front door of the Islamic Center, which hadn't been changed since the scare after 9/11. The Prestonsburg chief of police, who also happened to be Dr. Budgy's patient, called him to say, "I just want to let you know, given this march coming up, we're keeping an eye out for you." Meanwhile, as she placed her cellphone back in her purse at the end of our evening, Ruth Mullins repeated that she planned to lock her front door. Slowly, deliberately, she gave voice to an idea they all shared: "You don't want someone stirring up the fringe."

PART TWO

Faces in the Crowd

6

Bootstrap Pride

In April 2017 the stage seemed set. Pikeville was preparing to protect itself from a band of white nationalists who were preparing to march into it. The protectors were at their desks making calls. The marchers were standing in formation on a field an hour's drive away. Potential victims had locked their doors. In addition, anti-white-nationalist activists were planning to drive en masse from Louisville to Pikeville, including some associated with the Antifa (anti-fascist) movement and a group called Redneck Revolt. But what about everyone else? I wondered. How might they take measure of Heimbach's appeal to the region's distress?

So I set out to talk with a range of residents, top to bottom—and, politically, side to side. Among these faces in the crowd was a forty-year-old man named Alex Hughes. In his life experiences and concerns, he seemed to me to fall near the center. A large, long-striding man with a friendly, open, thoughtful manner, Alex had graying blond hair tucked under his company cap. An aspiring blue-to-white-collar Republican, he was part of the 80 percent of Pike County residents who voted for Donald Trump in 2016 and 2020.

Our talk together began with a surprise. We were walking along the sidewalk of Pikeville's Main Street on our way to a small café, when Alex stopped short, his eyes fixed in a frozen stare at something across the street.

"See that parking lot? That's where I got *this*." Alex tilted his head to reveal a scar extending five inches from his right ear to near his chin. "Four inches down, and the guy would have gotten my neck and me."

Once we were settled before our sandwiches in the café, he explained further. "I was in my early twenties and me and a bunch of my friends were hanging out one Saturday night in the 1990s. A lot of us had been scrounging for work and there wasn't that much to do here on weekends. So we parked our cars in that lot and walked around. Later that evening, we heard two drunk guys in the lot talking loudly. So we thought we'd get our cars out and drive around until they got bored and left. But when I tried to walk past one drunk to get to my car, he blocked me, then hit and slashed me. I punched him in the face but fell down back onto the pavement, bleeding badly. Luckily, a friend pulled him away and stopped him from cutting my head off. The police came and arrested him. He got assault with a deadly weapon, ten years. That was the dark side of the nineties around here."

Alex's American Dream was not to own a coal company, but to earn a bachelor's degree—which required money his family lacked—or to become a government administrator like Ruth Mullins. Alex's dream was to provide well for his family, perhaps as a small business owner, and the economic downturn had been holding a knife to that plan.

As for the march? "Oh, I heard about it, but I don't need to know more," Alex told me. "I'm three emergencies past a deadline at a job that I worry I could lose. I don't want racial strife. But sometimes you have to keep your head down and put first things first. I have a wife and three kids, hers, mine, and ours—and they come first."

As a small child, Alex had found his life unsettled by his parents' divorce. "All I remember of my mother before she left was my asking her for a soda pop. After that, no cards, no calls. She just left. So, my stepmother became my actual mother." After his father remarried, Alex became the middle child of three. He had an older brother from his father's earliest marriage, and a much younger sister from the marriage of his father and stepmother. Family life could shift without warning for reasons beyond a child's control.

And work brought great uncertainties too. Alex's grandfather had been a coal miner, and Alex grew up with stories of the dangers inside coal mines. The historian Harry Caudill recalled the routine hazards of mining in the 1960s and earlier: "The miner strapped thick rubber kneepads to his knees, and, kneeling, began to peck at the coal in a strip of some eight inches above the slate floor . . . as far back as the pick handle would allow." He picked out a line of rock beneath, "undercutting" the coal seam. Then it was time to "drill and shoot" the coal. "Pressing heavily with his chest and turning the auger handle, the miner drove the shaft deep into the coal. A line of such holes was drilled. Then charges of black powder were affixed to fuses and shoved far back into the holes. The holes were tamped with 'dead men'—tightly rolled paper cylinders filled with earth. The miners then removed themselves and their tools to a safe place and waited for the 'shot fired.'" A foreman checked the preparations, made sure the workmen were out of danger, then "the flame of a carbide lamp was applied to the ends of the fuses and the hissing trail of fire went blazing into the powder charges. With a roar that shook the tunnels, the shots exploded, and the coal was thrown in a glittering heap onto the floor of the mine."

Highly volatile coal dust could be accidentally set afire by the flame of a miner's lamp. "Flashing like lightning and booming like massed cannons, the explosion raced down headings, entryways and working places," Caudill writes. "Picks, shovels, sledgehammers, rocks, lumps of coal, empty coal-cars and human bodies were flung down the tunnels like pellets in the barrel of a shotgun."

For all the danger of mining, it paid well, the community of miners was close, and it had entered the ledgers of history as a source of pride. Like the legendary whale hunters of nineteenth-century New England or the cowboys of the Great Plains, miners faced danger, even death. In an era of disregard for safety, at a time when mine owners were suspicious of labor unions and regulations, it was a matter of pride to avoid injury and risk the dreaded disease, black lung. To this day, the Pikeville Medical Center has a special wing devoted to the disease and offers free chest X-rays to current or former coal miners to screen for black lung.

The Art of Improvisation: Yes-Sure-ing It into the 1990s

Alex's maternal grandfather had been severely injured in the mines and warned Alex's father and Alex himself to find safer work. So Alex's father became a long-distance coal truck driver. At age sixteen Alex moved in with his grandparents and started painting houses. By nineteen he had started a small business painting houses and married.

In his dream of becoming a business owner, Alex was inspired by his paternal grandfather, a brilliant jack-of-all-trades who improvised his way into the American Dream. "My grandfather was teased for being a dreamer—which was not a proud thing among those in his family," Alex mused. "From age fourteen, my grandfather learned to tinker with the cars that came in to be repaired in his own father's small garage business." Later, Alex's grandfather taught himself to paint and bend glass to create neon signs. In addition to car repair and sign making, Alex's grandfather loved animals and ordered books from which he taught himself veterinary medicine and got a mail-order diploma. Everyone called him "Doc."

Alex's grandfather was a Renaissance man, multiply gifted, a dreamer turned doer. Such a man might well have prospered before the Industrial Revolution, in a world like that described by the Scottish philosopher Adam Smith in The Wealth of Nations. Such a man, Smith wrote, was far more versatile than one who left the countryside to toil lifelong at one specialized if better-paid task in a city factory. But while the rural man may have had a more inventive mind, Smith argued, the urban man became part of a more dynamic economic system. And so it was with Alex's grandfather.

Like his grandfather, Alex started out as a jack-of-all-trades, gifted in many ways, specialized in none. Beginning during his early and brief marriage at nineteen, Alex painted houses. "When the job offers slowed down, I tried elevator repair. Then I found I could pick up jobs from coal companies fixing machines. I got a job with a little company out of Ohio that sold large-format HP printers that print maps of coal mines," Alex recounted. "As the rotary blades carve into mine walls, the enormous wall maps change daily. Coal is a very 'hurry-up-do-it-fast' culture. So they asked me, 'If we ship you the printer and the instructions, can you install it?' I didn't know how to do it, but I can read an instruction manual and I needed work. So I said, 'Yes, sure.' Then I 'yes sure-ed' my way into a job as a locally based technician for a company in Canada, editing video for Massey Energy, and into another job for a guy who ran a national advertising campaign on Facebook."

But by the 1990s Alex's bootstrap "yes, sure" strategy no longer brought in steady work. As with his buddies, his parents didn't have money to put him through college, nor was it common among his friends to go; by the latest estimate, 16 percent of Pike County adults hold bachelor's degrees. So Alex turned to the idea of starting his own business—a small tattoo parlor in Pikeville. To do so, and "to pursue some computer networking ideas," he said, "I took out a sizeable loan to start it up, and I made money, at first."

But Alex continued, "I didn't catch the signs of the downturn soon enough and didn't know how worried to be. My tattoo parlor and computer business went under. Since I was a small businessman, I didn't qualify for unemployment insurance or food stamps. I had to move in with my parents.

"At first, I scrambled to put a lot of little jobs together. But then those little jobs began to dry up. I tried refrigerator repairs, printer repair, 3D imaging. But those jobs also got fewer and fewer. There was *nothing* for me. I applied for a job as a bagger at a grocery store down the road, but no one returned my calls.

"And now I had to pay both my bills and my business loan. By then I was divorced and had my daughter to care for. So when I lost my business and got in debt for $128,000 to the IRS, that's when things really got bad.

"The house? Gone.

"The car? Gone.

"The furniture? Gone.

"My wife's and my wedding rings? Pawned.

"I was in free fall. I felt like there was no place for me. I had to ask myself, 'What did I do wrong?'

"I went to church.

"I prayed.

"I felt *to blame*.

"I leaned on my pastor, and he helped me keep my courage up," Alex said, but he also recalled, "One day at church I spoke with a board member at the local hospital and asked him if they needed any tech help. The next Sunday the pastor gave a sermon about not using the church for business. I felt awful."

Alex thought about leaving eastern Kentucky. "You've got a lot of people who want to say, 'I love the mountains, and this is where my family is from, and I'll never leave.' I admire the heck out of someone who feels that way. But I feel the mountains wall me in. Still, you can't just pack up, move, be homeless, and hope to get a job in Detroit, Toledo, or Chicago. To leave, you need money and contacts, and I didn't have either one."

Everyone I came to know in the 5th Congressional District felt they were living in a region that others—often young and educated—were leaving. They were "stayers" in communities increasingly depleted of well-paid jobs and workers. Despite a recent countertrend for some, since the year 2000, larger cities of the nation have gained population as small towns and rural areas lost theirs. In Kentucky, Jefferson County—which contains Louisville, where Alex Hughes would wind up moving—gained the most population between 2010 and 2021. Pike County—where the marchers were coming—lost the most.

Indeed, Alex was considering joining the white analog to the Black Great Migration. Between 1900 and 1970, 8 million whites had already migrated from the Lower and Upper South. In 1910, some 1,488,000 whites and 442,000 Blacks who were born in the South (including Kentucky, Arkansas, Tennessee, and West Virginia) had moved elsewhere. By 1990, 7,451,000 southern-born whites lived outside the South, as did some 4 million Blacks. Before migrating north, typically a first-time migrant would visit a relative up north. Then, leaving debt-burdened farms, dead-end jobs, shuttered mines and mills, they ventured north on the "hillbilly highway" to settle in poor white ghettos such as Chicago's Uptown, Muncie's Shedtown, and Dayton's East End.

But by the 1990s, many white migrants were turning around. For by then Midwest factories were automating and offshoring, and jobs had become hard to find. Every five years, 6 to 12 percent of all white Americans who migrated out of the Upper South, as the labor historian Max Fraser calls it, returned. In some decades between 1900 and 1975, it was as much as 20 or 25 percent.

At the time, Alex was a stayer watching migration from home. But even as a stayer, Alex saw what leavers saw. "Looking for work outside of here, I got to see how the city looks at us. I started calling people in Pennsylvania, but guys would say, 'Okay, but when I think of cutting-edge technology, I don't think of eastern Kentucky.' So I went to Lexington, Kentucky, and an employer there asked me, 'Do you live here in Lexington? No? Well, there's no job here.' So even *within* Kentucky the city looks down on the country." Alex looked at me long to make sure I grasped this key point. "Then when I hear Facebook, Instagram, Twitter posts with city liberals criticizing rural people, I absolutely"—he drew his head back as if restraining himself—"*do not* need that.

"I don't know if it was a coincidence or not," he went on, "but after six months of looking for work, I began to get gray hair. So I shaved my beard because I didn't want the gray to show."

Then, Alex recalled, he came upon a temptation. "When I got stabbed, they gave me a lot of opioids for pain. Drugs give you a choice—stay sober and live in hell or take a pill." OxyContin was moving into eastern Kentucky just as coal-related jobs—mining, trucking, fixing trucks—were moving out, a hazard for the tempted and cash for the drug companies.

"I got to thinking, if society is rejecting me, its rules don't apply to me. And I thought how easy it would be to make meth in my backyard and pay off my bills and loan." Again, he spoke slowly. "You can get to a state of mind where you think, 'There's no place for me in this society.' I hit bottom. I didn't want to live. I went back to my minister and prayed."

All this was eighteen years behind him now, but Alex was solemn. "The stabbing was a weird drunk on a Saturday night in the 1990s. That was bad. But losing my job was worse. It changed me more than anything else. You *never get over* losing your job."

Journey in Self-Blame

At the same time, Alex felt responsible for the financial woes that followed the failure of his business. "Nobody *wants* to blame themselves for the bad things that happen to you, even me sitting here at the lunch table, looking back at all that happened. But ultimately a lot of that was my fault. I should have seen it coming. I should have told myself, 'Wait a minute. I'm spending too much time on this one single client—I better make sure I've got others.' But I didn't. So ultimately the fault is mine. I put my family through that. For me, that's difficult to admit that I have myself to blame. The buck stops with *me*."

Taking responsibility for his failure meant to Alex that he was a mature, strong, stand-up guy. He wasn't the sort of person to make excuses, or weasel out of responsibility, or point to some larger circumstance. That would be taking the easy way out. He was quietly proud of being this kind of guy. It was a sign of real character: if you succeed, you can feel proud, but if you fail, you "man up." Indeed, across many of the conversations I had in the course of writing this book, if people offered criticism of others, it was often for being lazy, dependent on the government, or a "complainer."

"I don't hold myself responsible for the decline of coal," Alex clarified, "or for forces like that. But I was running a business and I do hold myself responsible for not keeping a hawk eye on those forces as they impacted the number of customers who walked in the door of my tattoo parlor." The loan officers had it right, Alex felt; it was on *him* to pay up.

At the same time, there was shame to be managed, and also anger. "When I was out of work, I was angry. I understood why I was angry, but I had to force myself to admit I was to blame." He'd been forced to pawn his honor.

As a small business owner, Alex was up against tough odds. With the rise of Amazon and Walmart, which were taking mom-and-pop stores off the Main Streets of America, the national rate of small business failure was 20 percent after the first year and 50 percent by the fifth year. Given hard times in Pike County, the chances of small business failure were probably even higher than elsewhere in the United States. Alex could have had a better shot at the standard of living embedded in the American Dream, as the World Economic Forum's 2020 report on global social mobility reported, if he had lived in Denmark, Norway, Finland, Sweden, rather than in the United States.

But like many other Republicans around the country, Alex embraced a stringent version of "bootstrap" individualism. Again, according to a nationwide survey, 71 percent of Republicans but only 22 percent of Democrats believed that people get rich because they work harder. Likewise, only 31 percent of Republicans agree, in contrast to 69 percent of Democrats, that people are poor due to "circumstances beyond their control."

The poll also showed that even among those with household incomes of $30,000 or less—and in the midst of his crisis, Alex fit there—36 percent credit "hard work" as the main route to success. As for believing that poverty was the result of "circumstances beyond one's control," the difference between rich and poor was remarkably small—overall, 46 percent of the rich (those earning $75,000 a year or more) and 56 percent of the poor (those earning $30,000 a year or less) agreed. The idea was this: Don't blame the class standing of your parents, or race. Blame your lack of devotion to work. For Alex, keeping an eye on his customer count was the relevant hard work and he blamed himself for not doing it. There Alex was, dead center inside the pride paradox.

Meeting Margaret

To get away from it all, Alex sometimes took vacations in the Dominican Republic. After Alex's first marriage collapsed during his debt and unemployment, he met and fell in love with a beautiful, warm-spirited woman. "Margaret is Dominican, has Spanish ancestry and olive skin. We have three children. One much older girl is mine. And one is ours—and he looks white just like me. Our third child is my stepson. His biological father has African ancestry, so the boy is very dark. His biological father is uninvolved, no birthday cards, calls, letters, nothing." Then Alex, speaking slowly, said, "I'm not my stepson's biological dad, but his biological dad is out of the picture. I'm all he's got. . . . So, he's . . . like mine. He *is* mine. He needs me. So, I have to help him go through an experience I haven't had to go through; that's my challenge."

Alex paused. "In science fiction you've got people with tentacles on the back side of their head. I wonder why in real life we can't handle a slightly different shade of skin color."

On our way back from lunch, Alex stopped on the sidewalk to summarize the trap he felt the issue of race put men like him in: "I understand what Detroit has gone through. What happened wasn't their fault. And when nobody is coming to help you, I can understand getting mad at the world. And then Black people are being killed by cops in the street. I get that too. But then eastern Kentucky wants to stand up and say, *We've been forgotten too.* But I feel like I can't do that." Alex didn't just feel ignored;

he felt silenced—a feeling to which Matthew Heimbach was hoping to appeal.

The Grass Police

I asked Alex what he felt about the local government of Prestonsburg, where he lived, a half-hour's drive north of Pikeville. He pushed his chair back from the table, took a sip of his coffee, touched his cap, and said: "I get mad about some things. My brain locks up. You forget that you might get over your anger. But the next time it happens to me, it all snaps back— that feeling of there being no place for me—and you get angry all over again. I felt like forces were pushing me and others to whatever edge we're close to. You feel like something out there is designed to keep you down. There's no specific person to get mad at. But I start thinking, whatever system is in charge here, I *hate* it and want to throw it out."

Alex wasn't looking to shift his frustrations to anger at Blacks or immigrants. He was married to his beautiful Dominican bride who had a half-Black child from an earlier marriage, a boy he loved as his own. He wasn't prone to paranoid accusations of a deep state. Nor was he inclined toward wholesale blame of large companies; indeed, he wouldn't mind running one. The private sector seemed to him to be the giver—of jobs, goods, and services. It was the government that took his taxes and freedoms. Alex was being strict with *himself*, he felt, but the local government wasn't being strict with *itself*.

One incident stood out. "I got a bill for my *grass*! I popped a cork. I called them, and it turns out they had the wrong lawn. But why are they billing anybody for long grass? The town government charges absurdly high fees for infractions of useless rules. They complain about your faded address label in your mailbox. There are so many rules, it's hard to live with them all."

Why was Alex Hughes getting a notice about his grass? I too wondered. Alex didn't live in a community with a homeowners' association, which might have its own rules of neighborhood appearance. Prestonsburg fined people for overgrown grass around homes in foreclosure, and maybe there were a number of such homes, but at the time Alex's house wasn't in foreclosure. Instead, it occurred to me that Alex may have run into a hidden economic logic. As coal mines close, coal extraction tax funds dry up. As they do, some towns try to make up for declining funds by hiking fines for minor infractions. So a man like Alex can feel squeezed by a declining economy on one side and squeezed by his local government, which is compensating for lost funding, on the other. Maybe this explained the grass police and the "popped cork."

Alex was angry at the federal government as well. "I get a nasty letter from the IRS saying, 'You didn't make your last payment and if you don't make it quick, we're going to fine you.' I called up the IRS. Their system messed up." He moved on to other government requirements, such as the state mandate to have car insurance: "I get the point of car insurance. But you force me to have it, okay? Then the insurance company ratchets up the price, okay? How do they calculate the rate? And why do they always hit me with slightly more than I can afford? It's based on where you live. So, I've got to pay more car insurance just because I live in eastern Kentucky. How am I supposed to feel about that?" Each brush with the government seemed to feel to him like a scolding finger, a touch of shame.

Turning his thoughts to escape from the authority of local government, Alex said, "I never wanted to live in the city limits because each city has its own rules and never ones that help me. They pull you over in a jalopy. Under your hood every part is a different color, so the cop tickets you. You drive past in a new Cadillac, the cops don't look twice. These rules, these authorities, sometimes I feel like I'm going to lose it." With all Alex had endured, he found himself already at his emotional limit. But it was at what Alex saw as governmental overstepping that he got mad.

Alex was caught in the pride paradox. He was living in a hard-hit red state and his business had failed. But his old-school pride included accepting blame for failure. So if he felt it was the right thing to be hard on himself, shouldn't the government be hard on itself instead of patrolling his grass? As for his government doing good things for him, over many conversations examples of that didn't come to mind. Meanwhile, "feeling forgotten" was a wedge Matthew Heimbach was hoping to drive; the pride paradox was another.

Worrying About Harry

Before all this happened, Alex had begun to worry about his beloved friend Harry, a truck driver. Harry shared Alex's philosophy of life. He had suffered hard knocks in the job market, as had Alex, but his increasingly agitated talk had begun to worry Alex. "Harry's a solid, hardworking, all-around great guy. He's Republican like me, voted Trump like me, but he's got a shorter fuse than me. And honestly, these days I worry about him," Alex said. "I don't know where he's picking up his news online, but he's talking strangely about conspiracies. I've known Harry all my life and I'm not sure what's going on."

Harry doesn't just hate big government and Democrats; he *despises* them. He thinks they've rigged things. He doesn't like all the violence caused by Black Lives Matter. On one side, he thinks, are all the rural people, and on the other side are all the big city free-handout people. He thinks the whole nation is going to war soon. Texas and California will each be on their own and the rest will shoot it out. Harry says he's about ready to pack up his truck, bring his guns, and leave for somewhere else—he doesn't know where. A steady voice of restraint for Harry, "It'll be okay, Harry," Alex told him.

After lunch, Alex and I walked back along the sidewalk past the parking lot where the drunk slasher had attacked him years earlier. I wondered if Alex's attacker might be getting out of prison about now and how he might feel about Heimbach's forthcoming appeal to white nationalism. "That might be just the kind of guy to go for a neo-Nazi," Alex remarked. But would his friend Harry, too? I wondered.

Meanwhile, Alex recounted what for him had been a life-changing event. "I saw an advertisement for a paid six-month training program for applicants sponsored by a Louisville-based company called InterApt." It was partly funded by the Appalachian Regional Commission, as mentioned, which directs federal dollars to programs lifting hard-hit regions. The program was designed to train unemployed coal miners and others, like Alex. Work formerly outsourced to Bangalore, India, the InterApt CEO reasoned, could be insourced to eastern Kentucky.

Alex would be paid, the ad explained, to learn to code, with the aim of being able to program cellphone applications to do such things as order food online or reserve movie tickets. Eight hundred Kentuckians applied for a slot. Fifty were accepted and thirty-five graduated, among them an elated Alex Hughes. "The company pay would be enough to cover all my bills, and I'd learn a needed skill. It sounded too good to be true. But I was chosen, and I left for Louisville," Alex said. "It was a whole new experience for me, being paid to learn. My fellow students became close friends. We helped each other and got very good; a lot of my fear and pessimism dropped away. Honestly, it *transformed* me."

From his desperate struggle on the edge of the receding rural middle class, Alex had "manned up" and taken responsibility for having missed the signs of failure of his tattoo parlor. Caught in the pride paradox, he did not move to transform shame into blame of others (though he could quickly pop his cork at the "grass police" and the IRS). In fact, for a bleak period, he was on the edge of turning his shame inward and questioned the value of his life. Now well paid, happily remarried, a baby newly arrived, new job offers coming his way, Alex didn't have to move shame in or out; he felt proud.

The program that trained Alex was a private-public venture, and the cost of his training had been paid for by the federally financed Appalachian Regional Commission, whose mission is to aid the Alexes of the region.

As we parted, Alex said he had no time for the Pikeville march, and returned to his concern about his friend Harry. "Harry feels the same as me about politics, only a lot more strongly. I'm glad he's not coming to the march."

7

Outlaw Pride

"Did you hear about the white nationalist march in Pikeville?" I asked Wyatt Blair, who was sitting across from me in a well-guarded meeting room in the Southgate facility overseen by the Kentucky State Department of Corrections, Division of Probation and Parole, Reentry Service.

The director had granted me permission to interview inmates so long as I protected the identity of the facility and prisoners, which I have done by using pseudonyms. I was led to a meeting room, where I sat at a long table. In a few minutes, a short, cocky, elfish man with gray hair and a bushy white beard entered the room, walking with a limp, and seated himself with care, as if older than his forty-three years. He had a lame left leg from a motorcycle accident dating back to his biker days. Once seated, however, his manner was open.

"Oh, sure, I heard about the march. The guys were talking about it back in the yard. It's being led by a neo-Nazi, ain't it?" he asked. "We got neo-Nazis in the yard. They say they're for the white man but they ain't really. They're just selling meth. I'm Klan and the Klan used to hate the neo-Nazis in the past. But I got a swastika tattoo. In prison, it's useful. If I'm walkin' around without my shirt on, I use it to keep guys away—like a fire stick."

Wyatt had thin lips, dark, straight eyebrows over slightly squinting blue eyes, and tousled gray hair. Wyatt had served almost all of a five-year sentence at Eddyville, Kentucky's only supermax prison—nearly half of that, he said matter-of-factly, in solitary confinement. But he'd volunteered for

Southgate's three-month habit-changing life-preparation program that, if he fulfilled its requirements, would permit him an early release. "This program is makin' me clean up my mouth," he said, looking sideways, "but that's a good thing."

"If you were out of prison, would you have wanted to join the march?" I asked.

"Oh, sure. I'd have walked up, shook hands, and said, 'How y'all doin'?' Neo-Nazis are a really violent bunch. But it's good to have them on your side. Not as polite as I am."

When I asked Wyatt if he could share a bit about his background, he relaxed into his chair, elbows on its arms. "I was born in Janine, Kentucky, but raised up at Left Fork. You know Left Fork? No?"

Then, as if to locate himself on a different map, Wyatt explained, "I'm distantly related to the McCoys!" He was referring to one side in the legendary McCoy-Hatfield feud that once terrorized eastern Kentucky and West Virginia. "My granddaddy was related to a seventh-generation McCoy. Daddy was related to an eighth-generation McCoy. His name was Shotgun McCoy Blair; they called him Gun. And I'm ninth. I feel lucky."

I asked Wyatt how he had gotten involved with the Klan, and he began: "My mom was thirteen when I was born, my dad was seventeen, and Mom left when I was three. So my daddy and my stepmom brought me up. I took my problems to my daddy, and he was Klan. After I graduated high school, my daddy inducted me into the Christian Knights of the Ku Klux Klan in Pocahontas, Virginia. It was preached to me. I've gone to every Klan rally in the country, till they got so weak. We had a march in the 1990s in Janine, with a group from Indiana. The Hammerskins [a skinhead hate group] did our security. It was peaceful except for when we walked through Mount Holly, North Carolina [a Black community], and there were altercations. The Klan's a religious organization, you know, dead set against drugs, not like the neo-Nazis."

Both Alex Hughes and Wyatt Blair were prime-age white male residents of eastern Kentucky. Both had come to maturity in a post-1970s blue-collar, rural region facing an economic downturn. Their grandfathers had mined coal, and both had hardworking male relatives in the skilled trades. Wyatt's male relatives were mostly welders and construction workers—he himself had "hung iron" on buildings rising in Cleveland, Ohio. Their families were both conservative Republicans. Coincidentally, both were raised by remarried parents. Both became leavers—Alex to Louisville, Kentucky, and Wyatt to Cleveland and Cincinnati, Eddyville, and beyond.

But there the commonalities stopped. Alex was working hard to support his family in a region of loss and self-blame, where the anguish of the pride paradox loomed large. Much like Donovan Blackburn, Mayor Andrew Scott, and others, Alex Hughes set his whole heart on being able to honorably support his wife and children. He was a man of bootstrap pride. By contrast, Wyatt took a casual interest in work, was long divorced, and had never met his daughter, born out of wedlock; and in a long interview, the term *provider* never came up.

Like Matthew Heimbach, Wyatt was proud to be a moral outlaw. His standing would depend on the potential rise or fall of white nationalism itself. Like Matthew, Wyatt Blair believed that Donald Trump had given the nod to the Klan. Before and during Trump's presidential campaign, Trump professed ignorance of Klan leader David Duke, and to a Bloomberg News anchor he dismissed the topic, saying, "A lot of people like me." But Wyatt concluded that "Trump's in it for the white man. He ain't in it to help the n—— because he knows they're getting all the help they need from the federal government. I think we should build a wall all the way around the whole place. Send all immigrants and Blacks out. Trump wouldn't mind that. I love him."

Nonvoting "Citizens" in Congressional District KY-5

Why was I talking with Wyatt Blair? Often in inquiries about civic engagement, prisoners are left out of public surveys, community studies, and even the pages of history. Yet a great many Americans are, for a period, in prison. According to the Prison Policy Initiative, "Kentucky's incarceration rates stand out internationally" at 930 per 100,000 people, compared to 664 in the United States as a whole, 129 in the United Kingdom, and 104 in Canada. The vast majority of prisoners are American citizens who will one day be released. New policies are also now connecting the inhabitants of rural prisons to population counts and votes. So it seemed important to include them as "faces in the crowd."

Wyatt had been brought from Eddyville to the Southgate facility, where I met him, to participate in a progressive diversion program run privately but overseen by the Kentucky State Department of Corrections. For a prisoner like Wyatt, it seemed like a good deal. One could volunteer for it, and by graduating from its rigorous three-month behavior modification program, which taught honesty, responsibility, and consideration, the volunteer could receive reduced time behind bars. The therapy program (called Moral Reconation Therapy or MPT) was teaching Wyatt to "clean out his mouth." For addicted prisoners, the program also offered an opportunity to prisoners to detox; nationwide, 65 percent of all prisoners have substance use disorders, and another 20 percent were under the influence of drugs or alcohol at the time of their crime.

Wyatt was also part of a little-noted nationwide trend. Over the last forty years, the prison population has been relocating from city to country. Today 53 percent of all American prisons are located in small towns or rural areas. For example, New York convicts far more prisoners each year than Pike County, but most of those convicted in New York serve their sentences in rural areas upstate.

Under Kentucky's new redistricting laws, Wyatt now counted as a resident where he was imprisoned and not where he had lived. So, for purposes of legislative redistricting, Wyatt was helping "repopulate" a depopulating rural area, even though he himself was ineligible to vote.

This prison gerrymandering boosts rural census tallies, and so also the proportion of members of the House of Representatives and state legislators representing such areas. Rural America tends to lean Republican, so the more rural votes, the more Republican votes. In 2016, the 2,623 small and rural U.S. counties that voted for Donald Trump had greater jail populations and higher incarceration rates than the 489 counties that voted for Hillary Clinton.

Two other forces lay behind Wyatt's incarceration. As coal declined, so did coal severance taxes that help fund local government. In Pike County, for example, funding derived from coal mining (coal severance tax revenue) plummeted from $2.6 million in 2015 to $486,000 in 2020. All the more welcome, then, were government funds to construct prisons, hire staff (guards, cooks, drivers, administrators); the prison seemed a lucrative form of rural job development, many reasoned.

Rural counties can also earn extra money by building and renting out jail beds that serve as a waiting room for state prisoners awaiting their trial dates. Between 1970 and 2017, the rate of pretrial incarceration rose 436 percent. And, increasingly, the state gives revenue-depleted counties in eastern Kentucky per diem payments to feed and house those sentenced to state prison.

Ominously, the Kentucky state legislature also recently passed more bills increasing felony penalties rather than reducing them—fifty-nine bills increasing penalties, ten reducing them. So as prisons move to the countryside, those awaiting trial face longer waits, and sentences for felony crimes have been getting stiffer—potentially adding to the headcount used in redistricting.

Then there is race. In 2017, the year of the planned march, as whites became a declining part of America's population outside of prison, they were becoming a higher proportion—now 50 percent—inside it. For, since 2000, the rate of incarceration rose 41 percent among whites and declined 22 percent among African Americans, making prisons increasingly white. Just as race was a hot issue in the nation's decreasingly white world outside of prison, the population was growing whiter inside it. All these trends had put Wyatt Blair in the seat across from me in the meeting room at the Southgate facility.

"Real Bad Racist"

"I'm a real bad racist," Wyatt said, tossing off the comment in the spirit of a boast. "My mom [actually, his stepmother] wasn't as bad. She and my gramma worked as maids at Days Inn with Black ladies, and my mom and gramma hung out and talked and laughed with them. I called my mom's mom 'mammy.' Later in the [prison] yard, when I said that, some Blacks looked at me funny: 'You're calling your grandma *mammy*?' They told me, 'That's a Black thing.'"

Wyatt continued, "Daddy's daddy, and his daddy and my uncles, were all coal miners and members of the United Mine Workers. My granddaddy could remember the 1930s when blood ran down the streets of Harlan. When they got out of the mines, they went into the trades. Daddy was a carpenter and granddaddy a Baptist preacher too. I'm a welder, and my brother's an electrician.

"But," Wyatt continued, "when I was fifteen, me and my daddy left for Columbus, Ohio, and for a year, every day on the school bus I got beat up. I was the only white boy, and the Blacks didn't like how I talked because I was white. They called me a 'billy goat.' I'd fight. I didn't show no weakness."

I asked Wyatt, "Did the Black kids know your dad was with the Klan?" Wyatt didn't recall whether they did, nor did he indicate that he thought it would have mattered. When you had two races, you had fights. Indeed, for Wyatt, fights were frequent, violent, and a source of pride. "I worked as a bouncer in a bar in Lexington and was told to get some drunk Blacks out," he related casually. "So I took a flashlight and cracked a guy in the back of the head a time or two. He came back with a gun, and we got into it." Another encounter was yet more extreme. "When I was nineteen in a bar, a white guy asked me to watch his beer cooler while he run to the bathroom. While he was away a n—— asked me to give him a beer, and I said, 'I ain't got no beer that belongs to me.' Well, two or three of his buddies circled around me. I got my straight razor and caught him across his ribs, cut him plumb in two. I didn't know I'd cut him that bad. He hit the floor like a rock and his buddies flew." And, not for the first time, Wyatt went to prison.

By age forty-two, prison was as much home for Wyatt as it had been for his maternal grandfather—half of his adult life. "My grandpap killed someone out in Indiana back when Mom was a kid, and my pap stabbed a Black man, though he didn't go to prison for it." While each of Wyatt's own sentences had been for several years, once in prison he got into fights in order to "get respected," each fight lengthening his sentence: "One time, I joined in to help my prison brothers—the Supreme Alliance and the Royals. I'm also a vet of the 2010 Eddyville riot, Black on white. I jumped in and stabbed the guys and got respected. I had a four-year sentence, and they upped it to ten and put me in the hole. That's an eight-by-ten cell. You don't see nobody. You can't talk to nobody. You can't see out. You don't know if it's day or night. It's hard on the mind. I done fifty-two months in the hole."

"President Obama signed a law limiting a person's time in solitary to thirty days. That would have reduced your time in the hole by a lot, right?" I suggested.

"Yeah," Wyatt conceded. "But he done it for his own."

Inside prison or out, for Wyatt, race was primary. A fellow prisoner named Dan (a pseudonym) in Wyatt's program later described to me his own life behind bars. "In the yard you've got your Peckerwoods, your Aryan Brotherhood, your Mohawks, your One Percenters. Then you've got your Blacks, your whites, your southern Mexicans, your Mexicans born here— and they hate each other," Dan told me. "You've got Blacks who hate Mexicans and whites or who just hate whites. It varies for each person. The best way not to get your ass beat is to team up with your own race.

"See these black dots on my knuckles?" Dan explained. "They mean,

'I'll fight with [on the side of] whites.' We call it the 'N dot.' It's the sign of a racist. I got mine young in jail, and when you're in there you ain't got much choice. A true racist won't mess with anyone from another race—even to transact business. You can't be in prison without being a racist because the guys in the yard are going to need to know who you'll fight with."

At the same time, cross-race prison friendships occasionally formed. As Dan, now an ex-racist, explained, "I fell for a Filipina woman, the baby mama of my kids. They're not my biological kids, but they call me Daddy and call my dad Granddaddy and they're waiting on me to get out. Inside prison, I was a racist; I remember my buddy praising me for beating the crap out of a Black guy, 'doin' it for your race brothers.' But even as that guy said it, I couldn't feel it. And when I got out, I realized it was all bullcrap." But what was bullcrap for Dan was for Wyatt the way to "get respected."

Good to Be Bad

I wondered about Wyatt's praising himself as "bad." In passing, he had described his stepmother as "not as bad" as his father, and his son as "not as bad" as himself, but he called his prison-bound daughter "bad like me." Was it good—honorable, a matter of pride—to be bad? Indeed, to Wyatt, "bad" meant worthy of respect, which generally meant being violent and even (when the superiority of whites seemed threatened), murderous. Murder did not signal a lapse from a higher moral code for Wyatt; willingness to kill *was* the basis of his outlaw code of ethics. His time in "the hole," he said, was for being *that* bad.

Outside of prison too, it was good to be bad. "I was with the first group to march in our robes through Louisa in the early 1990s. I didn't show my face, had a pistol on my hip. But I can't stay out of prison long enough to rally anymore. I'm not as bad as I was." This he said as if confessing a lapse, a matter of shame.

At the same time, Wyatt felt the Klan was "goin' downhill nowadays"—as he said this, he tightened his brows—"because they's afraid to be sued and your more serious people are staying silent. And now men at the top of the totem pole are in their sixties, seventies, and eighties and just layin' back and collecting dues. These days, the Klan's all about profit." He felt other conditions were also on the decline: "Now you have to pay dues, $35 a month to get a three-page monthly newsletter, all watered down. The young are listening to rap music and idolizing n——s. . . . We're not even allowed to wear our masks. We can wear a hood but we have to button or pin up the hood, so we show our faces, or else it's considered a terrorist act. When's the last time you saw a cross being burned?"

It's true that the KKK has declined, both locally and nationally. In 1925 almost thirty thousand Klansmen publicly marched up Pennsylvania Avenue in Washington, DC. But by 2016, the KKK had dwindled to an estimated 130 active Klaverns (local chapters)—and in 2021, only eighteen—even as other white nationalist groups were on the rise.

Still, some I spoke with in the area saw the Klan as a dormant presence. A young woman in Inez, an hour's drive from Pikeville, told me she was astonished to discover upon the recent death of an uncle that he had secretly been a local Grand Wizard of the Klan. Sitting with me in her living room, the niece recalled, "My family was *shocked*. He'd kept it a close secret because my family strongly disapproved. But when he was dying, I went to visit him in the hospital. I saw only two other family members there. But around his hospital bed was a large gathering of strange men. It was as if they were his *real* family."

One retired fumigator told me, "I used to work helping people get rid of lice in their homes. I'd spray their stuffed chairs. But those lice hibernate in the stuffing; when it's warm, they come out, and they're hard as hell to get rid of. To me, the Klan are like lice."

As for Wyatt, it felt harder to "get respected" for being bad: "The fed got ahold of our code and infiltrated us and now the government is preaching there's good and bad in every race. And to talk publicly you have to say,

'This is a good Black man and that's a bad Black man.' But I hate Black men, the way I got beat up."

Now even prison authorities seemed to Wyatt to be discriminating against the Klan. "All my tattoos made it through security screening except for the KKK on my chest. So I got classified as STG [security threat group], and the prison stopped us from getting our literature [in] as 'Christian Identity' [a religious ideology popular among right-wing extremists]. They're cracking down. If you do something to a n—— they'll hit you with a hate crime and take it from a state to a federal charge. And if you get a federal life sentence, you come home with a toe tag." Nowadays, things seemed all backward to Wyatt: it had become bad to be bad.

Confusions of Racial Identity

While Wyatt was coping with challenges to his bad-boy pride, his early life reflected a series of internal contradictions concerning his own racial identity. For one thing, he said, according to Klan rules "you don't eat or sleep with Black women because it's not natural." At the same time, in high school Wyatt had had a strong crush on a girl who was partly Black. "Me and her had a great time. I'd take her for rides through the hollers on the back of my Harley. One day I invited her home for dinner. My stepmom was fine with it, but my dad had heard she was part Black and wouldn't let her stay for dinner. I had to take her home." He said nothing of the girl's experience of this, nor the contradiction it seemed to reveal; if separation of the races was part of a natural order, why would it require strict—let alone any—discipline to limit his attraction?

Beyond this, Wyatt himself was racially mixed—a fact that emerged accidentally, as I was asking him to tell me about his tattoos. He pulled up his sleeve and held out his right arm. "My right side is my dad. So, this is my tattoo of the Mystic Insignia of a Klansman. See the white square in the center and a drop of red blood? That's the blood shed to protect the white race. And next to it, on my right, is my rebel flag. So I've got my Klan and Confederate flag on my dad's side. And I got me a little blurry swastika," he added, because "we had to draw them in the pen, and not make them look too swastika-like."

Then, matter-of-factly, Wyatt drew up the sleeve on his left arm. There he pointed to a bear's paw with five long claws. "That's my tribal tattoo. I have Cherokee in me. My mom's mom was half." Pointing to his upper left arm, he continued, "Up here I have my old eagle, and my steel trap tattoo." This was the image of a round black band from which hung a series of sharp spikes transected by a rod, a chain hanging down the arm at one end; he explained it as a Native American symbol for "catching the bear." So, the tattoos on his right arm represented his father and Anglo-Saxon identity, while on his left arm he boasted of his mother's Cherokee identity. Although his parents separated when Wyatt was small, his tattoos seemed to have united them at last.

"On one arm, I see Klan symbols, and on the other, Native American symbols," I observed neutrally. "What are your feelings about the relationship between whites and Native Americans?" Wyatt raised his eyebrows in surprise and fell quiet for a bit.

Eventually he replied, "Yeah, the white man marched our people from south Kentucky, Illinois, Missouri, all the way to Oklahoma, and we lost thousands due to the white people. Did you ever hear about the Trail of Tears?" Wyatt was referring to forced removal, under President Andrew Jackson, of sixty thousand Native Americans between 1830 and 1850. He shook his head. "It was a terrible thing."

As I was puzzling out his shifting use of *we* and *our*, Wyatt volunteered, "I don't hold no resentment to the whites for kicking us off our land because to them, the Indians were an inferior race. Still, this was our land at one time." He went on to explain that "we" don't resent the white man now because "we've" got casinos and don't pay federal income taxes on the revenue. "I have a problem with the Klan on the Trail of Tears," he added finally. "Whites was awful mean to the Indian." Then he repeated, "My mom left when I was three, and my dad raised me up. He's the one I went to with my problems. The Cherokee was on my mom's side, and she was gone." On this confusing point, Wyatt ended the matter.

Yet another inconsistency arose. Wyatt had declared he wanted to build a wall around the United States and keep out Blacks and immigrants. Scratching his white beard, he also let on, "I ain't got no problem with Mexicans; they is hardworking, trying to take care of their families. And in the yard, they'll fight with [on the side of] the white man. They're loyal. They was my buddies on the street too." He paused. "The Klan don't approve of that, I guess."

When I asked Wyatt his views of the 9/11 Muslim hijackers, yet another inconsistency emerged. "I hate Muslims," he declared, but then he again raised his brows to consider what he'd just said. "9/11 was bad. All of them dead lying on the sidewalk." He shook his head. "Probably a lot of good Black people died in 9/11, and I won't say the *n*-word. I do respect some." Then Wyatt considered the 9/11 jihadists. "They *believed* in their mission, pretty hard-ass, dedicated. Strapped bombs on themselves, ya know? The Klan may not be on the same page as them, but maybe we're in the same book."

Classifications that at first seemed clear and hard had melted in Wyatt's mind into a puddle of contradictions—between his right arm and his left, his loyalty to whites and his sympathy with Native Americans, his call for a totally white nation and his affinity for Mexican prisoners, his admiration for "hard-ass" 9/11 hijackers and his sympathy for their white and Black victims. But while such contradictions might alarm others, Wyatt seemed to accept them with good-natured tolerance.

Meanwhile, Wyatt found challenges to his racial views at home. "When my son was young, he tried to get like me [like the Klan], but I could tell his heart wasn't in it. And my son's wife is dead set against the Klan. She's blond and blue-eyed but she won't have the *n*-word used in her house. Got the kids cracked down on that too. No sir. My little granddaughter tells me where I can stick my views. My brother don't like the Klan either. We're all Republicans for Trump, but we don't talk race at their kitchen table." At home, the Klan brought shame.

The only child Wyatt had won to his side was his daughter, Krista. "She's got a rebel flag tattooed over her whole back," Wyatt boasted, his tone becoming more somber as he went on. "She's in prison now for robbery, possession of meth, and hit-and-run. She's . . . lookin' at nineteen years in prison and will probably get her sentence down to twelve or fifteen years. Krista's been in trouble as long as I have, done about year-for-year with me. Every time I call home, she's in jail. She's been selling meth all over the country and out of the house. She's young but she could easily get life. All you have to do is stab and kill someone, then you're a persistent felony offender and you're done."

While in prison, Krista had married the president of the local prison chapter of the Aryan Circle, a whites-only prison-based criminal gang with members in nine states. Referred to as the "Family," members are required to "attend church," or convene where they could in prison to conduct gang business, which went on in and outside of prison. Summing up "badness" in his family, Wyatt Blair said, "Krista's bad like me, and I'm worse than my brother and son."

Pride Hierarchies

According to one pride hierarchy, if Wyatt had been a peaceful, law-abiding welder, he could have found access to a mainstream "bootstrap" source of pride—upheld by former governor Paul Patton, city manager Donovan Blackburn, Mayor Andrew Scott, and high-striving Alex Hughes, not to mention those vulnerable to the violence he threatened, including Ruth Mullins, John Rosenberg, and Dr. Budgy. But with its gangs, tattooed knuckles, and race fights, prison offered Wyatt its own—to him more compelling—theater of pride, where you "got respected" for being called "a pit bull . . . fighting for your own." There, pride was based on brawn and race.

Even among fellow prisoners at Southgate, Wyatt found himself near the bottom of the totem pole. As a counselor in that program was to tell me, "Near the top of the hierarchy would be your guys in for lack of child support, regular guys except for that. Then you have your big-time drug dealers, who run national, international drug chains. Under them, you have your small-time vendors, then your users, addicts, drunks. At the *very* bottom are child molesters" and oddballs, the last a group where perhaps Wyatt found himself. Back home, except for the admiration of his imprisoned daughter, Wyatt didn't "get respected" either.

In contrast to Matthew Heimbach, Wyatt didn't refuse to be shamed. Heimbach had moved his emotional narrative from *They are trying to shame me* to *I won't be shamed,* which seemed to lead to *Neither I nor other people of German or American white southern heritage ever did those shameful acts.* And from there, it seemed to be a short step to *The Holocaust never happened.* In this way, Matthew became an anti-shame warrior. Wyatt Blair, by contrast, seemed to deny nothing, not even injuries or killings; for these he sought to be "respected" by his brethren. In the 1920s the Klan was out in the open, its crimes proudly shown off. But these days, the Klan was increasingly out of fashion, even as Wyatt held on to the vestiges of its outlaw pride.

Whatever the psychological origins of the two extremists, Matthew Heimbach and Wyatt Blair both understood themselves to be shamed within the larger American pride economy, and sought respect within small, extremist circles, a respect that was largely confined to those circles. Matthew Heimbach, fiercely denying the Holocaust and pain of slavery, dreamed of heading an anti-shame militia. But Wyatt Blair seemed casually resigned to the shame many attached to his racism.

Outside the circles of the neo-Nazis and the Klan, both men understood themselves to be reviled. Currency in pride earned in a criminal subculture could not be "cashed in" for higher standing in the wider pride economy. If Alex Hughes felt proud to bootstrap his way to the American Dream, Wyatt Blair, like Matthew Heimbach, based his outlaw pride on barring others—the Ruth Mullinses, John Rosenbergs, and Dr. Budgys of the world—from that dream. Curiously, the dream itself, with its elements of rising up, working hard, the car, and the house, wasn't in the picture Wyatt drew of himself. But conking a Black man on the head with a flashlight outside of a bar—he was proud of that.

Improbable Connections

On the sidelines of the violent brawls that fractured the boredom of prison life, some prisoners dared to form dangerous bonds. As a white man who was a fellow inmate of Wyatt's later recounted, "I was locked in a cell 24/7 for a year with three men so close to me I could tell each one by how they breathed—a Black guy with the Cincinnati Crips, a Mexican, and a white Iron Horseman. My two best buddies were the Black and the Mexican, and it was dangerous to be friends with them. My Black buddy watched my stuff when I was gone or sleeping, and I watched his. He put money on my books [spending money in prison], and I put money on his. Me and him are kind of brothers to this day."

A towering, broad-shouldered man named Willie, with jet-black hair drawn into a ponytail, strong tattooed arms, and a luminous smile, overcame even more. Like Wyatt, Willie was part Native American and a veteran of racial fights in the back streets of Detroit. "I'm a dark-complected Cherokee and get mistaken for Hispanic. In the winter I'm lighter, in the summer I'm darker. So I don't fit in anywhere," he said with a relaxed smile. "So I had a lot of 'just because' fights with Blacks. Growing up, we lived in a Black neighborhood of Detroit and because I wasn't Black, every day when I got out of the school bus, this Black guy would beat me up. Most days I'd come home with a black eye. But I lived with my Cherokee grandpa, who was a violent man. And he told me I had to fight harder, be a brave. If I came home with another black eye, he told me he'd whip me hard. I'd gotten staples from one of his whippings and didn't want another.

So I didn't know who I was more scared of—the Black guy at the bus stop or my grandpa at home."

Willie explained, "Growing up, my emotions got all messed up. If I was mad, I lashed out. If I was sad, I lashed out. If I was confused, I lashed out. I couldn't tell one feeling from another. On TV I'd seen movies of Indians scalping whites. So one day I put a knife in my pocket, and when I got off the school bus and this Black guy started hitting me, I took it out, tried to cut his scalp, and sliced his arm. After that, he laid off me, and so did my grandpa.

"Decades later, when I was working off twenty-year sentences in a supermax, that Black guy was working off a long sentence there too. He saw me, came up to me slowly, and asked, 'Do you remember me?'

"I looked at him and said, 'Yeah . . . '

" 'Remember when I beat you up every day when you got off the school bus?'

"I told him, 'Yeah.'

" 'I'm really sorry I beat you up like that.'

"I told him, 'Okay.'

"Then he said, 'I know you're not going to understand what I'm going to tell you, because it don't even make sense to me. But when I beat you up, that meant I liked you. I respected you. But I know that's a strange thing to say, and you're not going to understand.'

"I looked him in the eye long and hard. Then I told him, 'Actually, I do understand.' That's how we became friends."

Such unusual reach-outs on either side of prison walls not only knitted a new friendship between old enemies, but also erased an understanding of pride once based on being highly ranked in the bad-boy hierarchy.

In a far less insightful way, Wyatt Blair had also crossed the racial fence. According to Wyatt's Southgate counselor, Wyatt was doing KP together with a Black prisoner named Caleb. "Wyatt and Caleb were both at the bottom of the local totem pole, Wyatt because he's crippled and a bit odd, and Caleb because he was a convicted sex offender. Others leave them alone."

I asked Wyatt if Caleb was his friend, and he answered offhandedly, "We're both felons here. We have to do three hours of KP together in the cafeteria, and sometimes we hang out." But then he added, "At Southgate, if anyone does something wrong, we're supposed to 'check' that person. Caleb's healthy, so he can stand and work. I have to do my KP sitting down because I'm crippled up. But Caleb was going slow, and I checked him for hum-hawing, being lazy and watchin' me work. When I checked him, Caleb hollered that I done it because he's Black. Now I ain't allowed to check nobody who's a person of color for anything. That's PC for ya, the race card."

Wyatt's disgust at political correctness fit smoothly with his lifelong view that when there was shame to be felt, the thing to do was to turn it to blame—blame on Blacks, immigrants, and "out of place" women. Wyatt based his pride outside a culture of the Protestant ethic—personal responsibility, hard work—and the American Dream, the main basis of the national pride economy. He was not striving, like Alex Hughes, to make a way to that dream in hard times. So Wyatt seemed unbothered by the strains of the pride paradox. He wasn't basing his pride on striving for the American Dream, just on loyalty to a movement whose aim was to bar others from it. For some possible faces in the crowd, the white nationalist message Matthew Heimbach was bringing to town might seem to offer escape— "someone to blame"—for their difficulties in reaching the American Dream. But for Wyatt, the main idea was to widen the appeal of outlaw pride.

Ignored by others, but doing daily KP together, after a while Wyatt and Caleb began to patch it up and hang out, talking, laughing, smoking together. As with Wyatt's tattoos, irreconcilable things could be made to fit together.

"See this pack?" Paying homage to that other moral code he knew existed out there, Wyatt held out a crumpled pack of cigarettes from which one hung out. "I gave Caleb my near last cigarette."

8

Survivor's Pride: Hood and Holler

"You know that white nationalist guy who's leading the march? He's coming to eastern Kentucky because he thinks we're poor, dumb white hillbillies who don't know any better than to follow him, okay? *I am* poor and I *am* dumb and I *am* white, okay? So, he's coming for who he thinks I am. But I'm not who he thinks I am. I may be a hillbilly, but I'm not a redneck. I don't mistake my heritage for who I am. I have my *own* opinions." David Maynard, age thirty-four, was explaining the reason for his strong distaste for the white nationalists soon to march into Pikeville.

Sitting behind the wheel of a blue Subaru, eyes on the road, David had long dark brown hair that was drawn into a ponytail, sideburns edging his round, serious face. He was wearing a monster T-shirt over his heavyset frame. Leaning forward from the back, David's gentle blond wife, Shea, wore a matching monster T-shirt over her own heavyset frame. With a liquid giggle, Shea explained, "We bought the car from a used car lot, as is." Continuing the train of thought, David added humorously, "So we quickly got to learn all about carburetors." Block by block, they seemed to build the conversation together. Later Shea was to remark good naturedly, "Some people tell us we're like the same person."

We were retracing hidden moments of the couple's courtship—forbidden, it was to turn out, because David's family was poorer than Shea's. Our destination, about twenty-seven miles northeast of Pikeville, was a small movie theater in a mall where, eight years ago, the two had joyously married. It was in a town a few miles upland from the Tug River, bordering West Virginia, where the McCoys and Hatfields once feuded, and where now a drug crisis was felling many young, white, poor men like David Maynard.

Along the way we were talking about the relationship between their personal lives and the appeal to them of political candidates to the right and left of them.

The two were good friends with Alex Hughes. Shea had been one of the thirty-five trainees who graduated with Alex from InterApt, after working a string of low-wage jobs that barely paid their bills, and now earned good money as a UX designer and Android developer. Each now had a portable skill that allowed them the choice to leave or to stay. While Alex was restless to seek his fortune in Louisville, Shea and David Maynard chose to remain in their cozy trailer outside Prestonsburg, Shea driving to a nearby public library to do her online work.

Alex Hughes was trying to ignore the upcoming white nationalist march because he had far more urgent things to do, and keeping a protective eye out for his dear friend Harry, who seemed to be going off the deep end. He was also guiding his biracial Caribbean stepson into the reality of the American racial setup and beyond. At the other extreme, Wyatt Blair, a KKK extremist and felon, wished none of that American Dream for Blacks. For his part, David Maynard took great interest in the similarity between the lives of poor Blacks and poor whites ("hood and holler," as he put it)—a similarity that he felt was being ignored by both parties.

As David explained, "When the marchers come to town, we'll lock our doors and I'll get out my gun. Apart from the danger, there's a really bad idea behind it. The leader of this march is following Donald Trump. And Trump is trying to create a poor-white-ization of America. He wants to make all of America seem like they come from around here and to think like he imagines I think. But I don't think like he thinks I think. I come from around here, but I don't fit Trump's stereotype of me."

If You're White and Poor

Poverty was David's scarlet letter. Attached to it were two problems. First, as a child, being poor meant being scared, going without, and feeling ashamed. Second, it meant that, in the eyes of Shea's parents, David shouldn't marry Shea—the reason their courtship was forbidden. As both David and Shea saw it, David's parents were very poor. "I'm trailer trash, okay?" David said. "My uncle dealt drugs behind our trailer. A woman was murdered three trailers down because the robbers believed a false rumor that she had inherited money. I was in special ed. So I'm learning disabled. Shea's parents hated me. They called me trailer trash. They called *her* trailer trash for associating with me."

"Yeah, my mom and dad and grandma thought I could do better than David," Shea confirmed, leaning forward from the back, "but that's not what I thought, so we snuck around," she said with a giggle.

Both thought Shea's family was "upper class." "Her grandma owned two Subway shops and drove an old Cadillac," David explained. "My uncle could have been walking along the side of the road, and it wouldn't have occurred to Shea's grandma to stop the Cadillac and pick him up."

Still, Shea's family had suffered many divorces—Shea's father had married twice, and her mother had married three times and was now single again. Despite their disdain for David's family, Shea's father also had financial struggles. When Shea was a baby, her mother left and her father cared for her at his workplaces whenever he could at jobs that never paid more than $10.50 an hour. When he got a job as a guard at a coal mine, Shea played in a playpen he set up in the guard shack. When her father was the assistant manager of a Dollar General store, Shea did her homework in the stockroom, where her father homeschooled her. But Shea's father worked, which David's father, disabled by muscular dystrophy as a child, did not.

"Around here, when you're poor, you marry to escape," David said, glancing out the car window at a sheer drop down a mountainside. "Marry the person you're sleeping with until they sleep with someone else. That's on our side of the hill. The rich side of the hill, where some teachers live, is not so bad. So, by Shea's and my age, people on our side of the hill are on third marriages and have a kid with each one." For Shea and David, their happy marriage was a deep source of pride, because stable, happy marriages were so rare.

Tracing Their Romance: School, Library, Store

Dipping around a bend, the Subaru turned off into the parking lot of a large red brick building, the Warfield Elementary School, where the two lovebirds had met in Head Start. It was here six years later that nine-year-old Shea would sit next to David on a bench where he had often been sent for time-out.

"Isn't that our bench?" Shea said. "Let's go look."

David cautioned, as if even still he was being disapproved of, "I don't think we should stay long. They'll wonder what we're doing on the school grounds."

"It's okay," Shea reassured him.

As they walked toward the bench together, both dressed in their monster T-shirts, the two recalled other times together. "Remember where we first kissed, in the hallway at Warfield Middle School, with lollipops in our mouths?" Shea asked David. Without Shea nearby, David found school trying: "What I liked about school was not being home. Later I was diagnosed with a learning disability, and they placed me in the Carl D. Perkins [Vocational Training] facility with the mentally ill, the drug-addicted, and other special ed students. . . . Mainly, I stayed in my room." While David had described himself as "dumb," the irony was hard to miss. "After No Child Left Behind," he explained, "they got extra funding, so a lot of kids from poor homes got stuck in special ed mainly because the school officials wanted the funding. They told me, 'If you come into special ed, you get to go to museums and see dinosaurs and fossils and archeology.' I said, 'Don't you mean paleontology?'"

Shea's family had ambitions for her which did not include David. "After I graduated from high school, I told my maternal grandma, 'I'm working two jobs and I'm not on drugs.' She told me, 'Shea, that's not enough.'"

Looking out the window at the unfolding green mountains to one side and the other, I commented, "This looks lovely." But David corrected me: "You drive down this road, life expectancy drops around twenty or thirty years." He pointed left, where homes seemed slightly larger, indicating that there, "people live—what?—eighty years? But you go a mountain over, where I grew up, people die early—of drugs, alcohol, rough lives. If it wasn't for the violence and rampant poverty in Martin County, this would be an interesting place to live." Shea had grown up on one side, David on the other.

Now David was pulling off the road into the parking lot of a small red brick building, the Rufus M. Reed Public Library in the town of Lovely. "Shea's dad and grandma and mom all wanted Shea to study in the library—where her parents didn't expect me to be," David explained. "So we snuck meetings there." As we walked into the library, David and Shea politely greeted the librarian, new since their past visits, and glided quietly past the nearly empty main room to stacks along the back wall. "Here's where we roamed the shelves," Shea whispered. "And behind the stacks, and if no one was there," David added, "we'd kiss a little."

We returned to the Subaru and drove for a while before David turned into the parking lot of a Dollar General store. To one side of the front door stood a plastic "all-year-round" Christmas tree with tireless, colorful decorations. A blue plastic wading pool leaned against it, next to a grill and folding lawn chairs on sale, suggesting the idea of summer fun.

As we stepped inside, Shea pointed out the room where she'd done her homework when her dad was the assistant manager. "When David's parents came to shop, I'd secretly follow behind them." Past the chips and canned soup aisles, we were now facing an entire glassed-in cooler three-quarters of the length of the store, stocked with bottled soft drinks.

"David and I would look through the glass at the Coca-Cola, Diet Coca-Cola, Sprite, Diet Sprite, Dr Pepper, Diet Dr Pepper, Mountain Dew, Diet Mountain Dew, Fanta, Fresca. We'd compare our favorites," Shea recalled fondly. Other times when David visited the Dollar General, the two would help Shea's dad unload his truck and sort the shelves.

We returned to the car, heading now to their childhood homes, three miles apart, still in Lovely. David drove us slowly over a charming wooden bridge into a sylvan meadow, three trim, tasteful homes all shouting distance apart, where Shea once lived with her dad and stepmother, next door to her grandma and one house away from her aunt and uncle. It was just outside this holler that Shea's grandmother would cross the small wooden bridge to wait at the road for Shea's school bus and daily hear David call out from it, "I love you, Shea!"

As we headed for David's home, he began to recount a very different life, beginning with his mother's ordeal: "My papaw [his mother's father] drove a truck in the military. When he got out, he ran a truck repair shop while my mawmaw [grandmother] worked at Tyson's chicken factory, and I'm not sure she could protect my mom from Papaw. He was harsh, and my mother needed to escape.

"So my mom got pregnant and married my dad when she was twelve and he was seventeen. She lost that baby and had David when she was fourteen. They were so young that one day when my parents came to pick me up at school, the principal called Protective Services, because she thought my parents were my siblings pretending to be my parents," David recalled. "I also remember coming with my mom to get her driver's license."

"My dad's been crippled since he was a child," David added, "but he got around, even hunted . . . honestly, I don't know how he did it." Still, although they never married, David said, "until my dad died of a stroke at forty-two, they held hands wherever they went. They were happy with each other."

As we passed a Marathon gas station, then a Subway, David began to speed up. "Wait," Shea called out, "slow down! Number 13. Isn't *that* it?"

David slowed the car, his face frozen. We were passing a rusted, vine-covered roadside trailer, his childhood home.

"It's all torn to crap now. It's the first trailer I lived in," David said somberly.

As the car rolled past the trailer, he recalled, "Growing up, I had to stay in the trailer because they didn't want me to be influenced by a close relative who was often drunk, broke, out of his mind on drugs, or dealing drugs in the yard behind our trailer. This relative respected my dad and my dad tried to help him as much as he could. Other addicts knocked on the door too, to ask for money, but we didn't answer."

As a victim of muscular dystrophy, David's father had lived most of his life on disability. "My parents rented the land and kept up a mortgage on the trailer. Dad finally paid off the mortgage months before he died."

Then David glanced back at Shea. "I don't feel good here." He sped up and after a while said, "I was always scared."

David graduated from high school with poor grades and failing health—ulcers, diabetes, and early signs of a weak heart. He tried a series of jobs—at a Walmart, a Boost Mobile/Sprint call center, a Subway, and a McDonald's where, he said, "I had to carry heavy trays of potato fries to the kitchen from the freezer." Shea added, "But, carrying the tray, David collapsed unconscious, and after his second collapse, McDonald's fired him, and he was declared unable to do manually taxing work and put on disability." When I later asked if the couple planned to have children, Shea answered softly, "Given David's heart condition, I don't know how long I have him for. So we decided not to."

David tried a semester at Big Sandy Community College but found that it wasn't for him. Now he explained, "I do digital online art on my cellphone. I specialize in monster pictures and superheroes." The frightening pen-and-ink images he posted on Facebook were of zombies with rotted faces, purple or eyeless. He spoke respectfully of director George Romero, the "father of zombie films," who animated terrifying infected corpses. He revered *Night of the Living Dead*, the first zombie apocalypse film. In 2021 David set up a table showing his work at the Pikeville Comic and Toy Convention at the Appalachian Wireless Arena. He posted pieces of his art on Instagram—Godzilla, a red face exploding from the top, melting faces, astral scenes inspired by *Star Wars*, a cyborg cowboy, a fish eating its tail, and the mystical silhouette of a lithe woman in free fall. Mainly the faces expressed dread and fear.

While David continued his monster art, the largest purpose in his life was to help Shea in doing what they considered her two-person jobs. Before she trained for a far better-paying job coding apps for cellphones, Shea got a job staffing the front desk at a Motel 8 alone at night. David came along, seating himself in the breakfast nook in front of his computer. "I had a homeless guy ask if he could use some hot water for his ramen noodles and stay overnight," Shea explained. "I let him rest and eat there but then he settled in, so I called the police, who came, discovered he was a registered sexual predator, and took him away. David makes me feel safer." Meanwhile, David gamely chatted with hotel guests at breakfast. "One guy told me I could lose weight if I bought a grease-reducing broiler pan. Another told me to accept Jesus Christ as my personal savior."

Detroit Ghetto and Moore's Trailer Park

News of politics came to them through their cellphones: Twitter, TikTok, Facebook. In the breakfast nook at the Motel 8, at his desk in their trailer, waiting in the doctor's office, David checked his cellphone. But on the large monitor at home, both of them tuned into a young, speed-talking Gen-X-friendly YouTuber, Philip DeFranco, a cultural liberal who was anti-tax. If DeFranco's news report became too upsetting, they took a break.

"On the news you hear a lot of talk about race, but not a thing about poverty," David noted as we headed to our next stop. Neither party was telling it like it really is, he thought, about what whites and Blacks had in common—the pain of poverty.

Growing up, I asked David, had he gotten to know any Black kids? "In our elementary school, we just had a few Black kids. One was Alan. Our bus driver adopted Alan out of foster care. Alan always told me that the way I talked about Moore's Trailer Park, where I grew up, made it sound a lot like the neighborhood in Detroit where he grew up. I've never been to Detroit, Michigan, but I'll bet Alan's family's street is a version of Moore's Trailer Park. If you look at a white trash person and you look at a ghetto trash person—there's no difference," David explained. "Bad jobs, if any. Drug addiction. Drug trade. Crime and jail. Ripped-up families. Fights. When I was a baby, I had a gun pointed right at me. Cops are harsh here like cops are harsh in Detroit. A lot of them [Detroit residents] are on government assistance; so are we. Blacks scam the government; we scam the government. When I heard Reagan complained about welfare queens, I didn't know that applied to Black women with a lot of kids. We have welfare queens, my family included. One cousin of mine had to adopt his own sister because his mom kept having lots of babies and going to jail for drugs. My family is full of alcoholics, drug addicts, dealers, murderers. I don't talk to them.

"You know the Black comedian Dave Chappelle?" David asked. "He jokes about the 'poor Black experience.' You see a toddler asking for crack. It's the same in Martin County—maybe not crack, but pain pills." He continued, "People could think I'm a Moore's Trailer Park sort of person, okay? And that's pretty much like a Black ghetto sort of person—a poverty person. But, saying that, I would be dismissed as a communist among my conservative neighbors, and as racist by the left."

In his comparison, David was not alone. "Hood to the Holler" was a campaign theme of Charles Booker, the Democratic African American Kentucky state representative who sought Kentucky's U.S. Senate seat and lost to the Republican Rand Paul in 2022. Booker begins his own story with parents who dropped out of high school to care for their younger brothers and sisters, and his mother going without food to feed him and his siblings in east Louisville, where fair wage jobs, real food, and safe water had been scarce.

The "hood to holler" comparison led me to wonder what the difference is, in fact, between the whitest and the least white of the country's 435 congressional districts. The nation's whitest district—Kentucky's 5th Congressional District, containing David's and Shea's birthplaces and those of all others in this book—is 94 percent non-Hispanic white and 0.7 percent foreign-born. By contrast, New York's 15th Congressional District, located entirely in the Bronx, is 2 percent white.

The two racial pockets are in some ways very similar. The median household income in white KY-5 is $38,000, and in Black and Hispanic NY-15 it is $34,000. The proportion of families with children in poverty is 31 percent in KY-5 and 35 percent in NY-15. The proportion of adults with bachelor's degrees is 8 percent in rural white KY-5 and 12 percent in urban Black and Hispanic NY-15. In both districts, a high proportion also rely on government assistance.

But there are differences too. Appalachian whites are slightly older (in KY-5, 18 percent are over age sixty-five, versus 12 percent in NY-15), and working-age people are more likely to receive disability pay (12.5 percent versus 6 percent; in Appalachia, much disability was related to mining lung disease and accidents). They are less likely to get food stamps (26 percent of households compared to 47 percent), and relatively fewer are on Medicaid (46 percent versus 57 percent). Fewer poor adults of working age are likely to work or be looking for work: Among those ages twenty to sixty-four, 57 percent in mainly white KY-5 were working or looking for work, compared to 69 percent in mainly Black NY-15—both figures contrasting with 78 percent for the United States as a whole.

Taking the nation as a whole, 26 percent of Blacks but only 9 percent of whites live in poverty today. For a century after the Civil War, Jim Crow laws and practices reserved better-paying factory and office jobs for working-class whites. The reforms of Roosevelt's New Deal and union victories brought higher pay and better hours to many. But Social Security excluded domestic and agricultural workers—categories that included most working Blacks at the time. Today, Blacks own 12 cents in household wealth for every dollar owned by whites, and the wealth gap remains today the same as it was in 1968.

As David continued with his own list of similarities between Black poor and white poor, he declared: "The only thing different between Blacks in the hood and whites in the holler is *the music*. We got twangy tragic. Blacks got rap." In later talks with other people, I asked what they felt about David's comparison of hood-to-holler. Many nodded, first in surprise, then in easy agreement.

But one young man responded brightly, "Oh no! Haven't you heard of *hillbilly rap*? You've got Colt Ford [whose videos feature Blacks and whites partying], Haystak, Demun Jones, Jawga Boyz, Kid Rock, Knuckles, Lenny Cooper, Mikel Knight, Mini Thin, Moccasin Creek, Moonshine Bandits, and the Lacs."

He continued, "White guys like rap, but some aren't at ease liking it. I saw a friend get out of his truck and I heard hillbilly rap coming out of his truck window. So I asked him about his music. 'Oh, that's just my girlfriend's tape,' he told me. His girlfriend wasn't there, but he was listening to it. No, even the music's the same."

According to the lyrics of one white West Virginia rap artist, Mini Thin: "Times were tough, but we made ends meet . . . Daddy, what's a food stamp? And what's 'white trash'? Mr. Jones hit his wife, but I was too scared to ask." Another hillbilly rap artist, Colt Ford, sings of "not being ashamed" of who you are, in the course of taking sweet revenge:

There ain't no trash in my trailer
Though you might find an empty can of beer
No, there ain't been no trash in my trailer, oh no
Since the day I threw you outta here.

In both music and daily life there were many similarities between the poor of both races. "So are you picturing poor, white and Black, joining forces to push for better job training, jobs, health care?" I asked David.

He looked out the car window for a while, then answered slowly, "It's a fine idea, but it won't work."

How to Be "Really Something": A Missing Narrative

"We think in narratives. We've got two main ones, and people like me don't fit either one," David began. "First, you've got a white middle-class narrative. You hear these success stories: a person comes from nothing and gets to something. So you say, 'Congratulations. You're smart, hard-working, really something.' But you look at the guy who says he came from nothing, and you see something he had to start with. He's got a story of going from being something to being something better, and that's the normal narrative for whites.

"Then you have a second narrative for Blacks. And people say, 'Oh, you're a Black person. That means you're poor. You didn't have something to begin with and you don't have something now—and that's because you're a victim of racism.'

"But that leaves a problem for people like me. If I'm a Moore's Trailer Park white trash person . . . the only narrative I have tells me that I'm white, so I'm privileged. That's the something I have and that must put me ahead. But what if it doesn't put me ahead? I'm not left with nothing because of racism. I'm left with nothing because I'm lazy and stupid. There's no excuse. If you're white and poor, people think, 'What's wrong with you that you're stuck at the bottom?' If I just look at my own life, I came from nothing and I got to nothing and I'm not a victim of racism because I'm white. So, to most Americans, I'm less than nothing. If it's such a privilege to be born a white male, what could explain me except my own personal failure?"

Growing up in a poorer red state, many like David Maynard walked a rougher road to the American Dream. At the same time, they tended to apply a stricter ethic to themselves, thinking, *If I fail, it's probably my own fault, a matter of shame*. David was talking about the pride paradox, but adding something new: race and its role in popular accounts of success.

Others I talked with were busy coping with it. Alex Hughes had trepidatiously but proudly forged a path to the American Dream, earning bootstrap pride. Wyatt Blair wasn't even trying for it, since he wanted to notch points in bad-boy pride. David Maynard continued his zombie art while helping Shea in her work and life and felt deeply, privately appreciated for that. But he feared the pride paradox; it was a shame trap. He couldn't be seen as a bootstrapper but couldn't, like Wyatt, disregard the pride most Americans based on being one.

"On TV, I heard one Black person say, 'I don't think any white person could understand what it's like to be poor.' I'm like, 'Buddy, you don't get *my* life.'" David paused. "But if I were a Black person looking at me dressed as I am, I might not get that I'm poor because I can go to Target, buy a shirt and pair of pants, and look middle-class and skip the explanations. A Black in the same pants and shirt can't escape like that. I walk around poor in disguise. So, I get how a Black person might see me in my Target clothes and think, 'If you're white, you're probably fine.'

"Shea's mother always talked as though I should pull myself up by my bootstraps. But where are those bootstraps?" David asked. That was the missing piece, a source of continuing frustration for David.

The missing narrative raised the issue of pride. David felt shamed as a potential groom for Shea, not because of the racism that had barred Ruth Mullins from the Bobby Sox Grill, but by something that he felt neither political party dared clearly name—social class.

If Alex Hughes looked to mainstream bootstrap pride and Wyatt Blair to outlaw pride, David Maynard claimed the pride of a survivor. He was thoughtful, married, helping Shea, doing his monster art, but the big achievement in his life is that he had made it out of Moore's Trailer Park alive. Still, survivor's pride, it turned out, didn't have much currency in the eyes of his disapproving in-laws, nor did it have cash-in value with other Americans whose opinions were the basis of a national pride economy.

David also felt invisible to politicians on the left and on the right. "All the Democrats care about is color identity, gender, and sexual identity. So I'm not a Democrat. All the Republicans care about is patriotism and taxes. A lot of them are racist or rich, don't believe social class exists, give me bootstrap stuff. So I don't fit there either.

"And the politicians on both sides take money from the super-rich. I think all politicians should go to work in orange jumpsuits covered with buttons pinned to them—the more money the donor gave the politician, the bigger the button."

In the absence of political representation that he could trust, David turned to the job of giving himself his own identity. In Jennifer Silva's fine study of young working-class couples, *Coming Up Short: Working-Class Adulthood in an Age of Uncertainty*, she found they made up their own versions of the American Dream. Instead of describing their journey to the dream as getting richer, buying a house or car, they describe an ascent from abuse to full recovery—a journey to the emotional American Dream. Pride could be based on recovery.

David was struggling to find a place of dignity in an emotional American Dream too. Online, people clicked appreciatively on his monsters, and there were some creators who measured their position in the world by the dozens, hundreds, or thousands of clicks they got for a post. In response to this unpredictable accounting, David's mood went up and down.

Meanwhile, David had found himself doing the emotional labor of defending himself—even privately to himself—against public stereotypes of the white rural poor. As he explained, "It's like you're always having to say: 'Yes, we're poor rural whites, but no, we're not really racist. Yes, I speak with a regional accent, but no, I know the name of the president of the United

States. Yes, my mother had me young, but no, she's an intelligent person. Yes, I'm on disability, but no, I really have a disability. Yes, I grew up on the wrong side of the mountain, but no, I'm not blind to how you see me.' It's exhausting."

It would be nice, David felt, if the stereotype people have about you didn't make you squirm. You can't escape your social class—or the need to explain it, David felt. "It's exhausting."

Even by talking about exclusion from a dominant narrative, David felt vulnerable to imagined shame-trappers. "If I were to go outside this area and say what I just told you? They'd call me a racist. I'm not a racist, but I feel like I could be viewed as one, so it makes me scared to be around people in the mall or anywhere who would take me as a racist redneck. They'd mistake me for the guys coming to this march in Pikeville, and that makes me mad."

I'm a Fake Racist

"I'm between two racisms," David continued. "You've got Donald Trump trying his poor-white-ization of America, okay? The real racists call themselves free speech advocates. And I'm a free speech advocate, but don't lump me in with your racist nonsense."

Shea put in, "The right wing thinks whites are better, which we don't believe."

"But you've got a new form of racism from the far left. People are saying if you're white you have no right to talk about race or your own experience of being put down," David went on. "And they would call me a racist for saying just that. It's a stereotype laid on us—not by the Trumpers, who are racist themselves, but by liberals. We're their 'deplorables.' The left thinks people of color are better and makes the case for separation. I saw on Facebook that Uber might start a service just for women or just for Black women. Isn't that racial separatism?" David asked in a tone of exasperation.

Shea added, "They [the far left] want attention drawn to them and will call me a racist if I don't agree. They say it's bad to be color-blind because then you're taking away a person's heritage. Just because a person has a different heritage doesn't mean they're essentially different from me."

"The far left will ruin your life over thought and word crimes," David said. "Our friend Emily is white but increasingly hard to be around because she is so easy to offend—on race, on trans [rights], on LGBTQ."

Speaking on the basis of the Facebook pages they saw, Shea added, "A person can ruin a whole conversation with an accusation that you're a racist. It's sometimes best to say nothing. Because if someone thinks you're a racist, then it gets on Facebook, and public opinion turns against you. So I'm inclined to avoid situations that raise the question. I hate that I avoid people of color because I'm afraid I'll offend them. I wasn't like that when I was young. I was brought up to be friendly whatever a person's skin color."

In their attitude toward Facebook posts. David and Shea found themselves caught between the two major political parties. On the issue of economic help for the poor, they found themselves on the Democratic side, but on the issue of race, they weren't so sure. In a 2023 national survey, only 5 percent of Democrats saw "a lot more discrimination [than in the past] against whites," while 49 percent of Republicans said they perceived such increased discrimination.

"In a high school around here, some kid put up signs that said it's okay to be white," Shea said.

"And did they shut down the school?" David asked.

"No, they just ripped down the signs and said it was racist," Shea replied. "So now you can't say it's okay to be white."

Feeling rejected by both conservatives and liberals, David devised a label for himself: "I'm a fake racist."

"What's a fake racist?" I asked.

Looking out the window, David answered slowly, "A fake racist is what the left would make of me because I don't go along with them." It was a mocking self-denigration, a protest against being misunderstood. The word "fake" seemed like an answer to some leftist who accused him of racism in order to shut him up about his own deprived childhood.

When I mentioned the term "fake racism" to Mayor Andrew Scott of Coal Run, he paused, surprised. "I never heard the term," he said, "but it's interesting. These days talk about race is taking all the oxygen out of the air." Why did it seem like no oxygen was left for poor whites? David's mysterious term—"fake racist"—seemed like a placeholder for a larger missing idea: the link between public narratives and personal struggles for pride.

The Wedding

At last we'd arrived at the South Side Mall, in South Williamson, on the Kentucky side of the Tug River—the site of David and Shea's wedding. Williamson was divided in two. On the West Virginia side, it was nicknamed "Pilliamson," for in this former coal mining town, two pharmacies had dispensed over 30 million highly addictive prescription OxyContin pills. This made the state of West Virginia the number-one state in the nation for fatal drug overdoses; Kentucky was third, as we shall see.

But on the Kentucky side of the border, the Williamson mall held fond memories for David and Shea. As a teenager, Shea had accompanied her father to his job managing a small theater there. "If David wasn't there, I'd sneak out of the mall to Kmart," Shea explained, "and call him to see if he could join me." When they could, at thirteen, fourteen, fifteen, the young couple roamed the halls listening to their favorite music on headphones. "I'm excited to be back! I wasn't sure the mall was still open!"

Now, stepping inside the mall, Shea greeted the shops as long-lost friends. "Hey, this used to be the Fashion Bug; now it's Room 22. There's the Bumble Bee, but it's closed. Oh no! Claire's is shut down. Hallmark is still here, and Little Brothers jewelry store. The Dollar Tree and Shea's Style Nails are all still here." Shea recognized about a quarter of the stores in the declining mall; the rest were new or closed, reflecting the difficult environment for small businesses, which Alex Hughes had encountered. "I hope the mall isn't down on business because Amazon is taking over," Shea reflected.

Finally, as we arrived at the far end of the mall's esplanade, Shea called out, "There it is!" She was staring at the door of a small theater. "As a kid I'd nap on a pile of popcorn bags in the stockroom," she recalled with a happy giggle.

"Her dad used to make me wait and sit outside the theater for hours," David recalled.

Like many of the young people I met, David and Shea were not church-goers. But they loved films, so they decided to marry in a movie theater. When Shea approached the theater manager, new since her father's days, the warm-hearted manager was delighted and immediately offered to close the theater for one showing and provide a tablecloth, sodas, and popcorn for guests.

Happily recalling the wedding now, David said, "I wore a shiny black suit that I bought at a tiny flower shop that ran out of the side of a woman's house. I looked like a game show host! My sister brushed my hair into a ponytail."

"I ordered my wedding dress from eBay," Shea recalled. "Then I sent my measurements and the dress to a tailor in China for adjustments and got it back barely in time." On their wedding day, when all the guests were seated, they were shown slides of David and Shea, an Appalachian Romeo and Juliet, as children, as sweethearts. As the images flashed on the screen, a song was played, perhaps for disapproving ears: "Don't Rain on My Parade."

Next came a slow song, "Storybook Bride" from the movie *The Princess Bride*: "My love is like a storybook story but it's as real as the feelings I feel . . ." Slowly Shea walked down the aisle in her white wedding dress to where her bridesmaids, David's best man, and David awaited her. With her divorced, multiply remarried, and disapproving parents watching, the two exchanged vows, kissed, and became husband and wife.

Afterwards, guests ate popcorn, pizza, and a cake her grandmother had ordered. The remaining cake they took home and froze, to be ceremoniously eaten on their first anniversary.

David felt seen as a "nothing" unable to get to a "something," a prime target for shame. There seemed to him no honorable narrative for a poor white guy like him. He was a survivor and proud of it. But survivor pride felt like a fragile thing, a source of pride he'd need to defend against detractors. And the way things were, David also saw no way to bring poor Blacks and poor whites together: poor Blacks were Democrats and poor whites were Republicans and what could you do?

Meanwhile, as David drove us back to Pikeville, the joyful memory of their triumphant marriage burst like sun through a cloud. "Shouldn't we start thinking about planning a commitment ceremony?" David said to Shea.

As they looked back at their wedding, now nearly a decade later, only one memory marred the magical day—a jarring overheard remark, signaling another shame trap, passed between Shea's mother and grandmother: "Did you notice the Maynards? They can actually dress up nicely."

9

"I Could Have Become a White Nationalist"

"Watch the march? No.

"I was forty-two, senior year, in my second try at college. President Webb recommended all us [University of Pikeville] undergrads to go home, since the march might bring violence. So, I stayed home," Tommy Ratliff would tell me later. I was talking to him in the home he shared with his wife, a rented trailer, tidy but with uncertain flooring in one room, in Johns Creek, twenty miles east of Pikeville. "But when I was younger, there was a time when, if you talked to me like a kind dad and told me who to blame for hard times, I could have been open to marching with those guys."

A tall man with long, wavy brown hair fanned across broad shoulders, gentle and direct in manner, Tommy Ratliff was wearing his favorite black T-shirt, which said NOT PERFECT, JUST FORGIVEN. We'd been having a series of conversations about his life, education, and political views.

"In college," Tommy began, "we had a guest speaker who gave us a lecture on the American Dream. He told us all we had to do was to work real hard, stick to a plan, and open a bank account. We should save a little money each month for our kids' future education. At the time I was earning $9.50 an hour behind the counter at a hobby shop and had to repay a loan I took out to pay for college and child support. Part of me just felt like telling the guy, 'Shut up.'"

Then Tommy described how the man's speech sounded in his ears.

"Maybe I could earn my way to the American Dream if nothing else went wrong. That's if I don't get sick, if I don't need a new heat pump, if my electric bill weren't $400 a month, if my ex-wife didn't get hooked on drugs, if my parents weren't alcoholics, if my disturbed brother didn't move in with me and raid my refrigerator while I was at work. Sure, the American Dream is all yours if nothing goes wrong. But things go wrong."

Alex Hughes had found his "sure-I-can-do-that" way to the American Dream; Wyatt Blair tried to whiten that dream; David Maynard wanted pride to go to poor whites barred by their class from it and accused by the left of being racists. But Tommy felt blocked from the American Dream for another reason—one that would lead him beyond talk of narratives to anti-racism.

One day Tommy and I were walking through maple, redbud, and pines around his natal family's quietly sheltered valley enclave, once home to his grandparents, uncle, aunt, and parents. We walked by the home of his uncle Roy, now widowed and seldom home. Roy had gotten Tommy out of scrapes, bought him a car, lent him money, and raised him. Roy's wife, Tommy's aunt, became the "one I was closest to" when words became slurred and voices were raised in his own home next door.

Walking from home to home, we passed a shed used by Tommy's paternal grandfather, now deceased, a former miner and World War II vet who had been present in Iwo Jima as American GIs raised the flag. He had been decorated with a Purple Heart long proudly kept like a holy icon in a glass cabinet in his grandfather's hallway. A nearby shed held his grandfather's beekeeping equipment and a wooden cane that his grandfather had made in his retirement, together with a long wooden chain miraculously carved from a single piece of wood.

Visiting the small hillside cemetery near the end of a logging road where Tommy's ancestors had long been laid to rest, we ran into Tommy's aunt Loretta washing family gravestones and restaking the VFW flag by his grandfather's grave. It was part of a lingering tradition in the region to yearly pause the life of the living to lay flowers for the dead. A retired nurse, Loretta enjoyed Civil War reenactments—favoring Confederate ancestors, Tommy surmised—but was uninterested in Pikeville's upcoming white nationalist march. "Those guys come and go. I don't pay them mind," she said.

Discovering the Ladder He Was Climbing Down

"The very idea that I had a place on a class ladder came to me slowly," Tommy mused. "First, I thought of my family as middle class, and I was proud of that. As a kid, class was a matter of the kinds of toys I got at Christmas. Don't get me wrong. I was happy to get what I got—GoBots, Action Max, Conan the Barbarian, Turok, the Warlord. But the kids at school had better-made versions of the toys I got. So, in toys, I felt somewhere below the middle." Then when Tommy's mother's Texan relatives came to visit, he said, "I could see they looked around and thought my mom had married down and felt sorry for us. One cousin asked me, 'What do you think a redneck is?' and I wondered why she asked me that. Did she think *I* was one?"

Tommy's father worked as a guard at a coal mine, as Shea Maynard's dad had. But, Tommy explained, "after he lost that job, dad got a job in a lumberyard and we fell behind on taxes." To pay them, we sold half of the land that had my old home and my grandfather's on it, to a junk dealer who ran a strip club." Now along the edge of the Ratliffs' property line were rusted machines of different sizes—one of them an ancient wheel-less Cadillac crisscrossed with vines, a still-life testament to fading hopes for the American Dream.

We were walking now along a dirt path to a gurgling stream in back of Uncle Roy's and Aunt Loretta's homes—a wondrous wooded childhood haunt, filled with pine, poplars, birch, and pawpaw trees, that Tommy had long ago christened "Fairyland," a term he still used with reverence.

"After fourteen or fifteen, I used to spend a lot of time in this forest," Tommy recalled, looking around at the trees as if at the faces of dear friends. "George [a childhood pal] and I would fight monsters and trolls, and orcs and talking animals, like we saw in films about Narnia. We wore rounded strips of tree bark as body armor and used sticks as swords. A tree stump with a rock was my 'headquarters.' I'd catch salamanders, frogs, and crawdads from the stream and let them go. We didn't fish or hunt; we thought everything should be left the way it is. We hated logging roads and only used dead trees. If you listened really close to the crickets and frogs sing to each other at night, first a song would come from one bank of the stream, then we'd hear an answer from the other. In the winter, we'd walk up the frozen streambed on the ice, then slide all the way down." Listening to Tommy, I was reminded of a passage in Wendell Berry's *Jayber Crow*: "Aunt Beulah could hear the dust motes collide in a sunbeam."

"Growing up, my world was real small—Elkhorn, Dorton, Belcher, Millard, Lick Creek, places around our holler. I didn't know what was going on outside my family and neighbors and these places," Tommy said. "Elkhorn only had one red light, but it was a city compared to Dorton, nothing there except the school and a pizza place. Dorton was tough. In a lot of hollers people only come out once a month [to shop or visit] and don't like outsiders. Nearly everyone in my world—my parents, my two brothers, my best friend George, my neighbors and schoolmates, and the action figures we played with—were all white."

When, after finishing high school and working a few jobs, Tommy enrolled at Clinch Valley College in Wise, Virginia, he made his world smaller still. "Dad never liked me or my brothers to talk. If we were at dinner, he told us, 'Don't talk.' If we were in the car, it was 'Don't talk.' If we had company, 'Don't talk.'" So at Clinch Valley, Tommy sat in the back of a large classroom, was assigned to no discussion groups or advisor, feared going to his professor's office hours, and never talked. "The only guy who would talk to me was a quiet Chinese guy, the first Asian person I ever met, who also sat by himself and didn't talk." At the end of the first semester, Tommy flunked out, imagining that he, not the college, had failed, and that this would be his last try.

Blacks in a White Boyhood

As Tommy looked back at his nearly all-white world, he recalled befriending one of his two Black schoolmates. Also, he said, "I invited Missy [who was half-Black and whom he described as "uppity Dorton"] to our homecoming senior prom. Everybody thought she was a model." But Tommy added, "I just dated her a few months, since she went back to her jealous ex-boyfriend."

As for Black history, Tommy hadn't learned much about it. "I'm not sure if I wasn't paying attention or if it wasn't taught. But before college, honestly, I wasn't very sure how Blacks got to America. I learned about slavery from seeing *Amistad* [a film about a slave ship rebellion in 1839] and *Twelve Years a Slave* [about a free Black man kidnapped and sold into slavery], and about the Holocaust from *Schindler's List*."

Tommy also learned about Black life through television: "For a while we didn't own a TV. Dad would rent one in his name and when the bill got too high, Mom would put it in her name. I watched *The Cosby Show* [a sitcom about an affluent Black family] and thought those kids were a whole lot better off than I was. They got an allowance, and all they had to do was save it. Their parents didn't yell or drink. They lived in a nice house, and the dad was fine with them talking."

Yet in one program about Black family life, Tommy suddenly recognized his own. "I watched and loved every episode of *Good Times*," a 1970s sitcom about a Black family in Chicago that struggled with such things as job losses, a car breakdown, and an eviction notice. "In one scene," Tommy recalled, "the wife, Florida, is talking to her girlfriend, who confides, 'I can always tell when it's Saturday morning because I wake up with a black eye.' That meant that the husband of Florida's friend got paid on Fridays, got drunk on Friday night, came home, and beat up his wife.

"But what got me wasn't the story. It was that people *laughed* at it. Florida's friend laughed. Florida laughed. On the TV soundtrack, the audience laughed. As a kid I remember wondering: *Why did they all laugh?* At night, I'd crawl into bed with my older brother. I could hear my dad downstairs drunk, yelling and cursing at Mom, hitting her, shoving her against the wall, and shouting, 'That didn't hurt!' Mom was yelling at Dad, 'Stop it!' I was scared. I wanted to cry."

Cascading

As Tommy grew up, his parents' lives spiraled down. "In the 1980s, when I was in high school, Dad lost his job guarding a mine and got a job as a supervisor in a lumberyard. When the lumberyard closed, Dad worked for my uncle Roy's road crew cutting grass along public roads with a dozer at minimum wage. That's when we fell behind in taxes. When my father fell off the dozer and injured his back, his doctor discovered he had cancer." As funds ran down, Tommy said, "we went from three cars to one which we could barely keep running. We applied for food stamps, which bothered my dad terribly. I wondered: had we become *that* class of family? We felt ashamed."

Then Tommy's parents began to drink themselves farther downward. "Dad drank Early Times whiskey with Tab and Mom drank vodka with Sprite—all day long. By 6:00 p.m. I'd try to leave. They argued. Mom would cry. Dad would get mad at her crying. That's when I heard him shout 'That doesn't hurt.'"

The family house fell into disrepair and his parents moved out of it into a trailer, then asked to move in with one troubled son after another until, one by one, they died.

In this tragic decline, Tommy also saw shame. "The more ashamed and angrier my dad felt about himself, I think, the angrier he got at Mom, it seemed—and at me." But such emotional turns were expressed privately, inside the shell of his father's public reputation as a "great guy" and even as a "great dad." "My dad was popular with neighbors and friends, and he was nice to my two older brothers. But he never liked me. He was disappointed I wasn't into sports. He was disappointed I didn't fish. He was disappointed I wasn't a guy's guy. I couldn't find a way to get him to approve of me. It's like he was prejudiced against the kind of man I am. When I was between ten and fifteen, he was real mean and whipped me angry-hard. I could never guess why."

"We All Have Different Bottoms"

In the wake of his parents' decline, Tommy's own ordeal unfolded. An acquaintance asked him if she could move into his trailer to save on rent. The two became involved, she became pregnant, and at nineteen Tommy married and briefly imagined he was glimpsing a life of satisfaction and pride. "I got baptized at the Free Will Baptist Church in a creek one midnight in December, total immersion. One man held my back, another my head. It was cold and I got sick. When I got better, I got a union job at Kellogg's biscuit factory. We moved near her folks in Jenkins, and I thought, 'For my American Dream, this is good enough,' and it would have been if she'd been the right woman."

But she was not. The baby was too much for her. The house was left in disarray. Tommy's addicted brother moved into a spare room. Returning late from his job at Kellogg's, Tommy had a head-on car collision. When, after his medical leave, he tried to return to his job, Kellogg fired him.

Jobless, with a wife and child to support, with $225 due monthly for rent and $100 for power, Tommy began scavenging aluminum cans out of ditches to recycle, $25 per bunch. Other luckless neighbors competed for the good cans. "I knew people looked down on me because I knew how *I* looked at other people scrounging cans. But part of me still thought, 'I'm not that kind of person.' I'd spend a few hours visiting with Uncle Roy before I got around to asking to borrow money. He'd know why I came, which was embarrassing. I'd borrow his car if mine broke down or I was driving mine with dead tags [expired license plates]. I looked for work, but you had to pass the drug tests first and for a while I was trying muscle relaxants, Valium, Ativan. Then it got to half a case of beer, then more." After Tommy's marriage dissolved, his loving and nondrinking in-laws took in Tommy's son. Now, with Tommy on his own, his heavy drinking grew worse, from occasionally to every day, from with someone else to alone, to alone and a lot.

Drinking had its own pride system, Tommy discovered. "At the top were guys who could hold a lot without getting sloppy drunk, pay for the drinks, and share the high. In the middle ranks were angry drunks. There was a rule to never talk politics, so angry drunks would be mad at 'the man keepin' us down.' At the very bottom of the hierarchy were the crying drunks. I was a crying drunk," Tommy reflected.

Our walk through Fairyland was taking us to a cluster of branches, a long-ago-collapsed teepee Tommy and his pal George had once built as boys in a moment of childhood triumph, and Tommy began to relate the hardest moment of his life. "We all have different bottoms," he reflected softly. "I reached my bottom when my marriage broke up. I had a head-on car crash. I lost my job at Kellogg. My dog died. Then at a holiday gathering, I overheard my dad—whom I'd always assumed was my real dad— call me his *stepson*. I was shocked; I'm not his real, biological son? Maybe *that's* why he never liked me, seemed prejudiced against me. I'm the wrong blood and can't do a thing about it.

"The world went dark. I gave up. All I saw was a wall of night. I had failed. That was my bottom. I was drinking alone, a quart of whiskey a day. I dreamt of driving fast into oncoming traffic. I had an appointment with a doctor to check on the beginning stage of cirrhosis of my liver. I was heading toward my own death."

One of Tommy's favorite musical artists was Jelly Roll, a white, Tennessee-born rapper of southern hip-hop and country rap who put Tommy's feelings into words:

All my friends are losers.
All of us are users,
There are no excuses, the game is so ruthless.
The truth is the bottom is where we belong.

In *Deaths of Despair and the Future of Capitalism,* Anne Case and Angus Deaton report a surprising finding, one in which Tommy—after reading the book—saw himself. Although the United States had long been among the world leaders in extending its citizens' life spans, since the turn of the twenty-first century there has been an unexpected rise in premature deaths of white people in the prime of life, ages forty-five to fifty-four. The main causes are death by drug overdose, suicide, or alcoholic liver disease, which together claimed the lives of six hundred thousand people between 1999 and 2017. Especially hard hit have been white, blue-collar men without a bachelor's degree.

Such men were not dying in heroic wars, battling fierce storms at sea, or toiling in coal mines. One by one, they were—and are—dying in solitary shame. In the obituary section of the *Appalachian News-Express,* I began to notice death notices showing young faces, sometimes listing young ages, but nearly always omitting the cause of death.

Tommy could name a number of local suicides. "The younger brother of a fifth-grade friend of mine shot another and then himself in the head. One guy drove drunk into a tree. My own brother Scott drove drunk off the road, and I believe that was a suicide. At one point, you could have almost counted me."

"Biting the Bait"

Tommy tried to imagine how he might have turned into a racist. He had read Christian Picciolini's *White American Youth: My Descent into America's Most Violent Hate Movement—and How I Got Out,* the autobiography of a boy who was converted by a neo-Nazi. Picciolini was fourteen, smoking pot with a pal in a Chicago back alley, he writes, when a man in a muscle car drove up, stopped, and got out. The friend fled, but the man confronted the young Picciolini, took the joint out of his mouth, and said, "Don't you know that's *exactly* what the Communists and Jews want you to do, so they can keep you docile?" By sixteen, now clean of drugs and with a purpose, Picciolini had become the leader of a group of Chicago-area skinheads, which he then merged with the yet more violent white supremacist Hammerskins.

"If I had been fourteen and smoking in an alley and a man showed interest in me," Tommy mused, "what if he dressed in camo, wore his ball cap back-to, and took me in? What if I began spending time at his house to get out of mine? And if my dad was beating me hard, and my parents were drinking, and I felt like they didn't really know me or care? I ask myself: what would have happened? I could have felt the guy in the muscle car really cared about me.

"And what if that guy told me, 'Your dad lost his job at the lumber mill because immigrants were coming in, or because a Jew closed it down'? I might have said, 'Oh yeah . . . ,'" Tommy continued. "Or when I was going out with Missy [the mixed-race girl whom he invited to his high school prom], what if he'd said, 'Missy dumped you for that other guy. Black girls do that'? I might have said 'Oh yeah . . . ' Or when I flunked out of Clinch Valley community college and I couldn't go home—my stepdad had converted my bedroom into his hobby room to make fishing lures—the man could have said, 'Colleges are run by commies.' I might have said, 'Oh yeah.'"

In these ways, Tommy speculated, an extremist might offer recruits a raft of imagined villains onto whom to project blame and relieve the pain of shame. David Maynard had focused on a missing national narrative that might protect poor whites from the shame of failing to achieve the American Dream. Tommy was focused on something else: the shamed person's vulnerability to those offering to blame a world of "outside" enemies.

The Carrier Ant

When Tommy entered the recovery center, he sat before a kindly intake clerk who asked him questions about his life. "She asked me if my parents drank, and were they alcoholic? I told her both were, and she told me, 'This isn't your fault.' I cried."

On the third day of Tommy's detox, he walked outside and seated himself on a patio chair, miserable. "My head was hung low, and I was staring at the ground between my legs. Then I suddenly noticed a trail of ants. Each ant was carrying a tiny load—a crumb, a bit of leaf, a piece of dirt. Then I saw it: one ant was carrying another ant as big as he was. That dead ant was useless, not doing its part, being a load instead of carrying a load. I thought, 'See that dead ant? That's me, right there. I could be that carrier ant. *I do not want to be that dead, carried ant.*' That was one of the greatest moments in my life. That carrier ant brought me back."

As I noted earlier, the Latin term *prode*, "to be of use," is the origin of the word *pride*. Alex Hughes wanted to be of use providing for his family. Tommy's grandfather had been honored for his bravery in the mines and on the battlefront. Donovan Blackburn was to be honored for protecting Pikeville from harm, and Mayor Andrew Scott for providing school backpacks to the children of Coal Run. All were carrier ants. And for Tommy, it would be through helping others out of drink and drugs that he was to carry a load himself.

Tommy had hit bottom: shame. But he had rejected a move to shift blame to all the racial targets Matthew Heimbach was to offer up, and came to see how blame, placed like a covering over disappointing life events, might falsely seem to relieve his pain. He was to find his way forward to creative repair. By the time I was walking with Tommy through Fairyland, he had happily remarried to a medical researcher and earned a bachelor's degree, graduating on UPike's dean's list. He'd also taken a job at the Southgate Rehabilitation Program where he counseled recovering addicts, including the KKK felon Wyatt Blair.

Now, imagining the leader of the upcoming march, Tommy reflected, "That guy's selling white nationalism as a quick fix to make a guy who's down on himself feel like he's strong and going places. With racism, that guy would just be handing anyone like I was another drink."

10

At the Grave's Edge

"That white nationalist march? No, at the time I hadn't heard of it. And if I had, I wouldn't have cared. I was a homeless heroin addict who had overdosed three times and was heading toward a fourth."

A thoughtful man of forty, James Browning had a blue bandana bound tight around his forehead, edging the top of his eyebrows, sunglasses lifted over his brow. A trim brown mustache edged his mouth, below which was a pointed beard with a streak of gray; long brown hair hung down his back. James spoke slowly, succinctly, as if carefully lifting and laying down precious instruments with which to build an idea. He sat at a desk in a nearly empty homeless shelter, where he'd been hired as a guard and workman. It was several years after the march had taken place, and COVID had shut down hotels, shops, travel. We were talking by Zoom about his life in the period leading up to the march.

"As a teenager, I wore a big chain wallet, bracelets, purple spiked hair; I looked ridiculously alien for around here," James said with a gentle laugh. Then, in a soft tone, he added: "I'm in recovery now."

Shortly after James had arrived at an emergency room unconscious from his fourth heroin overdose, the phone rang in the apartment of his devoted sister, Ashley, a graduate student at the University of Tennessee. "I'd received emergency calls three times before, and every time my phone rang," she would tell me later, "I dreaded it would be *the* call: 'James is dead.'

"One day a medic did call," Ashley recounted, "to say, 'We found James without a pulse. But we did CPR and revived him.' I just sobbed," Ashley recalled, "I took a breath, got online, and spoke to James: 'James, are you ready this time?' He said, 'I'm so sorry, Ashley; yes, I'm ready.' So I looked for the best recovery program in eastern Kentucky and found Southgate [the facility at which Tommy Ratliff worked and where Wyatt Blair "cleaned up his mouth"]. They usually only accept clients through their prisoner sentence reduction program, but I got James covered by a separate grant to help addicts recover," Ashley explained. This was how James Browning met Tommy Ratliff, and the two bonded.

"Tom Ratliff became my counselor," James told me. "He took me for walks with him in a forest behind his house. We liked the same seventies punk rock bands—the Ramones ["I Want to Be Sedated"], Black Flag ["Nervous Breakdown," and "Fix Me"], and the Misfits ["Scream!" and "Die, Die, My Darling"]. By tradition, when a recovering addict graduates from Southgate, he offers a gift to his counselor. Tom told me he liked my Misfits T-shirt, so when I graduated from Southgate, I gave it to him.

"Tom told us about how he hit his own bottom and saw the line of ants, each carrying its tiny burden, one live ant carrying a dead ant. I understood. Tom Ratliff became the carrier ant willing to carry the dead—or nearly dead—ant, me. The man saved my life."

The National Pride Economy, Bottom-to-Top View

Like everyone else I came to know, James saw the 2017 march and the larger political moment surrounding it through the unique prism of his immediate world and its ideas about pride. Prisoners such as Wyatt Blair and drug addicts in recovery programs like James Browning might not normally find their way into a rough survey of community opinion such as this. But, again, it may be from those who've fallen through the bottom of the national pride economy that we learn the most about how to see beyond it—to politics, race, and human dignity.

James would awaken from the nightmare of his addiction a man with new eyes. He was not like Rip Van Winkle, who returns to us from the past to view modern life through the eyes of a previous age. Rather, James was like a man who at one point lost a sense of how to feel his emotions, then recovered that sense with a keen understanding about what it is to be alive to our emotions—including those of pride and shame.

"Where did you grow up?" I asked. "Turkey Creek," James answered, "A tiny holler of ninety-eight, and they are basically good, *good* people." He also described his parents as "good, good, good people and *good* parents. They had nothing to do with my addiction and tried all they could to stop it."

When James thought of pride, he thought of his dad. "I think my dad is a good, proud, strong man. He'd rather chop his arm off than reach out to Uncle Sam for financial help. Other guys around here, too, are proud they work. And if a guy isn't working himself at the moment, he's proud his dad worked, and especially proud if he mined coal. He's proud of his skills. He'd be ashamed if he couldn't move a wrench around a lug to fix a flat tire, or hunt and fish. Or he's proud of being an American, and proud to live in Appalachia.

"When my dad was real young, he got up to feed the chickens and hogs before walking to school. My grandfather had been a coal miner at Swan Creek mine in Logan, West Virginia. I think he was a day laborer, shoveled coal. But when Dad was twelve, a wall inside my grandfather's coal mine collapsed on him and my grandfather was crushed and killed.

"So my dad and his two brothers and two sisters all helped my widowed grandma get by. In addition to feeding the chickens and hogs, when Dad was fifteen he got a job afternoons pumping gas, and after that my dad never stopped working. He fixed most everything that broke and worked all the time. He just retired from forty-one years as an engine driver on the Norfolk and Southern Railroad and as local chairman of the United Transportation Union. Dad raised me and Ashley middle class—the American Dream, country style."

His father's pride was based on strong family ties and independence from government authority. "My dad told me to think of our male cousins as brothers and to honor our ancestors. Generations of Brownings are buried in our family plot, where I hope to have my ashes laid too. When a family member dies, we stay up with the body for three days—someone always awake—and we dig the earth ourselves. The family is proud not to have strangers dig Browning graves. I don't consider myself a traditional guy and I don't love all our traditions, but I love that one," James told me.

"At reunions, Christmas, and Thanksgiving, the men always sit down first at the men's table. Women serve the men, then seat themselves at a side table. My grandma said this didn't make her feel 'less than men' since in the old days men would come in from heavy work in the fields. But for my sister, Ashley, and my ex-wife, Kara, it was agony to hold their tongues. Ashley was the first family member anyone can remember to go to college, and around the table, the idea was, 'Don't brag about it.' To this day, they keep a close eye on how Ashley talks: 'You go off to college and now you can't talk right anymore' is what she'd hear. Ashley's getting a PhD in sociology at the University of Tennessee," James said proudly. "Formally, women here have a secondary place, but when the door's closed"—here James laughed lightly—"Appalachia's a matriarchy. Miners get injured or die, and women have to be prepared to raise large families on their own, like my grandma did."

James also described his family as prizing self-sufficiency, away from the government's probing eye and authority. "It was always said that if a problem arose in the family or holler—someone was breaking the law, beating their wife, or stealing—we didn't call the police. We took care of it ourselves." This was to pose a personal problem for James and others. "In the culture I grew up with," James added, "Blacks and immigrants lived somewhere else, gay people hardly existed, women had their place, and we loved our culture. On my birthdays, my dad gave me CDs of Dolly Parton and Johnny Cash."

As a thirteen-year-old, James said, "I shot beer cans in the river. I was a metalhead listening to the Ramones, Black Flag, raw, fast, intense. Later in South Williamson we'd slick up our cars and buzz the avenue, a four-block radius, with music, beer, and pot. That was the action."

This "action" took James past the South Williamson mall where David and Shea Maynard had married, and where James's mother worked at the Fashion Bug and his sister, Ashley, at Coffee Corner. Ashley stayed late on Fridays to hear bluegrass music and watch clogging, a quick-stepping collective Appalachian tap dance. The action for thirteen-year-old James was not far from where John Rosenberg and Dr. Budgy drove in from Prestonsburg to attend services, one at a synagogue, the other at a mosque. James was cruising, too, through territory in which the wider action a century back had been the bitter feud between the McCoys and Hatfields. But as James was growing up in this part of Appalachia, another silent war was becoming far more deadly.

Two Secret Shames

Two secrets fractured James's childhood. One was a series of deeply shaming events perpetrated by two adults repeatedly on James as a child between the ages of eight and eleven. It was feared that alerting local authorities might bring public shame to the community, so by local tradition, such matters were to be resolved privately or, better still, kept hidden. This way shame would stay confined to the family. James told no one. "I couldn't tell my parents. If I'd told my dad, two men would have been shot dead, and my dad would be in prison for their murder. So I kept quiet. But I began to feel that I didn't belong where I was."

The second secret was kept from James, his parents, his sister Ashley, the paramedics who years later would revive him, the good people of Turkey Creek, and, through the 1990s from the largely white, coal-mining rustbelt of blue-collar America. Indeed, this second secret was in the hands of the criminal owners of the Connecticut-based pharmaceutical company Purdue Pharma—the Sackler family. At the time,

the Sackler family paraded under their proud reputation as generous donors to such institutions as New York's Museum of Modern Art, Yale University, and Harvard University. But Purdue Pharma's actual business was
to promote a lie—that the pain reliever OxyContin was nonaddictive and
therefore superior to other pain-relieving opioids. The company targeted
vulnerable populations, including injured coal miners and their struggling
families in eastern Kentucky and West Virginia.

Corporate Investments, Regulation-Averse States

Starting in 1996, Purdue began an aggressive campaign marketing Oxy-
Contin as a nonaddictive solution to pain. First, it increased its sales force.
In 1996, Purdue had 318 sales representatives. Four years later, the number had risen to 671. It dispatched 78 sales representatives to Kentucky
alone. In 2000, Kentucky had only 1 percent of the U.S. population, but
it was especially vulnerable to the Sacklers' aggressive marketing—first
because it had a higher than usual proportion of coal miners who had
suffered injuries and needed pain relief.

But second, Purdue focused on regulation-averse states. That there was
less regulation in these red states was a point of pride among right-leaning
politicians (who routinely called for "cutting government red tape"). For
each drug purchase, such states called for only two receipts documenting
the purchase—one for the pharmacist, a second for Purdue. A handful of
more closely regulated states, mostly blue states, called for three copies—
the third going to a state medical official monitoring the prescribing of
controlled substances.

The requirement of that third copy had an astonishing effect. As later
research would reveal, OxyContin distribution was 50 percent higher in
the loosely regulated states (requiring two copies per drug purchase), such
as Kentucky, Tennessee, West Virginia, than it was in more tightly regulated states (requiring three copies per purchase), such as New York,
California, and Illinois.

Within these "freer" states, Purdue targeted doctors who were already prescribing large amounts of opioids and the pharmacists from whom those high-prescribing doctors ordered drugs. And it offered its sales force exciting vacation conferences. Health care professionals were given Oxy-Contin fishing hats, stuffed plush toys, and music CDs (*Get in the Swing with OxyContin*). Ominously, Purdue offered free, limited-time prescriptions for a seven- to thirty-day supply of OxyContin—a drug that, it was found later, in habitual users, produced similar withdrawal cravings and symptoms as heroin. Between 1996 and 2001, Purdue invited more than five thousand doctors, pharmacists, and nurses to forty conferences on pain management, all expenses paid. Crucially, Purdue offered its salespeople large bonuses for increasing OxyContin sales. In addition to the average sales representative's annual 2001 salary of $55,000, annual bonuses ranged from $15,000 to nearly $240,000. That year, Purdue paid its sales reps $40 million in incentive bonuses.

It created "prescriber profiles" on the nation's doctors and pharmacists. And its "physician call list" included 94,000 combined "prescriber profiles," detailing the number of drugs each doctor prescribed, along with their zip code, county, and state. The more a doctor prescribed, the more frequently Purdue sales reps would visit them. Sales skyrocketed. In 1996, when the company first introduced it, sales were $48 million. By 2000, sales had hit $1.1 billion. By 2004, OxyContin was a leading drug of abuse in the nation.

Along the "abandoned ghost shops" in pill-saturated Williamson, on the West Virginia side of the river, cars lined up at pharmacy drive-through windows, the author Chris McGreal has written. A while back a patron at the local Moose Lounge in Boone County, West Virginia, not far from where James once lived, could pay a tab with half an Oxy. Parking lots filled at the so-called pill mills—Williamson Wellness Center, the Tug Valley Pharmacy, Hurley Drug, and across the river in Kentucky at Family Pharmacy—reaching the James Brownings of the region, who held secret their shame and sorrow.

Back in the sales division of AmerisourceBergen, a large drug distribution company, a lawsuit forced confidential company files into public view.
Drug salespeople had secretly emailed each other about the rising rate of
addiction in a spirit of hilarity. One wrote a shaming parody of the *Beverly
Hillbillies* theme song about Florida victims:

> Come and listen to a story about a man named Jed,
> A poor mountaineer, barely kept his habit fed,
> Then one day he was looking at some tube,
> And saw that Florida had a lax attitude.
> About pills, that is, Hillbilly Heroin, "OC" [OxyContin].
> Well the first thing you know ol' Jed's a drivin' south,
> Kinfolk said Jed don't put too many in your mouth,
> Said Sunny Florida is the place you ought to be,
> So they loaded up the truck and drove speedily.
> South, that is.
> Pain clinics, cash n' carry.
> A Bevy of Pillbillies!

Between 1999 and 2021, more than 1 million lives nationwide were lost
to drug overdose. In Appalachia the hit was harder. In 2021, the rate of
deaths from drugs in the United States was 32 per 100,000. In Kentucky
it was 56 per 100,000. The counties in which I talked to people about
the march had their own hit rates, so to speak. For Wyatt Blair's native
Bath County, the annual drug overdose rate in 2022 was 156 per 100,000.
For Tommy Ratliff, James Browning, and others in Pike County, the rate
was 91 per 100,000. Wherever they lived, a disproportionate number of
victims were prime-age, white, high-school-educated men living in rural
areas. Beyond this, the Purdue sales pushers were probably not thinking
about the number of babies who were born to drug-addicted mothers and
later suffered developmental problems.

Once the state of Kentucky sued Purdue in 2007, the public began to gasp at the full damage Purdue Pharma had caused. Some 1,600 legal cases were brought against it by cities, counties, Native American tribes, hospitals, and others. Purdue lawyers argued that it couldn't receive a fair trial in Pike County, and to show why, they pointed to a company-commissioned study revealing that 29 percent of Pike County residents reported that they or a family member personally knew someone who had died from an overdose of OxyContin. "My own first psychotherapist was indicted for trafficking in OxyContin," Tommy Ratliff told me.

On the heels of economic loss, KY-5 has suffered terrible losses to family and community through drugs. Between 2016 and 2018, Kentucky had the nation's highest rate of children living with relatives other than their parents—9 percent. Another 5 percent were in foster care. "Sure, the American Dream is all yours if nothing goes wrong," Tommy Ratliff had told me, recalling hearing a college guest speaker advise students on how to get there. "But things go wrong."

Upon the heels of one drug scandal came two others. Astonishingly, recent research suggests that the lawsuits against Purdue did not dissuade competing drug companies from themselves promoting their own opioids to suspect doctors. In a recent study, David Tan of the University of Washington discovered that "competitors did not attempt to distance themselves from Purdue's OxyContin promotion or its association with communities suffering from the opioid epidemic." In 2015, the year after Kentucky sued Purdue, the company's budget for sales representatives promoting OxyContin fell by 94 percent, but the following year, the sales budgets of Purdue's competitors—spent in some of the same areas—*increased* 160 percent.

In addition, Tommy and James began to have suspicions around the widespread and longterm use of Suboxone, a drug that is used to treat opioid addiction by easing withdrawal symptoms and reducing dependence over time. It is advertised as "nonaddictive." But many recovering addicts feel the need to stay on it," James explained. "Recovering addicts line up for it and don't stop using it. "It takes seven to fourteen days to get heroin out of your system, but thirty days for Suboxone. U.S. Department of Health even declares an addict cured while he or she takes Suboxone daily. The officials are calling you cured but you're still on the stuff," James said, shaking his head. One day a while later, as James and Tommy and I were riding in a car, James slowed the car and called out, "Look!" There was a large sign in front of a small storefront clinic, which read: FAMILY SERVICES, WEIGHT LOSS, SUBOXONE.

Invidior, the manufacturer of Suboxone, has been sued, much as Purdue Pharma was, for false advertising about the "less addictive" nature of its drug. And as part of Massachusetts' lawsuit against Purdue, it highlighted evidence that in 2014 and 2015 Purdue explored entering the "attractive market" of addiction treatment drugs like buprenorphine and naloxone (the components of Suboxone). "Big Pharma is at it again," James said.

Tragically, the two secrets—James's secret of childhood abuse and the Sacklers' secret targeting of victims such as James—collided. In the material economy, the Sacklers amassed billions and depleted public coffers now desperately needed to fund services such as foster care, rehabilitation services, the police force, prisons, treatment programs, government staff to implement the regulation of such drugs, and the public upkeep of graves. In the pride economy, the drug crisis plunged James's loving family, his community, and his struggling region further into a painful pride deficit.

Shame Cycle

I asked James how drugs had affected his sense of pride. He answered with a clarity he credited to his recovery. "I felt shame about what happened to me when I was a kid. When I dressed up with my chain wallet and huge blue mohawk, I was saying 'Bring shame on! Laugh. Point. Go ahead, I'm ready. Put me to shame.'

"To hide from my shame, I turned to drugs. Then I was ashamed of being on drugs. So, I was part of a shame cycle. I took drugs to suppress shame, then felt shame for taking drugs. I disappointed my mom. I destroyed my marriage. I hurt my kids. But with Tom Ratliff's help, for the first time in my life, I recovered from my fear of shame."

Looking back at his descent into drugs, James observed how he had slipped down a hidden status hierarchy among fellow users, parallel to that Tommy Ratliff had discovered among the inebriated. "At the top of the hierarchy was the guy who can manage his drug habit and not get caught, and at first I was that guy. I thought drugs were an adventure. I tried marijuana at fourteen, moved to pain pills in high school, and said to myself 'I'm just doing pills.' Then when I was a husband and father and could hold down a job, I was proud of managing my habit. Then I was a divorced father. When my ex-wife wanted to move eight hours' drive away to live near her sister, I moved into a drug house with five buddies and began my homelessness.

"We worked out our own way of judging ourselves and other addicts," James commented. "When I was snorting oxycodone and hydrocodone, I told myself, 'I'm just snorting. I'm holding down a job. I'm not a junkie.' And that worked for a while. But then I got dopesick [slang for having opiate withdrawal symptoms] and I wasn't holding down a job. And a guy came around, obviously a heroin pusher, and said, 'Hey, I can make you feel better.' But we looked down on heroin, and my buddies and I told him we were broke and ran the guy off. But in a few weeks, I was dopesick again and the pusher came back saying, 'I'll give it to you free.' We took some heroin and felt better—for a while.

"Then I told myself, 'I'm *snorting* heroin, not *shooting* it.' I snorted heroin for four or five years telling myself, 'If you snort, you're okay, but if you shoot up, you're a junkie.' But then I found the effect was stronger if it was shot into me. I didn't like needles, so I asked a girl to shoot it into me, and I wasn't shooting it myself, so that was better. But then two years later, the day came when I shot myself up. I became a junkie."

From the top of his drug-den hierarchy of pride James had slid, over twelve years of heroin addiction, to its bottom. "Of my five buddies," he said after a long pause, "three of them are dead. One of them is my son's godfather and was my best friend. His parents told people he died of a 'heart condition.'

"In recovery," James said, "I discovered that I was doing drugs instead of feeling my feelings. So I had to start all over to learn to feel them. I felt like I was four years old. One time, driving, out the car window I saw a stunning sunset and had to pull over and weep at the beauty. I didn't know what to call what I felt. Later, my twelve-step fellowship sponsor told me, 'James, that's awe.'" Newly awake to his emotions, he began to think about emotions, and over many discussions he shared his insights about them with me.

Kinds of Pride

James distinguished between two kinds of pride. One was direct pride— such as he felt looking at the life of his father, his PhD-bound sister, Ashley, and after recovering and discovering himself to be a gifted healer, himself. Pride was based on being "of use" and "of help" to others. For both James and Ashley, it was also important to try to help both those in the family and those beyond family—people out there whom you don't happen to know personally, the poor, addicts, people of different races.

James also distinguished between humble pride and puffed-up pride. Having journeyed to the bottom of the pride hierarchy and back up, James said, "Do I dare feel proud? Around here you're not supposed to claim too much pride, because we don't approve of puffed-up, arrogant pride—pride you demand. We approve of humble pride, the kind a person deserves but never asks for. When I die, I want people to say nice things about me and"—here he chuckled—"to be telling the truth."

James's father was, as his grandfather had been, a proud union man. And although James was not himself a union member, he felt the pride of membership almost as a heritage from his father. Dangerous as mining was, the work of organizing the United Mine Workers, the strongest union in the United States in 1921, had many dangers of its own. "Have you heard of the Battle of Matewan?" James asked. "Matewan is sixteen miles southeast of Turkey Creek in West Virginia and should be a national monument." In 1920, miners at the Stone Mountain Coal Company were paid low wages in scrip (a certificate representing company money they could spend nowhere else except the company store) to work long hours in its dangerous mines." In the stand-off between workers and company-hired detectives sent to evict them, ten died," James said. The incident in Matewan set off a cycle of violence that culminated in the Battle of Blair Mountain, in which a pro-company sheriff hired private planes to bomb the union headquarters and at least sixteen died.

"You know the origin of the term *redneck*?" James's sister asked me later. "In the coal wars, you could tell a loyal union man from a company-hired scab because the man fighting for the union wore the company uniform—which came with a red scarf. And if you were a white union man, Blacks and immigrants were your union brothers and sisters. So being a redneck was a proud thing."

In addition, James credited his dad's work with the railroad union as responsible for his dad's financial success in life, a ladder to the American Dream. "The railway union is why my dad could grow up dirt-poor and me and Ashley grow up middle-class. But the unions went out of here when the coal did," James added, "and I'm not sure my grandkids will even know what a labor union is."

Comparing himself to his father and other local men of his generation, James ranked himself lower in the pride economy. "My dad grew up poor, but by the time he was my age he had a new truck, a double-wide home, and summers he took us to the beach. He did it to provide for us, and not for himself," James added. "Well, a little for himself; when he got an old clunker to fix up, he called it his toy."

But James's pride was not based on things he'd earned the money to buy. "Most guys around here want to be providers, and I appreciate that," James said. "As for what about their work they take pride in, apart from the money, it's usually not much. If a guy at a bar gets asked, 'What do you do?' and he answers, 'I work for [the building company], I'm a construction worker,' the other person will say, 'Oh . . . ' Or if the guy says, 'I work for [a tree removal service], the other person will say, 'Oh . . . ' Or if he answers, 'I work for the gas company. I lay line,' the other person will say, 'Oh . . . ' And if I say, 'I work in addiction recovery,' they'll say, 'Oh, good for you.' So I get 'Oh, good for you,' to feed into my pride bank account," James said with a chuckle. "I think it's because the region really needs the recovery work people like me do."

Immigrants and Blacks: How Different Are We?

In 2017, the marchers about to descend on Pikeville wanted a white America. "Keep immigrants out. Keep Blacks down. That's their idea," James declared later. "But some of us are migrants out of eastern Kentucky, and in places we migrate to, at least back in the day, hillbillies were unwanted, like Blacks were."

James had faced three options—stay, leave, or leave and return. "Most of us love it here, our families, community, our mountains, and traditions. But even as a kid, I wasn't sure I could stay. I loved whales and sharks and water snakes and wanted to be an oceanographer, but where's the ocean around Turkey Creek? It can be rough to stay but also rough to leave," he explained. Often relatives urged their young to stay. "You always know your people want you to come home," Ashley Browning later told me. "When I got accepted to the University of Tennessee to earn an advanced degree, my aunt said, 'We're real proud of you, Ashley. But we need someone to teach kindergarten here. You're not going to *stay gone*, are you?' "

"If you're returning home from being away," James continued, "people get teased back into talking 'regular.' A lot of my high school class did leave the region but came back. For one guy, college didn't work out. For another, his job didn't; another came home with an injury. I came back to live at home after my wife left me."

A curious parallel exists between the stayers and leavers of eastern Kentucky and those in Mexico, Central America, and South America. Eastern Kentucky and other rural areas of the United States have played the role within the domestic economy that such poorer regions have played in the world economy. In the domestic economy of the U.S., KY-5 functions somewhat as a Mexico.

Those who leave Mexico to get jobs in the United States are frequently questioned about their accent and dress and asked to explain where they came from, as Ashley Browning was asked to explain her birthplace to the Boston bookstore employee ("When I said eastern Kentucky, he leaned over the counter to see if I was barefoot").

Those who stay back in Mexico are left to mourn the loss of the "leavers" and await their return. In a parallel way, family and village contacts form part of a "chain migration" from one locale to the other—from a small town in Chiapas state, Mexico, to Modesto, California, or from Turkey Creek, Kentucky to Cincinnati, Ohio. In both cases, a "better life" is often imagined in a stronger economic region somewhere else.

Former president Donald Trump popularly focused on stopping Mexico's leavers, whom Trump has accused of "poisoning the blood of our country." Many who were taking Route 23 out of eastern Kentucky were voting for building a wall against immigrants coming in from the world's South.

"How ironic. Trump is asking us to hate Mexican migrants," James observed, "but precious few Mexicans come here into eastern Kentucky. Even if they were, some of us are too busy packing up to leave eastern Kentucky to notice. And we're being asked to look down on people leaving their country just like some of us are leaving our region. Whatever kind of border regulation you want, why are we asked to look down on or hate migrants? We don't like it when people look down on us."

Hood to Holler, Migrant and Stayer

James summed up his own views about Blacks and Appalachian whites: "There's a connection to Blacks a lot of whites around here don't see. Coal companies took our labor, blackened our lungs, killed guys like my grand-dad, messed up the water, and cut out with the profits. We were taken for dumb hillbillies. I wouldn't go so far as to say they were treated as badly as slaves. No. But we were used and thrown away. A lot of Black boys grew up like my dad, without fathers, and had to work at an early age and didn't make it to college, like my dad and uncles. With coal jobs gone today, my white male relatives have almost taken the place of what would have been last-in-line Black men if they'd been here." On the parallel of whites to Blacks, James seemed to echo David Maynard. He also saw many in his community in the position of migrants. "Isn't that ironic," James mused, "that the two groups Trump is asking us to look down on—immigrants and Blacks—are the two groups we have quite a bit in common with. And we're voting for Trump. He's calling immigrants 'rapists' and calling Black Lives Matter activists 'thugs.'"

In James's family of white "stayers," Blacks were warmly welcomed. "My parents are not prejudiced people," he said, weighing his words carefully. "Dad grew up isolated from Blacks, but the *n*-word has never been heard at our dinner table. He worked forty-one years for the railroad, and he came to love a Black union buddy, a gifted artist named Clyburn Dodson. He bought Clyburn's artwork as gifts for the family and welcomed him into our home. I dated a half-Filipina girl all through high school and my dad was fine with that. One of dad's brothers came home from the Korean War with a Korean bride, so three of my nephews are biracial. The whole family is fine with that. But one of my biracial cousins got teased at school every day, grew up prejudiced against Blacks, and voted for Trump.

"In school I read *Uncle Tom's Cabin*. We saw all of Alex Haley's *Roots* series, and read about segregation and the civil rights movement in history class." I asked if he'd ever heard about the 1919 expulsion of Blacks from Corbin, a three-hour drive away. "Yes, vaguely," he said and then recalled: "Before we moved to Turkey Creek, we lived in Burnwell, Kentucky, eleven minutes' drive south of Williamson [where David and Shea Maynard married]. My best friend Trey's family had a big old house his deceased great-uncle later used for storage. When I was about eleven, Trey and I rummaged around inside it. We discovered a box of letters from the 1940s and '50s with notices where and when to meet. We knew they were *bad*; it turned out Trey's great-uncle was KKK. We also heard that decades back the house of a Black family was burned down, right there in Burnwell." Like Tommy Ratliff, James sensed the menacing presence of a once-active Klan. "I wish I could talk with Trey about all this now." James paused for a moment. "But Trey overdosed."

"One day around the dinner table with all our cousins and uncles," James's sister, Ashley, told me, "I raised the term 'white privilege.' And almost everyone around the table had a conniption fit. It was that word *privilege* that got them furious. They took it as an insult," Ashley recalled. "My dad laughed me right out of the house. He told me, 'I went to work at age fifteen and never stopped. I never owned a *toothbrush* until I was sixteen.'" The word *privilege* seemed to carry the idea of a person of leisure, hoity-toity, puffed-up—someone undeserving of pride. To Ashley's relatives, that was the kind of person they couldn't relate to and didn't like. Perhaps they were offended, too, because of what the word seemed to erase—any acknowledgment of suffering, of stiff-upper-lipping-it, of endurance, and the decency not to toot one's own horn. "Around here, and a lot of places," James said, "a lot of people think if Blacks rise, whites fall. And when your region's on the skids, you don't want to fall any more than you already have."

As political scientist Christopher Parker has argued, many on the extreme right see in these groups a "status threat"—a potential loss of pride in the national pride economy.

One painful hit to community pride has come from economic divestment—the closing of mines, lumberyards, tattoo parlors. Other hits had come from disappearing unions, lower wages, more leavers, incoming drugs. Meanwhile, new calls for pride in the mainstream media were going to women, Blacks, immigrants, LGBTQ people. While to some such calls were welcome, to others it only added to a sense of loss or even erasure and replacement. "Not all change is good change," one man declared with feeling.

An Underground Connection

In the world of drugs, James discovered a hidden connection between the races, one that he felt left scars of shame. Reviewing his twelve years of heroin addiction, he observed another, more personal parallel, this time to the Black drug underworld, that involved a man I will call William. "When I did heroin, I needed to pay for it. First, I bought it from a Black drug dealer and resold it to others. Then the dealer noticed I was buying more heroin than I could use, so he said, 'You're a sub-dealer. You could drive me to Cleveland and I'll give you a commission; be my mule.' At the time I thought it was a dream come true, so I drove him six hours each way. He trusted me and I kept his secrets. He was a friend. But one time when I was dopesick and I asked him to get me off it, he didn't dare. He was afraid a girl would tell on him and he would get ten years [in prison], so he didn't help me."

A girl? I wondered. Later, asking James about the tattoos on his hands, I discovered who that girl might be. On the knuckles of his left hand, he had tattooed letters: N T T S. "I tell people it means 'never trust the system.' But when in my active addiction I was paid to drive from Pikeville to Cleveland for William, we brought five or six women addicts with us, whom William paid in dope. If the cops saw us and signaled us to pull over, the girls quickly stuffed the dope up their vaginas, for some six hours, a risky practice at best. The letters on my knuckles mean 'never trust the stuffer.' William didn't trust them because they could have told on us. I don't know where any of them are now."

Most of James's fall into and journey out of the drug underworld occurred in a mainly white world. Curiously, a remarkably similar targeting of the discouraged inner-city unemployed hit African American communities in the 1970s and 1980s. Midlife deaths from drugs and alcohol (although not suicide) spiked in Black communities in the 1980s, when, as the sociologist William Julius Wilson has explained, offshoring of factory jobs deprived blue-collar Black men of a path to the middle class, just as mine closures did in the 1990s for Appalachian whites. In each case economic losses were followed by a wave of deaths of despair. While the rate of Black mortality was higher than that for whites to start with, after 2000 rates among Blacks began to drop and rates among whites began to rise. This lasted until 2013, when the Black rate began to rise again.

Looking at his left hand, James reflected, "I don't want to remove those tattoos; they remind me how far down I fell and how far up I've come." Then, pointing to his right hand, he said, "I have four rings on it. One is a tree of life. One is for my twelve-step fellowship. The next is my high school senior class ring. On my pinky is my black gem ring, onyx, for healing. There you have it," James said after a pause, "I have a shame hand and a pride hand."

Like other "faces in the crowd," James Browning had grown up with a pride paradox standing, as it were, in front of the American Dream— limited opportunity to achieve the American Dream, and maximal responsibility for failure to do so. And before the young James could face it fully, a drug company had run off with his American Dream, nearly taking the dreamer with it.

Meanwhile, the perpetrators were shamed but unequally punished. According to the *Appalachian News-Express*, in 2022 a local drug dealer was sentenced to twenty years in prison for the death from overdose of a Pikeville resident to whom he sold drugs. Yet at the time of this writing, no member of the Sackler family, owners of Purdue Pharma, has ever gone to prison. The farther down the class ladder, it seemed, the heavier the punishment. But the very act of being sent to prison, wearing handcuffs and prison uniform, all this in itself brought additional shame to the local dealer and his family. So the farther down the social class ladder, it seemed, the more shame. The very logic of money seemed a hidden way to steal pride.

Rock Climbing

But James was back. Under Tommy Ratliff's guidance, James would move into a homeless shelter, get a job as a guard, and enroll in a community college. He was hired on at a recovery center, where he flourished as a healer.

"Before my addiction, I used to love rock climbing," James Browning told me during one of our conversations. "After my recovery, when I realized I had an actual life ahead of me, I started to climb again. And there's this one cliff I know pretty well. It has certain holds where I realized my right foot needed to go where my right hand was, and I'd get discouraged. And with all those years of drugs, I'd lost my self-confidence. But then I did get my foot to where my hand was and to a place almost at the top. I almost began to feel proud. Given all I'd been through, it was hard for me to feel that." He paused.

"But when I finally lifted myself to the top, and looked out at these glorious Appalachian Mountains, some sawed off, gouged out, I didn't want to take them for granted. They'd been through a rough time like a lot of us had. I looked down and saw Tommy Ratliff, who saved my life, holding the ropes below. I thought about all the friends I'd buried. And it occurred to me I could start a new outfit called Recovery Climbs. It could help addicts. But a lot of us are addicted to things other than drugs, like to things politicians say.

"Looking out at these mountains on one of my first post-recovery climbs," James said, "I felt part of life. I felt big. And I felt good. But as time went on and I began to feel more re-attached to the world, when I reached the top, I realized I felt something different.

"I felt small and I felt good."

PART THREE

The Roll of Thunder

11

Trial Run

On April 30, 2017, the temperature at midday in Pikeville was 90 degrees, and the marchers were already an hour late. Along the forty-mile route from outer Whitesburg, where Heimbach's band had camped, to Pikeville, local radio stations were reporting on the thirty-five-vehicle convoy of heavily armed white nationalist men coming from out of town to Pikeville.

In the town office, Donovan Blackburn had worked out a plan. First, get the citizenry out of harm's way. Empty streets. Close shops. UPike students had been urged to leave campus, and a student-initiated counter-rally was postponed. The marchers had been banned from campus, and in response, Burton Webb, the president of the University of Pikeville, had received an anonymous death threat. He had been taken to an undisclosed room guarded by police, where he was preparing to watch the march on a computer monitor linked to a security camera on Main Street. A religious group called Mountain Mission sent prayers imploring all to maintain peace. Most signs of armed readiness were hidden. Anti-riot vehicles and ambulances were stationed out of sight in a large armory at the edge of town, on standby, as were the Pikeville police, state police, Fish and Wildlife, the Pike County Sheriff's Office, police from neighboring cities, and the National Guard.

Matthew Heimbach's various supporters and opponents had cleverly been instructed to enter and leave town along different routes. Main

Street itself was lined with two sets of concrete barricades and bicycle racks behind which a boisterous crowd was already restlessly lined up. "We added barricades to prevent cars that might come in with detonation devices," Blackburn explained. In a bulletproof vest, walkie-talkie in hand, he stationed himself with the FBI in a tactical unit upstairs in a former sheriff's office overlooking Main Street. One concerned citizen we shall meet stood on the street, pistol on hip.

Meanwhile, Matthew Heimbach was hoping to shock the town with the appearance of muscle: Nazi-style tall jack boots, shields, tattoos, tinted sunglasses, and visible guns. At a 2016 Trump rally in Louisville, as noted earlier, Matthew had shoved and yelled at a Black student, Kashiya Nwanguma, and had been arrested and charged with misdemeanor harassment. But before the court could serve papers ordering Heimbach to appear, he had disappeared out of Kentucky, and out of reach of Kentucky authorities. Now, still wanted, he was back in the state.

Faces Missing from the Crowd

Of all the citizens who might have lined the sidewalk to watch Heimbach's men march into town, a great many were absent. Ruth Mullins, who had integrated Pikeville High School but been unwelcome at the Bobby Sox Grill, was sitting at home, her front door bolted, her television tuned to the local news. John Rosenberg, the Holocaust survivor, was home with his wife, his anti-hate speech tucked in a nearby drawer. Inside the Masjid Al-Farooq Islamic Center of East Kentucky, on Masjid Avenue outside Prestonsburg, sat Dr. Syed Badrudduja's assistant. The sheriff had reassured Dr. Budgy, the Indian-born physician who was acting imam at the mosque, that he had the mosque under watch.

Others were missing from the crowd for different reasons. Alex Hughes, the struggling achiever, was busy at his new job in Louisville. Wyatt Blair with the KKK tattoo was still behind bars. David Maynard, who had married his sweetheart in a movie theater, stayed inside his locked trailer, gun ready. Tommy Ratliff, who had found inspiration in a line of ants, was studying hard for his final exams. James Browning was, at the time, a homeless heroin addict. These were some of the faces who were not in the crowd on this day.

Present instead was the press, local, regional, national, and international: *The Guardian,* Associated Press, ABC, *Appalachian News-Express,* and West Virginia Public Broadcasting.

Impatiently waiting, too, were some two hundred boisterous Antifa protesters in red and black scarves, some armed with whistles, drums, and bullhorns. With them were members of Redneck Revolt—a largely white, left-leaning, anti-racism, pro-gun group wearing red neck scarves and holding up a large sign: REDNECKS AGAINST RACISM. They stationed themselves opposite equally impatient and punctual members of the League of the South, who had long been waiting for the delayed Matthew Heimbach and his band. Nearly all the marchers and protesters were from out of town, many from out of state.

"If fascists make the trains run on time, where are your people?" an Antifa protester taunted.

"Time to take a bath!" came a scoffing retort from the League of the South.

Around 2:55 p.m. the police began lining the middle of Main Street. They wore uptilted plastic face shields over their black helmets, guns on black belts, gray shirts (some with protruding bellies). Legs apart, elbows akimbo, eyes impassive, officers formed a line between marchers and protesters, one officer facing the extremists, the next officer facing protesters and onlookers, and so on in a line down the street, an implacable wall conveying the unspoken message, *Don't even try.*

At last, at 3:00 p.m., the caravan arrived. The heavily armed extremists climbed out of their vehicles, lined up to form a phalanx, and marched into the center of town. At the sight of them, whistles, drumming, and amplified slogans, taunts, and counter-taunts clashed in the air over the wall of police officers.

"The white man built this country! Only those of pure white blood may be members of the nation! A second secession! Diversity equals white genocide!"

From behind the steel four-foot-high bike racks, counterprotesters yelled back: "Appalachia comin' atcha, Nazi scum. We're gonna smash ya! Punch a Nazi in the face! Every nation, every race!"

Back from the marchers came: "Race traitor cucks! White rule! We built it. We rule it!"

More temperate slogans steadied the atmosphere: "We celebrate diversity. Injustice anywhere is an injustice to all. You're not welcome! No one wants you here!" A small sign to one side read PIZZA FOR PEACE.

Some counterprotesters wore gently worded T-shirts: NO HATE IN MY HOLLER. Chalked in blue on the sidewalk was NO TO NAZIS IN OUR COMMUNITIES. One Antifa protester, an earnest, large African American man in glasses and red shirt, Daryle Lamont Jenkins, had traveled to Pikeville from Philadelphia and now carefully seated himself on a chair to the side of the street before a laptop set on a card table. There he noted down names and affiliations of various extremist marchers. He was doxxing (short for "documenting and exposing") them. The founder of One People's Project, which monitors hate groups, Daryle explained to an ABC reporter in measured tones that marchers escaping public attention may "sooner or later [become] your police officers . . . your politicians . . . your teachers . . . people you cannot touch. And I don't want that to happen."

Dressed in a white clerical robe, purple velvet stole, and knitted white cap, with a blond beard and mustache, Robert Musick, the University of Pikeville campus chaplain, calmly strode apace alongside the heavily armed Matthew Heimbach. Musick had asked former Kentucky governor Paul Patton about engaging the extremists on campus, evoking his furious reply, "Absolutely not!" Now the irrepressible Musick was trying a different approach.

"Hey Matt! It's Rob here . . . Hi . . . It's nice to see you, brother . . .

Remember, we started dialoguing a few days ago?" Musick called out to the forward-facing Matthew Heimbach. From the marcher behind him, Heimbach could also hear: "Heil Heimbach! Heil Heimbach!" Perhaps enjoying the glory of command, and fearing to seem "soft" in front of his men by responding to the kindly cleric, Heimbach marched grimly past the chaplain.

Finally, before a microphone, one by one, the speeches began. Neo-Nazi Matthew Heimbach, Jeff Schoep, former leader of the National Socialist Movement, and other leaders punched out headlines sprinkled with words: *Forgotten. White. Our.* Off and on, an Antifa member slyly disconnected the extension cord of their loudspeaker, sending the extremists scrambling to reconnect it. Among the neo-Nazis, a winsome young woman in high-cut shorts and a top that revealed a swastika on her belly sat in ostentatious flirtation on the knee of an older man in Nazi uniform.

Pride-Shame Showdown

An hour and a half later, the event was over. The marchers returned to their vehicles parked at the edge of town. As Heimbach opened the door of his car, however, a young police officer dashed up to hand him a sheaf of white papers—a criminal summons. Matthew would now have to appear in a Louisville court. As the white nationalists departed, a block past the crowd, out a car window flew a single concussion grenade, which failed to explode, much like the march itself. Altogether, just three people were arrested.

"How did we do?" everyone asked themselves. Removing his bulletproof vest, noting the complete absence of violence, the city manager, Donovan Blackburn, shared relief and pride in his team, his region, his culture. "I grew up in Greasy Creek, right here in the region, and I love the people here," he told me. "We're brought up to believe in the Lord, say please and thank you, believe in the First and Second Amendments. Today we protected the free speech of people we strongly disagree with. I feel proud to live here."

The federal Department of Homeland Security learned that their prediction of three thousand to six thousand marchers had been wildly over the mark. The march of some one hundred white nationalists had attracted about two hundred counterprotesters—mainly Antifa—and very few local recruits. The African American head of UPike student affairs later told me, "I spotted only three locals who marched with the white nationalists, and one of them is mentally challenged." Meanwhile, the extremists declared themselves a success, the neo-Nazi NSM website praising the marchers for "making no effort to conceal our identities." It produced an exaggerated estimate of 250 new recruits from the march.

The march had been a pride-shame showdown. Through their tattoos, weaponry, and catcalls, the white nationalists were attaching pride to whiteness. Through their callouts and signs, Antifa activists, Redneck Revolt, and unaffiliated attendees shamed the marchers.

Reverend Musick worried that Pikeville itself had been shamed by the marchers' very presence. One town government worker later questioned me sternly, "Why are you even *interested* in that march?" as if the interest itself was tainted with the desire to shame. Ruth Mullins was later proud of Pikeville for "sending the rascals on their way."

Several stories swirled about the Islamic Center. UPike President Webb, who, as noted, had been sequestered due to the death threat, relayed a version of the story he'd heard: "A truck with two men pulled up with a shotgun sticking out an open window on one side. It parked in front of the Islamic Center. The imam [Dr. Budgy] walked cautiously up to the men, worried, to ask the men what they wanted. 'We're guarding the place for you!' came the reply." Dr. Budgy's son-in-law, a professor at the University of Kentucky in Lexington, had heard a second story: two highway patrolmen who were vets of the Iraq War—one a native Kentuckian now returned home, the other a former Iraqi interpreter who had been given U.S. citizenship and who was a close friend of the first man and now his neighbor—had dropped around to reassure Dr. Budgy they had the mosque covered. The third story came from Dr. Budgy himself: "The sheriff came by and told me he had added police protection."

The march itself was summed up by a friendly Prestonsburg car dealer and Trump enthusiast as a "big nothingburger." Andrew Scott, the mayor of Coal Run, quipped with a smile, "In handling extremists, maybe Berkeley should take some lessons from Pikeville."

Later that day, as the hot afternoon melted into evening, Matthew Heimbach's celebratory caravan wove its way back into the mountains, where earlier the band had drilled, to eat, drink, and sing white supremacist songs.

What did they imagine themselves gathered to celebrate? They had—as the NSM website said—shown their identity openly, imagining themselves to be ridding Nazism of its worldwide shame. Imagining a new public tolerance for violence, that website suggested, NSM was "coming out." The march was a stand which they hoped would raise the value of white skin, so to speak, on the national pride stock exchange.

Meanwhile, the history of one white supremacist song the men sang that night curiously paralleled the racial politics of the nation: "Which Side Are You On?" The tune originated, it is believed, as a Baptist spiritual hymn called "Lay the Lily Low" or "I'm Gonna Land on the Shore." And it was known to Black sharecroppers like those recruited from the South to work in the Appalachian mines.

The melody was later accompanied by new lyrics written by Florence Reece, the widow of a slain Harlan County union organizer, during the time in the 1930s remembered as "Bloody Harlan." In the Great Depression, more than one out of every four Harlan County miners was jobless. Even those who found work earned as little as 80 cents a day, some for just a few days a month. Food was scarce. The strike in which Reece's husband was killed was protesting a 10 percent pay cut.

Union coal miners—white, Black, native-born, and foreign-born—fought together for fair wages, and were, together, tear-gassed, beaten, and evicted from their company-owned homes on the orders of the pro-owner sheriff, J. H. Blair. The oft-sung lyrics go:

Which side are you on, boys?
Which side are you on?
They say in Harlan County
There are no neutrals there.
You'll either be a union man
Or a thug for J. H. Blair.

The song took on new life during the 1960s civil rights movement, when it was performed by the folk singer Pete Seeger as a civil rights song. In 2012, folk singer Ani DiFranco added new lyrics to the song, addressing the sense of hope some felt at the dawn of Barack Obama's presidency:

Come on all good workers
This year is our time
Now there's folks in Washington
That care what's on our minds.
Which side are you on now
Which side are you on?

Are we living in the shadow of slavery
Or are we moving on?
Tell me which side are you on now
Which side are you on?

Other themes from the 1960s and later—like opposition to the Vietnam War, opposition to the Iraq War, protests of the response to Hurricane Katrina—were added later:

We voted for an end to war
New direction
And we ain't gonna stop now
Until the job is done.

It was also used to criticize the free market:

Lord knows the free market
Is anything but free
It costs dearly to the planet
And the likes of you and me.

As Heimbach and his white nationalists drank into the evening, they sang the same tune with lyrics rewritten by an alt-right songwriter:

They say that in this country.
There are no white jobs there
You'll either be a pusher
Or die of your despair.

Over the lyrics of a southern hymn had been layered lyrics about striking Kentucky coal miners, to be overlain by verses from 1960s civil rights and other protests, and now white nationalist ones—one atop the other, like the ancient striations of rock inside the ageless mountains surrounding the celebrating marchers. Each set of lyrics reflected moments in American history and, with them, different understandings of pride.

In the end, the marchers had pitched white nationalism to the townspeople and the townspeople had said no. But Matthew Heimbach and the Pikeville march's co-organizer, Jeff Schoep, were soon at work with others to organize a far more dangerous march—with numbers, as it would turn out, much more like what Homeland Security had mistakenly predicted for Pikeville. This torch-carrying Unite the Right march was to take place three months later and attract fifty extremist groups from around the nation, five and a half hours' drive northeast in Charlottesville, Virginia.

Pikeville had been their trial run.

12

Liquid Politics

"I'm sorry to be late. I try to be on time, my German heritage, you know."

Matthew Heimbach was meeting Tommy Ratliff and me in a Pikeville restaurant lobby. "We've been six and a half hours on the road from Chattanooga," Matthew explained. This was where he had moved now that he was in divorce proceedings and living with Diane, a Navy-trained electrician from Florida. Dressed in his usual black, hair clipped to a bristle, Matthew now weighed 220 pounds. Three years after the white nationalist march down Main Street in Pikeville, the memory of the day had faded and a raft of new permit requests had crossed a new Pikeville city manager's desk. In 2018, honking jalopies rolled slowly through town, carrying celebrants wearing overalls and straw hats atop wild hair, sporting grins revealing blackened teeth, banjos in hand. A truck carried a portable jail. Another offered moonshine tasting for the Hillbilly Days festival. The town was having fun with stereotypes of itself.

Later that year, Hope in the Mountains, put on by the Kentucky Baptist Convention, brought a chorus of five hundred to town. That year, too, Pikeville's first LGBTQ parade brought with it multicolored flags. In 2020, a Black Lives Matter parade attracted nearly all white attendees, mostly students, followed by a Rally for Public Grief to honor victims of police violence and some policemen came as participants. Later in 2020, Roger Ford, proud member of Pikeville's Fraternal Order of Police, Lodge #29, had organized a follow-up event, Back the Blues. Twice a year, Pikeville also holds its Gun and Knife Show in the Appalachian Wireless Arena on Main Street—admission cost nine dollars and it prohibited loaded guns.

But the same three years had gone differently for Matthew Heimbach. His march had been followed up by the far larger Unite the Right march in Charlottesville, which left one person dead and thirty-five injured.

Things had changed in Matthew's political life as well. The violent confrontation Homeland Security had predicted for Pikeville had happened three months later in Charlottesville, Virginia, where Matthew, its co-planner, had appeared. He had arranged for two violent skinhead groups, the Hammerskins and Blood & Honour, to "add muscle" to the melee, and he had railed against "white genocide." After a neo-Nazi comrade gunned his car backward into a crowd of protesters and killed counterprotester Heather Heyer, Heimbach was asked by a PBS news reporter, "Do you feel at all responsible for the death of Heather Heyer?" Referring to it as a "car accident," Heimbach answered, "Not at all. I think it's regretful when any person loses their life, but I'm also not going to cry over someone that was trying to kill me and my comrades just a few hours earlier."

Now, several years on, Matthew had written me that he saw things differently. But how differently? Tommy Ratliff, now a graduate of his recovery program and the University of Pikeville, was counseling clients at Southgate. As a man he had tried to imagine how extremists might have recruited him to their cause. So Tommy was eager to meet Matthew Heimbach and compare the "old" Matthew with the "new" one.

To all outward appearances, Matthew's tumultuous and violence-prone life seemed to continue. After Charlottesville, Matthew had to deal with the old, suspended sentence he'd received for shoving a Black protester at a Louisville pro-Trump rally. "I got a $145 fine and 90 days' jail time, waived if I didn't re-offend for two years," Matthew had explained at the time. But in March 2018 he was arrested again.

In a bizarre, violent domestic attack that occurred in and outside his trailer in Paoli, Indiana, Matthew had grabbed his then wife by the cheeks, thrown her on the bed, and knocked his father-in-law to the ground, pushing his arm on the man's neck, causing him to twice fall unconscious. Matthew had had an affair with his father-in-law's young wife, which had been discovered; Matthew then enraged at the discovery. It was this new love interest, Tommy and I later realized, who was carefully studying the menu at the corner table at which we were all seated. Both Matthew and Diane had now split from their spouses, and later would be married for a time.

After being arrested for domestic abuse, Matthew Heimbach was expelled from the Traditionalist Workers Party, which he had founded, and the group itself disbanded. He was also expelled from the National Socialist Movement, for which he'd worked as an outreach officer. In August 2019 he found himself sued for having co-led the deadly Charlottesville march. A local judge sanctioned Matthew for failing to attend hearings or comply with court discovery orders. Discovering that their client was unable to pay his legal fees, Matthew's lawyers had dropped him, though not his obligation to pay them over $12,000. So Matthew was focusing on paying his bills, which now, most importantly, included child support.

"So I got a job," Matthew said after we had ordered, "trucking cake snacks and chips to stack shelves in truck stops. It's all high-fructose corn syrup in plastic bags—junk food—so during COVID, I don't know why they classified me as an 'essential worker.' But I worked on commission, so when sales dropped, I lost work. Since I was self-employed, I couldn't file for unemployment. It was rough." Recently, though, he had found a well-paid job at Volkswagen in Chattanooga. "I look for dirt in the paint, and sand and buff each car and mark it with tape. I get $14 starting pay on ten-hour night shifts; it's mainly young, divorced guys." Now he was earning $15.50 an hour, "50 cents more than I got at Amazon, nights." Also weekly, "to help with my $1,000 monthly rent, I sell blood plasma."

After Charlottesville, "fifteen plaintiffs raised $15 million to sue me personally as well as James Field [the twenty-year-old fellow neo-Nazi who had driven his car into Heather Heyer]. They could take half my paycheck for the rest of my life."

Changing What He Hated or Changing Hate?

Matthew had helped lead a large, deadly Unite the Right march that riveted the nation in 2017, had assaulted his wife in 2018, now was divorcing her and cutting ties with political groups once core to his identity.

"A lot has happened to you since the last time you were in Pikeville," Tommy ventured. "How have you changed?" Matthew answered slowly. "I used to be full of hate and against diversity, and now I'm full of hate and I love diversity. I want to be part of a movement, but one that's cross-racial. In retrospect, it probably would have been better if I'd come to Pikeville to point out the atrocities of the coal bosses."

But Matthew insisted on the partial nature of his change. "I don't like people who say, 'Once I was bad and now I'm good. I once was full of hate and now I love.' I'm not like a caterpillar that suddenly turns into a butterfly. But I have broadened my perspective. For one thing, I used to drink too much. We all did. Probably two-thirds of white nationalists are alcoholics. Every event we'd end up binge-drinking. It's the only way guys know how to bond."

Matthew also feared the U.S. government. "To be honest, it's scary times right now to be on the right." As a neo-Nazi activist, he had been banned from traveling to the United Kingdom. "Two weeks ago in Greece, they declared the Golden Dawn a criminal organization. Now some parliamentarians have had their immunity retroactively removed and are heading to prison for fifteen years! I have good friends who are Golden Dawn. That could happen here. What if five years from now, I'm put on trial for the murder of Heather Heyer?"

Matthew felt ostracized. At home, he had earlier been banned from the Antiochian Orthodox Christian Archdiocese of North America, with which his small local church was affiliated and in which his oldest son would, he hoped, serve as an altar boy.

Then came the fury of his former comrades. He summed up his

dilemma. "If they put me in jail and I'm an ex-white nationalist, God forbid. White nationalists don't trust me now. I'm Matt the traitor. Liberals don't trust me. I'm Matt the fascist. Blacks don't trust me. I'm Matt the racist. "I've always liked Appalachia because I thought I'd fit in here. Now here I'm Matt the outsider."

Matthew remained estranged from his father and older sister, who had changed her last name to avoid association with him. Meanwhile, the sister of the new partner sitting beside him, he said, had married an African American and had two light-skinned children who called him "Uncle Matt."

"I feel more alone now than I have in my entire life," he said. Only Matthew's mother had reached out to him, but with a complaint: " 'I wish your name didn't come up so much in the news connected to extremism and fights.' And now I'm getting death threats"—he glanced around at fellow diners—"by email. Actually, the best thing that can happen to me, I've thought, is if I could die for my cause like a kamikaze pilot."

Some time lapsed before any of us spoke again. It was hard to take all this in. Matthew was trying to change—but what, we wondered, had actually changed? The outer part of Matthew—his name, his look, his reputation—was with him still. But how had he changed inside?

Then Matthew mentioned a surprising positive experience. "I was hard up for work. So I took a $12-an-hour job at a private Jewish nursing facility. I was the only white guy on the night shift. Most of its residents think Donald Trump is Hitler. I'm strong and they need workers who can move and bathe a patient or change them at night. It's a sad place, a holding pen for neglected elderly. But the job's fulfilling," he added, seemingly almost to his own surprise. "One old man has two kids, a son who never visits and a daughter who only comes when her dad gets into a diabetic coma. So the man eats candy to raise his blood sugar, get himself hospitalized, so his daughter will visit. It was a daily struggle to get him to eat his diabetic snacks and make him feel life was worth living."

Another patient had greatly surprised Matthew. "I help an eighty-five-year-old Jewish woman bathe," Mathew recounted. "She has real bad dementia, and she is convinced I am her nephew. It is a very intimate, embarrassing moment for her when I bathe her. You've messed yourself—you know, the frailty of the human body—there as the Lord made them and you've got some random guy helping you." This was the first time in many meetings that I'd heard Matthew tell a story from a Jewish or Black person's point of view.

Later, Matthew also spoke of a new possible line of work—nursing. "I come home from my shifts in the nursing home feeling I did something good today. Maybe I could get a nursing degree. I have a BA. With two more years in community college, maybe online, I could get a nursing degree, or be a nursing assistant. With an extra five-day course on medication aid, I could hand out pills. Then if I work in a nursing home or hospital for a year, I could qualify for tuition reimbursement." Searching his mind for other sources of funds, Matthew added, "My credit is garbage, no family member will co-sign a loan, and I don't qualify for a Pell Grant. In Germany or Sweden, the government helps transition extremists by paying for education and housing, but not here." The United States offered no easy off-ramp from what seemed, then, like the sticky shame of extremism.

Matthew looked into finding work deprogramming young extremists such as he had once been and tried to recruit. For a while he co-hosted a YouTube podcast called *Light upon Light* with an ex-jihadist, Jesse Morton. They covered what Matthew called the "classic works" of the far right. But here he ran into the obstacle of his private disdain for many of the "formers," as comrades who renounced extremism were called. "I hate former skinheads; they have zero intellectual depth. Just because you put a swastika on your bomber jacket doesn't mean you're read up on the Belgian right."

But his focus was on racist thought, not on the humanity of those hurt by it. "They want me to rend my garments, be a player in a morality play,"

Matthew complained, "and fit into the liberal narrative of repentance. I don't want to do that."

Matthew also took an immense personal dislike to the former white nationalist extremist Christian Picciolini, author of the bestselling *Breaking Hate: Confronting the New Culture of Extremism.* "Christian got millions of dollars in U.S. grants to combat extremism, and I asked him what he could do for me," Matthew explained, "because I'm in a hole; I need more education and a better job, right? But Picciolini doesn't offer anything to new 'formers'—no services, no programs, no help. All he offers is tattoo removal. A buddy of mine had an SS bolt tattoo on his face lasered off so he could get a job. He said it hurt like hell, took forever to heal, and never really did. My swastika is on my chest, where only my girlfriend can see it. I'm like, 'Dude, I need to go to school. I need a job. I need help to reintegrate.' And Picciolini was like, 'Well, we don't do that. We remove tattoos.'"

But how much, Tommy and I wondered, had Matthew Heimbach really changed? He was struggling with his finances, but how was he struggling with his identity? It wasn't clear.

"Money for de-radicalization comes from the Department of Homeland Security," Matthew explained. "They require us to *accept* what's told, and I didn't pass the DHS definition as 'de-radicalized.'" I was wondering what those criteria were when Matthew said in passing, "North Korea's prison system is a model for the world." He also described China as "free and democratic," and praised Vladimir Putin for "getting things done."

Since Matthew's greatest animus had previously been toward the Jews, I asked if he saw them any differently now. He replied, "Yes, I used to think that all Jews were rich, but now I can see that some aren't rich." And how about the Holocaust? Tommy asked. "A lot of Jews were killed," Matthew answered slowly, "but I'm not sure about the gas chambers." Similarly, southern plantation life had "many positive features."

Then, as we were lingering over dessert, Matthew shared a startling doubt about his own racial identity. "You never know about your heritage for sure," he said. "I have very dark hair, nothing blond about me. I sent in a sample of my saliva to 23andMe and found my genes go back to Germany—that would be my father—and Ireland—that would be my mom." Neither genetic story promised blond hair, so about this he was reassured.

A curious repartee then arose between Matthew and his partner, Diane. As noted earlier, Matthew had moved from Indiana to Tennessee, where he now lived with Diane in Chattanooga. "I want to make a home here in Appalachia," he said.

But Diane teasingly challenged him, studying his face for a reaction. "Matt *says* he feels like a real Appalachian, but he was born in a Mc-Mansion in Montgomery County, Maryland. Of the two of us, *I'm* the *real* Appalachian." Matthew took the challenge good-naturedly. But while proudly reaching out to his "Appalachian brothers" during the 2017 march in Pikeville, it turned out, Matthew was to be privately teased at home for being a wanna-be hillbilly.

Matthew had changed his views about race: Blacks were in. Jews, he wasn't sure about. And one-man rule still looked preferable to him than messy democracy. It seemed that Adolf Hitler was to be replaced in his pantheon by Vladimir Putin.

Moving "Left" as the World Moves Right

A movement for racial justice was on the rise. A Black Lives Matter protest on June 6, 2020, became one of the largest one-day protests—half a million people in 550 places—in U.S. history. More than 40 percent of the nation's counties held protests, and most of the participants—as in Pike County—were white. Ninety-three percent of the 7,750 Black Lives Matter demonstrations following the murder of George Floyd between May 26 and August 22, a study showed, were peaceful. But those I spoke to in Pike County were tuned to media focusing on the 7 percent that were indeed violent.

Violent groups were stirring into action on the right as well. Between 2015 and 2020, 405 attacks and thwarted plots by domestic extremists were reported, more than double the number in the previous decade, two-thirds by white supremacist and far-right extremists. Inside the right, some older groups, such as the KKK and NSM, seemed in decline, while new groups such as the Proud Boys, the Oath Keepers, and the Three Percenters were on the rise, and finding support in high places for their movement to preserve, protect, and expand the pride of white Americans.

The Republican Party itself had split between "the MAGA populist Republicans," as people described them, led by Donald Trump, and the "country club Republicans" affiliated with Republican figures such as Mitch McConnell and former Republican presidential candidate Mitt Romney, who now seemed too tame for some.

Especially on the right, loyalties were dividing. Back in Pike County, Heimbach's message had fallen on deaf ears, and the memory of the Pikeville march was of a model of exemplary restraint in the protection of free speech. At the same time, three years on, there was talk of civil war. In 2021, Representative Thomas Massie, a Kentucky Republican, hinted at secession. And his colleague in Congress, Representative Marjorie Taylor Greene, called for "a national divorce," with some 23 percent of Americans in agreement. Senator Lindsey Graham of Georgia threatened "riots in the street" if Donald Trump was prosecuted for improperly retaining classified government documents. Many were shocked and appalled—assuming the national "marriage" solid enough.

Reality itself had come to seem splintered into zones of harmony and conflict. For example, Alex Hughes, who was now based in Louisville, told me, "Sometimes it's hard to really know what's going on. On Facebook, I see family members and friends denouncing each other. So, I thought me and my wife could get away from it all, place a bet, have some fun at Churchill Downs [a horse racing track]. But as we got out of the car in the parking lot, we noticed several large vans with heavily armed Black paramilitary guys in balaclavas over their faces, getting out of their vehicles—part of a group called Not Fucking Around Coalition [not affiliated with Black Lives Matter]. Across the lot, we saw police with their eyes on them. We got back in the car and left. But on the way home I stopped at the grocery store and inside people were friendly, polite. 'Excuse me, thank you.' Facebook page, parking lot, grocery store—I didn't know which scene was normal."

Politically Homeless

As the four of us finished our dinner, Matthew shared two final quandaries. One was about his last name, Heimbach. "My mom hates it that my name keeps appearing in the papers with bad news. I wish I could change it."

"You could change your name," Tommy replied encouragingly.

"No," Matthew replied. "If I did that, it would get into the news: 'Matthew Heimbach changes his name.'"

Thinking it over later, Tommy mused, "Maybe Matthew has reached his bottom."

A day after our dinner, Matthew contacted me about a second thing on his mind. "Maybe before getting a nursing degree, I should get a job working with Tommy at the Southgate Rehabilitation Program. I could do something good for a change," he wrote. I forwarded Matthew's message to Tommy, who thought it over with care. Can a leopard change some spots but not others? Tommy wondered. In such a job, would Heimbach urge Wyatt Blair to abandon his racism, or would he stir it up? As the song that miners used to sing went, which side are you on? In the case of Matthew Heimbach, Tommy didn't know and didn't respond.

But Matthew was happy to find a union job in an auto plant for $16.50 an hour—until he ran into problems. "Antifa chased me down and doxxed me in an effort to get me fired. They discovered where I worked by finding my name on an overtime application list. So the company fired me, and through the union I grieved it. Now that I'm not a white nationalist anymore, how does Antifa think I'm supposed to adjust back into society?

The Labor Relations Board is [so] backlogged that I'd have to wait a year before my case came up. But I have to support my family, so I quit." He later found a job "using my social skills": working the front desk in a medical office.

Meanwhile, as the memory of the Pikeville march slowly faded, a collective excitement had been growing about someone else.

13

Lightning in a Jar

Hello Trumpsters! The number of vehicles surpassed 5,500 and we estimated there were approximately 13,000 people in the total caravan. In addition, estimates put the number of fellow Patriots that lined the intersections, overpasses, and sides of roads through our caravan route at 2,700. Our caravan had participants from all 30 counties in East Kentucky, as well as several Kentucky counties as far away as Bowling Green and Louisville and from all bordering states of Indiana, Illinois, Missouri, Ohio, Tennessee, Virginia, and West Virginia; plus, other states: Alabama, California, Georgia, Louisiana, Maryland, Mississippi, North Carolina, New York, and Texas. . . . At one point we stretched as far as 20+ miles.

So read the triumphant post of Roger Ford in October 2020 on the Facebook page of the East Kentucky Patriots, based in Pike County, where 80 percent of voters would a month later vote for Donald Trump. Vehicle parades set off to travel through Perry, Hazard, and Knott Counties in eastern Kentucky as well, American flags waving and horns honking. Skydivers and a helicopter joined a pro-Trump boat parade on the Ohio River in western Kentucky.

At 10:00 a.m., elbow out the window, MAGA cap on, smiling to a cellphone camera, Roger Ford himself led the caravan out of a Coal Run parking lot, between Sam's Hot Dogs and Kentucky Fried Chicken, past waving pedestrians, some dressed in red, white, and blue. "We were bumper to bumper at first and didn't get back until 6:00 p.m.," Ford exulted. "When you have a man like Donald Trump, you have lightning in a jar."

An energetic man of fifty-three dressed in a white shirt and pants, with thinning blond hair and a restrained smile, Roger Ford was happy to explain his view of life. While some spoke propulsively, as if this were the very last chance to get in a word, and others spoke vaguely or avoidantly, Roger talked in a direct "let-me-tell-you" kind of way. As an adult, he described himself on the Greasy Creek Elementary School Facebook page as "Kentuckian by birth, Southern by the grace of God, Freemason and Shriner." He was pro-life, pro-gun, pro-police, anti-tax, anti–public schools, pro-wall, anti–affirmative action, and anti-regulation. On a car trip through the hollers, Roger explained to me that we were more likely to get hurt wearing the required seatbelts than if we were not wearing them. A highly imaginative entrepreneur, well-read, ambitious to reverse the woes of his region, Roger in 2010 had run unsuccessfully as a Republican candidate for the Kentucky House of Representatives, and he followed politics with keen interest.

Behind the Anger

By 2019, most Americans felt their country had become more divided and angry. A national Barna survey found that 70 percent of Americans agreed that hate crime and hate speech had "increased in the last five years." When asked why, two-thirds said it was because "politicians are encouraging or feeding it" and social media and the internet amplified it. Sixty-seven percent of whites and 80 percent of Blacks also thought hate crime had increased.

A "Stop the Steal" movement had grown out of the Republican Party, and while internally cohesive, those in it seemed increasingly angry:

at Republicans who were not part of it, at Democrats, and at the federal government in general. Those I had come to know had a variety of relationships to this movement. Ruth Mullins, John Rosenberg, and Dr. Budgy watched it from the sidelines, apprehensively. Alex Hughes and his family, stout Republicans, were watching it in a more neutral way, though Alex was now worried about his friend Harry, who seemed to Alex overinvolved with it. Wyatt Blair was enthusiastic about it but was still behind bars. Tommy Ratliff and James Browning, now working as counselors in recovery programs, were watching from the sidelines. Andrew Scott, a strong Republican but mindful of his role as mayor of Coal Run, didn't want to appear "too political" so as not to offend constituents, and was trying to help me as best he could to understand why some local people were mad.

I wanted to understand how local citizens had arrived at a point of anger and hate, with some even characterizing it—as had Roger Ford—as the "last straw." What had led them to that? Those I was getting to know didn't seem in the least hateful. After the Capitol riot on January 6, 2021, many were avoidant of all outsiders, since the FBI was tracing down January 6 participants and the mood was one of extreme caution. In a sense, I was looking for an angry person who was considerate enough to explain to me why he and so many others were so angry. By good luck, I met Roger Ford.

The Beauty of Order

After a number of initial conversations, Roger invited me on a daylong tour around the hollers where he'd been born and raised. So early one morning, he drove us just south of Pikeville along increasingly narrow, winding mountain roads. We passed the Greasy Creek Volunteer Fire Department, the Freewill Baptist Church, Mountain Firearms, Adam's Affordable Homes, and Ford's Branch to a hillside cemetery. We were passing places of his childhood, homes and small shops belonging to his kin. Along the way we sat down to lunch at a diner, and he said about the friendly proprietress, "We're related. I'm related to everyone around here," Roger said with a smile. Lingering at the counter to speak to her while I was seated in the booth, he told her which hollers he was showing me. "Oh, don't take her there," she'd advised—something he told me as we returned to the car. One never knows what a stranger might think.

As we were driving on a hillside road to the small community cemetery, the road narrowed to one lane. "What happens when a car comes from the other direction?" I asked. "Each driver knows the distance they'd have to back up to the nearest turnout, and the driver with the shortest distance to back up does. We're neighborly here," Roger told me. Later he observed, "Some people in Pikeville look down on people deep in the hollers, and then Louisville looks down on Pikeville, just like Kentucky is put down in Washington."

Walking along a pathway to the graveyard of Roger's ancestors, I noticed, as I had in some other graveyards we visited, an empty, open-sided wooden shelter with benches. There one could sit, meditate, perhaps sing. These were used, more in the old days than now, by a community of mourners.

We came finally to a small white wooden non-denominational Protestant church. The door was open, the pews empty. We walked to the front, where on some future Sunday a minister would stand before a diminishing congregation. (By church rules, this minister would be a man, and by custom, heterosexual.) We sat. "Do you notice that to the back of the pews, there are no hymnal racks? In the old days, we had no hymnals. We were illiterate," Roger explained. "The minister sang the lines of a song, and worshippers repeated after him." To illustrate, Roger sang the first line of "Amazing Grace": "Amazing grace, how sweet the sound . . ." I followed along.

Poverty and illiteracy were matters of history, and Roger was a historian. But I came to understand that he was also a custodian of a code of honor, a way of being for which he did not want to be shamed.

When I asked about his family, Roger began by describing his great-great-great-great-grandfather, centuries back, a man after whom he was named and who was given a land grant for his service in the American Revolutionary War. Indeed, Roger knew his genealogy in astonishing detail ("My great-grandmother's father fought in the Kentucky 45th Infantry, Company C, Union side").

As with many others, Roger's ancestry also linked him to coal. "My grandpa was a coal miner before becoming a Church of Christ minister in Greasy Creek. My dad was a Pike County sheriff and taught sixth- through eighth-grade math and science at Greasy Creek Elementary—and he was especially strict with me so he wouldn't be accused of favoritism," Roger recalled without a smile. As a young man, his father had worked as a grave digger. Several uncles worked for the railroad. One was a minister, another a barber, and yet another an English professor at the local college.

Born into a stable middle-class family, Roger did not worry, as David Maynard did, about being born on the wrong side of the mountain. Nor was he forced to overhear the alcohol-fueled, late-night arguments of his parents, as Tommy Ratliff had. Instead, Roger was forging ahead to a career as a businessman with hopes of bringing back good jobs to Pike County. Roger Ford and others like him were part of what I came to think of as the elite of the left-behind. As I discovered in my earlier study of Louisiana Tea Party enthusiasts, those most enthralled with Donald Trump were not at the very bottom—the illiterate, the hungry—but those who aspired to do well or who were doing well within a region that was not.

The Shame of Disorder

Roger tended to associate Democrats with permissiveness and disorder. Black looters at the Black Lives Matter march in Portland, Oregon, women accusing men of the slightest sexual advance, hordes of undocumented migrants, mainstreaming transgenderism—all seemed like forms of unraveling, a frightening disorder that the Democrats were doing little or nothing to set straight.

But perhaps it was the permissiveness or even encouragement of gender fluidity that most disturbed Roger. At one point Pikeville held a small gay pride parade, which ended up at the town park. "There were men dressed up as women there, right where little children could see them," Roger said. In a later conversation he turned to his cellphone, to show me a video of a transgender woman and activist, Rose Montoya, during a celebration of Pride Month on the White House lawn, grinning into the camera, topless, and jiggling her breasts. Biden was then shown, describing gay and transgender individuals as "some of the bravest people I know." Montoya was later banned from the White House and apologized, but not before Fox News brought forward the shocking image to its cast of shamers.

For Roger, transgender identity was not a matter that applied, in 2023, to only 1.03 percent of Americans, nor was it simply a matter of accepting difference. In a region facing too many disruptions, this seemed like one too many. Much of his beloved region felt to him like it was under siege— lost jobs, departures, ruptured marriage, drugs. "With all we're coping with here, we're having a hard *enough* time," Roger told me. "Then you make it fashionable to choose your gender? Where are we going? I blame the Democratic Party for most of that. The church can help stabilize us, but where is the Democrat Party's support of the church?" Indeed, Democrats seemed to him the party of looseness, permissiveness, and what they led to: shame.

Roger was proud to be a "law and order" man, a member of Pikeville's Fraternal Order of Police, Lodge #29, and, on the heels of a Black Lives Matter parade in town he had helped organize a public rally called Back the Blues. But some laws also had to be questioned, he felt. "My wife and I love to eat at a fabulous Mexican restaurant here and we've made friends with a waiter—I don't want to mention the restaurant or guy. José [a pseudonym] is the younger brother of the owner, a nice guy, and he works night and day. He buses tables long hours, and on weekends I see him mowing his lawn. He works harder than a lot of people around here." José shared many qualities Roger so greatly admired in his own ancestors and wished he saw more of among Americans. "When José first crossed the border illegally at age fourteen with no money, no English, he walked and hitchhiked from El Paso to Nashville, where he thought he'd find his brother, but his brother had moved to Pikeville, so he hitched his way here. Now he works eighty-hour weeks and pays taxes on his pay.

"Then," Roger continued, "José got COVID and didn't dare see a doctor. I told him to 'call me if your temperature gets over 103, I'll arrange for medical care.' [And in 2016] when Trump was elected, José told me, 'I'll have to leave.' But I told José, 'No, just the criminals need to leave.' He told me he talked to the other illegals and the criminals left. I told him we'd pay for him to get a lawyer. After that José told me, 'I will kill for you.' I think that's his way of saying I'm like family to him." Roger chuckled. "I gave him a Trump sticker for his truck. Now I see a four-by-eight plywood sign up in his front lawn: 2020 TRUMP." Later, Ford disregarded Donald Trump's talk of immigrants as "vermin" poisoning the "blood" of Americans and his plans, if reelected in 2024, to deploy the army to remove the Josés of the nation. "We disagree on some things."

Curiously, too, the idea of law and order was not the first thing that came to mind when Roger learned of the January 6, 2021, break-in at the Capitol. First he imagined that it was members of Antifa who had been the lawbreakers, trying to give Trump supporters a bad name. Then he felt the media was blowing the break-in "all out of proportion." Similarly, an editorial in the *Appalachian News-Express* dismissed January 6 as "just another staged stunt" for the cameras. Indeed, unless I brought it up in a two- or three-hour conversation, the topic of the Capitol invasion seldom came up. Lively talk seemed to bubble up on many issues—guns, abortion, the price of gas, a Biden misstatement, a man with hairy legs walking into a women's bathroom, accusations of "wokeness"—but, with one exception over two weeks in the summer of 2023, I heard not a word about the January 2021 attempt to overturn by force a legitimately won election. When I did bring it up, one person said, "All we're hearing from the Democrats these days is about the hearings regarding the January 6 break-in." Another man commented, "That's a top-of-the-holler [rich peo-ple's] issue, and we're struggling to pay for gas that's getting more expensive by the minute. Bring inflation down and then let's talk about other things." During two and a half weeks of talking to people in Pikeville in 2023, the only person who spontaneously raised the issue of January 6 violence with grave concern was a Lebanese-born pharmacist who recalled a memory from her childhood: her dad, wounded, driving her in a car through a dan-gerous crossfire that occurred during a political coup in Beirut.

Certain outside forces seemed to be bringing the world of Roger Ford to this point of bitter division. For the right, alarm bells were ringing first at the "Democratic" war on coal, the unimpeded long-term economic ero-sion, and unchecked (and even promoted) "cultural decline" into gender confusion. To this they added the more immediate issue of inflation. On some Kentucky gas pumps you could find a sticker showing an image of Biden and the words I DID THAT! No one I talked to mentioned the record-breaking profits made during this period by oil companies Chev-ron, Shell, and Exxon. Meanwhile, for the left, alarm bells were ringing over the unprecedented violence of January 6.

There had for decades been a growing polarization of wealth—legitimated by both political parties, exacerbated by the decline of labor unions. Once this issue had been the big connector between workers and the Democratic Party. In their book *Winner-Take-All Politics: How Wash-ington Made the Rich Richer—and Turned Its Back on the Middle Class*, Jacob Hacker and Paul Pierson argue that since the 1970s, under both Re-publican and Democratic administrations, lower taxes on the mega-rich, the deregulation of corporations, and the decline of organized labor have greatly widened the gap between the rich and everyone else.

The issue of the class divide seemed both curiously alive and dormant in conversations I was having. A 2023 cri de coeur song by a country and western song writer, Anthony Oliver, shot to #1 on the Billboard Hot 100, lamenting "bullshit pay" and "nothing to eat" while wealth lay in the distant hands of "Rich Men North of Richmond"—which was, he sang, "a damn shame." But as a political issue, class inequality, as opposed to poverty per se, seldom came up among the Trump supporters I met.

Meanwhile, the non-charismatic Joe Biden spoke of the rich "paying their fair share" and passed legislation to try to regulate monopolies, protect labor unions, and increase taxes on the 1 percent—all measures many feared might scare away the industries they were trying to lure.

Also, the media continued to divide and concentrate each side's voters in their own media sphere, since companies increase profit by focusing on division and conflict, and some networks on the right, such as Fox News, knowingly promoted false reports that the 2020 election was "stolen." These, then, were the larger circumstances when in late 2020 Donald Trump made his appeal to the residents of Kentucky Congressional District 5, and to those like Roger Ford.

Hair in a Biscuit

What, I wondered aloud with Roger, was the reason Trump excited so much enthusiasm in the Pike County vehicle parade? Over coffee one June afternoon, I asked him, "What do you think of Donald Trump as a person?" He answered with a pleased chuckle, "Trump's got a big personality. He needs to get heard to feel important. That's a good thing because we need a big microphone. A lot of people think Donald Trump is highly self-centered, a narcissist, and he is. But when he's running *for us*, that's to our advantage." What to many seemed like disqualifying character flaws—selfishness, narcissism, vengefulness, cruelty—was to Roger Ford, Andrew Scott, and others useful. This meant that there was one set of rules of good character for Appalachian schoolchildren but another for the man with the "big personality" who would lead them. He took license. This made him useful, people told me, "for us."

Of course, there are many on history's list of strong personalities: Father Charles Coughlin, the populist Catholic who preached in the 1930s to the nation's unemployed; Huey Long, the governor of Louisiana in the late 1920s and early 1930s who preached a "chicken in every pot" but took many himself; Theodore Roosevelt; and many more. To Roger, Donald Trump was in this league.

Not only was Trump a big personality, but he was tough. At one point Roger pointed out, Trump had hired the infamous lawyer Roy Cohn. Cohn had been the lead lawyer for Senator Joe McCarthy's 1950s investigation of alleged communists, and had a reputation not only for getting his way but also for being ruthless. Before his death, Cohn had been indicted and disbarred for obstructing justice, perjury, and extortion. But Ford seemed to feel that for a good cause—protecting a vulnerable region and way of life—it wouldn't have been bad for Trump to have a guy like Roy Cohn by his side. The ends seemed to justify the means.

I was surprised to hear Roger explain at the same time that "God sent Donald Trump as a messenger to straighten out matters on earth. Trump is solid, unalterable, tenacious." Roger added cheerfully, "Why, he's like hair in a biscuit—baked in." And, he declared, "there's only *one* Donald Trump."

"The Lord sometimes picks flawed messengers to carry out His work," Roger continued. "The Bible tells us about a lot of flawed people God chose for His purpose. Noah was a drunk, and so was Abraham. David murdered the husband of the woman he married. They were flawed, but God used them all for His purpose. According to this reasoning, each of Trump's moral flaws—narcissism, stubbornness, vengefulness, and his refusal ever to be shamed—"were God's instruments." Appalachia had been left behind. God had found a human instrument to recover its lost pride.

In this view of Trump as God's messenger, Roger Ford was joined by many local Republican men of the cloth. Roger himself was a lifelong member of the Greasy Creek Church of Christ, where his father and grandfather had served as pastor and where, as a boy, Ford had played the piano every Sunday. Rob Musick—the lively pastor and religion teacher at the University of Pikeville—offered to introduce me to Trump-supporting pastors. In talks with two local evangelical pastors I met through Rob, I discovered a variety of ways—some more pragmatic than others—that Donald Trump's supporters linked their candidate to God.

One day we drove to a café in Elkhorn City, a community half an hour's drive southeast of Pikeville, where we met Reverend D. R. Harrison, a large-framed bald man with dark glasses. He leaned intently forward over his plate and, focusing on Reverend Musick, spoke as if his words were propelled by some inner force. "To my eyes," he said, "Trump does not act like a Christian man, but he has helped the church a lot." Pastor Harrison had taken a leave from his position at the Elkhorn City Baptist Church to do a tent ministry—including many revivals—around the country; at the moment he was on a short stay at home. "The average Christian is discouraged, distressed, depressed. He feels like the devil has taken over," Reverend Harrison explained. "The 2020 election was stolen and I want it back, all back, and through our revivals around the country, we're taking our nation back."

Reverend Harrison was assisting a nationally known evangelist from Tennessee named Greg Locke, whom he described as "the pope of the Independent Baptist movement" and a man close to Trump. Indeed, Locke had stood on a podium with Donald Trump to lead a prayer before thousands gathered in Washington, DC, on January 6. Harrison explained that he handled "all the music" for Locke, later noting that his trailer and living expenses were paid by Locke. "We did an Awakening in Washington, DC, for thousands," Harrison said, "and a men's revival in Georgia. And we put shoes on four hundred kids. We have a special trailer filled with Jordans. At the men's revival in Georgia, we had runners go out and ask people what color and size shoes they wanted. We gave out $150 boots to farmers. Sometimes we have to take the tags off because the parents will take them back to get money to spend on drugs," he added. When floods hit Kentucky in 2020, Harrison said, Reverend Locke "sent out checks."

But there seemed to be a frightening side to this. For Greg Locke was also part of the Black Robe Regiment, a group of "Christian nationalist" clergy who believe the 2020 election stolen and have committed themselves to the armed defense of Trump if necessary. A high-school-educated son of an Oklahoma policeman and a former Blue Dog Democrat, Pastor Harrison was about to get back on the road with his wife and four children, three of whom were adopted ("If I preach pro-life, I have to walk the talk," he added) to do the music for Locke at appearances in which Locke would speak in defense of Trump.

A local pastor of another Elkhorn church, Dan Fraley, followed Trump for reason beyond usefulness to the church: "Things are going on behind our backs and Trump is trying to stop it," Dan Fraley, a gentle, dark-haired man of forty, told me. Reverend Musick and I had met him at a picnic table in a small public park in Elkhorn. The son of a coal miner and also a former Democrat, Pastor Fraley had retired after three deployments with the Army Special Forces and had seen horrors he could not forget. Living a quieter life now, Fraley had proudly built up his Church of Christ congregation from four worshippers to twenty on Wednesdays and up to sixty on Sundays.

For news, Fraley watched Breitbart on his cellphone, and through the Telegram app got more "news" from Qanon, the voice of an imagined insider revealing the evil doings of a deep state. He too believed the 2020 election had been "stolen." He also believed the January 6 protesters were actors, and that Hollywood was "controlled by China." Dark forces, he felt, were at work—the CIA, the National Security Agency, even Delta Force and the Navy SEALs. He believed Democrats were "drinking the blood of children" and thought of Trump as the great unmasker, the knower, the man to follow. But there was a limit to Fraley's belief in Qanon. "I was following Qanon pretty closely for a while," he told us, "until they began talking about lizard people. Now that didn't make sense to me."

The Deep Story: Good Bully, Bad Bully

In *Strangers in Their Own Land*, I proposed that, underlying the political rhetoric and beyond statements of ideals and notions of truth, all of us hold a "deep story." This is a feels-as-if story—a story that feelings tell. It removes judgment. It removes facts. It tells us how things feel through a story. I came to believe there is a deep story for the right and another for the left.

In the right's deep story, the principal figure is a man patiently waiting in line, facing toward the American Dream set atop a high hill. His feet are tired. He feels his turn should be coming up, but the line isn't moving. He is quite far ahead in line but seldom looks back to notice how very many people, especially people of color, wait in line behind him. Then the man spots some people stepping in line ahead of him—line-cutters. Who are they? They are educated women and Blacks propelled, it seems to him, by affirmative action. It's also immigrants, refugees, and well-paid public servants. Then the man sees a Democratic president waving to the line-cutters. *Is he encouraging them to bypass me?* he wonders. In another moment of the right's deep story, someone ahead of him in line whirls around to criticize the man patiently waiting: "Ignorant, sexist, racist, homophobic, redneck!" the critic says. For the man in line, this is the last straw.

I tried this deep story out on the Louisianans I was then interviewing. Many responded, "I live your story" or "You read my mind." Others added their belief that those waiting in line "are paying taxes that go to the line-cutters."

When I related this deep story to Mayor Andrew Scott, he said presciently, "Sure, that story fits us Appalachian Trump supporters, too. But it doesn't say it all. You need to add a new chapter to the story that goes like this: 'Among the line-cutters is a bully. He pushes everyone around and lets his friends cut in line, and roughs them up if they complain. He's the *bad* bully.

"'Then the line-waiter sees a second man, full of himself, kind of mean—a bully too. He has obvious flaws, but you forgive them, because he's a *good* bully, strong enough to push around the *bad* bully. He's protecting you; he's *your* bully. So, when others criticize the second bully, you defend him not because he's perfect but because he's your bully.'" In fact, in late 2022 a Trump organization began selling digital trading cards—NFTs, non-fungible tokens—at $99 per card. One features his face attached to a red-caped hypermuscular superman with laser eyes; in another he is a baseball hero, in another a cowboy—all suggesting the "good bully."

When I offered this account of the good bully to friends on the left, they were baffled. Who was the *first* bully? What was he doing that was so bad? Wasn't Joe Biden's Build Back Better bill giving good jobs to people nationwide to rebuild the middle class? Didn't that bill actually help workers in red states more than blue states? What could they be talking about?

But to Roger Ford, the first bully was strong and clearly in focus. In fact, the first bully was a gang of bullies: the Democratic Party, CNN, the federal government (apart from the military), and the defenders of urban America who rudely dismiss rural America. Together they had walked away with power and pride. Having surveyed CNN and MSNBC, Roger also noted critically, "Not one day goes by without them beating up on Donald Trump." To Roger, the bad bully was beating up the good bully. Appalachia needed a "good bully" because, as Roger saw it, the Democratic Party and federal government were bigger and badder.

The Story of Stolen: Loss to Stolen, Shame to Blame, Victim to Avenger

Why, I wondered, were Roger Ford and many others drawn to defend Trump's claim that the 2020 election was stolen, in the face of the powerful accumulating evidence that it was not? Ford was a thoughtful man who prided himself on looking at an issue from all sides. He sensed the great enthusiasm for Trump in his own vehicle parade, and he knew of others in the area who were similarly enthusiastic. But he knew that KY-5 sometimes didn't get the candidate it wanted even without anything being stolen. He had also seen Appalachia get the candidates they voted for—Democratic presidents Jimmy Carter in 1976 and Bill Clinton in 1992 and 1996—and along with much of the nation's Republicans, he accepted news of these results philosophically. He pointed out that some elections had been contested—for example, that of George Bush versus Al Gore in 2000—so doubting election results was not new in America. Still Roger agreed, this was something new.

Two trends seemed to proceed apace. One was the widening acceptance of the narrative of "stolen." The second was the accumulation of legal evidence that the 2020 election had not, in fact, been stolen, a belief that remained fixed in spite of the mounting evidence.

Starting in 2012, Donald Trump gave many speeches and wrote many messages using the word *stolen* or conveying the suspicion that something was "stolen." He declared Barack Obama's presidency a "total sham." Before Trump won the 2016 election, he claimed that if he didn't win, the election would have been stolen. The idea caught on. Shea Maynard's family members, Tommy Ratliff's aunt and uncle, James Browning's uncles and cousins—all came to believe the election was "stolen." Hal Rogers, the Republican representative from Kentucky's 5th Congressional District, which includes Pikeville, said he believed it was "stolen." By May 2023, CNN found, 33 percent of all Americans, and 63 percent of all

Republicans, believe that the 2020 election was stolen. A movement arose: Stop the Steal.

To be sure, not everyone I met in eastern Kentucky agreed with Roger Ford. When I shared this remark with Roger Ford, he too laughed, but he soon returned to his conviction that "the 2020 election was stolen."

Another man suggested that Republicans had lost the 2020 election because "the Democrats outmaneuvered us with young voters." When I repeated this to Roger, again he listened with interest and laughed, but shook his head: no, the vote was "stolen."

Continually repeating the claim that the election was "stolen," President Trump himself even called for the "termination" of the U.S. Constitution so as to reinstate himself as president. According to a December 14, 2022, Quinnipiac University poll, taken after Trump made this statement, the survey asked, "As you may know, former President Donald Trump called to terminate the Constitution so that he can be reinstated as President of the United States. Do you think those remarks should disqualify him from running for president again, or don't you think so?" Fifty-one percent said it should disqualify him—85 percent of Democrats, 52 percent of independents, but only 17 percent of Republicans. Nor did Roger Ford feel this should disqualify Trump, because the election had been "stolen."

At the same time, legal evidence was accumulating that confirmed definitively that the election had not been stolen. In an Associated Press review of millions of votes, only 475 cases of illegal voting were found. Even research on voter fraud conducted by firms hired by the Trump 2020 campaign confirmed the finding: not stolen. Donald Trump's own attorney general, William Barr, declared the election had not been stolen. Vice President Mike Pence declared that it had not been stolen. The Supreme Court declared it not stolen. The most powerful Republican in the U.S. Senate, Mitch McConnell, declared it not stolen. Others within Trump's own administration testified under oath that the election was not stolen. Ivanka Trump, the former president's daughter, said that she accepted the word of Attorney General Barr that the election had not been stolen.

In the weeks after the 2020 election, Trump's backers filed sixty-two lawsuits against a range of state election officials. Sixty-one of these suits were dismissed, and the remaining suit found no evidence sufficient to alter the election result. During this period Trump also famously called Georgia's secretary of state, Brad Raffensperger, himself a Republican, asking him to "find" votes favorable to him, but the Georgia vote too was declared not stolen. Wisconsin and Arizona conducted partial recounts that resulted in an actual *increase* in the number of votes for Joe Biden. A January 6 congressional committee was formed and held ten televised hearings; in this, the public witnessed sworn testimony by a series of Republican officials, including virtually all those in Trump's inner circle, including his personal chief of staff, Mark Meadows, that they believed and had personally informed Trump that the election had not been stolen. Commentators on Fox News later admitted that even at the time they reported on the election, they did not believe it was stolen.

As counterevidence mounted, the proportion who claimed "stolen" seemed to stay steady, and more and more people wondered why. This included a number of non-MAGA Pike County residents I came to know. "Even before Donald Trump was first elected," James Browning told me, "he claimed that if he didn't win, it would be because the election was stolen [a statement Trump repeated in 2024]. Now, if a guy wants to sit down with me to a game of chess, and he tells me before we begin, 'If you win, you must have stolen the game from me,' am I going to play chess with this guy? *Seriously?*" His eyebrows rose and his face circled around a smile.

When the topic of "stolen" came up among my neighbors or friends in Berkeley, they said they were baffled. The first thing that came to mind was the media. One man told me, 'MAGA election deniers live in a right-wing media bubble which lies to them." Beyond that, explanations suggested election deniers "may not be informed," "don't believe in evidence," were "hoodwinked by Donald Trump," or had a cult mentality. Whatever their ideas, they usually ended by saying, "I don't know."

No one ventured to compare the exuberance of the car-honking, flag-waving drivers in Roger Ford's pre-election vehicle parade that left from the Coal Run parking lot with the apparently deadpan expression of President Biden seen in newspapers. For they were comparing a charismatic candidate whose appeal was based on who he was against a rational, bureaucratic candidate whose appeal was based on what he did. And few on the right were looking at the get-out-the-vote efforts of the generally more progressive young.

The Redheaded Stepchild

So why did Roger Ford and so many others stand firm with "stolen"? Perhaps Roger Ford was predisposed to believe the election was stolen because he distrusted everything the federal government did. Ford had, in fact, expressed a general doubt about "the federal government"—it was the "bad bully." But Democrats, too, distrust the federal government in roughly equal measure, studies find, and distrust tends to rise when the opposite party is in power even as it declines when one's own party is in power.

So was there, I wondered, a *culture of plausibility* that was based on truths about loss? In a highly revealing study, *New York Times* investigative reporters Michael H. Keller and David D. Kirkpatrick compared two kinds of Republican voter. Some lived in the congressional districts of the 139 Republican House members who had voted not to certify the election results—who voted, so to speak, "stolen." Others lived in the remaining 64 Republican districts whose representatives voted to certify the results—in other words, who voted "trust." Those in districts voting "stolen" were on average poorer—their annual incomes 10 percent lower—than those in "trust" districts. Voters in "stolen" districts had fewer college and also high school diplomas per capita. They suffered higher rates of deaths of despair, such as suicide, drug overdoses, and alcohol-related liver failure. Voters in "stolen" districts were more likely to be evangelical Protestants. They were also more likely to find themselves residing in areas in which they were a decreasing racial majority. Of the twelve Republican districts in which whites had become a racial minority, ten out of twelve representatives voted "election stolen." Many districts voting "stolen" were in former Confederate states, home to large Black populations. Republicans who believed the election was stolen were also more likely to watch Fox News.

Curiously, none of these characteristics described Roger Ford. He was a well-informed graduate of the University of Pikeville with a master's degree in national security studies from the American Military University. He was a widely traveled businessman. As for media exposure, he said, "I watch Fox but I check MSNBC and CNN, just to see what's going on over on that side, and I listen to the BBC." As noted, Roger's Pike County had not seen any influx of African Americans or immigrants. Indeed, as a small businessman eager to recruit from the best and the brightest, Roger bemoaned the loss of potential hires and secretly championed an illegal immigrant. For him, the problem wasn't that unwelcome people were entering Pike County but that welcome people were leaving it.

Roger seemed to be both grieving and aggrieved. He often compared what rural counties like his didn't have to what urban counties did have. He was an energy entrepreneur and his job involved travel. So he regularly traveled to Wyoming, Missouri, West Virginia, Mississippi, and California, allowing him to continually compare urban to rural, blue states to red, and to feel anguished at the contrast. "Other regions got their electrical grid, standard plumbing, freeways, internet services, vast industrial parks way before we did. We're last in line to get *anything*. We're the redheaded stepchild of the nation."

Roger took an anguished interest in the very cities for which leavers had headed—Lexington, Louisville, Chicago, and coastal cities beyond, focusing his gaze on what those cities have that rural areas do not. Some of his own relatives and friends had taken to Route 23, heading, as the Pikeville-born but Los Angeles–bound Dwight Yoakam sang, "to the jobs that laid a-waiting in those cities' factories." In serious tones, Roger said, "My own brother left for Lexington, and I don't think he's ever coming back. And my cousins left for factory jobs in Ohio." Yoakam himself took his singing career from Pikeville to Nashville.

Roger Ford's anguished pride was not based on surviving poverty (as was David Maynard's), nor on protecting whites from it by foisting poverty onto Blacks (as Wyatt Blair wanted to do). Nor was it based on recovery from personal addictions (as it was for Tommy Ratliff and James Browning). His was based on fighting to make Pike County one of those better-off places people didn't have to leave. He based his deepest sense of pride, it seemed, on his role as defender of his imperiled rural homeland, from which so much had been lost—or, as it could feel, "stolen."

In a 2018 editorial for the *Appalachian News-Express* entitled "Farewell Kentucky," Roger Ford wrote that Pike County was in "a rapid population decline—from 59,000 to 48,000 projected by 2040," leaving stayers to "suffer a brain drain, youth drain, mentally-fit drain, leaving behind those in need of help, and reducing political influence and their ability to qualify for federal and state funding."

In Pike County, Roger was seeing a local version of a national trend, for between 1988 and 2008 nearly half of the nation's 2,050 non-metro counties had lost residents. And in the decade from 2010 to 2020, the working-age population in these counties declined by another 4.9 percent due to outmigration, while the population sixty-five years of age and older grew by 22 percent. Roger felt it was a painful story of talent loss.

At one point, Roger remarked in passing that "my wife and I will stay . . . probably."

Loss to Stolen to Betrayed

As Roger Ford described his region, there seemed to be three distinct kinds of loss—the loss of coal-related jobs (absolute loss), a reduced value attributed to what one still had, such as heritage, land, and ingenuity (devaluation), and a declining value of rural life compared to a rising value of city life (relative loss). In his frequent travels, Roger enviously eyed more populous, fortunate cities that were attracting rural people off the land and into cities where the rural people who stayed home seemed of diminished importance. Added to these losses was the indignity of gratuitous insults pitched from somewhere that seemed to Roger to be more urban, liberal, and rich. All this added up to multiple kinds of loss of pride, which was filtered through a painful reality: they were more prone to blame themselves for failure, but they lived in states with fewer economic opportunities—the pride paradox.

Most hidden and, I believe, most painful, was devaluation. When a man went to apply for a job in the countryside, he could present himself as "Harry's son" and be hired based on local reputation or firsthand knowledge of a man's knowledge and character. But at home, that knowledge at least, was of less use. And in the city, such a man was unknown, degreeless, "just a hillbilly."

Coastal or city people, Roger felt, often saw rural people like himself as behind the times. Being modern was good; being traditional was bad. "But if a culture is going the wrong way, isn't being behind sometimes a *good* thing?" Roger quipped, jokingly recalling Mark Twain's remark: "'Kentucky is twenty years behind the rest of the world. So when the world ends, I want to be in Kentucky.'" On family size, college education, we can seem behind people in other regions," Roger clarified. "But behind doesn't always mean wrong."

Perhaps most of all, memories of past suffering and hardship seemed in danger of being devalued: the memory of men like James's grandfather, who died in a coal mine, or Alex's grandfather, who had been maimed. Embedded in the lament was the thought that the appreciation for all the fortitude once summoned to withstand that loss would itself be lost.

Loss on the Hollywood Screen

The movie screen was putting them down too. As Nicholas Jacobs and Daniel Shea insightfully trace in *The Rural Voter*, some of the sense of stolen pride in areas like Appalachia surely derives from the movie screen, viewed by urban and rural viewers alike. On that screen the view of rural life was shifting from positive to negative. For the first half of the twentieth century, the image of rural America was a backdrop to images of the heroic: take Hopalong Cassidy, who comes to town to save the widow's ranch from outlaws. Or rural America was imagined as a place of nostalgic return to "Grandma's house" (as the Christmas carol says, "the horse knows the way to carry the sleigh"), a pastoral refuge from capitalism and immigration. In such ways, rural places were places of pride. After World War II, the authors note, the image shifted to the comic and ridiculous—a figure who shoots rabbits with a Civil War–era musket, as in the television show *The Beverly Hillbillies*.

Then, the cultural view took a deeply dark turn in *Deliverance*— a 1974 hard-to-watch box office hit in which Appalachians were portrayed as lawless, incestuous, and violent. By the 1990s there was the rise of the fearsome rural monster. Dan Shea, co-author of *The Rural Voter* and a professor at Colby College, asked his students if they could think of a horror film that wasn't set in rural America. "None of them could come up with one," he said. What came to mind instead was *The Texas Chainsaw Massacre*, *The Blair Witch Project*, Stephen King's *Cujo*. And in 2016, the negative view of rural life could be seen in 127 "reality shows" with rural settings, from *Ax Men*, *My Big Redneck Family*, *Moonshiners*, and *Here Comes Honey Boo Boo* to *Swamp People*—none of which were based on reality.[3] When asked how often movies and television portray people who live in their area in a fair and accurate way, half of those living in urban places said yes, but less than a quarter of those living in rural areas said yes. In the back of some minds, perhaps Hollywood could seem to have "stolen" a positive image of rural people.

As much as or more than Roger felt himself middle class and white, he felt himself Appalachian and, more broadly, *rural*. In this he closely resembled the farmers and small-town residents of Wisconsin whom the political scientist Katherine Cramer describes in her excellent book, *The Politics of Resentment*. The adults she met at gas stations and lunch counters in rural Wisconsin complained that Hollywood moguls, newscasters, professors, and government officials had given America's urban centers the notice, the appreciation, and credit belonging to rural people. Reflecting on conversations she had with thirty-nine groups across a sample of twenty-seven Wisconsin communities, Kramer found that many saw government workers as lazy, inefficient, overpaid, and represented by "greedy" unions. Cities, they felt, drained the countryside of tax money and kept it for themselves.

Roger Ford felt that, relative to city people, rural residents were wrongly portrayed as racist. "When I hear some CNN commentator claim that all Republicans are racist, I feel enraged! Why, we had the first interracial cemetery in the entire region"—referring to the Dils Cemetery, which holds 130 African American graves. "Our schools also integrated early and well," Ford declared. He felt that the rest of the country knew nothing about this proud history. And in truth, outside of Pikeville's tourist bureau, this local pride in racial integration did seem lost.

Still, when it came to earning pride in the eyes of the nation, Roger Ford felt that Blacks were beating out whites. On his personal Facebook page, he posted a bitter cartoon contrasting elite Blacks such as billionaire Oprah Winfrey ("Worth = $2 billion, Oprahssed") with a hapless, grimacing white comedian, Ed O'Neill ("Worth = $2.32, Privileged"). The posted iconic Black heroes were, of course, "outliers"—as Malcolm Gladwell called them in a book by that name. But to Roger, the contrast stung. Roger's post did not imply that whites were superior to Blacks; on the contrary, whites weren't doing financially as well as Blacks. Of course, the "joke" entirely misrepresents the facts, for in family wealth today, as mentioned, Blacks are vastly poorer and, relative to their credentials, earn lower wages than whites at all levels of education. But apart from country singers and rich former coal mine owners, where was the heroic narrative of the Appalachian white man? Roger wondered.

Then came the urban put-downs. In 2016, Hillary Clinton had called Trump supporters a "basket of deplorables." In 2021, the actress Bette Midler had reviled West Virginia senator Joe Manchin, saying he "wants us all to be just like his state, West Virginia. Poor, illiterate and strung out." Indignities appeared on Facebook pages—*hillbilly, redneck*—to be endlessly played up by right-wing media, which further infuriated the already incensed.

The Hunger Games

"Have you ever seen *The Hunger Games*? That's us! We have 120 rural counties in Kentucky, and they are just like District 12 in *The Hunger Games*. They're rural, poor, exploited, and sacrificed to the interests of the ten urban counties of this state. *The Hunger Games* is art imitating life," Roger declared.

Based on a bestselling dystopian novel about a post-apocalyptic nation called Panem, the 2008 film describes how a wealthy city and its fascist commanders dominate its twelve poor rural districts. Yearly the leaders hold ghoulishly cruel "hunger games." With callous cheer, a garishly made-up top bureaucrat, Effie Trinket, struts about in stilt-like high heels to select a boy and girl as "tributes" from each district. The two must then fight rival tributes to the death for the greater glory of a despised state. In the end, one tribute couple remains.

When a young girl is selected from among the oppressed of District 12, her older sister, Katniss Everdeen (played by Jennifer Lawrence), heroically volunteers to replace her younger sister for the dreadful mission. As Katniss goes to the central stage of the arena, she looks out at her co-inhabitants of District 12 standing—abject, fearful, ragged—below a huge sign in bold type: CAPITOL COAL.

The audience is invited to champion the heroic Katniss Everdeen—Appalachian stayer in coal country—and to hate the evil Trinket, whose pride has soured to arrogance. Katniss is forced to feed her family with small game she hunts with bow and arrow, illegally hunting a forest in ways the state forbids. The heroic girl is defending her beloved family by secretly defying the blind and heartless Capitol. *The Hunger Games* was a story told through women which very much spoke to men. Roger Ford saw it as a fiction that "told the truth" about his region and himself. Did a fiction about an election outcome bear a similar sort of relationship to the truth of loss for some of the post-1970s "losers" of globalization and automation? Though an idea that is surely disconcerting to many, it occurred to me it might have contributed to the culture of plausibility that led many to conclude "stolen."

For Roger, *The Hunger Games* and Pike County were a perfect fit. In an op-ed in the *Appalachian News-Express*, Roger wrote of those in the "Golden Triangle"—Lexington, Louisville, and northern Kentucky: "They [sit in their] high perches and never venture outside the Golden Triangle. How many times have the pontificators from the *Courier-Journal*, or the *Herald-Leader* [Kentucky's two main newspapers, one based in Louisville, the other in Lexington] traveled beyond their confines to the far reaches of rural Kentucky? Could they find Woodman or Wingo in daylight?" Ford wrote. "They snub the contributions of rural Kentucky in music, writing, and the arts." Weren't these urban centers of Kentucky shaming the District 12 of Pike County?

And money: "Those enlightened ones [Golden Triangle residents] sit on their high perch, peering down their noses at the rest of us unenlightened folks," Roger wrote. "[They] pillaged our coal severance tax for their benefit . . . revenue that helped build their [urban] roads and bridges, their arenas." Meanwhile, counties such as Pike—like the fictive

District 12—lacked good roads, clean water, and internet service for all residents. Of the coal tax revenue, Ford wrote, "[We] received a paltry 7.6 cents on the dollar while 50 percent went into the 'General Fund'"— money to be distributed across the whole state.

"Isn't this a local version of a larger story?" Roger wrote. "[People living in] the government Zip Codes are richer than Manhattan." (Here he was not counting the twelve thousand well-paid corporate lobbyists who live in those neighborhoods.) If Roger had to put a face to the problem, it would have been that of Barack Obama. "In 2014, Obama passed national legislation to cut carbon emissions and that killed coal around here," he stated.

On this last point, others differed. For example, Andrew Scott, the mayor of Coal Run and an ardent Republican, saw rural Kentucky as hurt, but not in the manner of *The Hunger Games*. When asked why coal had declined in his area, the former coal mine owner and ex-governor of Kentucky, Paul Patton, answered matter-of-factly: "We took out the best coal, then the okay coal, and we're left with the barely okay coal."

More important, while the cost of coal has been relatively stable, the costs of natural gas, solar energy, and wind rapidly declined, to the point where they came to undersell coal. In short, natural gas and renewables became cheaper. On average, the marginal cost of running and maintaining a coal plant is now $36 per megawatt-hour, while the marginal cost of solar is about $24 per megawatt-hour—about a third cheaper.

But probably most of those I talked to blamed the federal government and the Democratic party and their desire to reduce one cause of climate change. By proposing to regulate carbon emissions, first Barack Obama and then Hillary Clinton were said to have declared a "war on coal." In 2016, presidential candidate Hillary Clinton famously said, "We're going to put a lot of coal miners and coal companies out of business." The rest of her speech—about funding job retraining and incubating new businesses—was lost to memory. When I asked one man about his vote in 2016, his immediate answer was, "you heard what Hillary said." Signs on the back of trucks that once read "War on Coal" began to read "Trump Digs Coal."

Others point out that the federal government has long directly and indirectly subsidized coal. Indeed, according to an Environmental and Energy Study Institute, the U.S. government spends $20 billion a year on direct fossil fuel subsidies, with $16 billion going to oil and gas and $4 billion to coal. Within Kentucky, Pike County also received more federal funds than counties in Roger Ford's "Golden Triangle." District 12 was in trouble, but it could not all be blamed, so to speak, on the Capitol.

Angie Hatton, at the time the lone Democratic state senator representing Pike County (and replaced in 2022 by a Republican), pointed out that 40 percent of Kentucky's state budget comes from the federal government, which is, she said, "a good thing because we need it." In Pike County itself, about 22 percent of residents receive SNAP (Supplemental Nutrition Assistance Program) benefits, also known as food stamps, and nearly half are on Medicaid. "We have a lot of older, disabled people," Hatton said. "My job is to make sure we get what we *need*." As she saw it, the federal government wasn't taking resources from Pike County; it was giving the county resources. Indeed, the federal government didn't look to Hatton like the dictatorial Capitol in *The Hunger Games* at all as it was giving money to coal and to those in the region who needed it. Still, to many I spoke with, the federal government seemed like the "taker" while the people were the "makers," and the act of "drawing"—receiving federal help—was associated with shame.

Four-Moment Anti-Shame Ritual

A scene had been—and is—set. Through circumstantial loss, shame had been fed into the pride paradox, like meat into a cultural grinder. Given a very proud culture and a strictly held ethic of individualism—*if I succeed, I take credit; if I fail, it's my fault*—the painful result is shame. In a culture oriented toward achieving the American Dream, losers are left to suffer shame. Regional loss comes to be carried as personal shame, acting as a magnet for other unwanted forms of shame—a phenomenon sometimes baffling to those who most often endure it.

It was into this setting that the big personality, the good bully Donald Trump, set foot. In him, many like Roger Ford saw a master anti-shame warrior. Even before Trump ran for president, his anti-shame public ritual was in place, becoming gradually more extreme over time. When jihadists attacked New York's Twin Towers on September 11, 2001, he claimed, people "on the other side of New Jersey, where you have large Arab populations . . . were cheering as the World Trade Center came down." Immediately the pundits objected to his blanket categorization of "all Arabs," giving him the chance to roar back at the shamers. When Barack Obama ran for president, Trump questioned Obama's identity as an American and condemned the election as a sham. In April 2015, after Baltimore erupted in protests regarding Freddie Gray's death in police custody, Trump responded on Twitter, "Our great African-American president hasn't exactly had a positive impact on the thugs who are so happily and openly destroying Baltimore!"

The ritual is made up of four moments. In moment 1, Trump makes a public statement which provokes. It defies the rules of political decorum. In announcing his presidential bid in 2015, for example, Trump declared, "When Mexico sends its people . . . they're bringing drugs. They're bringing crime. They're rapists."

In moment 2, the punditry shames Trump: "You can't *say* that!" After Trump's Mexican rapists remark, NBC—which was then airing his programs, *Celebrity Apprentice* and the Miss America and Miss Universe contests—announced it was severing ties "due to the recent derogatory statements by Donald Trump regarding immigrants." Univision also announced that it would not air the pageants. New York City mayor Bill de Blasio called Trump's remarks "disgusting and offensive" and said he would review ongoing contracts the city had with him. Macy's announced that it "stands for diversity and inclusion" and would discontinue Trump's menswear line. In a conversation aired on CNN, Ana Maria Salazar, a blogger and radio host, said, "I'm outraged. I can't understand . . . how is it possible that [a man] who wants to be president of the United States can . . . use hate language?" Trump was shamed.

In moment 3—more important as time went on—Trump poses himself as the victim of shaming. Look what they are doing to me. I am good. They are bad. And this could happen to you so stand with me. This is the message of moment 3.

In moment 4, Donald Trump roars back at the shamers. "If NBC is so weak and so foolish to not understand the serious illegal immigration problem in the United States, coupled with the horrendous and unfair trade deals we are making with Mexico, then their contract-violating closure of Miss Universe/Miss USA will be determined in court." Trump sued Univision for $500 million for the cancellation of the Miss USA broadcast, for breach of contract, defamation, and stifling free speech. It is this fourth moment that is key, for it is at this moment that the overly shamed feel, I believe, a strong cathartic release. It's the *our* bully in action.

Sometimes Trump expresses the 1-2-3-4 in a direct shame-to-blame line of statements, with little time spent dwelling on his victimhood. As David Keen points out in his fine book *Shame: The Politics and Power of an Emotion*, in a 2016 campaign debate with Hillary Clinton, for example, Trump was asked about the Access Hollywood tape in which he boasted groping women. In his astonishing answer he said, "Yes, I'm very embarrassed by it. I hate it. . . . But it's locker-room talk and it's one of those things. I will knock the hell out of ISIS."[359] He then moved on to Bill Clinton who was "so abusive to women" and to Hillary Clinton who "attacked those same women and attacked them viciously." From there Trump broad-jumped to the claim that the Clintons and President Obama were to blame for ISIS. Indeed, Trump claimed that Obama was the "founder" of ISIS. Trump *displaced* his own shame onto Hillary Clinton and Barack Obama.

Trump has applied this four-part anti-shame ritual emphatically again and again. No matter what its object was, the anti-shame ritual became a way to gather right-leaning followers. And shaming, getting shamed by, being a victim, and countershaming were not simply a show Trump's followers turned on and watched. He continually invited his followers into it. With the January 6 break-in, Trump conducted the 1-2-3-4 de-shaming ritual on a grander stage: First was the break-in. Second, the public shock and indictments. Third, outrage at the shamers. And later followed an embrace of those who broke into the Capitol. Added to this was the message of bonding, "When they shame me, they shame you," and implicitly, "So together we should get revenge."

When I proposed this 1-2-3-4 shame ritual to Roger Ford, he laughed out loud. "Right, Trump *can't* be shamed," he agreed. I asked Roger, "Do you think Trump sometimes pokes the bear?" By this I meant provoking liberal/left critics (moment 1) so that they will move into a scold (moment 2), enabling him to claim victimhood (moment 3) and roar back (moment 4). Again, Ford laughed and replied, "Oh, yeah." When asked, Mayor Andrew Scott too said, "Sure. Trump eggs on the liberal media to taunt us, and the left falls for it every time, and the networks make money covering it. To the networks, any fight is a moneymaker. So we're seeing this all the time."

As a personal matter, for Trump, exposure to shame also seemed an extremely serious matter. The annual White House Correspondents' Association Dinner had been since 1914 a ritual for presidents, high officials, and the journalists who cover them. The occasion calls for telling jokes about others and oneself—in other words, shaming others and oneself. Donald Trump refused to attend this dinner and forbade all his cabinet members to do so. For Trump, you couldn't kid around about shame. You couldn't play around. Shame was *serious*.

Before evangelical leaders, Trump declared himself *free* of shame. For example, at a Family Leadership Summit in Iowa, Trump was asked if he ever asked God's forgiveness, to which he answered, "Why do I have to repent or ask for forgiveness if I am not making mistakes?" For Trump, shame seemed deadly serious, something to almost never admit.

One might speculate about what in Donald Trump's childhood accounts for this sensitivity. He was the son of a highly demanding father—an explanation offered by his niece Mary L. Trump, in *Too Much and Never Enough: How My Family Created the World's Most Dangerous Man*. Weaknesses of all sorts, she reported, were considered shameful. But whatever the causes—I won't speculate further—Donald Trump's anguish about shame seemed to match that of the wider population to whom he so strongly appealed.

"Stolen": The Right to Something Gone

In the absence of a strong national or Democratic narrative that effectively spoke to the anguish of the pride paradox, Roger Ford and many like him, I believe, came to be persuaded by a certain emotional narrative. Over time this narrative was repeated with regularity, shifted focus, and grew more extreme. But it seemed a narrative his followers were predisposed to hear. It shifted the Protestant ethic notion of the responsible party to a focus on victimhood, shame, blame, and revenge. When something is lost, the question arises: *Why is it gone? Did I* (or *we*) *lose it? Or is it lost because it was stolen?*

For many Americans, things they believed in or treasured actually *had* gone missing. Such losses created a sense of plausibility that made it possible for so many otherwise thoughtful people in the District 12–like regions of America to feel like the idea rang true.

Through his daily rhetoric of victimhood, Trump guided the emotional needle from "loss" to "stolen." Over time, it grew into a master narrative, and like a magnet, it gathered further losses to the idea of "stolen."

Election: stolen.

Appalachian land: stolen.

Proud region: stolen.

Good jobs: stolen.

Community: stolen.

Story of heroic America: stolen.

An undisputed concept of human sexuality: stolen.

Honorable country culture: stolen.

White power: stolen.

Recognition of one's struggles and accomplishments: stolen.

Visibility itself: stolen.

Right to guns: watch out or it'll be stolen.

Pride: stolen.

Stolen became a master narrative. Those who are stolen from are victims. And rich, famous, and powerful as he was, Donald Trump became for many a powerful symbol of victimhood. He was a victim of the press that questioned his version of the truth. He was a victim of the Democratic Party. Later he was to become the victim—through four indictments and ninety-one felony charges—of state and federal courts. In his role of victim, Trump reached out to followers who felt like victims too but saw no better way to express it. After one indictment, Trump said, "I was indicted for you." Here the emotional narrative seems to have been, "I'm carrying your shame. When I win my pride back, you'll have yours."

"They're trying to go after him," one waitress explained to me. "They're trying to bring him down." And in his role as victim, Trump won sympathy from many who'd felt brought down, put upon, ignored, taken from too. Trump seemed to offer himself as a quasi-religious figure of sacrifice for his many followers who had themselves suffered loss. Through him, they could grieve their own stolen pride.

Meanwhile the local political pageant continued. In October 2022, a Republican gathering, the Mountain Freedom Fest, took place in Pikeville's Appalachian Wireless Arena, featuring Eric Deters, a Republican candidate for governor of Kentucky. The music was on, admission free. The crowd of some two hundred were middle-aged and older, all white. A table sold T-shirts saying SOCIALISM SUCKS, FAITH OVER FEAR, and WE THE PEOPLE . . . ARE PISSED. At another table, stickers were on sale that said I'M PRO-CHOICE. PICK ONE over images of different types of gun. Another sticker said YES ON 2, referring to a legislative measure that would remove any protection of the right to abortion by altering the Kentucky constitution. Bikers for Trump provided security. Hung on the wall was a sign: 2020 STOLEN.

What had happened? Materially, for hourly wage earners, wage packages were slightly down. As James Browning observed, coal didn't come back; pride itself was down too.

The abiding talk was of the American Dream, a finger pointing to exemplary blue state prosperity. But where was the red state story about equally hardworking, bright, stoic, blue-collar would-be bootstrappers for whom the dream had been largely squeezed out?

For them, there seemed a secret buried beneath the story of pride and shame: terrible loss without redress or mourning. Men who had based their identity on skills and lifeways that had since been devalued were men holding back grief and without the means to mourn it. Indeed, where in eyes-on-the-prize America was the cultural space for the displaced rural blue-collar man to mourn? In this forgotten region, there was an urgent call for good jobs, new roads, steady internet access—material resources to lift KY-5's niche in the material economy—what Anthony Flaccavento and others call a "rural new deal." But there was also a call for an emotional new deal to restore losses in the pride economy. This would require a place in the nation's memory to tell the rural story and mourn its losses, a national version of the sheltered wooden benches found on hillside cemeteries south of Pikeville.

In the absence of it, there appeared an emotional vacuum that long preceded Donald Trump. Abandoned as many felt by both political parties, and without a larger narrative speaking to their dignity and invisibility, a narrative of "stolen" rose up.

To the bafflement of most Americans, a mountain of counterevidence was in but the narrative of "stolen" stuck. It had become a powerful magnet for other losses and sources of unwelcome and undeserved shame. It was a move out of the pride paradox.

On the surface, Trump was restoring pride among his followers. He had offered them what a majority of Americans saw as a lie. *But he had paired the lie with a truth—the truth of lost pride.* And he had bonded—even fused—with his followers, saying to them, in essence, *All those who shame me shame you.* Through the alchemy of his repetitions, the list of things that had been "stolen" grew longer. As items passed from "lost" to "stolen," matters passed from shame to blame. With each shift of shame to blame came a parallel shift from grief to anger, and from depression to rage. It felt electric.

Maybe this was the "lightning in a jar."

14

Pride on a Dangerous Ride

"Everyone around here's looking at the rising price of gas," Mayor Andrew Scott told me in late 2020. "It was $1.70 a gallon in 2016, and now under Biden it's $3.20. The liberal media is talking nonstop about the January 6 break-in but the down-holler news is the rising cost of gas." For the first time in American history, an American president has been accused of obstructing the peaceful transfer of power. For the first time since 1814, the U.S. Capitol was breached, this time by U.S. citizens. These events would not have occurred without grassroots support. Yet among the residents Andrew was in touch with, that wasn't the real news.

There was the economic news. Looking back at economic life in Pike County during Donald Trump's first term, January 2017 to January 2021, I wondered, had Trump filled their pocketbooks, and Biden emptied them?

In answer to this question, James Browning reflected, "For us, nothing improved—not coal jobs, not other kinds of jobs, not better pay." Government reports told the same story. From 2015 onward Donald Trump had publicly vowed to "bring back coal," but during his presidency coal jobs in Kentucky fell from 6,460 in 2016 to 3,911 in 2020. One commentator observed that under Trump, we saw "the fastest decline in coal-fuel capacity in any single presidential term, far greater than the rate during either of President Barack Obama's two terms." Assuming the presidency in 2021, Joe Biden touted renewable energy, but paradoxically, while he was in office, the number of the nation's coal jobs actually rose due to surging natural gas prices linked to Russia's invasion of Ukraine.

Similarly, under Trump, American hourly workers saw their pay and fringe benefits fall slightly. In Kentucky's 5th Congressional District, as in the whole nation, most workers (58 percent) are paid by the hour. During this period, hourly workers' total compensation—including both wages and fringe benefits—fell 0.2 percent. In 2016, average real hourly wages were $22 an hour; in 2020, they were still $22 an hour. But during that time, fringe benefits fell from $9.52 to $9.41 per hour. This was true even in the manufacturing sector, in which average total hourly compensation went from $37.96 in 2016 to $36.31 in 2020—a decline of 4 percent.

To be sure, the stock market rose; the Dow Jones Industrial Average had grown 40 percent under Obama, 35 percent under Trump, and 10 percent under Biden. But the stock market rise thickened the wallets of CEOs and stock owners, not many of whom lived in KY-5. To be sure, inflation, which ran low (1–3 percent) under Trump, indeed rose in a frightening way under Biden, until it fell.

Meanwhile the political news had moved from "stolen" to the imagined rightness of "stealing." And to most of the nation, the January 6 takeover of the Capitol in Washington, DC, loomed large. A young Louisville-born legislative assistant, Harper White, explained in an interview how he learned this from his own family. "I come from a very hardcore conservative Kentucky Republican family, but I work for Democratic congresswoman Rosa DeLauro [of Connecticut], chair of the House Appropriations Committee, and we're working on the Working Families Tax Relief Act—it's great for all parents; the right should love it."

Harper described where he was on January 6, "I was sitting in my office on January 6 and suddenly heard gunshots. I was worried about my *life,* our lives. I hid inside a closet for four hours with my cellphone and heard people shouting threats right outside my door. People I didn't know called me every twenty or thirty minutes to see if I was okay, and they were consulting with the Capitol Police. Rosa was on the House floor for the vote to certify the Electoral College and I feared for *her* life or anyone's there. Rosa called my cell, and I overheard her tell someone, 'We're not leaving without Harper.' That's what I'll always remember."

Security officers eventually escorted Harper and Rosa DeLauro to safety. After the ordeal, Harper returned home to Louisville to recuperate, and to discover how his conservative grandparents perceived the January 6 break-in. "My grandparents are hard-core Trump defenders. But to them, I'm Jimmy and Donna's son, and they're proud of me. They listen to Fox News. Its reality is their reality. So, they think the January 6 break-in was a passing event, easy to forget. I felt like I was suddenly thrown into a war zone. Rosa or I could have gotten *killed*. But to my grandparents, it was like 'January 6? Oh, Harper had a bad day.'"

As later video and testimony revealed, the January 6 siege was deadly serious. Four protesters and five police officers died of events related to the break-in. There were smashed windows, beatings, dragging, weaponized flagpoles, a hangman's platform with dangling noose, video recordings of protesters shouting "Kill Mike Pence! Kill Nancy!" The House investigation shared recorded phone conversations in which the security officers protecting Vice President Mike Pence called family members to say goodbye in case they were killed. According to Capitol Police figures, in 2021 alone some 9,600 threats had been made against federal government officials that the police force is charged with protecting. In the nation as a whole, 72 percent felt the January 6 attackers were "threatening democracy." As of this writing, 150 people have been convicted for crimes related to the break-in.

Among those who broke in, racism was also on full display. Four officers, two from the U.S. Capitol Police and two from DC's Metropolitan Police Department, detailed the hostile bigotry expressed to them in the Capitol assault. When African American Capitol Police officer Harry Dunn told rioters that he voted for Biden, pointing out that his vote should be counted, "one woman in a pink 'MAGA' shirt yelled, 'You hear that, guys? This n—— voted for Joe Biden!'" he recalled. "Then the crowd, perhaps around twenty people, joined in screaming 'Boo! F—— n——!'" Dunn testified. He said that before this, no one had ever before called him the *n*-word while he was in uniform.

All of this presented Roger Ford with a troubling dilemma. Most of the Capitol invaders were not from rural areas like Pike County. But he feared rural whites would take the blame for the invasion.

Pride Slide: From Proud Patriot to Dangerous Criminal

"I disapprove of violence and racism," Roger told me, "but what the cameras caught of it wasn't typical of everyone there. He had led a group, the East Kentucky Patriots Coalition—many of whom had joined the honking, waving pro-Trump vehicle parade, and whose Facebook page lists some nine thousand members. Some of them had traveled to Washington to hear Trump speak. Roger explained, "They are all innocent, good, patriotic, decent people. No one from the East Kentucky Patriots delegation entered the Capitol. They went to Washington and stood on Pennsylvania Avenue to save America. He added, "I wish I'd been able to go."

But after the event, deaths and injuries counted, the damage from shattered windows and ruined paintings assessed, in the theater of national opinion many fiercely proud patriots found themselves under the axe of public judgment, shock, horror, and anger.

For many like Roger Ford, a firm law-and-order man, January 6 presented a moral crisis. Members of the East Kentucky Patriots (whose Facebook page lists some nine thousand members) had driven to Washington to express their support of Donald Trump—a matter of great pride to Ford. They had not joined the invaders but were now burdened with carried shame. Like Roger Ford, they found themselves at the center of a confusing national pride-shame mashup. After the break-in, they returned to their like-minded circle of friends.

But things had gone awry. "It's terrible," Ford told me. "Now every person who came to Washington is suspected of being violent and racist. And if they were violent, they should be punished. But our people have nothing to do with that," Ford said. Later research by University of Chicago political scientist Robert Pape on Americans who were arrested or charged in the insurrection suggests that most of those who broke into the Capitol were, indeed, not extremists such as Matthew Heimbach or Wyatt Blair. Eighty-seven percent of those who came to Washington, DC, on January 6 were unaffiliated with extremist groups, such as the Proud Boys, Oath Keepers, or neo-Nazis. In general, too, rural residents—such as those from the East Kentucky Patriots—were less likely to embrace violence than were residents drawn from suburban or urban areas.

When, in 2023, Fox News commentators admitted that they had publicly announced the election "stolen" on the air while privately knowing this was a lie, the revelation made no difference to Roger. He had stopped watching Fox News. Newsmax, to which many on the right were switching, was sticking with "stolen." Roger checked Newsmax, but he continued to "check CNN, the *Washington Post*, the BBC"—stations which did not characterize the election as "stolen." He was nevertheless still convinced the election was stolen.

And Ford was hardly alone. Three years after January 6, a 2023 CNN/SSRC poll found that 63 percent of Republican and Republican-leaning people also believed the 2020 election "stolen"—half because they thought the evidence "solid," and half because they had a suspicion. Over 70 percent of all Americans believed the election fair and the break-in a danger to democracy.

Addressing a Pride Slide

To this public judgment, there seemed three ways to respond and some I spoke to combined several at once. The first response was outright denial: *Violence did not occur.* Tucker Carlson, then at Fox News, edited a lengthy tape of the day, eliminating any shows of violence, and making January 6 appear as a respectful walk of true patriots touring the Capitol. In that video, no one was blowing off steam, smashing windows, or erecting a hanging platform. Violence didn't occur at all.

A second approach was to say, *Violence did occur, but people like us didn't do it.* Yes, things got smashed up, but our people did not do it—they were Antifa. As a first guess, Roger suspected that fake protesters were dressing up as patriots in an effort to pin shame on MAGA supporters.

A third approach was to say, in effect, *Some people committed violence, but it wasn't serious.* Harper's grandparents claimed that while the roughnecks were true Trump supporters, they "weren't seriously violent." A Prestonsburg car salesman summed up his view of January 6 to me: "It was wrong to destroy property but the guys who did it were just being guys, like at a football game where the fans climb the fence. Boys will be boys." In the same spirit, a neighbor told John Rosenberg, "January 6 was just guys blowing off steam." It was bad, but it wasn't seriously bad. It was shameful, but not *that* shameful.

Three years after the event, sitting over coffees in a Pikeville hotel lobby, Roger commented to me about the platform and scaffold on which a hangman's noose had been placed—a stage setting for the execution of Vice President Pence for refusing to authorize "alternative" vote totals. At the time, protesters were calling out, "Kill Mike Pence! Kill Mike Pence!" "You remember that hangman's noose?" Roger said. "That platform the hangman's noose was on wasn't as big as it was portrayed on television. You see that?" He pointed out the window at a bus stop passenger shelter. "The platform was only that size—not very big." To him, the smaller size apparently made it seem less threatening and shameful.

In *The Origins of Totalitarianism*, Hannah Arendt pointed to "crimes committed in the spirit of play . . . [and in a] combination of horror and laughter." This applied, the writer David Keen observes, to the kind of carnival atmosphere of the break-in: an intruder's feet on Speaker Nancy Pelosi's desk, the "laughter and animal masks" that coincided with beatings, window smashing, and ultimately, five deaths. If violence went with fun, the idea was, it wasn't "serious" violence and if it wasn't serious violence, it wasn't shameful. If there was laughter, who could be getting hurt? In all three of these responses to the violence of January 6, there was a strong resistance to shame or what seemed to Trump's supporters like "too much" shame.

But in other instances, something else was going on. As David Keen wisely observes, "When large numbers were laughing together . . . often at some kind of cruelty that [Trump] was embodying or encouraging [as in the ridicule of a disabled man] . . . it was as if shame had magically evaporated for both Trump *and* his audience. In the act of ridiculing [subjecting someone to mockery and derision] and in the act of laughing along, there is a kind of instant escape from being mocked or derided."

The Indicted: Patriotic Hero or Treasonous Villain?

After the mayhem of January 6, FBI notices went up in public places like post offices. Search warrants went out. Facebook posts and cellphone calls were checked. Some of the intruders' faces had been caught by video camera inside the Capitol. By January 2024, the Department of Justice had indicted 1,265 people for breaking the law, and 718 had pled guilty. One day they were heroic patriots rescuing democracy from a "stolen" election; the next morning they were reviled criminals. One day patriotic, the next day treasonous. One day proud, the next day ashamed. Or so it was for some.

Of the 1,265 who were charged, thirty were residents of Kentucky. From supporters at home, they received a sympathetic reception. In fact, to some the indicted themselves now seemed victims, for some of those charged were fired from their jobs by shocked employers. And while they waited for trial, they languished in jail. "I feel sorry for the arrested who are kept waiting a long time in jail. Good people are being hunted down like criminals. And now good people are afraid," Ford said with alarmed sympathy. "Hunted down by our cellphones? It's like we're living in a police state."

Of the thirty Kentuckians charged with entering the Capitol, seventeen have pled guilty to one or more charges so far. The court asked all of the defendants to submit personal statements and "character letters" (written by oneself or others) to the sentencing judge, letters he was to consider in determining sentences. In the government file of a twenty-four-year-old University of Kentucky junior, Gracyn Courtright, were publicly available cellphone selfies posted on social media from inside the Capitol. In messages on Instagram, Courtright denied seeing any damage being done to the Capitol and exclaimed, "I can't wait to tell my grandkids I was here!" Later, in the courtroom, she told the judge abjectly, "I have so much shame from this, I hold my head down and don't make eye contact with my neighbors."

At the other extreme, Lori Vinson, a fifty-year-old nurse from Morganfield, Kentucky, described herself in her character letter first by what she owned—thirteen apartments, eleven mobile homes, four houses, and a commercial pizza business—and expressed minimal regret. After January 6 but before her indictment, she had publicly declared herself "proud to be there." In a television interview, she'd said, "I'd do this all over again tomorrow." In addition to detailing her wealth in the character letter, Vinson added other points of pride—her long marriage, her six children, her nine grandchildren, her nursing degree, her hard work. In her final statement she said, "In reflection, I regret entering the Capitol building." Then she quickly shifted to points of shame that did not apply to her. "I did not encourage others to do such things. . . . It wasn't until I returned home and watched the news that I realized the details and the magnitude of what was happening further inside the building."

Both Gracyn Courtright and Lori Vinson formally expressed regret for invading the Capitol, but very different degrees of shame—one seemingly too much, and one too little. One was abject, the other defiant.

The defendants who pled guilty also appealed to different bases of pride. Some pointed to "bootstrap pride." As one man wrote: "My best accomplishment[s] are my two associate degrees that I completed with Honors." Another said, "I've managed to build a small business, purchase a house, pay off two cars, a semi-truck, semi-trailer and still have plenty left over." Another said simply, "I enjoy working hard and enjoy the simple things." Yet another appealed to "survivor's pride": "Although being dragged through the belly of the beast, I hold my head higher now than I did." Having worked on himself and learned from his mistakes, he noted poignantly, he is "proud of the man I have become."

On the national stage, Donald Trump was faced with his first indictment. What followed initiated bigger, far bolder versions of his 1-2-3-4 de-shaming ritual: the provocation, the public's shaming, his posture as victim, and the roar-back. Trump was indicted for calling the Georgia attorney general and asking him to falsify voter records. (In a recorded phone call, Trump said, "I just want to find 11,780 votes.") It also included coordinating with others to set up substitute electors to falsely represent the state's real voters.

After the provocation came the shaming: Trump was indicted in Fulton County, Georgia, for his attempt to falsify voter results. This was followed by a public shaming: criminal indictment itself. Third came victimhood. Fourth came Trump's roar-back. For this he now posed for a memorable mugshot. Beneath his blond comb-forward hair, lowered brows, and locked jaw, Trump squinted furiously at the camera, counteraccusing the legal world that had brought him to justice. So now the roar-back was on the face of the "victim," making the image that of the "vengeful victim." There it was—the 1-2-3-4 anti-shame ritual writ large.

The Trump scowl became a shame-averting talisman. It soon went on sale, reproduced on mugs, T-shirts, and posters, and was announced by Trump himself in a Truth Social post: "Due to the great Excitement and Success of my previous TRUMP DIGITAL TRADING CARDS . . . the

MugShot Edition, available RIGHT NOW." An image of the suit and tie he wore that day went on sale separately. Like the other NFTs, these were on sale for $99 each, plus transaction and service fees. The object provided a symbolic restoration of pride. Of the 1-2-3-4 of the de-shaming ritual, it was number 4 in the form of an object. It could magically protect you.

On the Sidelines: Battered Voter Syndrome

Some I talked with were dismayed by the events of January 6, listened carefully to the testimony of witnesses at the House of Representatives hearings, disliked the escalating rhetoric, were not compelled by the 1-2-3-4 de-shaming ritual, and so felt honestly conflicted. Andrew Scott, the mayor of Coal Run, introduced me to a retired male friend and neighbor who wanted to remain anonymous and whom I'll call Peter. A retired railroad worker and former maker of moonshine, Peter was tall and robust, but he sat down with care and spoke in a thoughtful, mild-mannered way.

"I voted for Trump in 2016 and 2020 and have—or had—thought I'd vote for him in 2024," Peter said. "Now I feel like I'm driven from one crisis to the next and the next. It's like I'm part of battered voter syndrome. That's why I'm talking to you like this [anonymously].

"Say a woman marries a guy who is steady, decent, but doesn't pay enough attention to her, so she's a bit restless. A very exciting guy comes along. He seems to really understand her, and tells her she's the most beautiful woman he's ever met. So she leaves the dull, steady husband for the exciting new guy. And everything goes fine—for a while.

"Then the new guy goes to a bar, drinks too much, beats up some illegals. A cop arrests him, roughs him up, shoves him into the car. He calls her and asks her to bail him out. She's mad at him for getting into a brawl but sorry that the cop roughed him up and she bails him out. He gives her flowers and promises her a Florida vacation and a wonderful life after that. She gets that old love feeling for him back.

"But then it happens again: he picks a fight with the jailer, threatens to bring down the whole jail system, and complains she isn't supporting him enough. She thinks to herself, 'He's bringing this on himself.' Still, she tells herself, 'he's doing all he does for me and he needs me.' She bails him out again, because, poor guy, he's a victim. Things are fine again for a while. Then he lights a fire in the jail. She's exhausted. But who else can he turn to? He needs her. She thinks she needs him. So she tries to downplay the fire in the jail, and bails him out.

"I feel like that woman. First I thought, 'Okay, Trump's my guy— pro-coal, pro-life, pro-gun, anti-tax, and lovable, right? But then he picks fights with decent people, and at first I thought, 'Well, never mind, he's my guy.' Then came January 6! And I thought, 'That's it; I'm done.' But I hate seeing the Democrats gang up on him. Each time they do, I go back to him.

"I liked Mitch McConnell okay, but Trump felt betrayed by him and turned against him. I don't like that he hates Mitch, but I say, 'Okay.' He turns on Vice President Mike Pence. I don't like that he turns on Mike Pence, but I hate how the press beats Trump up, so I say, okay. Each time I'm done with Trump, the Dems bear down on him and I'm back to rescuing him. Then he talks about immigrants as 'poisoning the blood' of America? I'm done with him again. But then he needs me, and I'm back. I'm miserable, but I'm married."

After Trump's indictments, his legal expenses mounted and now a portion of any donations to the Republican National Committee was directed to his personal lawyers. This bothered some of his supporters. But Peter said, "it's like having a partner, good friend, or relative sent to jail. You're not going to like it, but you're going to go down to the county lock-up and put money on his commissary account.

"A lot of local and state officials are in this boat too, I think. If you were to have an honest conversation with most Republican officials around here, they would tell you they can't stand Trump, but they also know they could never get elected if they said that. They don't fear him; they fear the voters. So they're quiet. But that isn't just cowardice or careerism. They don't want to be replaced by a true believer who may be caught up in this battered voter syndrome."

Listening to Peter, it occurred to me that Donald Trump's anti-shame 1-2-3-4 ritual had a fifth, final step. By slamming the shamers, Donald Trump solidifies his base of support for an oft-promised "retribution" against his opponents. All new officials, the idea is, will be required to be loyal not to the Constitution or to the rule of law but to Trump himself. I asked Peter: if it came down to a choice between Donald Trump and Joe Biden, who would he vote for? For a very long time Pete said nothing. Then it dawned on me: maybe his pause was his answer.

For many who believed Trump's 2020 victory and pride "stolen," the story began with the unresolved pride paradox and the desire to throw off the undeserved shame it produced. For some, the feeling of being unjustly shamed was experienced as a certain mild background noise. For others, it had grown intolerably strong, propelling a feeling of shame to blame to desire for revenge—the electricity in a jar. Bypassed were other Republican candidates whose policy packages were loaded with different emotional tones, promising something short of the catharsis of Trump's 1-2-3-4-5. Certainly bypassed was the emotionally dull-toned candidate, now in the White House, who had steered more public money to lifting America's sinking middle class than any other since President Franklin Delano Roosevelt.

To Roger Ford and many others, Donald Trump at first seemed utterly different from Matthew Heimbach in appearance, rhetoric, dress, sense of normality, and most of all, in his association with history and his focus on America. True, Trump talked rough. In a review of Trump's public utterances, his use of such words as "kill, destroy, fight" contrasts sharply with words used by the nation's last five presidents." But many, like Roger, felt Trump tossed such words about in a spirit of bravado and horsing around, and even found such language a breath of fresh air.

But the fringe itself increasingly felt inspired by Trump's talk of revenge.

In a 2023 ABC review of police reports and court records, researchers identified at least fifty-four cases in which a person was arrested for a violent crime motivated by Donald Trump. One Florida man punched a Latino gas station attendant saying, "This is for Trump." On the eve of an indictment in the New York court of law in 2023, Trump predicted "death and destruction" if he were to be indicted. Hours later, those in the mailroom used by Manhattan District Attorney Alvin Bragg discovered a threatening letter addressed to Mr. Bragg containing white powder. The letter read, "ALVIN: I AM GOING TO KILL YOU." The question arose: was Trump preparing to use the violent fringe as a weapon against his enemies, even as he used MAGA enthusiasts to pressure their national Republican representatives?

But by 2023, Donald Trump had himself embraced extremists. He invited Kanye West, admirer of Adolf Hitler and Holocaust denier, to dine with him in Mar-a-Lago. He embraced the Proud Boys, Oath Keepers, and Three Percenters. Trump offered to help pay the legal defense fees of those found guilty for the January 6 break-in of the Capitol. If reelected, he has promised to grant them full pardons. At a 2023 campaign rally in Waco, Texas, hand to heart, Trump sang the national anthem along with those jailed for the break-in, the so-called J6 prison choir—made up of extremists jailed for violence—recorded by iPhone singing from prison. Trump created a "charity record" of the song called "Justice for All," with proceeds slated to benefit the families of January 6 arrestees.

What had happened? The 2017 marchers had dressed like storm troopers, fierce, gun-toting, a potential right-wing paramilitary. They had knocked on the back door of American culture, calling for a white Christians–only America, and violence as a means of achieving it. Roger Ford had folded his arms in a gesture of "no." Pikeville, too, had listened politely, folded its arms, and said "no." The 2017 march through Pikeville had failed. Moreover, Matthew Heimbach himself later disavowed his racism, and was considering a degree in nursing, if he could get the money to pay for it.

Meanwhile someone else—voluble, expressive, the American Dream incarnate, wearing a red MAGA hat—was knocking on America's front door. He dressed normally and promised better times. There was just one thing: his rhetorical 1-2-3-4 was calling for all to join him on a dangerous pride ride. Twelve New York jurors indicted Donald Trump as a felon and he countered that he was a victim and vowed revenge. Trump had helped move shame to blame. Now increasingly he was adding an appeal to fear, dotting speeches with fiery words such as "crisis," "invasion," "total disaster," "catastrophe," and posing himself as the sole answer. To some this has struck a nerve, and for many it has created an unsettling legacy which may last for years to come.

Meanwhile Roger Ford, a law-and-order man who believes in rule of law and disagreed with Trump on "good" hardworking migrants, told me in 2024, "If Trump runs for president of the United States, I'll vote for him."

15

An Empathy Bridge

Beneath the heated public rhetoric of the day, I discovered hidden foot traffic across what we might call an "empathy bridge" spanning opposing views on "stolen" January 6, migration, climate change, sexual identity, and race. The more hostile the two sides, the less talk of crossover there is, and the more getting to know those who disagree comes to be confused with "betrayal" or "caving in." But such barrier-crossers quietly weave a stronger national fabric that increasingly we need.

Curiously, Republicans and Democrats share more views than they think they do, studies show. The average man or woman on the street tends to be more moderate in view than party leaders. At the same time, each side holds an exaggerated view of the other. In one study, Democrats were asked how many Republicans earn $250,000 a year or more, and answered 38 percent. It's actually 2 percent. Republicans were asked what proportion of Democrats believe "most police are bad people" and answered 50 percent. It's actually 15 percent.

Such findings suggest that it might help to reach across the political divide. But does everyone want to do that? Interestingly, liberal Democrats are more likely than conservative Republicans to cut off contact at first signs of a difference in political opinion. At the same time, for conservatives, personal contact makes more of a difference in their degree of tolerance than it does for liberals.

Despite a nationwide communicational impasse, crossover goes on in some of the least explored locales. In my time in Pike County, I discovered a number of quietly inspiring models for how to move forward.

Take race; among many divisive issues, race has become key. Since 2020, at least thirty-five states—including Kentucky—have passed or have considered laws restricting education on race in classrooms or state agencies. Legislators felt that "educators are indoctrinating students with certain lessons on race that make people feel discomfort or shame," one Kentucky newscaster reported. House Bill 14 addresses "any classroom instruction or discussion that incorporates designated concepts related to race, sex, and religion." If such "designated concepts"—which the bill did not specify—are taught, the Kentucky attorney general is authorized to impose "a penalty of $5,000 for each day a violation persists . . . [and] require the commissioner of education to deduct the penalty from funds distributed to a school district." While the bill did not advance out of committee, it expressed great anxiety about race and shame. In 2022, the Kentucky state legislature considered bills banning diversity training and negative claims about U.S. history, with the threat of loss of school accreditation.

But what exactly are our differences about race? Interestingly, three quarters of both whites and Blacks—and 65% of Republicans and 85% of Democrats—agree that "it's good for the country that the U.S. population is made up of people of many different races and ethnicities."

Where the parties divide on the issue of race is the point touching the pride paradox. Republicans, far more than Democrats, believe that if someone fails to achieve the American Dream, whatever their color, it's not because of class or race but because they didn't work hard enough. A hardworking Black and a hardworking white have the same crack, the idea is, at the American Dream. The idea of "white privilege" seemed to many to subtract credit from "hard work" and so from pride.

But how about the impact of slavery and discrimination? A 2020 national survey of voters posed a statement: "Generations of slavery and discrimination have created conditions that make it difficult for Blacks to work their way out of the lower class." When asked if they agreed, 75 percent percent of Blacks and half of whites agreed. But the two political parties were more widely split: 76 percent of Democrats and 28 percent of Republicans agreed with this sentiment. Among rural white Americans, it was 59 percent of Democrats and 19 percent of Republicans. That is, those hit hardest by the pride paradox—rural, white Republicans—had the least sympathy.

So who, I wondered, in this statistically least probable group, becomes the incidental ambassador across the divide on this core issue? How does one person understand how another person got to feel the way he or she did? To empathize is not to agree, or seek common ground, though these can more easily follow. It is simply to empathize.

Some bridge-crossers, I began to notice, fit two biographical patterns related to pride and shame. One life pattern is to "rise up, give back, reach out." Such a person *rises above*—or feels above—the fear of shame, enabling him or her to get on with reaching out. A second life pattern is to "hit bottom, rise up, reach out." Such a person doesn't rise above shame. He or she *goes through* shame, suffers it, loses fear of it, and proceeds from there. Those in-between these two extremes are, it seems, less likely to reach out, perhaps because somehow, they haven't gotten shame enough out of the way to develop empathy with others.

Rise Up, Give Back, Reach Out: The Upper Deck

The University of Pikeville chaplain, Rob Musick, exemplified the life story of those on the "top deck" of the bridge. Bright-eyed, forty, bespectacled, balding, and wearing his white clerical collar, Rob sat in his office chair in front of his orderly desk. Often students were waiting around outside it, wanting a brief chat, the solution to a problem, a word of encouragement. Rob was a man of connections. He shepherded students struggling with addiction to twelve-step fellowship meetings at the local Methodist church and led yearly missions in Nicaragua and Costa Rica.

One day, sitting at his office desk, hands folded, he began to reveal his life's story. Many people I interview about their life sit back and relax in their chair, presuming the availability of time to tell their story, but Rob spoke rapidly, as if to get his story out before time was up.

"I was born in a trailer park in Barn Hill, Ohio, poor, struggling, lots of drama. My dad's mom was volatile, chain-smoking, and my dad's dad was one of ten kids, in and out of foster care, and got his only Christmas gifts from the Salvation Army. Almost all his siblings—my aunts and uncles—ended up on drugs, idle, on welfare, and looked down on. As a kid my dad struggled for every inch of his dignity. He told me, 'Never make a person feel like a loser.' "

Each bridge-crosser differs in motivation from the next, of course, but I began to sense Rob's in his admiration for his father. Despite his child-hood hardships, as an adult, Rob's dad made a success of himself, build-ing up a small business repairing heating and cooling units. On Sundays, he washed and polished his 1986 Thunderbird. Rob went on, "Every day he took great care to wear a fresh, clean pair of pants and shirt, care-fully combed and parted his hair, and wore cologne. "He always told me, 'There's no excuse for a man not to dress neat and be clean.'" As the ulti-mate symbol of his bootstrap climb to the American Dream, Rob added, "Dad even took my mom to Hawaii."

But Rob's dad's dream slowly collapsed on him. As Rob explained, "Dad shared his business with my sister's husband, and when that marriage fell apart, the heating and cooling business did too. Dad ran into debt, became sick, and had to apply for disability, which shamed him terribly." Rob drew a long breath before hesitantly adding, "When my dad was only sixty-two, he took his own life.

"But," Rob continued after a while, "in my own life, I've been lucky. My parents and my mom's mother gave me a secure and loving childhood, and I did very well in school," Rob reflected. "My dad felt like an outsider to school, never checked my homework or met my teachers, but he loved know-ing I was doing well. As a senior, I got elected president of my high school class. From there, I went to college, graduated from seminary, and became a Protestant minister. I became secure and relaxed enough within myself that I'm not afraid of being looked down on, and I've ended up reaching out to people who are. You could say it's something I want to do, my mission."

One day, atop a flower-edged knoll on campus, next to an American flagpole, Rob discreetly placed a wooden "peace pole" with a different language on each of its four sides. Beside it was a small figure of St. Francis. Beside St. Francis, Rob set a small figure of Buddha. "I thought it would expand our horizons a bit here in Appalachia," he said with a smile. But to the school authorities, this seemed a step too far. A few weeks later, Rob was politely asked to remove the Buddha. "It was explained to me that that was 'too controversial.'"

Rob's outreach extended to Black students on campus, for whom he was the go-to guy, and also to white students, who often hesitated to talk about such issues as Black Lives Matter. "I have some great students. Their dads are like my dad. When there's talk of government help to Blacks, they get stopped. They say, 'We're poor. We're forgotten. Why should we care about Blacks because the government's already helping them? They don't need more. We do.' It's not that my students don't care. It's that, given our own circumstances, the issue of racism feels too far to go. So I want to help them try to connect to the experience of Black people.

"Sometimes it's a challenge to get them to empathize with George Floyd or understand the Black Lives Matter movement. They understand that George Floyd was arrested for giving a store clerk a fake twenty-dollar bill for a pack of cigarettes. They understand that a Minneapolis police officer handcuffed Floyd, pinned him down, pressed his knee on Floyd's neck, and killed him. They understand that other police offiers stood by while he died.

"I've been trying to get my students to see that situation from everyone's point of view—the store clerk, the police officer, the bystanders, George Floyd himself. They could feel compassion for the store clerk who lost money. They can understand the bystanders. They all agreed the cop who murdered George Floyd was guilty and should go to jail. But then they say, Floyd himself had previously robbed someone and served time in prison. So this turned Floyd into an entirely different kind of person, a criminal. What with our opioid crisis, we experience a good bit of crime in the area. We have police officers visiting schools warning kids off drugs, arresting robbers and dealers who are on drugs, and a lot of us are victims of crime. So that's the context.

"But I thought I'd try something new," Rob said. "I asked them to think about George Floyd as a man crucified like Jesus.

"They were shocked. 'George Floyd was a criminal.' I told them, 'You're absolutely right. A crime is a crime. Floyd was a criminal. And we don't want crime. But let's think back to Jesus Christ in ancient times. Back in the day, for a different reason, Jesus was considered a criminal too.'"

Hit Bottom, Rise Up, Reach Out: The Lower Deck

If Rob Musick's life story was to rise up, give back, and reach out, James Browning's was to hit bottom, rise back up, and reach out. When I spoke with him three years after we first met, a trim beard edged his face and the bandana across his forehead was gone. Now he was forty-three, his short hair lay under a cap, and he wore a small ring to the side of his lip, perhaps a reminder of the old punk days. It had now been six years since medics had brought him to the emergency room and restarted his heart after a fourth heroin overdose. And it had been six years since he'd entered the Southgate facility and met Tommy Ratliff, whom he credited with "saving my life."

"I took drugs instead of feeling my emotions. In my recovery, I had to learn how to feel and even name my feelings again. And one of those feelings was shame." James had not forgotten the fall from "just pills," to "junkie." Now in his recovery, he reflected, "As for shame, I faced it down and I'm not afraid of it anymore." It felt new to him but these days, when one of his clients seemed to be improving, he caught himself feeling pride.

After graduating from Southgate, James found a job as a guard at a homeless shelter. On weekends he dug ditches. Eventually, he found work at a nearby addiction recovery center, New Beginnings. "I love it here because I'm helping people," he said. He married a fellow recovering addict, a mother of two, and regained part-time custody of his own two children. "I'm three years clean after eighteen years of active addiction, and during two of those, I was homeless," he recalled. Now James had started taking classes at a nearby community college and had received a raise and promotion to assistant director of New Beginnings.

James invited me to a conversation with the twenty-two men at his center, three Blacks and nineteen whites. Sitting in its large, comfortable living room, drinking coffee, they talked first about feeling misunderstood and put down as "hillbillies"—a topic on which all agreed—and turned next to the 2020 election, on which they also seemed to agree. "I voted for Trump," one voluble Black man offered, to nods around the room. The main difference that arose concerned whether felons could vote. "I'm a felon and I voted," one man volunteered, while others looked perplexed. "I thought we couldn't vote," one replied. In what states could a felon vote? As the talk circled around one issue and another, James seemed in his element, inviting exiles from society back in.

Through his twelve-step program, James had begun to reach out to African American recovering addicts. At a Louisville-based twelve-step meeting, he had an encounter that greatly affected him. "In twelve-step meetings you don't shake hands, you hug," he explained. "And I met this seventy-three-year-old African American woman who told me she'd never hugged a white man. She said whites had gone through the same pain of drug addiction she had but hadn't endured the same ordeal of segregation. She felt that white men didn't *really* understand her non-drug life. I got that. In Appalachia we've had crippling accidents, black lung, poverty, coal towns with their company stores. If your husband got killed, you had to move out of your company-owned home so the next worker could move in."

But, James added, "the boss didn't *own* you and yours for four hundred years. I got that." Then, he continued, "that lady heard a white man tell about his life as a foster kid and all that happened to him on the streets. She got up from her chair in our circle, walked over, and gave him a long hug. She'd come a long ways to give that hug. I was inspired to reach out myself. I work full time, have my kids with me and have had to drop community college for now. But I'd like to get going with Recovery Climbs. I'd like to get some Louisville folks I met here down to the mountains, climb together. Who knows what we all could see from the top."

Hints of a National Story?

While I was getting to know Rob Musick and James Browning, two men in one town and region at one point in time, I wondered if these two kinds of biographies suggested a larger national pattern unseen on the empathy bridges. We might call them upper deck patterns "noblesse oblige" and the lower deck, "in the same boat." The results of the 2020 American National Election Studies (ANES) suggested to me and Kirstin Krusell, my research assistant, that perhaps Rob and James are not alone. As mentioned above, in a survey of over eight thousand eligible voters—including six thousand whites—respondents were asked whether they agreed with the following statement: "Generations of slavery and discrimination have created conditions that make it difficult for blacks to work their way out of the lower class." Answers vary widely but provide hints that certain social conditions seem to foster the two paths across the empathy bridge.

The upper deck: among the nation's white adults, the most affluent (annual household income of $150,000 and higher) and the most highly educated (bachelor's degree or more) are much more likely to agree with the statement about slavery and discrimination than are their poor, less educated counterparts. Among the richest and most highly educated, two-thirds counted slavery and discrimination as an obstacle for Blacks. Of the poorest and least educated, only a third did. It's likely that at the top, shame didn't get in the way for they felt above it. In fact, the upper deck elite might have felt proud to be reaching out to the less fortunate—in the spirit of *noblesse oblige*.

The lower deck: what seemed to put people on the "lower deck" of the empathy bridge was the experience of great insecurity. "How worried are you about losing your job in the near future?" respondents were asked. The more financially precarious a white person felt, the survey suggests, the more empathy they express for Black people, *together in a shaky boat*.

White responses to a statement about government aid to Blacks reveals a further clue. The survey asked how much they agreed with this sentiment: "The government in Washington should make every effort to improve the social and economic position of Blacks." Most likely among whites to favor government help for Blacks were, as before, the richer and more educated on the upper deck (53 percent compared to 33 percent among the poor and least educated). But the highest white support for help to Blacks was among the precarious poor whites, those who most feared losing their jobs, at 66 percent. It seemed an echo of David Maynard's comments about the link of "hood to holler." This cross-race, bottom-to-bottom channel is, perhaps, thin and chancy, but I believe that, for the Jameses, the David Maynards and others of the world, it's there. (See Appendix 2 for more details.)

Accompanying his new wife to a large twelve-step fellowship conference in Louisville, James joined many other recovering addicts, white and Black, in the large conference hall. "It was the first time I'd been to a large meeting like that—with maybe eight hundred to a thousand people; over half were Black. After a general session there were many breakout circles. As people were walking the halls to get to one, I got talking with this tall, middle-aged Black guy, friendly. He asked me where I was going. I told him the name of it, and we said goodbye. But funny thing—when I sat down in the circle of some twelve to fifteen people, it turned out *he* was the leader and I was the only white.

"The man stood up, moved to the center, and nodded to all of us in the circle. He was holding the big book [the NA book, based on the similar Alcoholics Anonymous book] in his right hand, as he would a Bible," James noted, "and he talked distinctly and loud to us all, as if he was preaching in church.

"The leader began, 'When I was a kid, I didn't know many people my age in my neighborhood who acted like they had some future in mind.' Around the circle, I could hear a murmur: 'Oh yeah . . . I know . . . mmm-mmm . . .'"

James explained, "After coal was out, it was like a funeral parlor around Turkey Creek. I knew what he was talking about. So I joined in and said, 'Me too.'

"'I saw friends doing drugs and it looked cool,' the man continued. The circle was with him, saying, 'Yes . . . yeah . . . I know what you're saying.'

"I remember my own high school. Pills were cool. So I said, 'Me too.'

"The speaker went on: 'I saw some of my friends getting strung out. But I told myself, oh, that can't happen to me. I don't need help.'

"I thought of how Trey ended up, and what I thought. I said, 'Me too.'

"'Then I thought I could quit, but I discovered I couldn't quit. Then I felt beyond help,' the leader said.

"And I thought to myself, 'I know what you mean,' and said, 'Me too.'

"Then the speaker looked around the circle slowly at us all and told us, 'A great evil has come upon us. But now I'm on the other side of it. Now I'm stretching my hand out to help people I've never met in my whole life, but who've gone to hell and come back just like I have.'

"I thought about burying Trey, and all of us together that day in that circle, making the recovery climb together, and I said, 'Me too.'"

16

Overburden

On a last drive through the rolling mountains of Pike County, I went down a road that began to pass between giant walls of thinly layered ochre sandstone cliffs that suggested the quiet presence of some forgotten ancient civilization. It occurred to me that I was driving through a history of ideas about pride. I had begun with the 2017 march in Pikeville—its leader, the town's protectors, its potential victims, its "faces in the crowd"—all grappling with ideas about the race, religion, and natality of the "real American," now a leading issue on the national stage.

The mountain slopes were dotted by well-tended graveyards which remind the visitor of similar conflicts in our past. In some lay the graves of McCoys and Hatfields, two enemy clans laid to rest in separate but nearby spaces as in the case of the Dils graveyard in Pikeville. Such graveyards also held the remains of soldiers who fought in the Civil War, mainly on the Union side. It was in a small graveyard on a mountainside behind his old home that Tommy Ratliff and I discovered his aunt cleaning and laying flowers at the grave of his grandfather, a veteran of World War II and winner of a Purple Heart. What, I wondered, might we learn from these struggles about the role of loss and aggrieved—and as it might seem, stolen—pride? For years now, Pike County had become my schoolhouse and I wanted to gather the lessons from my sojourn there.

Pike County had been home to the feuding Hatfields and McCoys. In my travels, I had found myself retracing the area once marked by narrow horse trails the rival families had traveled, now marked by highway signs such as: Indian Burial Ground, Hatfield-McCoy Rest Area, Little Coal River, Burning Fork, Church House Hollow, and Lost Trail Road. Could this local feud offer us a lens through which to move forward more wisely on our modern-day "lost trail"?

The Hatfield-McCoy feud began as a dispute over a stolen pig. It ended as the longest and fiercest clan fight in the nation. Between 1863 and 1891, deadly horseback raids had crossed and recrossed the Tug Fork of the Big Sandy River some thirty miles northeast of Pikeville—past where later stood the South Williamson mall where James Browning's mother and sister had worked and where David and Shea Maynard married. It was this area that later became the epicenter of a tragic drug crisis which nearly killed James Browning. A murder case from the feud had been tried in the old Pikeville Courthouse, past which Matthew Heimbach and his white nationalists had marched. Over a dozen died; one was executed. The feud had shifted from local gunfire to national legend, and from there to quaint tourist trinkets—such as a Hatfield and McCoy shot glass, mug, and dog tag key chain.

The families had long ago settled their differences. Outside Pikeville, at the Hog Trail Cabin, a log home with a front porch on well-kept grounds with a historic marker, the descendants of the McCoys and Hatfields gathered in 2003. It was in this same spot that Randolph McCoy brought charges against Floyd Hatfield for stealing the pig, and where, in 1888, one of the worst revenge attacks had occurred. At the gathering, Paul Patton, governor of Kentucky, and Governor Bob Wise of West Virginia proclaimed June 14, 2003, to be Hatfield-McCoy Reconciliation Day. The Hog Trail Cabin became a local voting center. In a 2017 regathering of the clans, Reo Hatfield declared that if the McCoys and the Hatfields could settle their differences, "there has to be a way for America to get back together as one."

So why did the two clans fight? The dispute began, most agree, when

Randolph McCoy accused Floyd Hatfield of stealing his pig. At the time, to accuser and accused alike, the pig seemed like the problem. But was the deadly fight over a stolen pig really about a stolen pig?

What, for instance, were the relative positions of each clan in the material and pride economies at the time? Both clans were landowners when land was the main measure of pride, and as landowners both probably counted as members of the local elite. In both clans, families were large and in need of land to grow food for themselves. But due to a legal dispute over property rights, one clan became more prosperous (the Hatfields) and the other clan less so (the McCoys).

It was the McCoys who were outraged about the stolen pig. They had lost a legal battle with the Hatfields over land and were left with more sons than land on which to settle them. Meanwhile, the Hatfields timbered their land, made money from it, and settled their more prosperous sons and families on it. Some McCoys, it seems, were forced to work as hired hands on Hatfield land. Indeed, Selkirk McCoy—who voted against Randolph in the pig trial—had to work on Anse Hatfield's thirty-five-to-forty-man timber crew along with his two sons. And as the historian Altina Waller writes, "Devil Anse [Hatfield] . . . provid[ed] his partners and employees with economic rewards and social status that most Tug Valley farmers were actually losing . . . a situation ripe for resentment, aggression and violence." In this feud, one man heightened the tension between the clans—a McCoy cousin, Perry Cline. For his time, Cline may have been the lightning in a jar. As tensions rose, governors of both Kentucky and West Virginia called in the national guard.

Did a Hatfield steal the McCoy pig? We don't know. But whether or not they did, it was the idea of "stolen"—perhaps symbolizing other losses—that took on a life of its own. At a time when land was a measure of status and when one's personal pride carried that of one's clan, hard-earned pride was lost, surely grieved, and might have seemed stolen.

From Local to National

In the graveyards of Tommy Ratliff and Roger Ford were also ancestors who had fought in a very bloody Civil War. While it ended over 150 years ago, commemorations of that war tell their own story. Of all the Civil War–based reenactments staged in 2023, more have taken place in the South (thirty-five), which lost, than in the North (twenty-three), which won. Apart from Abraham Lincoln, the characters most reenacted are from the South: General Robert E. Lee and Confederate President Jefferson Davis. Far more monuments, too, have been dedicated to the losers than to the winners, with some forty-five Confederate monuments going up after 2000.

In Kentucky, which fought with the North, there exist far more Confederate monuments than Union ones. Among them is a giant 351-foot obelisk dedicated to Jefferson Davis, who ironically called on the defeated South to "lay aside all rancor" after the war.

We might expect the survivors of the winners of this war to commemorate their victory more than we might expect the losers to commemorate their loss. But fifteen years after the Civil War, Wolfgang Schivelbusch noted in *The Culture of Defeat*, the South had "become the nineteenth-century equivalent of the Third World . . . more controlled by and dependent on the North than ever before." More powerful than the joy of victory, it seems, is the sting of humiliation, the need for healing, and the restlessness of lost pride.

From National to Global

Buried in the cemeteries Roger Ford took me to visit were also those felled during World War II. In what is the worst global conflict to date, "stolen" pride looms large. When Germany surrendered to the Allies in November 1918, concluding the First World War, many Germans were deeply shocked and shamed. Only a few months previously, their troops had been close to the gates of Paris and held vast amounts of land in Russia. Despite Allied advances, German newspapers were predicting triumphant victory. The kaiser had declared a holiday to celebrate German advances. So at the signing of the Treaty of Versailles, many Germans felt a hard-won victory was being precipitously and egregiously "stolen." The losses were enormous: 1.8 million were dead and more wounded. Due to rampant inflation, Germany's currency had become nearly worthless. Photographs show men pushing wheelbarrows filled with devalued German marks. In the realm of German pride, many Germans must have felt they were wheeling about loads of devalued identity.

The Treaty of Versailles forced Germany to accept complete blame for the war, to disarm, give up its colonies, and pay huge reparations, shaming and enraging Germans across the political spectrum. It was in the face of this shame that a strong personality rose to power who pinned blame on traitors, Jews, Gypsies, homosexuals, reds, all who were not of "true" German blood.

In *Shame: The Politics and Power of An Emotion,* David Keen explores the underlying role of shame in Germany, Sudan, Sierra Leone, and Iraq's histories. To be sure, in conflict there is scarcity, ethnic competition, economic decline, and a mix of all these, but always, Keen argues, there is shame, resistance to that shame, and a desire for revenge.

Not all losses are losses of pride nor are all wars caused by bankruptcies of pride. A need to redress humiliation can exist without leaders able to mobilize rage against it. Current leaders will come and go. But those buried in these graveyards who died in conflict offer us a guide to what can happen in the future when we ignore lost pride.

America Divided

Our present conflict is not between one clan, region, or nation and another. It is between what we can imagine as a domestic version of the global North and South. Within the U.S., rural regions like Pike

County, Kentucky, have become akin to a global "South," a periphery to an urban "North." Millions of the rural poor have moved to urban America. Many in the upper South—Kentucky, Tennessee—have moved to the industrial Midwest or North. And those who stay back see how they are seen.

Is relief coming to forgotten parts of America? At the time of this writing, 2024, the economic arrow points up. The nation's GDP, employment rate, and personal incomes are on the rise—especially in the red states. In 2023, Kentucky's governor announced over twenty-seven billion dollars of new investment creating forty-eight thousand new in-state jobs, most with above-average wages. But did the good news reach Pike County? It wasn't clear. Hopes have been pinned to what stood behind a large sign saying INDUSTRIAL PARK. Standing on the edge of a three-hundred-acre plot, was a complex hosting two businesses: one makes aluminum truck fuel tanks, while the other, housed in a corporate office building, is a concrete business. But nearly all the remaining lots stood empty and waiting. A Hampton Inn front desk clerk, pointing out the window, declared, "If I won the Powerball lottery, I'd build a car factory *right* on that mountain." She and her family had left Pikeville for Cleveland, where her husband had worked in a factory and become injured. The family had resettled with her parents in Pikeville where she now wished a factory job would follow him.

Still, even in Pike County, there was positive news. The largest source of new jobs in town was the Pikeville Medical Center and a nearby university, and in Kentucky's 5th Congressional District jobs existed mostly in services, sales, administration, with only 7 percent in construction and extraction. Pike County boasted a new whiskey distillery with plans to age Kentucky bourbon in a repurposed underground coal mine. A Pikeville waitress I met harvests local ginseng, for which there was high demand in China. Another entrepreneur grew mushrooms in an abandoned coal mine shaft. The largest solar farm in Kentucky, employing former miners and built on a former coal mine, was also going up some three miles from David Maynard's old home in Lovely, Martin County. While about a quarter of Kentucky's 5th Congressional District remained poor, the median household income had risen from almost $36,000 to $38,000 from 2020–2021, a 7.6 percent increase. And a Virginia farmer had gathered activists to plan a "Rural New Deal" featuring ways public investment could boost rural communities, give them more say, and so help heal the national divide.

In talking with those I came to know in KY-5, however, I heard little about federal dollars newly directed to rural areas. Talk was of the cost of gas, trans people entering girls' bathrooms, retribution for a "stolen" election, the failing memory of a Democratic president, and most of all, the eight thousand migrants crossing the border daily. I heard little, too, about the congressional Republican turndown of funds to strengthen border control. The country seemed at an impasse. Eleven months before the 2024 election, half of Americans expected violence to result.

How Big a Personality?

In my talks with the Trump supporters I came to know, the word "fascism" almost never came up. But when, in early 2024, I googled "fascism, Trump, 2024," over ten million hits appeared. Many of these articles were in response to things Trump said. Some commentors have advised taking Trump at his word. And what has he said? He has expressed uncritical praise for Russia's strong man, Vladimir Putin. If NATO allies don't pay more into their militaries, Trump said, Russia "can do whatever the hell they want." He has suggested that the nation's top military officer who served under him should be executed, that a state judge and attorney general prosecuting him should be arrested. He's said that illegal immigrants are "animals" and are "poisoning the blood of our country" and should be turned away if they don't accept "our religion." He has said that his opponents should be "rooted out." He has said that, once back in office, he will invoke the Insurrection Act and dispatch the military to political demonstrations. Trump's lawyers have argued that "once back in the White House he would be able to order a SEAL team to assassinate a political rival and be beyond criminal prosecution." When, at the age of forty-seven, Alexei Navalny—a rival of Russia's Vladimir Putin—died suddenly while imprisoned in a Siberian jail, most of the world saw a tyrant eliminating his rival. In speaking about it, Trump said nothing about Putin.

Were fascism to enter the mainstream of American life, experts tell us, it would not appear in a Nazi-like, swastika-brandishing uniform such as Matthew Heimbach wore on his Pikeville march. It would not come in the "back door" through the fringe, or not only in that way. It would come in the front door through the ballot box. The conditions for it to do this would have to be ripe: low popular trust in the federal government, active civic opposition, fascist allies abroad, and unanswered discontent mobilized by "a big personality."

What might prevent such an event, now with our current cast of characters or in the future with others? In the short run, a bid for calm deliberation, and in the long run, relief from the uneven burdens of the pride paradox. This we could do both by revising the American Dream and by equalizing access to it. In the common conception of the American Dream, the young must earn, own, or do "more" than their parents. But maybe more isn't better. As a goal, we could instead strive for ample provision, robust community, care for our fragile earth. We could reduce extremes of wealth, rebuild the middle, and strengthen the guardrails protecting our democracy. We can also reduce shame where it hits hardest by equalizing access to that goal.

In addition, we can watch out for—the 1-2-3-4-5 shame ritual before it leaps to lash-out. And from whichever side of the political wall, we can see the appeal of this shield as a symptom of a deeper problem that, standing together, we can fix.

Down the Side of the Mountain

Imagining solutions, I invited Tommy Ratliff and James Browning to join me on a visit to the renowned Kentucky writer and philosopher Wendell Berry, who lives with his wife, Tanya, on the Lanes Landing Farm, three and a half hours northwest of Pikeville. The farm is near Berry's birthplace. Like Tommy and James, Berry is a stayer. He is also a farmer and writer, having written—in pencil—fifty-two books at his desk in a cabin by the side of a lake. Among his most influential books is his 1977 title *The Unsettling of America: Culture and Agriculture.* Seen simultaneously as a throwback, a visionary, and a critical commentator on modern life, Berry raises big questions about pride.

Berry, a tall, balding, lean, spritely man of eighty-two, sat us around his kitchen table. He composed his thoughts as he went along, as if slowly plowing a field. "We are living on the far side of a broken connection between humans and nature," he said. "It's an irony," Tommy commented. "The people who actually live closest to nature, like us, don't value it very much. In the stream in back of our house, my wife and I see beer bottles, soda cans, Styrofoam cups, plastic bags, as if people are throwing them onto nothing. And for their part, companies make stuff disposable so they can sell you more of it to throw away. We live out here in the country but we have taken on an urban and industrial view of ourselves."

City people don't know where their food comes from, Berry reminded us, and most Americans don't know where their energy comes from, Roger Ford had complained—in both cases, from the land.

In the car returning to Pikeville, Tommy, James, and I continued the conversation about broken connections between the American Dream and hopes of achieving it—between the salary of an American CEO and that of a median worker (now 399 to 1), between the rising temperature of the earth and our efforts to lower it, between government and people, between left and right, between the proud and the shamed.

In coal country, James said, "there's a broken connection between the top of some mountains and their bottoms." Indeed, as we drove home, we were passing some of the three hundred Kentucky mountains whose tops had been blasted off in a process called mountaintop removal. Tons of soil and rock are then bulldozed down the sides. It required the labor of few. It contaminates water, disrupts plant and animal life. It makes valleys vulnerable to flooding, and creates acres of bare rubble which become graveyards of their own. To protest this, Wendell Berry once sat with fellow activists in the office of the Kentucky governor to oppose it. While coal officials speak respectfully of mountaintop "development," nearly all of those I came to know pointed to their decapitated mountains with shaking heads and sorrowful faces.

There is a name for the mountaintop soil the machines dump over the side: overburden. The valuable stuff, in this view, is the coal inside the mountain. The throwaway stuff is all the life above it—the nutrient-rich earth that once held the rain, and nourished plants and fed the animals.

Many workers in America have come to feel like a human overburden. Like nature itself, such workers show the scars of an economic machine that has disrupted the ecology of their lives. Indeed, a whole strata of workers across America have felt themselves bulldozed off the mountain, their sense of purpose and pride crushed.

James had told me about a man at New Beginnings who had come to feel himself part of an overburden. He had been a coal miner and had suffered an accident on the job, had taken OxyContin to ease his pain, then became hooked on it. The man had lost his job, lost his marriage and custody of his children, and had only recently found his way into recovery. He watched Donald Trump give a stump speech in 2016, and told James, "When Trump told us he was going to bring back coal, I knew he was lying. But I felt like he saw who I was."

"Saw who I was": The first task in healing our growing divide is, it seems, to recognize the faces of the overburden. And there are many—inner-city

Blacks, small farmers, rustbelt low-wage workers, truck drivers vulnerable to automation, retail and service workers soon to be replaced by AI, underpaid teachers, childcare workers, attendants in homeless shelters, and the homeless, to name a few. For all Americans, the job ahead is to repair damages done, and expand access to a re-envisioned American Dream.

But the second task is to be on alert to the serious possibility of a lightning strike at American democracy itself. For a human overburden can come to feel distress, which, once prospected, can be set by political leaders to frightening purpose, and injury to many others. And such leaders can create a mortal challenge to the honest vote, the fair election, the government official who is loyal to a public office and not a given leader—all of which constitute America's own most precious resource.

There are guides among us who model a way out of our impasse. Tommy Ratliff once felt like human overburden, useless, broken, as his father before him may have felt. He had listened hopelessly, angrily at the guest lecture that described how to open a bank account, save for a future child's education, to arrive at a distant American Dream. Head on, Tommy faced the pride paradox, turning his shame inward. Then in his recovery, sitting outside on a chair, he noticed in a humble line of ants a carrier ant: a worker, a helper, driven by instinct but relevant to the present-day dilemma of highly evolved and wrongly shamed human beings like himself.

After his own ordeal, Tommy had set to work treating recovering addicts and sharing with them his "carrier ant" revelation. He counseled them on how to avoid retreating into shame or lashing out in blame, and how to move steadily, thoughtfully, forward. After a while, he was selected "Best Counselor," receiving more gifts than others from graduating clients. "I volunteered to drive groups of prisoners outside the grounds on Saturdays to visit Fairyland," he told me. This was the forest behind his old home where he had once escaped drunken quarrels at home to join his pal, poke about the stream, and listen to the orchestral frogs. "The guys love coming here, and we have great talks, walking out there among the trees, about how they got to where they were. I'm thinking of getting some of them to help me build tree houses for kids in the neighborhood. They'd like that. They're very handy.

"A hillbilly can make anything."

Goodbyes

By the end of 2023, the political landscape of eastern Kentucky seemed splintered. Andy Beshear, a Democrat, was elected to a second term as governor of Kentucky, a state that had voted 60 percent in 2016 and 2022 for Donald Trump and whose state legislature was in Republican hands. Still, although Pike County was not one of them, Beshear won seventeen of its eighty-five rural counties. In nearby Corbin, the town bearing the history of the 1919 forced exodus of African American railroad workers and once a "sundown town," had given birth to the "Sunup Initiative." There's "work ahead," an organizer told me, "but we're on it." Meanwhile, one central Kentucky county banned a hundred books from its school libraries, including a graphic novel based on *The Diary of Anne Frank*.

Matthew Heimbach:

To support his family, he was earning $23 an hour canvassing suburban Republican voters in Lexington, Indiana, for the Koch-funded Americans for Prosperity, a group that favored the Republican Nikki Haley as a 2024 presidential candidate. "They don't train or supervise us. It's a Republican Astroturf operation," Matthew reported, referring to corporate or political public opinion campaigns that are designed to appear as grassroots organizing efforts. "For the 'Libre Initiative' they pick up unemployed guys from the Walmart parking lot to leaflet Spanish neighborhoods." The Democratic canvassers pay $2 an hour less.

"I knock on the doors of retired people, homemakers, some home-based workers in their forties," Matthew explained. "A lot of them listen to local Christian radio and homeschool their kids because they think the public schools are satanic. A surprising number are apocalyptic; some are preppers. Canvassing these neighborhoods makes me feel like a moderate. These suburban retirees remind me of the guys I marched with in Pikeville."

As for the future, Matthew planned to move his family to Russia. "I love Russia and I love Putin," he said, "so I looked into moving there." "I got a job offer to teach English in a private school in Moscow, $20,000 a year. The guy I talked to said my background doesn't matter. They're offering to pay for two months of Russian lessons for my kids [Matthew has legal custody of his two young sons] and will pay for the kids' private school. They'll live like oligarch's kids."

Meanwhile, in another talk, Matthew said, "I've been thinking a lot about my father. He was adopted, and his dad died at ten, and he grew up a lonely man. I was trying to relate to him through history, I think." "Have you ever thought about some therapy?" I asked Matthew. "Yes, I tried it once, but the problem was I'm smarter than they are."

Alex Hughes:

For a while in Louisville, to help unburden the family from a "mountain of debt," Alex's Dominican wife, Margaret, took a 6:00 p.m. to 4:00 a.m. night shift at an auto plant and caught up on sleep in the first part of the day. For a while, he said philosophically, "I was Mr. Mom, did the laundry, and helped the kids with their Zoom classwork."

But now earning $150,000 at a new job, the debt was gone, though the desire to earn more wasn't. "We live near the race track and I heard gun shots in our neighborhood. I'd like to buy a house in a safer neighborhood, and that will take more money. He's still concerned about his beloved childhood buddy Harry, now worried the country was headed for a civil war.

Wyatt Blair:

Having graduated from Southgate, the KKK loyalist got time off his prison sentence, but within the year he was back in jail on a different minor charge.

David and Shea Maynard:

Shea's dad was now in a nursing home, and David and Shea have moved from their trailer in Prestonsburg to a cozy house thirteen minutes from David's mom and stepfather, who kindly drove over with a truck to help them move. As for David, Shea told me proudly, "his monster art is getting more hits on his TikTok site."

Tommy and Melanie Ratliff:

In July 2022, Tommy and Melanie suffered from the heavy regional flooding, which cost them thirty feet of their backyard, washed away by an adjoining creek. Timbering, mining and "overburden" had weakened the earth's resistance to the 2022 storm and others to follow, washing out bridges, roads, and uninsured hillside trailers and homes. Melanie Ratliff's Facebook page filled with complaints about a cartoon in the *Lexington Herald-Leader* which readers felt added hillbilly-shaming to tragedy. The cartoon depicted a family and dog trapped on the roof of their nearly submerged home, the man kneeling in a cap, arms outstretched in an apparent call for help, his frazzle-haired wife and baby crouched beside him. The caption read, "When it rains . . . it pours on poor people." But to Melanie and her Facebook friends, pride itself was being washed away.

Roger Ford:

The pro-coal organizer of the 2020 pro-Trump vehicle parade told me in a tired voice, "I'm not a climate denier. But I am into renewables in order to make money, get the U.S. energy independent, and to keep coal alive by mixing it with other things." As the CEO of the start-up Eureka Energy Corporation, he was trying to orchestrate a green energy plan. He had started the National Hemp Growers Co-operative. "We have sixty members who need an assured market for their hemp. We add hemp to municipal biomass and forest refuse and make a methane-rich sludge from which we extract natural gas. This we get processed and plan to sell to Delta Airlines to add to its fuel line. I also applied for a federal permit"—made available under President Obama—"to build a 20-megawatt solar farm on a reclaimed mining site. To handle grass growing around the panels, I'll get goats to eat it, and at the end of the year sell the goat meat to Muslims who observe halal—it's their bacon and sausage. The goats are free labor."

By early 2024 he'd visited seven European countries, scouting out companies interested in forming a joint venture. He'd formed Memoranda of Understanding with two Ukrainian companies. He had also visited Hungary, whose political policies of illiberal democracy he admired.

James Browning:

The last time we talked, James said, "After our visit with Wendell Berry, I thought about getting a vegetable garden going out back so the guys could grow their own food. It could help them to nurture plants." In the dark times of his addiction, James became divorced and his wife moved away to be near her sister, taking the children. Since his recovery, James had happily remarried a fellow addiction counselor and they'd moved with their children into a modest duplex in a charming development in an expanse of well-kept green lawn and flower beds. James was counting his blessings. "Four years ago today, I was high, homeless, and very alone. Today I am four years clean. I'm on step eight in my twelve-step program. Megan and I just celebrated our second anniversary and the idea of Recovery Climbs is in development." James smiled. "I can hardly believe it, but earlier today, my boss called me into his office, asked me to sit down, and told me I'd been doing a good job. He said I was helpful and had added good ideas to the program. Then"—James paused to gather himself. "He offered me the job as director of New Beginnings."

Acknowledgments

I owe so many thanks. First, thanks go to all those in Kentucky's 5th Congressional District who generously shared their time, lives, and perspectives in the faith that that something good would come of it, my heartfelt thanks. I am especially grateful to Reverend Rob Musick, not only for sharing his story but for introducing me to many people, and emailing me when Oliver Anthony's song "Rich Man from Beyond Richmond" hit the top of the charts. To Mayor Andrew Scott for getting me up to speed on the history and culture of eastern Kentucky. Thanks to sociologist Tom Ratliff, then at the University of Pikeville, for an early tour through Marrowbone, Rockhouse, Lookout, and Poor Bottom on the way to his grandparents' farm outside Prestonsburg, and to Roger Ford for visits to small hillside graveyards and the Big Branch Old Regular Baptist Church at Brushy Creek. Thanks also to Wendell Berry for kindly receiving Tommy Ratliff, James Browning, and myself at his farm in Port Royal, Kentucky.

When COVID hit in 2020, travel became unsafe and public accommodations closed but I kept in touch with people by Zoom. Tommy Ratliff became my on-the-ground "eyes and ears," alerting me to events and checking out such things as a convention for a Republican candidate for governor, occupants of the Kentucky Enterprise Industrial Park, and the location of Hatfield and McCoy graves inside the Dils Cemetery.

Back in Berkeley, thanks go to Tyler Leeds for early research on the economics of the region, and to Natalie Pasquinelli for her insightful analysis of legal testimonies of January 6 defendants from Kentucky, and her later research on many issues including shame and blame, and work, income, and benefits across time and regions.

Throughout the research and writing of this book, huge thanks for insight, carefulness, patience, and good humor to Kirstin Krusell. Especially helpful were her analyses of rural "prison gerrymandering," Purdue Pharma's focused sales of OxyContin, and regulation-averse states. Kirstin also conducted a superb analysis of dozens of surveys conducted by the American National Election Studies and the Cooperative Election Study (formerly the Cooperative Congressional Election Study) at Harvard University, which tested out ideas about the "empathy bridge" reported on in chapter 15 and elaborated on in appendix 2.

Once I had a draft of the manuscript, I gratefully turned to my dear and gifted friends. Elizabeth and Chuck Farnsworth gave me a loving and bracing read on a wandering early draft. For help on a later draft, thanks to Allison Pugh for her helpful insights. Thanks always to Ann Swidler for her careful read and for long breakfast conversations over the years at Saul's exploring the mysteries of culture, so elucidating I often bring pen and paper. And for a vital last-minute series of reads and rereads, my deepest gratitude to Deirdre English for her utterly masterful read of the manuscript's structural "sags," "tilts," and "feel," and who stuck with me so faithfully through anxious last minute redrafts.

Thanks also go to Claude Fischer and Mike Hout, buddy consultants on matters of empirical scholarship. To Anthony Flaccavento and Erica Etelson and fellow members of the Rural Urban Bridge Initiative for sharing ideas about healing the rural-urban split and bringing about a "rural new deal." Thanks to Hans Stahlschmidt, a friend and psychotherapist, for a conversation about the relationship of politics to mourning.

At The New Press, I'm blessed with a fantastic team, with special thanks to the ever-resilient Gia Gonzales and Jay Gupta, and further help from Susan Warga, Katherine Porter, Daniel Chasin William Fowkes, and Tate Schneider; and for publicity, many thanks to Derek Warker and Emily Lavelle. And a great big hug goes to Ellen Adler, editor-publisher queen of The New Press, who has seen me through *Strangers in Their Own Land* and now *Stolen Pride* with a magical combination of professional know-how, humane outlook, and great human warmth. Thanks also to Joan Cole, to whom I dedicate this book, for her capacity to share her wonder at very small things as well as large.

Most of all, daily thanks to my husband Adam who lived and breathed this book with me, and whose brilliant, acrobatic red pen marked, over multiple drafts, page-long arrows, cross-outs, daring paragraph-moves, and large, loopy question marks just where I imagined that I finally had things right—the ultimate gift of love.

Appendix 1:
Research

Research for this book began with a surprising phone call, which opened the door to the first of three stages of exploratory research on which this book is based. The call was from Congressman Ro Khanna of California's 17th District. He was a Democratic congressman who had "crossed the aisle" to talk to Republican Hal Rogers, who represented Kentucky's 5th Congressional District. One district was urban, the other rural. One was relatively rich, the other poor. The median household income in 2021 for CA-17 was $157,049, while for KY-5 it was $37,910. Khanna's district had plenty of good jobs; Roger's district had few. Khanna's idea was to train and hire unemployed Kentucky coal miners to code software and create a "Silicon Holler in rural Kentucky." Was I interested? Yes, I was.

So I flew to Louisville, Kentucky, to interview graduates of InterApt's coding training center, focusing on those from eastern Kentucky who were now working from home. We met at lunch places such as Billy Ray's in Prestonsburg, Frosty Freeze in Hindman, and—since one young man told me, "You won't find Hueyville on Google Maps"—at a gas station off a freeway that sold snuff. In 2018, I wrote an op-ed for the *New York Times* on the program, and two successful graduates of the program followed me into this book.

I realized I was getting to know people in the whitest and second-poorest congressional district in the country, a region that had rapidly shifted from the Democratic Party to the Republican Party, even as the split between regions, demographics, and parties was growing nationwide. And so I decided to begin an exploratory study of residents in one of the region's hubs, the city of Pikeville, and in surrounding Pike County.

Talking with residents, I had the impression of a perfect storm—the decline of coal (its main source of jobs), the rise of a drug crisis, and a white nationalist march about to hit town. I wanted to learn about local citizens' feelings about the march and politics in general.

So I began to gather what sociologists call a "purposive sample" of residents in Pike County and, to some degree, in the larger 5th Congressional District of eastern Kentucky. In contrast to an opinion poll researcher's random sample (in which the aim is to hold brief encounters with many people determined to be typical), I searched out people in one town, at the top and bottom in social status, and on one side or the other of the political spectrum with the aim of exploring their "pride biographies," with the goal of getting to know people as well as I could.

For the "top," I interviewed leaders—a former governor of Kentucky, the mayor and assistant mayor of Pikeville, the mayor of Coal Run, Republican and Democratic members of the state house of representatives, and the president of a local university. To represent the "bottom," I interviewed felons and recovering addicts. I also interviewed police officers, social workers, counselors, teachers, students, a judge, several business owners, ministers, prisoners, prison personnel, an electrician, a pipe fitter, a road worker, and a grass cutter, and I had long conversations with a hotel desk clerk, a waitress who together with her husband harvested ginseng to sell to China, and a party of friendly retired businesspeople who bought me a beer at a street fair in the summer of 2023. I talked to all of the principal figures in this book half a dozen or more times, in sessions that often lasted several hours.

For every interview, I inquired about the individual's close and distant family and friends so as to learn about each person's circle. During COVID, when I couldn't visit Pikeville from 2020 to 2023, I conducted many Zoom-based "check-ins." Later, I returned to Pikeville for several weeks to visit my principal subjects again. Over six years I interviewed eighty Kentuckians, some sixty-five of them in eastern Kentucky, congressional district KY-5.

I subscribed to the *Appalachian News-Express* and the *Courier-Journal*, through which I followed city council meetings, arrests, and obituaries. I read Appalachian history, listened to a great deal of Kentucky music, especially the songs of Pikeville-born Dwight Yoakam, and explored humor by, and directed at, hillbillies. I tried to see this Appalachian world—and the world outside it—through the lens of pride and shame.

I took many field trips. One was with the Paintsville-born sociologist and criminologist Professor Thomas N. Ratliff (not to be confused with Tommy Ratliff, the subject of chapter 9) who was then teaching at the University of Pikeville. I invited him to give a talk at the Berkeley Center for Right Wing Studies, and when I next visited Pikeville, he kindly took me on an extraordinary field trip to a known KKK Klavern hideout.

During COVID, when it was unsafe to travel, I asked Tommy Ratliff after I had interviewed him if he would also act as my "eyes and ears" in Pike County and work as my research assistant, reporting on such things as the layout of the Dils Cemetery, the business center, and a gubernatorial rally.

I traveled to western Kentucky with Tommy Ratliff and James Browning, two subjects of this book, to visit the Kentucky-based philosopher Wendell Berry. Mayor Andrew Scott kindly drove me to see the possible good use of mountain-blasting, to take pictures of a trainload of coal (production having risen in 2023 under President Biden); he gave me the present of a beautiful large block of coal. Roger Ford also invited me on an all-day trip to visit the small open-doored churches and graveyards on the hillside hollers where his ancestors had settled, and where his relatives still lived. I attended services at a small Baptist church, and interviewed the director—a documentarian and novelist, and the artist who designed "No Hate in the Holler" T-shirts—at the highly innovative nonprofit, AppleShop, in nearby Whitesburg.

As for the timing of my interviews, although I started talking to people in the area before the white nationalist march in 2017, I conducted most of my interviews after it.

In the third phase of my research, I worked with my research assistant, a PhD student in sociology at UC Berkeley, Kirstin Krusell, to see if upper and lower decks of an empathy bridge could be found in a national study as described in Appendix 2.

Appendix 2:
Upper and Lower Decks on
the Empathy Bridge

Rob Musick and James Browning were two men in one town, one region, one nation. They were not trained mediators, members of organizations devoted to racial or political harmony, nor had they signed grand treaties. They were regular people I met whose lives expressed what seemed to me unusual empathy, foot travelers across an empathy bridge. Did their personal journeys reflect a pattern true for other Americans? Kirstin Krusell, a doctoral student in Sociology at Berkeley, and I set out to examine the evidence.

In the 2020 American National Election Studies, we focused on the 5,963 respondents who identified themselves as "white, non-Hispanic." Kirstin created a large series of cross-tabulations in an effort to understand which circumstances for whites were correlated with answers to questions suggesting empathy for Blacks.

We began by analyzing responses to the statement "Generations of slavery and discrimination have created conditions that make it difficult for Blacks to work their way out of the lower class." The possible responses were "Strongly agree" "Somewhat agree," "Neither agree nor disagree," "Somewhat disagree," and "Strongly disagree." We collapsed the "strongly" and "somewhat" responses into a binary Agree/Disagree. We interpreted the answer "Agree" both as a sign of the individual's understanding of history, and as a gesture of empathy with those impacted by it. Given this, who, we wondered, were the empathizers? What social conditions might have fostered their empathy?

There seemed to be an upper and lower deck to the empathy bridge extending from whites to Blacks. On its "upper deck," so to speak, we found it was the most well-off ($150,000 annual household income and more) and highly educated (bachelor's degree or higher) whites who expressed the most empathy for Blacks (68 percent). The very least empathetic, at 26 percent, were the poorly educated rich (i.e., those in the highest income bracket with a high school education or less).

What seemed to put people on the "lower deck" of the empathy bridge was the experience of insecurity. "How worried are you about losing your job in the near future?" whites were asked. Combining both rural and urban respondents, 62 percent of those who felt the most precarious and 46 percent of those who felt the least precarious agreed with this statement sympathetic to Blacks. Among urban whites, the gap was steepest; 76 percent of the least secure whites (contrasted with 58 percent of the most secure whites) expressed empathy for poor Blacks (an 18-point margin). Among rural whites, precarity seems to have less of an effect on empathy: 38 percent of the most precarious but 29 percent of the least precarious white Americans expressed empathy (a 9-point margin).

A statement about government aid to Blacks revealed a stronger link between biographical journeys and viewpoint. The statement read: "Some people feel that the government in Washington should make every effort to improve the social and economic position of Blacks. Suppose these people are at one end of a scale at point 1. Others feel that the government should not make any special effort to help Blacks because they should help themselves. Suppose those people are at the other end, at point 7. And of course, some people have opinions somewhere in between." The statement said nothing of the needs or history of Blacks; it simply tested a person's desire for—and tacit belief in—government help. That is, the statement was aimed at both a person's understanding of a need and their feelings about the government's obligation to meet it.

Most likely to favor such government help, we found, were the most educated and economically better off, suggesting an "upper deck." The richest favored help more than the poorest by a 10-point margin: 48 percent to 38 percent. The most educated favored help more than the least educated by a 24-point margin: 51 percent to 27 percent. To be sure, a person can be highly educated and rich without having "risen up," and each person rises up relative to where they began. Still, there may be more Rob Musicks out there.

We also found trace elements of the "lower deck" empathy path. Asked "How worried are you about losing your job in the near future?" those whites who said "extremely worried"—that is, those who felt the most precarious—were also the most likely to favor helping out Black people. It was the poorest whites (with household income of $30,000 or less) and most fearful of losing their own jobs who most favored help for Blacks: 65 percent. Among the non-precarious rich, only 45 percent did. Researchers have found that cross-race empathy contracts in hard times and expands in good times, as mentioned earlier. But in addition to this, we report trace elements of certain underlying life logics—at the top, *noblesse oblige*, and at the bottom, *together in a shaky boat*. While our measures are crude and our findings partial, we invite other scholars to explore how life circumstances impact empathy.

Notes

Chapter 1

3 *ten were hospitalized with stab wounds* Eric M. Johnson and Justin Madden, "Clash at California Capitol Leaves at Least 10 Injured," Reuters, June 26, 2016.

3 *Kentucky's 5th Congressional District* KY-5 is the whitest congressional district in the country. In the United States as a whole in 2022, 59 percent of people are non-Hispanic white, while in KY-5's Pike County (where much of the action in this book takes place) 97 percent are. In the United States, 14 percent of people are African American, while less than 1 percent in Pike County are. U.S. Census Bureau QuickFacts, "Pike County, Kentucky," www.census.gov/quickfacts/fact/table/pikecountykentucky,US/PST04 5222, accessed March 1, 2023.

4 *the county had now become* U.S. Census Bureau, American Community Survey (ACS), 1-Year Geographic Comparison Tables, 2021, www.census .gov/acs/www/data/data-tables-and-tools/geographic-comparison-tables/. For a ranking of congressional districts by percentage of households in poverty, see Table GCT1701. For a ranking by percentage of residents who are white non-Hispanic, see Table GCT0209.

4 *such groups had marched in Seattle* Benjamin Woodard, "How the Shooting at the UW Protest of Milo Yiannopoulos Unfolded," *Seattle Times*, January 23, 2017.

4 *In Minneapolis, a white man shot* CBS News, "Minnesota Man Who Shot 5 Black Lives Matter Protestors Found Guilty," February 3, 2017.

4 *The white supremacist Knights Party* Lucian K. Truscott IV, "Slow Motion Civil War," *Salon*, November 17, 2018.

4 *$800,000 in damages* Emily Deruy, Thomas Peele, and David Debolt, "Milo Yiannopoulos' 15 Minutes in Berkeley Cost University $800,000," *Mercury News*, September 24, 2017.

4 *that number had risen to 954* Southern Poverty Law Center, Hate Map, www.splcenter.org/hate-map?year=2000. See also Peter Martinez, "Hate Groups Hit New High, Up 30 Percent in Last 4 years, Southern Poverty Law Center Says," CBS News, February 20, 2019.

4 *Kentucky alone was headquarters* Southern Poverty Law Center, Hate Map: Kentucky, www.splcenter.org/hate-map?year=2017&state=KY.

4 *Second Amendment sanctuary* Jonathan Bullington, "How a College Student, a Felon and 90K Followers Turned Kentucky into a Gun Sanctuary," *Courier Journal*, February 14, 2020.

4 *eligible to openly carry fully loaded guns* The Giffords Law Center to Prevent Gun Violence tracks gun laws by policy and state. It rates Kentucky as an F on its gun safety law scorecard. There are currently no laws in Kentucky prohibiting or regulating either concealed or open carry of firearms for those at least twenty-one years of age and eligible to carry a firearm. Further, there are no laws regulating assault weapons or high-capacity ammunition magazines. See "Kentucky Gun Laws," updated January 5, 2023, www.giffords.org/lawcenter/gun-laws/states/kentucky/. For an overview of federal and state requirements for purchase and possession of firearms, see "Firearm Prohibitions in Kentucky," Giffords Law Center, updated January 5, 2023, www.giffords.org/lawcenter/state-laws/firearm-prohibitions-in-kentucky/.

5 *As a "stand your ground" state* Giffords Law Center to Prevent Gun Violence, "Stand Your Ground in Kentucky," updated January 5, 2023, www.giffords.org/lawcenter/state-laws/stand-your-ground-in-kentucky/.

5 *And since 2010, gun deaths* "Kentucky Gun Deaths: 2019," Educational Fund to Stop Gun Violence, www.efsgv.org/state/kentucky/.

5 *anger at "the other side"* See Pew Research Center, "The Partisan Divide on Political Values Grows Even Wider," October 5, 2017, 1.

6 *In her research on preppers* Kirstin Krusell, "Political Subjectivity in a Risk Society: A Comparative Ethnography of Left- and Right-Wing Doomsday Preppers," dissertation prospectus, Department of Sociology, UC Berkeley, January 4, 2023. See, for example, Michael F. Mills, "Obamageddon: Fear, the Right, and the Rise of 'Doomsday' Prepping in Obama's America," *Journal of American Studies* 55, no. 2 (2019): 1–30, and Nellie Bowles, "I Used to Make Fun of Silicon Valley Preppers. Then I Became One," *New York Times*, April 24, 2020. While data on the political affiliation of preppers is not available, preppers are not more likely to be in either red or blue states. See Dr. Chris Ellis's research in John Ramey,

"New Statistics on Modern Prepper Demographics from FEMA and Cornell," *The Prepared*, August 4, 2021, www.theprepared.com/blog /new-statistics-on-modern-prepper-demographics-from-fema-and-cor nell-university/.

6 *An idea had gripped the American Right* Jon Greenberg, "Most Republicans Still Falsely Believe Trump's Stolen Election Claims," Politifact, June 14, 2022.

6 *But Trump declared it "stolen"* Domenico Montanaro, "Most Republicans Would Vote for Trump Even If He's Convicted of a Crime, Poll Finds," NPR, April 25, 2023. See also Ruth Igielnik and Maggie Haberman, "More Republicans Say Trump Committed Crimes. But They Still Support Him," *New York Times*, August 1, 2023.

6 *I wanted to move my focus* Combining the states of the old Confederacy with those in greater Appalachia, we have about 40 percent of those who voted for Donald Trump. The proportion of Trump voters in the thirteen states of greater Appalachia and the former Confederacy (Kentucky, Tennessee, West Virginia, Texas, South Carolina, Mississippi, Florida, Alabama, Georgia, Louisiana, Virginia, Arkansas, North Carolina) was calculated using data from the Federal Election Commission, "Federal Elections 2020: Election Results for the US President, the US Senate and the US House of Representatives," October 2022, 25–38, www.fec.gov /resources/cms-content/documents/federalelections2020.pdf.

6 *Each lent a different tone* Colin Woodard, *American Nations: A History of the Eleven Rival Regional Cultures of North America* (New York: Penguin Books, 2011), chap. 9.

6 *According to a 2023 analysis by the Cook Political Report* Paul Kane, "New Report Outlines Deep Political Polarization's Slow and Steady March," *Washington Post*, April 8, 2023. See also Cook Political Report, "The Cook Partisan Voting Index," www.cookpolitical.com/cook-pvi.

6 *"gave Donald Trump two of his five"* Kane, "New Report."

6 *80 percent of KY-5* In 1996, both the state of Kentucky and the eastern part of it (5th Congressional District) voted for Clinton. For the state it was 46 percent (Clinton) to 45 percent (Dole). Comparing the presidential vote in KY-5 in 1996 with that in 2000 is not straightforward, because the counties that make up the district change with each census; in 1996 KY-5 had thirty-eight counties, and in 2020 it had thirty. So Kirstin Krusell downloaded the Kentucky Board of Elections 1996 results for each county and then used the ICPSR database to "crosswalk" counties and congressional districts over time. If we look at the 1996 voting outcomes in the

thirty counties that now constitute KY-5, the vote would be 47 percent Clinton to 43 percent Dole. Whether we compare by county or district, the finding is the same: Democratic then, Republican now. See Andreas Ferrara, Patrick A. Testa, and Liyang Zhou, "New Area- and Population-Based Geographic Crosswalks for U.S. Counties and Congressional Districts, 1790–2020," Inter-University Consortium for Political and Social Research, October 19, 2022, https://doi.org/10.3886/E150101V4.

7 *last of all the nation's* Emma Roller and National Journal, "This Congressional District Ranks Dead Last for Well-Being." *The Atlantic*, March 25, 2014. https://www.theatlantic.com/politics/archive/2014/03 /this-congressional-district-ranks-dead-last-for-well-being/455913/.

7 *36 percent of KY-5 residents* U.S. Census Counts. https://datausa.io/profile /geo/congressional-district-5-ky.

7 *During COVID, nearly half* Following dramatic increases in enrollment due to COVID-era policy changes, as of August 2023 46.6 percent of Pike County residents were enrolled in Medicaid. See "Monthly Medicaid Counts by County," Department for Medicaid Services, Kentucky Cabinet for Health and Family Services, https://www.chfs.ky.gov/agen cies/dms/dafm/Pages/statistics.aspx.

The state of Kentucky relies heavily on federal funds too. During fiscal year 2019, prior to the pandemic, Kentucky received 39.8 percent of its state revenue from federal funds. Rebecca Thiess, Justin Theal, and Brakeyshia Samms, "2019 Federal Share of State Revenue Remains Stable," Pew Trusts, December 22, 2021.

In fiscal year 2021, that figure reached 46.2 percent, driven in part by federal pandemic aid. Rebecca Thiess, Justin Theal, and Kate Watkins, "Pandemic Aid Lifts Federal Share of State Budgets to New Highs," Pew Trusts, August 28, 2023.

7 *in 2020, 58 percent* CNN Politics, "Exit Polls," 2020, www.cnn.com /election/2020/exit-polls/president/national-results/46.

7 *Blue-collar men have proved most vulnerable* See Helena Norberg-Hodge, *Ancient Futures*, 3rd ed. (White River Junction, VT: Chelsea Green, 2016). See also Anne Case and Angus Deaton, *Diseases of Despair and the Future of Capitalism* (Princeton, NJ: Princeton University Press, 2020).

8 *Since the 1970s, red states* Robert Samuels, "Americans in Search of a Better Life Are Moving from Blue States to Red States—but It Could Backfire Big Time," *Forbes*, May 25, 2023. See also Rachael Kleinfeld, "Polarization, Democracy, and Political Violence in the US: What the

Research Says," Working Paper, Carnegie Endowment for International Peace, September 5, 2023, 29, www.carnegieendowment.org/2023/09/05 /polarization-democracy-and-political-violence-in-united-states-what-re search-says-pub-90457. In recovery from the 2008 depression, I'm using the difference between urban and rural as a proxy for the distinction between red and blue areas of the country.

8 *Pikeville seemed like an epicenter* For an excellent account, see Katherine J. Cramer, *The Politics of Resentment: Rural Consciousness in Wisconsin and the Rise of Scott Walker* (Chicago: University of Chicago Press, 2016).

8 *Only with ambivalence* At least since the nineteenth century, America has long harbored a "paranoid streak," as the historian Richard Hofstadter noted, citing the nineteenth-century Know Nothing Party and the John Birch Society of the 1960s. See Richard Hofstadter, "The Paranoid Style in American Politics," *Harper's Magazine*, November 1964, 77–86. Today this paranoia is apparent in the rise of the QAnon movement, which believes the "government, media, and financial worlds in the U.S. are controlled by a group of Satan-worshipping pedophiles who run a global child sex-trafficking operation." See PRRI, "The Persistence of QAnon in the Post-Trump Era: An Analysis of Who Believes the Conspiracies," February 24, 2022.

8 *In 1964, 77 percent* Pew Research Center, "Public Trust in Government: 1958–2022," June 6, 2022, www.pewresearch.org/politics/2022/06/06 /public-trust-in-government-1958-2022/. Here Pew combines data from various sources, with figures from 1977 coming from the American National Election Studies.

8 *But by 2023, this had shrunk* Pew Research Center, "Public Trust in Government."

8 *Central to Ronald Reagan's message* Nicholas F. Jacobs and Daniel M. Shae, *The Rural Voter: The Politics of Place and the Disuniting of America* (New York: Columbia University Press, 2023), 98.

8 *Over half of Republicans* Pew Research Center, "Americans' Views of Government: Decades of Distrust, Enduring Support for Its Role," June 6, 2022, www.pewresearch.org/politics/2022/06/06/americans-views-of-gov ernment-decades-of-distrust-enduring-support-for-its-role/.

9 *Democracy Fund Voter Study Group* Lee Drutman, Larry Diamond, and Joe Goldman, "Follow the Leader: Exploring American Support for Democracy and Authoritarianism," Democracy Fund Voter Study Group,

March 2018, www.voterstudygroup.org/publication/follow-the-leader. Another survey showed that 19 percent of Americans agreed strongly or very strongly that "it is more important for the United States to have a strong leader than a democracy." An additional 23 percent said they "somewhat" agreed. See Gary Winetemute, Sonia Robinson, Andrew Crawford, Julia P. Schleimer, Amy Barnhorst, Vicka Chaplin, Daniel Tancredi, Elizabeth A. Tomsich, and Veronica A. Pear, "Views of American Democracy and Society and Support for Political Violence: First Report from a Nationwide Population-Representative Study," UC Davis Violence Prevention Research Program, July 2022, 26, www.medrxiv.org/content/1 0.1101/2022.07.15.22277693v1.full.pdf.

9 *a 2017 global Pew survey* See Drutman, Diamond, and Goldman, "Follow the Leader," 18.

9 *27 percent of those on the right* The 24 percent overall figure is drawn from Drutman, Diamond, and Goldman, "Follow the Leader," 12. The right (27 percent) and left (14 percent) figures are from a 2017 Pew study, which puts the overall figure at 22 percent. The Pew study also reports figures for the center (20 percent). Therefore, the right and left figures do not average to 24 percent. Richard Wike, Katie Simmons, Bruce Stokes, and Janell Fetterolf, "Globally, Broad Support for Representative and Direct Democracy," Pew Research Center, October 16, 2017, 10, 27.

9 *"He's now president for life"* "Trump Says Maybe U.S. Will Have President for Life Someday," *PBS NewsHour*, March 4, 2018, https://www .pbs.org/newshour/politics/trump-says-maybe-u-s-will-have-a-president -for-life-someday. See Eva Illouz and Avital Sicron, *The Emotional Life of Populism: How Fear, Disgust, Resentment, and Love Undermine Democracy* (Hoboken, NJ: Polity Press, 2023), which argues that institutions and their underlying principles matter less, the personality of the leader more. Populism also elevates the idea of pride and exclusion based on national status, religion, or race.

9 *a post–World War II wave* Cas Mudde, "The Far-Right Threat in the United States: A European Perspective," *Annals of the American Academy of Political and Social Science* (January 2022): 101–115. Also see Cas Mudde, *The Far Right Today* (Cambridge: Polity, 2019); Michael Mann, *Fascists* (Cambridge: Cambridge University Press, 2004); Dylan Riley, *The Civic Foundations of Fascism in Europe* (Baltimore: Johns Hopkins University, 2010); and Dylan Riley, "Enigmas of Fascism," *New Left Review* 30 (November 1, 2024).

10 *to understand politicized emotion* Max Scheler, *Ressentiment* (Milwaukee: WI: Marquette University Press, 1994). As norms of civility give way—on the Internet or in the halls of Congress, for example—to insult, derogation, and talk of vengeance, it's useful to understand the pathological end of the emotional spectrum. This can include suppressed envy, and the desire not only to have an envied object (cultural primacy, affluence, freedom), but the desire to deprive others of having that which is envied and resented.

12 *a revealing 2019 Pew poll* Mark Jurkowitz and Amy Mitchell, "A Sore Subject: Almost Half of Americans Have Stopped Talking Politics with Someone," Pew Research Center, February 5, 2020.

12 *"set the people of this region"* Martha Elson, "Our History: LBJ Visits E. Kentucky in 1964," *Courier Journal*, April 17, 2015. See also Pam Fessler, "Kentucky County That Gave War on Poverty a Face Still Struggles," *Morning Edition*, NPR, January 8, 2014.

13 *Then, in April 2017, flyers began appearing* For an image of the leaflet, see "Counter Rally Planned to Oppose White Nationalists Canceled for 'Safety Reasons,'" WKYT, April 28, 2017, https://www.wkyt.com/content /news/Counter-rally-planned-to-oppose-white-nationalists-canceled-for -safety-reasons-420700463.html.

Chapter 2

16 *decline to 48,000 by 2040* Matt Ruther, Tom Sawyer, and Sarah Ehresman, "Projections of Population and Households: State of Kentucky, Kentucky Counties, and Area Development Districts 2015–2040," Kentucky State Data Center, University of Louisville, 2016, http://ksdc.louisville .edu//wp-content/uploads/2016/10/projection-report-v16.pdf.

16 *Wendell Berry* When COVID hit and I became unable to travel to Pike County, Tommy Ratliff agreed to become my research assistant, and came on this trip in that capacity. See Appendix 1 on my research.

16 *"A coal miner truly is a tech worker"* "These Ex-Coal Miners Learned How to Code with the Help of a Tech Company in Rural Kentucky," YouTube, posted by Business Insider, November 3, 2022, https://youtu.be /mSj_zNhS5l4?si=30hoKKnLh9NKidbG.

16 *"Motivation through starvation"* "Coal to Coding Entrepreneur Rusty Justice on Going from Coal Miner to Tech Worker," YouTube, posted by Kentucky to the World, August 7, 2021, https://youtu.be/eAo973oUL Z0?si=3IFHh5YuwjRBI57M.

17 *The American National Election Studies* American National Election

Studies, ANES 2020 Time Series Study Full Release [dataset and documentation], July 19, 2021, www.electionstudies.org.

18 *David Hackett Fischer* David Hackett Fischer, *Albion's Seed: Four British Folkways in America* (New York: Oxford University Press, 1989), 621.

18 *Arjun Jayadev and Robert Johnson* Arjun Jayadev and Robert Johnson, "Tides and Prejudice: Racial Attitudes During Downturns in the United States 1979–2014," *Review of Black Political Economy* 44, no. 3–4 (2017): 379–392.

18 *Red states generally* Kleinfeld, "Polarization, Democracy and Political Violence in the United States," 29, 30. As the author notes, "The idea that fear of economic scarcity exacerbates racism is corroborated by experiments showing that in a lab context, White Americans primed to be thinking about economic scarcity reduce resource allocations to Black Americans. The problem may be linked to the idea of relative deprivation: when individuals feel deprived of success they had anticipated achieving or felt they deserved, they can experience a sense that they deserve better than their current situation and that someone else is to blame. Usually these grievances must be articulated and exploited by a conflict entrepreneur or political leader, and until that person or movement comes along, structural inequality per se does not move people into extremism." See Amy R. Krosch and David M. Amodio, "Economic Scarcity Alters the Perception of Race," *PNAS* 111, no. 25 (June 9, 2014): 9079–9084; Amy R. Krosch, Tom R. Tyler, and David M. Amodio, "Race and Recession: Effects of Economic Scarcity on Racial Discrimination," *Journal of Personal Social Psychology* 113, no. 6 (December 2017): 892–909; Christopher Vito, Amanda Admire, and Elizabeth Hughes, "Masculinity, Aggrieved Entitlement, and Violence: Considering the Isla Vista Mass Shooting," *International Journal for Masculinity Studies* 13, no. 2 (2018): 86–102.

19 *by the Works Progress Administration* For a description of the WPA-built court house in Pikeville, see "National Register of Historic Places Inventory—Nomination Form for Multiple Resources of Pikeville, Huffman Avenue Historic District," August 8, 1984, National Park Register of Historic Places Digital Archive on NPGallery, National Register ID 84001927, https://npgallery.nps.gov/NRHP/AssetDetail?assetID=17acea18-d844-45d5-afe3-8b4068e6d010.

19 *the extraordinary Cut-Through* See "Pikeville Cut-Through Project," Pikeville–Pike County Visitor's Center, www.tourpikecounty.com/things-to-see-do/outdoor_adventure/pikeville-cut-through-project/.

19 *A bronze plaque there* "Pikeville Cut-Through," Historical Marker Database, updated January 4, 2023, www.hmdb.org/m.asp?m=212047.

19 *A tourism website* Andrea Limke, "This Tiny Kentucky Town Literally Moved a Mountain in One of the Largest Engineering Feats in the World," Only in Your State, July 13, 2023, www.onlyinyourstate.com/kentucky /pikeville-cut-through-ky/.

19 *Buried in tourist bureau write-ups* See the tourism brochure for the project at Pikeville–Pike County Visitors Center, "Pikeville Cut-Through Project," https://tourpikecounty.com/things-to-see-do/outdoor_adventure/pike ville-cut-through-project/.

20 *school built by the WPA* According to a study by the Kentucky Heritage Council, "approximately five WPA schools were constructed for Black Kentuckians in Hazard, Pikeville, Manchester, Harlan, and London." Rachel Kennedy and Cynthia Johnson, "The New Deal Builds: A Historic Context of the New Deal in East Kentucky, 1933–1943," Kentucky Heritage Council, State Historic Preservation Office, 2005, https://heritage .ky.gov/Documents/NewDealBuilds.pdf.

20 *then governor of Kentucky* Patton is one of only four governors since 1800 to win two terms—a possibility made significantly more likely after state laws regarding term limits were amended in 1992.

20 *Kentucky now ranks thirty-first* U.S. News & World Report, "Best States: Education," https://www.usnews.com/news/best-states/rankings/educa tion, accessed December 20, 2023.

Chapter 3

25 *Pride functions as an emotional* In Thomas Scheff's "Shame and Conformity: The Deference/Emotion System," Scheff links the experience of pride with attachment to others and shame with detachment. And there are different types of shame—differentiated shame and undifferentiated shame, overt shame and covert shame, bypassed (or avoided) shame and non-bypassed shame. See Helen Block Lewis, "Shame and Guilt in Neurosis," 1971.

25 *Shame also feels like a "skin"* One could do a parallel analysis of envy and entitlement which may underlie challenges to "deservingness"—of wealth, power, status.

25 *This is insightfully explored in David Keen's 2023 Shame* David Keen, *Shame: The Politics and Power of an Emotion* (Princeton, NJ: Princeton University Press, 2023). David Keen takes a political-science oriented,

world-comparative approach to shame (and pride) whereas I take a psychosocial approach to pride (and shame). As a pattern to explain, Keen focuses on political struggles and genocides around the world, while as an ethnographer I focus on a shifting political allegiance of one community and region, one that, I suggest, we find elsewhere around the United States and the world. We also develop the concept of pride in very different—and I think complementary—ways.

Many scholars have focused on the importance of shame and pride. See in particular Thomas Scheff, *Bloody Revenge: Emotions, Nationalism and War* (Boulder, CO: Westview, 1994), and his "Shame in Self and Society," *Symbolic Interaction* 26 (2:239–62). Also see Suzanne Retzinger. "Shame, Anger, and Conflict: Case Study of Emotional Violence," *Journal of Family Violence* 6, 1: 37–59.

Also see Jeffery Stuewig et al. (2011), who find that the most "shame-prone" are those who see in negative experiences a reflection of a defect in themselves, and who also are the most likely to externalize blame. Exploring psychotherapy, Helen Lewis (1971) notes the frequency with which shame comes up, is hidden, and comes caught in "feeling traps"—an idea. Lewis identifies two responses to shame—withdrawal and depression (as in my "move inward) and anger and aggression (as in my move of shame outward to blame).

Drawing on European history, Thomas Scheff (2000; 2014) posits a connection between shame, blame, and violence and through what he calls "recursive shame spirals" explores as shame "spirals." He posits that the shame must be sufficiently secret and sufficient in amount (p. 110) to act back on itself without resolution. Keen, too argues that "those who have been shamed en masse may be ripe for those seeking an exit (Keen pp. 9–10). For other thinkers on pride and shame, please see the Bibliography.

25 *Aristotle Merriam-Webster Dictionary*, "Pride: The Word That Went from Vice to Strength," *Wordplay* (blog), www.merriam-webster.com /words-at-play/pride-meaning-word-history.

25 *the word* pride See Harper Douglas, "Etymology of Proud," Online Etymology Dictionary, last modified December 27, 2020, www.etymonline .com/word/proud.

26 *often associated with remorse* Merriam-Webster's dictionary describes it as a "painful emotion caused by consciousness of guilt, shortcomings, or impropriety," and as a condition of "humiliating disgrace or disrepute."

26 *we experience secondary attitudes The Managed Heart: The Commercialization of Human Feeling* (Berkeley, CA: University of California Press, 1983).

27 *Barbara Kingsolver's superb novel* Barbara Kingsolver, *Demon Copperhead* (New York: HarperCollins, 2022).

29 *"rural purge"* Courtney Campbell, "Television's 'Rural Purge' is the Reason So Many Classic '60s Sitcoms Were Canceled," Wide Open Country, July 1, 2021, www.wideopencountry.com/rural-purge/.

30 *so-called mobility incubator* Mark Muro and Jacob Whiton, "America Has Two Economies—and They're Diverging Fast," *The Avenue* (blog). Brookings Institution, September 19, 2019.

30 *Between 2008 and 2017* Muro and Whiton, "America Has Two Economies—and They're Diverging Fast."

30 *In recent years* Daniel Wood and Geoff Brumfiel, "Pro-Trump Counties Continue to Suffer Far Higher COVID Death Tolls," NPR, May 19, 2022

30 *Studies of optimism* Carol Graham and Sergio Pinto, "Unequal Hopes and Lives in the USA: Optimism, Race, Place, and Premature Mortality," *Journal of Population Economics* 32 (2019): 665–733. See also Joe Neel, "Is There Hope for the American Dream? What Americans Think About Income Inequality," NPR, January 9, 2020. Also see Carol Graham, *"Why Are Black Poor Americans More Optimistic than White Ones?,"* Brookings Institution, January 30, 2018; Robert Kuttner, *Everything for Sale: The Virtues and Limits of Markets* (New York: Knopf, 1997).

31 *Over time, death rates* "Widening Gap in Death Rates Between Democrat and Republican in the US," *British Medical Journal*, June 7, 2022, www .bmj.com/company/newsroom/study-finds-widening-gap-in-death-rates -between-us-areas-that-vote-for-democratic-rather-than-republican -party/.

31 *sociologist Max Weber* Max Weber, *The Protestant Ethic and the Spirit of Capitalism*, trans. Talcott Parsons (New York: Charles Scribner's Sons, 1958). This core belief has become what Michael Sandel has called the "rocket fuel" of the economy. See Michael J. Sandel, *The Tyranny of Merit: What's Become of the Common Good?* (New York: Farrar, Straus and Giroux, 2020), 47, 60.

31 *More Republicans than Democrats* Frank J. Lysy, "Why Wages Have Stagnated While GDP Has Grown: The Proximate Factors," *An Economic Sense* (blog), February 13, 2015, www.aneconomicsense.org/2015/02/13 /why-wages-have-stagnated-while-gdp-has-grown-the-proximate-factors/.

31 *When asked in a national survey* Amina Dunn, "Partisans Are Divided over the Fairness of the US Economy—and Why People Are Rich or Poor," Pew Research Center, October 4, 2018.

32 *In a 2020 poll conducted by NPR* For both a summary of the poll results and a link to the full study report, see Neel, "Is There Hope for the American Dream?"

32 *In 2014, 47 percent of Republicans* Samantha Smith, "Why People Are Rich and Poor: Republicans and Democrats Have Very Different Views," Pew Research Center, May 2, 2017.

32 *one which broke free* See Kuttner, *Everything for Sale.*

34 *Eastern Kentucky coal companies* J. W. Randolph, "Impacts of Coal 101: Mountaintop Removal = Job Removal," *Front Porch* (blog), Appalachian Voices, January 21, 2011, www.appvoices.org/2011/01/21/impacts-of-coal-101-mountaintop-removal-job-removal/.

34 *Revelation Energy* Lisa Abbot, "Many Affected as Revelation Energy files for Chapter 11 bankruptcy," Kentuckians for the Commonwealth, July 9, 2019, https://archive.kftc.org/blog/many-affected-revelation-energy-files-chapter-11-bankruptcy.

34 *Blackjewel* Dan Radmacher, "Blackjewel's Catastrophic Bankruptcy and the Collapse of the Mine Cleanup System," Appalachian Voices, March 3, 2022, www.appvoices.org/2022/03/03/bankruptcy-mine-cleanup-collapse/.

34 *Wyoming, currently the main source* U.S. Energy Information Administration, "Coal Explained: Where Our Coal Comes From," last updated October 19, 2022, https://www.eia.gov/energyexplained/coal/where-our-coal-comes-from.php.

34 *With this shift came the loss of jobs* Randolph, "Impacts of Coal 101."

34 *the least educationally armed* An interesting study comparing white-collar workers in America and Israel found that the Americans more often took their inability to find a job as a personal failure, while Jewish Israeli job-seekers were more likely to understand their failure in structural terms, which helped them avoid discouragement and keep on looking. Blue collar Americans understood the job search as a "diligence game," or a matter of hard work and perseverance—perhaps evidence of the Protestant ethic at work. Ofer Sharone, *Flawed System/Flawed Self: Job Searching and Unemployment Experiences* (Chicago: University of Chicago Press, 2013).

36 *production rose and rose* Michael E. Long, "Wrestlin' for a Livin' with King Coal," *National Geographic*, June 1983, 795.

36 *By 1977 Pike County led* Greg Bone, "Kentucky Coal Facts, 17th Edition," Energy and Environment Cabinet, Kentucky Department for Energy Development and Independence, 2017, 12.

36 *"Within a ten-mile radius"* Long, "Wrestlin' for a Livin' with King Coal," 807.

36 *"lace curtains fluttered"* Harry M. Caudill, *Night Comes to the Cumberlands: A Biography of a Depressed Area* (Boston: Little, Brown, 1962), 110.

36 *a 1964 CBS News special called* Christmas in Appalachia "Christmas in Appalachia (1964)—Revisiting the CBS Special Report by Charles Kuralt with Updates," YouTube, posted by Real Appalachia, December 14, 2020, www.youtube.com/watch?v=4ECdhjJTHRc.

38 *In 2000 coal had provided 52 percent* See Harry Stevens, "America Needs Clean Electricity. These States Show How to Do It," *Washington Post*, April 12, 2023, citing data from the U.S. Energy Information Agency.

38 *"thirteen or fourteen miners"* Max Fraser, *Hillbilly Highway: The Transappalachian Migration and the Making of a White Working Class* (Princeton, NJ: Princeton University Press, 2023), 42.

38 *In 1990, Kentucky had 30,498* For statewide coal industry employment from 1927 to 2016, see Bone, "Kentucky Coal Facts, 17th Edition," 117. For employment figures from 2000 to present, see Quarterly Coal Dashboard, Kentucky Energy and Environment Cabinet, https://eec.ky.gov /Energy/News-Publications/Pages/quarterly-coal-dashboard.aspx.

38 *largely went out with them* Lainey Newman and Theda Skocpol, *Rust Belt Union Blues* (New York: Columbia University Press, 2023).

39 *Some companies, such as Blackjewel* Ken Ward Jr., Alex Mierjeski, and Scott Pham, "In the Game of Musical Mines, Environmental Damage Takes a Back Seat," ProPublica, April 26, 2023.

39 *The nation's most eloquent defender* Liz Judge, "Mountain Hero Gets Help from Author Wendell Berry," Earthjustice, June 25, 2012, https://earthjustice.org/article/mountain-hero-gets-help-from-author-wendell-berry. See Silas House and Jason Howard, *Something's Rising: Appalachians Fighting Mountaintop Removal* (Lexington: University Press of Kentucky, 2009). See also the Alliance for Appalachia, a coalition of local groups in several Appalachian states trying to challenge mountaintop removal: https://theallianceforappalachia.org/where-we-work/.

39 *musical legend John Prine* John Prine, "Paradise," MP3 audio, track 5 on *John Prine*, 1971.

40 *country-and-western musician Dwight Yoakam* Dwight Yoakam, "Readin', Rightin', Rt. 23," MP3 audio, track 5 on *Hillbilly Deluxe*, 1987.

40 *"After being one of the fastest growing"* Fraser, *Hillbilly Highway*, 115.

40 *the roughly 8 million whites* Fraser, *Hillbilly Highway*, 3.

40 *Uptown, Chicago* Fraser, *Hillbilly Highway*, 4–6, 110.

41 *Goodyear Tire and Rubber Company* Fraser, *Hillbilly Highway*, 81–82. Goodyear Rubber and other rubber companies in the 1920s recruited workers from Appalachia "regardless of local business conditions," Fraser notes, and local newspaper editors at the time wondered if this was "a method to insure a surplus of labor."

42 *A Kentucky Republican member* See Aila Slisco, "Is Kentucky Republican Thomas Massie Making a Case for Secession?," *Newsweek*, December 17, 2021. See also Brendan Cole, "Marjorie Taylor Greene Asks If US Should Be Divided Between GOP and Democrats," *Newsweek*, October 12, 2021, and Colby Hall, "Marjorie Taylor Greene Gets Sean Hannity on Board for National Divorce—Then Warns of Looming Civil War," MSN, February 22, 2023.

Chapter 4

45 *"had left New York City"* Lois Beckett, "Is There a Neo-Nazi Storm Brewing in Trump Country?," *The Guardian*, June 4, 2017.

45 *National Socialist Movement* Southern Poverty Law Center, "National Socialist Movement," Extremist Files Database, www.splcenter.org /fighting-hate/extremist-files/group/national-socialist-movement.

46 *But Donald Trump had not* Daniel L. Byman, "Assessing the Right-Wing Terror Threat in the United States a Year After the January 6 Insurrection," Brookings Institution, January 5, 2022.

46 *"If you see somebody getting ready"* Michael Finnegan and Noah Bierman, "Trump's Endorsement of Violence Reaches New Level: He May Pay Legal Fees for Assault Suspect," *Los Angeles Times*, March 13, 2016.

46 *Along with other protesters, Nwanguma* WLKY, "Protestor Pushed at 2016 Trump Rally," CNN, April 4, 2017, www.cnn.com/videos/poli tics/2017/04/02/protester-pushed-trump-rally-louisville-kashiya-nwangu ma-sot.wlky.

47 *"It is plausible that Trump's direction"* The district court dismissed all claims

against Trump except "incitement to riot." However, these claims too were dismissed by the Sixth Circuit Court of Appeals because Trump's exhortations to "get 'em out of here" were followed by "don't hurt 'em." For the appeals decision, see *Nwanguma v. Trump*, No. 17-6290 (6th Cir. 2018), www.law.justia.com/cases/federal/appellate-courts/ca6/17-6290/17-6290 -2018-09-11.html.

47 *Vlaams Belang and Nieuwe-Vlaamse Alliantie* See Adam Hochschild, "Another Great Yesterday," review *of Shadowlands: Fear and Freedom at the Oregon Standoff—A Western Tale of America in Crisis*, by Anthony McCann, *New York Review of Books,* December 19, 2019. However, the traditions that the political right defends can differ radically from one country to another. The Dutch leader Geert Wilders defends "as tradition" respect for gays and social welfare. See Jan Willem Duyvendak and Josip Kesic, *The Return of the Native: Can Liberalism Safeguard Us Against Nativism?* (New York: Oxford University Press, 2022).

48 *Others were bringing homemade shields* Ryan Wilson, "Detroit Lions Disavow Use of Their Logo During Violent Rally in Charlottesville," CBS Sports, August 16, 2017.

48 *Vegas Tenold* See Vegas Tenold, *Everything You Love Will Burn: Inside the Rebirth of White Nationalism in America* (New York: Nation Books, 2018).

49 *"inside a cogwheel"* The cogwheel is used in the iconography of some neo-Nazi groups as a callback to the symbol of Nazi Germany's labor organization. See FARE Network, *Guide to Discriminatory Practices in European Football*, Version 6, June 2021, https://farenet.org/uploads/files/2021 _Fare_guide_to_discriminatory_practices_UEFA_.pdf.

50 *95 percent white town* Census data indicate that the white non-Hispanic population in Poolesville was 78 percent at the time of the march in 2017 and 80 percent in 2021. Including white Hispanics, the figures are 88.5 percent in 2017 and 90 percent in 2021. Data USA, "Poolesville, MD," https://datausa.io/profile/geo/poolesville-md#demographics.

50 *eleventh-richest county in the U.S.* This ranking is based on median household income data from the 2010 U.S. Census Bureau. The 2020 census puts Montgomery County in the top twenty richest counties.

54 *"failed men"* Michael Kimmel, *Healing from Hate: How Young Men Get Into—and Out of—Violent Extremism* (Oakland: University of California Press, 2018), 20.

54 *"Battle was part of their very being"* George L. Mosse, *Nationalism and*

Sexuality: Respectability and Abnormal Sexuality in Modern Europe (New York: Howard Fertig, 1985), 124.

54 *white nationalism was a man's game* Adam Hochschild, "The Proud Boys and the Long-Lived Anxieties of American Men," review of *We Are Proud Boys: How a Right-Wing Street Gang Ushered in a New Era of American Extremism*, by Andy Campbell, *New York Times*, September 18, 2022.

56 *As one Black undergraduate later recalled to a journalist* Southern Poverty Law Center, "Heimbach," Extremist Files Database, www.splcenter.org /fighting-hate/extremist-files/individual/matthew-heimbach. For footage of Heimbach on "guard" patrol, see "White Student Union (Documentary)," YouTube, posted by Vice, June 4, 2013, www.youtube.com /watch?v=GJ_MHp8iqtQ.

58 *He was referring to Vegas Tenold's fine* See Tenold, *Everything You Love Will Burn.*

Chapter 5

61 *Effie Waller Smith* For the text of the historical plaque, see Christopher Beebout, "Effie Waller Smith," ExploreKYHistory, www.explorekyhistory .ky.gov/items/show/880. See also "Smith, Effie Waller," Notable Kentucky African Americans Database, last modified July 17, 2017, https://nkaa .uky.edu/nkaa/items/show/1033.

61 *Pikeville's Dils Cemetery* "The Dils Cemetery," Historical Marker Database, updated March 6, 2020, https://www.hmdb.org/m.asp?m=146196.

62 *The KKK had indeed appeared in Pikeville* William David Deskins, *Ginseng, Coal Dust, Moving Mountains: A History of Pike County, Kentucky* (Paintsville, KY: East Kentucky Press, 2018), 241.

62 *the Perry A. Cline School* Jerry Cline, "Hatfield-McCoy Feud: The Truth About Perry Cline's Involvement in the Feud," Cline Family Association, 2013, www.clinefamilyassociation.com/hatfield_mccoy_feud.

63 *county's schools were not fully integrated* "African American Schools in Pike County, KY," Notable Kentucky African Americans Database, last modified January 16, 2023, https://nkaa.uky.edu/nkaa/items/show/2794.

64 *five hundred companies* Ron D. Eller, *Miners, Millhands, and Mountaineers: Industrialization of the Appalachian South, 1880–1930* (Knoxville: University of Tennessee Press, 1982).

64 *fifty-four company-owned coal camps* Coal Camp Documentary Project, Appalachian Center, University of Kentucky, https://appalachianprojects .as.uky.edu/coal-camps.

64 *ranged in size* Kentucky Coal and Energy Education Project, "Pike County, Kentucky Coal Camps," www.coaleducation.org/coalhistory/coaltowns /coalcamps/pike_county.htm.

64 *By the onset of World War II* William H. Turner, *The Harlan Renaissance: Stories of Black Life in Appalachian Coal Towns* (Morgantown: West Virginia University Press, 2021), 6.

64 *The largest camp in the entire state* Turner, *The Harlan Renaissance*, 6, 168. See also Caudill, *Night Comes to the Cumberlands*, 106.

64 *"Up from the worn-out cotton fields"* Harry M. Caudill, *Night Comes to the Cumberlands: A Biography of a Depressed Area* (Boston: Little, Brown, 1962), 103.

64 *"The 900 new houses in Jenkins"* Caudill, *Night Comes to the Cumberlands,* 106.

64 *Happy, Sassafras, and Hi-Hat* Caudill, *Night Comes to the Cumberlands,* 105, 109.

64 *In "the Golden Age of the coal industry"* Caudill, *Night Comes to the Cumberlands,* 110.

65 *admitted 140 Black students as early as 1956* "African American Schools in Pike County, KY," Notable Kentucky African Americans Database.

66 *When once speaking about interracial friendship* Personal communication. Also see Porter Square Books, "Paul Farmer with Ophelia Dahl: Fevers, Feuds and Diamonds," Facebook, at 12:30–13:00, www.face book.com/Porter-Square-Books-112608362085830/videos/5307179 31197122/?refsrc=deprecated&_rdr.

66 *the Civil Rights Act forbade* See "Civil Rights Act (1964)," Milestone Documents, National Archives, www.archives.gov/milestone-documents/civil -rights-act.

67 *In 1860, Blacks made up about 20 percent* Campbell Gibson and Kay Jung, "Historical Census Statistics on Population Totals by Race, 1790–1990, and by Hispanic Origin, 1970–1990, for the United States, Regions, Divisions, States," Working Paper No. 56, Population Division, U.S. Census Bureau, September 13, 2002, https://www.census.gov/library/working-pa pers/2002/demo/POP-twps0056.html.

67 *a population of 7,325 whites* "Pike County (KY) Enslaved, Free Blacks, and Free Mulattoes, 1850–1870," Notable Kentucky African Americans Database, last updated January 10, 2023, https://nkaa.uky.edu/nkaa /items/show/2528.

68 *"The first generation migrated"* Karida Brown, *Gone Home: Race and Roots*

Through Appalachia (Chapel Hill: University of North Carolina Press, 2018), 2.

68 *Black Joe, Harlan, Hazard, Red Fox* Turner, *The Harlan Renaissance,* 165.

68 *Even today, Black reunions* Turner, *The Harlan Renaissance,* 103.

68 *Lynch County* Turner, *The Harlan Renaissance,* 7.

68 *In 1946, Harlan alone* Turner, *The Harlan Renaissance,* 70.

68 *a population that has now dwindled* United States Census Bureau Quick-Facts, "Harlan County, Kentucky," www.census.gov/quickfacts/fact/table/harlancountykentucky/PST045222, accessed December 5, 2023.

68 *sundown towns* James Loewen argues that, as a result of sundown laws, the Great Migration was followed by a "Great Retreat" of African Americans from towns and rural areas in the North to ghettoized neighborhoods in large northern cities. By Loewen's estimate there were about 10,000 sundown towns and counties in the United States, and not all of them are "long ago and far away," as we say. Guidebooks for cross-country Black travelers included advice on which towns to avoid. See James Loewen, *Sundown Towns: A Hidden Dimension of American Racism* (New York: Simon & Schuster, 2006).

69 *A mob of 125 white men* The L&N was an economic engine for Corbin, a town of some 2,800. The railway conveyed coal in hopper cars from the Kentucky coal mines south to Knoxville and Atlanta and north to Cincinnati, and in 1919 brought in two hundred to four hundred Black workers to help build a railyard. But when white men returned from World War I looking for work, they discovered Blacks already working at jobs many whites imagined as "theirs." There are several competing explanations of the immediate cause of the mob, but a number of alleged thefts and the mugging of a white man were attributed to Black railworkers. Many townspeople supported the terrorism perpetrated by some 125 armed white men, who banged on the doors of Black homes, smashed windows, and rounded up Blacks, walking them at gunpoint to the train station and forcing them to leave town. Some whites took Black neighbors in or otherwise defended them against the marauders. Elliot Jaspin, *Buried in the Bitter Waters: The Hidden History of Racial Cleansing in America* (New York: Basic Books, 2007), 169–179. See also: Kristy Owens Griggs, "The Removal of Blacks from Corbin in 1919: Memory, Perspective, and the Legacy of Racism," *Register of the Kentucky Historical Society* 100, n. 3 (Summer 2002): 293–310; *Trouble Behind: A Film About History and Forgetting,* directed by Robby Henson (1990, Cicada Films).

69 *William Hambley* See "Pikeville Cut-Through Project," Pikeville–Pike County Visitor's Center, www.tourpikecounty.com/things-to-see-do/out door_adventure/pikeville-cut-through-project/. See also "Pikeville Cut-Through," Historical Marker Database, updated January 4, 2023, www.hmdb.org/m.asp?m=212047.

72 *He was to end up as a trial attorney* Will Wright, "How This Jewish Attorney Escaped the Holocaust and Changed Eastern Kentucky Forever," *Lexington Herald-Leader,* April 23, 2019.

74 *Islamic Center of East Kentucky* Kevin Williams, "The Muslims of Appalachia: Kentucky Coal Country Embracing the Faithful," Al Jazeera America, February 21, 2016.

74 *"what Donald Trump says about us Muslims"* Reuters, "Donald Trump: I Was '100% Right' About Muslims Cheering 9/11 Attacks," *The Guardian,* November 29, 2015.

75 *Muslim Doctors' Association* Williams, "The Muslims of Appalachia."

76 *"The people of the southern highlands"* David Hackett Fischer, *Albion's Seed: Four British Folkways in America* (New York: Oxford University Press, 1989), 650.

77 *historian Isabel Wilkerson* Isabel Wilkerson, *Caste: The Origins of Our Discontents* (New York: Random House, 2020).

Chapter 6

83 *"The miner strapped thick rubber kneepads"* Harry M. Caudill, *Night Comes to the Cumberlands: A Biography of a Depressed Area* (Boston: Little, Brown, 1962), 116–117.

83 *"Flashing like lightning"* Caudill, *Night Comes to the Cumberlands,* 119.

84 *free chest X-rays* "PMC Expands Black Lung Screening Services," Pikeville Medical Center, June 22, 2018, www.pikevillehospital.org/pmc-expands-black-lung-screening-services/.

84 *Scottish philosopher Adam Smith* Adam Smith, *The Wealth of Nations: Books I–III* (London: Penguin Books, 1999 [1776]).

85 *16 percent* U.S. Census Bureau, American Community Survey (ACS), 5-Year Estimates, 2017–2021.

86 *Despite a recent countertrend* Kim Parker, Juliana Menasce Horowitz, Anna Brown, et al., "Demographic and Economic Trends in Urban, Suburban and Rural Communities," Pew Research Center, May 22, 2018.

86 *In Kentucky, Jefferson County* See "How Has the Population Changed in

Kentucky?," USA Facts, https://usafacts.org/data/topics/people-society /population-and-demographics/our-changing-population/state/kentucky.

87 *Between 1900 and 1970* James N. Gregory, "The Southern Diaspora and the Urban Dispossessed: Demonstrating the Census Public Use Microdata Samples," *Journal of American History* 82, no. 1 (June 1995): 112.

87 *"hillbilly highway"* Arlie Russell Hochschild, "The Black and White Southerners Who Changed the North," review of *Hillbilly Highway: The Transappalachian Migration and the Making of a White Working Class* by Max Fraser and *Black Folk: The Roots of the Black Working Class* by Blair L. M. Kelley, *New York Times*, September 27, 2023. See Fraser, *Hillbilly Highway,* 5–6.

87 *Every five years, 6 to 12 percent* Max Fraser, *Hillbilly Highway: The Transappalachian Migration and the Making of a White Working Class* (Princeton, NJ: Princeton University Press, 2023), 68.

89 *national rate of small business failure* Bureau of Labor Statistics, "Table 7, Survival of Private Sector Establishments by Opening Year," www.bls.gov /bdm/us_age_naics_00_table7.txt.

89 *World Economic Forum's 2020 report* World Economic Forum, "Global Social Mobility Index 2020: Why Economies Benefit from Fixing Inequality," January 2020, 7, www.weforum.org/publications/global-social-mobili ty-index-2020-why-economies-benefit-from-fixing-inequality.

89 *71 percent of Republicans* Amina Dunn, "Partisans Are Divided over the Fairness of the US Economy—and Why People Are Rich or Poor," Pew Research Center, October 4, 2018.

89 *36 percent credit "hard work"* Dunn, "Partisans Are Divided over the Fairness of the US Economy."

92 *Prestonsburg fined people for overgrown grass* City of Prestonsburg, "Vacant Foreclosed Property Registration," www.prestonsburgcity.org/wp-content /docs/CE_VacantForeclosedPropertyRegistration.pdf.

Chapter 7

97 *Southgate facility* This is a pseudonym to protect the identity of the program, as well as the clients in it.

97 *Eddyville* In Pike County in 2011 (the year Wyatt Blair was sentenced), 197 white men were put in prison, 27 white women, 4 Black men, and one Black woman. In state prisons, 35 percent of offenses were violence-related, as was Wyatt's. Steven L. Beshear, J. Michael Brown, and LaDonna Thompson, "2011 Annual Report," Commonwealth of Kentucky,

Department of Corrections, www.corrections.ky.gov/About/researchand
stats/Pages/default.aspx.

99 *"A lot of people like me"* Evan Osnos, "Donald Trump and the Ku Klux
Klan: A History," *New Yorker,* February 29, 2016.

100 *"Kentucky's incarceration rates stand out internationally"* See Emily
Widra and Tiana Herring, "States of Incarceration: The Global Context 2021," Prison Policy Initiative, September 2021, www.prisonpolicy
.org/global/2021.html. For the number of prisoners in Kentucky, see
Prison Policy Initiative, "Kentucky Profile," www.prisonpolicy.org
/profiles/KY.html.

100 *Moral Reconation Therapy* MRT is a trademarked cognitive-behavioral
treatment program developed in the 1980s for prison populations. The
term "conation" refers to the process of making conscious decisions. See
www.moral-reconation-therapy.com.

100 *nationwide, 65 percent of all prisoners* National Institute on Drug Abuse,
"Criminal Justice DrugFacts," last updated June 2020, www.drugabuse
.gov/publications/drugfacts/criminal-justice.

100 *Over the last forty years* Jacob Kang-Brown and Ram Subramanian, "Out
of Sight: The Growth of Jails in Rural America," Vera Institute of Justice,
June 2017, www.vera.org/publications/out-of-sight-growth-of-jails-rural
-america. See also Michelle Alexander, *The New Jim Crow: Mass Incarceration in the Age of Colorblindness,* revised ed. (New York: The New
Press, 2012).

100 *Today 53 percent* Kang-Brown and Subramanian, "Out of Sight," 8. As of
2013, the distribution of prisoners was as follows: 27 percent were housed
in large metropolitan urban areas, 20 percent in metro suburban areas,
33 percent in medium and small metro areas, and 20 percent in rural
areas—the last being the case for Wyatt in Eddyville.

100 *New York convicts far more* Vera Institute of Justice, "Incarceration
Trends," last updated February 14, 2023, www.trends.vera.org/. In 2019
all five boroughs of New York City housed only 162 prisoners for every
100,000 residents jailed locally. But in the same year, rural Pike County
had 1,117 jailed people for every 100,000 of its residents.

100 *This prison gerrymandering boosts* Hansi Lo Wang, "Most Prisoners Can't
Vote, But They're Still Counted in Voting Districts," NPR, September 26,
2021.

101 *In 2016, the 2,623 small and rural* Kang-Brown and Subramanian, "Out of
Sight."

101 *funding derived from coal mining* Will Wright, "Kentucky Coal Communities Are Bracing for Financial Crisis," *The Messenger*, April 10, 2020, www.the-messenger.com/article_a104a5b7-29d4-5101-a21a-69130435e4dd.html.

101 *All the more welcome* For a portrait of how declining coal revenues play a role in the growth of the Kentucky prison industry, see Jack Norton and Judah Schept, "Keeping the Lights On: Incarcerating the Bluegrass State," Vera Institute of Justice, March 4, 2019, www.vera.org/in-our-backyards-stories/keeping-the-lights-on.

101 *rate of pretrial incarceration rose 436 percent* Kang-Brown and Subramanian, "Out of Sight," 7.

101 *per diem payments* Norton and Schept, "Keeping the Lights On."

101 *fifty-nine bills increasing penalties* Chris Kenning, "Why Can't Kentucky Reduce Its Sky-High Prison Populations? Look to Lawmakers, Report Says," *Courier Journal*, December 29, 2021.

101 *Since 2000, the rate of incarceration* See Keith Humphreys and Ekow N. Yankah, "Prisons Are Getting Whiter. That's One Way Mass Incarceration Might End," *Washington Post*, February 26, 2021, citing Zhen Zeng, "Jail Inmates in 2018," Bureau of Justice Statistics, U.S. Department of Justice, March 2020, www.bjs.ojp.gov/content/pub/pdf/ji18.pdf.

103 *"I done fifty-two months in the hole"* There are no state laws limiting the duration of solitary confinement in Kentucky prisons. Under the current policies of the Department of Corrections, inmates can be placed in "disciplinary segregation" for up to twenty-two hours per day for thirty days per offense, and these terms can be served consecutively. See "Policies and Procedures, Chapter 15.2: Rule Violations and Penalties," Kentucky Department of Corrections, August 12, 2016, https://corrections.ky.gov/About/cpp/Documents/15/CPP%2015.2%20-%20Effective%201-6-17.pdf. However, in 2021 Kentucky passed a law prohibiting "restrictive housing" (solitary confinement) for women who are pregnant or in the "immediate post-partum period." The law also requires annual reporting to the legislature on the use of restrictive housing. A bill was also proposed in the House to limit the use of solitary confinement for youth, but it has not yet advanced out of committee. See Judith Resnik, Jenny E. Carroll, Skylar Albertson, et al., "Legislative Regulation of Isolation in Prison: 2018–2021," SSRN, August 20, 2021.

105 *In 1925 almost thirty thousand Klansmen* For a description of the 1925 march, see Terence McArdle, "The Day 30,000 White Supremacists

in KKK Robes Marched in the Nation's Capital," *Washington Post*, August 11, 2018.

105 *and in 2021, only eighteen* For a map of active KKK chapters, see Southern Poverty Law Center, "Ku Klux Klan," last updated 2021, www.splcenter.org/fighting-hate/extremist-files/ideology/ku-klux-klan. See also Vegas Tenold, *Everything You Love Will Burn: Inside the Rebirth of White Nationalism in America* (New York: Nation Books, 2018), 73.

106 *"Mystic Insignia of a Klansman"* Anti-Defamation League, Hate Symbols Database, "Blood Drop Cross," www.adl.org/resources/hate-symbol/blood-drop-cross, accessed May 28, 2023.

108 *"The Cherokee was on my mom's side"* We can't know the truth of these claims, as important as they are to Wyatt. Still, there is a burgeoning academic literature on why whites might claim Native ancestry. For an introduction, see Cecily Hilleary, "Going 'Native': Why Are Americans Hijacking Cherokee Identity?," Voice of America, July 23, 2018. See also Jessie Daniels, "Why White Americans Love to Claim Native Ancestry," *Huffington Post*, October 16, 2018, and Gregory D. Smithers, "Why Do So Many Americans Think They Have Cherokee Blood?," *Slate*, October 1, 2015.

109 *Aryan Circle* See a recent federal indictment of Aryan Circle members operating out of Kentucky and other state and federal prisons: *United States v. Farkas, et al.*, No. 7:20-CR-17-REW (E.D. Ky. September 3, 2020), https://www.justice.gov/opa/press-release/file/1327486/download.

Chapter 8

119 *"people live—what?—eighty years?"* In 2020, 18 percent of the Martin County population lived in poverty. For a comparison of socioeconomic statistics for Martin and Pike Counties, see Data USA, www.datausa.io/profile/geo/pike-county-ky?compare=martin-county-ky.

123 *"Hood to the Holler"* Hood to the Holler is also the name of an organization founded by Booker, with the aim of "building broad coalitions, breaking down barriers of race and class, and fueling a people centered movement" to transform Kentucky. See www.hoodtotheholler.org/.

123 *Booker begins his own story* Nicole Ziege, "State Rep. Charles Booker Visits Pikeville, Discusses Candidacy," *Appalachian News-Express*, February 18, 2020.

124 *The nation's whitest district* U.S. Census Bureau, American Community Survey, 1-Year Geographic Comparison Tables, 2021, www.census.gov

/acs/www/data/data-tables-and-tools/geographic-comparison-tables/. For a ranking by percentage of residents who are white non-Hispanic, see GCT0209; Black, see GCT0202; foreign born, see GCT0501.

124 *Appalachian whites are slightly older* U.S. Census Bureau, American Community Survey, 1-Year Estimates, 2021. The proportion of working-age adults receiving disability payments is calculated as a percentage of the civilian non-institutionalized population ages nineteen to sixty-four. See Social Security Agency, "OASDI Beneficiaries by State and Zip Code, 2021," https://www.ssa.gov/policy/docs/statcomps/oasdi_zip/.

124 *26 percent of Blacks* John Creamer, Emily A. Shrider, Kalee Burns, and Frances Chen, "Poverty in the United States: 2021," Report No. P60-277, United States Census Bureau, September 2022, www.census.gov/library/publications/2022/demo/p60-277.html.

125 *But Social Security excluded domestic* Blair L. M. Kelley, *Black Folk: The Roots of the Black Working Class* (New York: Liveright, 2023).

125 *Today, Blacks own 12 cents* Heather Long and Andrew Van Dam, "The Black-White Economic Divide Is as Wide as It Was in 1968," *Washington Post*, June 4, 2020.

125 *"We got twangy tragic. Blacks got rap"* The lyrics of country music, as Max Fraser notes, historically spoke of dispossession and dislocation—"a radical potential that, for a time . . . made . . . American country music a music of liberation." See Max Fraser, *Hillbilly Highway: The Transappalachian Migration and the Making of a White Working Class* (Princeton, NJ: Princeton University Press, 2023), 15.

125 *"Colt Ford . . . Haystak, Demun Jones"* See David Peisner, "Rhymes from the Backwoods: The Rise of Country Rap," *Rolling Stone*, January 24, 2018. See also Tressie McMillan Cottom's essay "Reading Hick-Hop: The Shotgun Marriage of Hip-Hop and Country Music," available at https://tressiemc.com/wp-content/uploads/2015/06/cottom-reading-hick-hop.pdf.

125 *hillbilly rap artist, Colt Ford* Colt Ford, "No Trash in My Trailer," MP3 audio, track 3 on *Ride Through the Country*, 2008.

128 *In Jennifer Silva's fine study* Jennifer Silva, *Coming Up Short: Working-Class Adulthood in an Age of Uncertainty* (New York: Oxford University Press, 2013).

130 *In a 2023 national survey* Stella Rouse, "Poll Reveals White Americans See an Increase in Discrimination Against Other White People and Less Against Other Racial Groups," *The Conversation*, July 1, 2022.

131 *pharmacies had dispensed over 30 million* Chris McGreal, "Why Were Millions of Opioid Pills Sent to a West Virginia Town of 3,000?," *The Guardian*, October 2, 2019.

131 *number-one state in the nation* "Drug Overdose Mortality by State," National Center for Health Statistics, Centers for Disease Control and Prevention, 2021, www.cdc.gov/nchs/pressroom/sosmap/drug_poisoning _mortality/drug_poisoning.htm.

Chapter 9

136 *lay flowers for the dead* Alan Jabbour and Kaen Singer Jabbour, *Decoration Day in the Mountains: Traditions of Cemetery Decoration in the Southern Appalachians* (Chapel Hill: University of North Carolina Press, 2010).

138 *"Aunt Beulah could hear"* Wendell Berry, *Jayber Crow* (Berkeley, CA: Counterpoint Press, 2000).

138 *Clinch Valley College* In 1998, Clinch Valley College was renamed the University of Virginia's College at Wise.

140 *Cascading* Social class cascade is a concept developed by Brandeis sociologist Karen Hansen. Cascading describes the "process of experiencing crisis and loss in ways that create potential for additional declines." For more about Hansen's Cascading Lives Project, including life histories of those who have suffered economic decline, see www.brandeis.edu/cas cading-lives/index.html.

142 *Jelly Roll, a white, Tennessee-born rapper* Jelly Roll, "The Bottom," MP3 audio, track 1 on *A Beautiful Disaster*, 2020.

143 *unexpected rise in premature deaths* Anne Case and Angus Deaton, *Deaths of Despair and the Future of Capitalism* (Princeton, NJ: Princeton University Press, 2020), 32.

143 *Christian Picciolini's* White American Youth Christian Picciolini, *White American Youth: My Descent into America's Most Violent Hate Movement— And How I Got Out* (New York: Hachette Books, 2017).

144 *"If I had been fourteen"* Meghan Holohan, "White Supremacists Recruit Teens by Making Them Feel Someone Cares," *Today*, August 21, 2017.

146 *"That guy's selling white nationalism"* In fact, evidence suggests that people attempting to disengage from white supremacism may experience it as a "struggle against addiction." See Pete Simi, Kathleen Blee, Matthew DeMichele, and Steven Windisch, "Addicted to Hate: Identity Residual

Among Former White Supremacists," *American Sociological Review* 82, no. 6 (2017): 1167–1187.

Chapter 10

152 *Four years later, the number had risen to 671* Art Van Zee, "The Promotion and Marketing of OxyContin: Commercial Triumph, Public Health Tragedy," *American Journal of Public Health* 99, no. 2 (February 2009): 222.

152 *It dispatched 78 sales representatives* See Shraddha Chakradhar and Casey Ross, "The History of OxyContin, Told Through Unsealed Purdue Documents," *STAT*, December 3, 2019, citing documents from Kentucky's lawsuit against Purdue.

152 *In 2000, Kentucky had only 1 percent* See comments from Kentucky lawyer Mitchel Denham in Patrick Radden Keefe, "The Family That Built an Empire of Pain," *New Yorker*, October 23, 2017. See also Beth Macy, "America's Other Epidemic," *The Atlantic*, May 2020, and Ron Formisano, "Addiction's Profit Stream Broad, Deep," *Lexington Herald-Leader*, November 19, 2017.

152 *Purdue focused on regulation-averse states* Van Zee, "The Promotion and Marketing of OxyContin."

152 *OxyContin distribution was 50 percent higher* Abby Alpert, William N. Evans, Ethan M. J. Lieber, and David Powell, "Origins of the Opioid Crisis and Its Enduring Impacts," *Quarterly Journal of Economics* 137, no. 2 (May 2022): 1139–1179.

153 *Purdue targeted doctors* Van Zee, "The Promotion and Marketing of OxyContin."

153 *Ominously, Purdue offered free* Van Zee, "The Promotion and Marketing of OxyContin," 222.

153 *Between 1996 and 2001, Purdue invited* Van Zee, "The Promotion and Marketing of OxyContin," 222.

153 *It created "prescriber profiles"* Van Zee, "The Promotion and Marketing of OxyContin," 221.

153 *"abandoned ghost shops"* Chris McGreal, "Why Were Millions of Opioid Pills Sent to a West Virginia Town of 3,000?," *The Guardian*, October 2, 2019. See also Chris McGreal, *American Overdose: The Opioid Tragedy in Three Acts* (New York: Public Affairs, 2018).

153 *pay a tab with half an Oxy* Vegas Tenold, *Everything You Love Will Burn:*

Inside the Rebirth of White Nationalism in America (New York: Nation Books, 2018), 164.

154 *"Come and listen to a story"* Chris McGreal, "Big Pharma Executives Mocked 'Pillbillies' in Emails, West Virginia Opioid Trial Hears," *The Guardian*, May 16, 2021. See also Lucas Manfield and Lauren Peace, "As Opioid Epidemic Raged, Drug Company Executives Made Fun of West Virginians," *Mountain State Spotlight*, May 13, 2201. McGreal reports, in "Big Pharma Executives," on AmerisourceBergen emails revealing that when Kentucky proposed legislation tightening regulations, executive Cathy Marcum wrote "One of the hillbillys must have learned how to read."

154 *Between 1999 and 2021* See data table for Figure 1 in Holly Hedegaard, Arialdi M. Miniño, and Margaret Warner, "Drug Overdose Deaths in the United States, 1999–2019," Data Brief No. 394, National Center for Health Statistics, Centers for Disease Control and Prevention, December 2020, www.cdc.gov/nchs/products/databriefs/db394.htm.

154 *32 per 100,000* "Drug Overdose Deaths Remained High in 2021," Centers for Disease Control and Prevention, August 2023, www.cdc.gov/drugover dose/deaths/index.html.

154 *156 per 100,000* For Kentucky's overdose death rate, see "Drug Overdose Mortality by State," National Center for Health Statistics, Centers for Disease Control and Prevention, www.cdc.gov/nchs/pressroom/sosmap /drug_poisoning_mortality/drug_poisoning.htm.

154 *Bath County* "Drug Overdose and Related Comorbidity County Profiles," Kentucky Injury Prevention and Research Center, University of Kentucky, https://kiprc.uky.edu/programs/overdose-data-action/county-profiles.

154 *a disproportionate number of victims* Shannon M. Monnat, "Trends in US Working-Age Non-Hispanic White Mortality: Rural-Urban and Within-Rural Differences," *Population Research and Policy Review* 39 (September 2020): 805–834. See also Thomas B. Edsall, "There Are Two Americas Now: One with a BA and One Without," *New York Times,* October 5, 2022.

154 *number of babies* Al Cross, "Kentucky Has Very High Rate of Addicted Mothers; Rose by Double-Digit Percentages Early in Decade, Seemed to Level Off in 2015–16," *Kentucky Health News*, September 3, 2018. Also see Egil Nygaard, Kari Slinning, Vibeke Moe, and Kristine B. Walhovd, "Behavior and Attention Problems in Eight-Year-Old Children with

Prenatal Opiate and Poly-Substance Exposure: A Longitudinal Study," *PLoS One* 11, no. 6: e0158054.

155　*Some 1,600 legal cases* Danny Hakim, Roni Caryn Rabin, and William K. Rashbaum, "Lawsuits Lay Bare Sackler Family's Role in Opioid Crisis," *New York Times*, April 1, 2019.

155　*29 percent of Pike County residents* Radden Keefe, "The Family That Built an Empire of Pain."

155　*Between 2016 and 2018* "Children in Kinship Care in United States, 2020–2022," Kids Count Data Center, Annie E. Casey Foundation, https://datacenter.aecf.org/data/tables/10455-children-in-kinship-care?loc =1&loct=2#ranking/2/any/true/2479/any/20161.

155　*Another 5 percent* "Children Ages Birth to 17 Entering Foster Care in United States, 2021," Kids Count Data Center, Annie E. Casey Foundation, https://datacenter.aecf.org/data/tables/6268-children-ages-birth-to -17-entering-foster-care?loc=1&loct=2#detailed/2/2-53/true/2048/any /15620.

155　*"competitors did not attempt"* Strategic Management Society, "New Study Shows Drug Manufacturers Actually Increased Opioid Marketing After Kentucky's Purdue Pharma Lawsuit," Medical Xpress, August 3, 2023, www.medicalxpress.com/news/2023-08-drug-opioid-kentucky-pur due-pharma.html. See also Lauren Kirschman, "Prescription Opi oid Companies Increased Marketing After Purdue Pharma Lawsuit, UW Study Shows," UW News, October 9, 2023, www.washington.edu /news/2023/10/09/prescription-opioid-companies-increased-market ing-after-purdue-pharma-lawsuit-uw-study-shows/.

156　*the manufacturer of Suboxone has been sued* Suboxone is classified as a Schedule III controlled substance in the United States—that is, a drug deemed to have medical value but with moderate risk for addiction. Mirroring the deceptive practices of Purdue Pharma in its marketing of OxyContin, the makers of Suboxone have come under legal scrutiny for presenting the drug as "less addictive" in an "illicit nationwide scheme to increase prescriptions." Manufacturer Reckitt Benckiser Group, for exam ple, agreed to pay the U.S. government a record $1.4 billion to settle fed eral probes into its marketing practices. See Soo Youn, "Suboxone Maker Reckitt Benckiser to Pay $1.4 billion in Largest Opioid Settlement in US History," ABC News, July 12, 2019.

156　*Purdue explored entering the "attractive market"* Alanna Durkin and Geoff

Mulvhill, "Purdue Pharma Family Sought to Profit Off Opioid Crisis, Filing Alleges," *PBS NewsHour*, February 1, 2019.

159 *organizing the United Mine Workers* William David Deskins, *Ginseng, Coal Dust, Moving Mountains: A History of Pike County, Kentucky* (Paintsville, KY: East Kentucky Press, 2018), 252.

159 *In the stand-off between workers* Lorraine Boissoneault, "The Coal Mining Massacre America Forgot," *Smithsonian Magazine*, April 25, 2017.

159 *Battle of Blair Mountain* Rachel Donaldson, "West Virginia Mine Wars," National Park Service, https://www.nps.gov/articles/series.htm?id =C8B39227-C269-2EE9-F318CA6374FA310F.

159 *"You know the origin of the term* redneck?*"* Others trace the origin of the term *redneck* differently. There is evidence that the term was used in the United States as early as the 1890s to denigrate poor rural people, particularly farmers fighting for populist reforms. See Patrick Huber and Kathleen Drowne, "Redneck: A New Discovery," *American Speech* 76, no. 4 (2001): 434–436. Various theories point out that "red perhaps [derives] from anger or from pellagra, but most likely from . . . labor in the sun . . . with the neck exposed." There is also evidence that the term was used as early as 1894 in South Africa as a Boer insult for those who did not wear broad-brimmed hats as the Boer did. See Harper Douglas, "Etymology of Redneck," Online Etymology Dictionary, www.etymonline.com/word/redneck.

161 *"poisoning the blood of our country"* Kate Sullivan, "Trump's Anti-Immigrant Comments Draw Rebuke," CNN, October 6, 2023.

162 *"he's calling immigrants 'rapists'"* For video of the speech in which Trump made these disparaging remarks about Mexican migrants, see "'Drug Dealers, Criminals, Rapists': What Trump Thinks of Mexicans," BBC, August 31, 2016. Trump expressed such views not only in public speeches but also in private meetings with border control officials. "Privately, the president had often talked about fortifying a border wall with a water-filled trench, stocked with snakes or alligators, prompting aides to seek a cost estimate. He wanted the wall electrified, with spikes on top that could pierce human flesh. After publicly suggesting that soldiers shoot migrants if they threw rocks, the president backed off when his staff told him that was illegal." Michael D. Shear and Julie Hirschfeld Davis, "Shoot Migrants' Legs, Build Alligator Moat: Behind Trump's Ideas for Border," *New York Times*, October 1, 2019.

163 *"when your region's on the skids"* Christopher Sebastian Parker, "Status

Threat: Moving the Right Further to the Right?," *Daedalus* 150, no. 20 (Spring 2021): 56–75.

163 *"status threat"* Parker, "Status Threat."

164 *"the girls quickly stuffed the dope"* "The Dangers of Hiding Drugs in Body Cavities," Recovery First Treatment Center, December 20, 2022, www .recoveryfirst.org/blog/treatment/the-dangers-of-hiding-drugs-in-body-cavi ties/.

165 *Midlife deaths from drugs and alcohol* See William Julius Wilson, *The Truly Disadvantaged: The Inner City, the Underclass, and Public Policy*, 2nd ed. (Chicago: University of Chicago Press, 2012 [1987]). Also see Wilson, *When Work Disappears: The World of the New Urban Poor* (New York: Vintage Books, 1997).

165 *This lasted until 2013* Anne Case and Angus Deaton, *Diseases of Despair and the Future of Capitalism* (Princeton, NJ: Princeton University Press, 2020), 5–6.

165 *in 2022 a local drug dealer* "Staff Report," *Appalachian News Express*, October 11–12, 2022.

Chapter 11

171 *A religious group called Mountain Mission* The Mountain Mission used the hashtag #PrayersForPikeville. Blake Montgomery, "The Far Right and Left Confronted Each Other in a Small Kentucky Town but It Remained Mostly Peaceful," BuzzFeed News, April 29, 2017.

173 *Present instead was the press* Dave Mistich, "'Surrender Under Protest': Another Take on Pikeville, Kentucky's White Supremacist Rally and Counter Protest," 100 Days in Appalachia, May 8, 2017.

173 *With them were members of Redneck Revolt* Cecilia Saixue Watt, "Redneck Revolt: The Armed Leftwing Group That Wants to Stamp Out Fascism," *The Guardian*, July 11, 2017.

173 *"If fascists make the trains"* Lois Beckett, "Neo-Nazis and Anti-Fascist Protesters Leave Kentucky After Standoff," *The Guardian*, April 30, 2017.

173 *At last, at 3:00 p.m., the caravan arrived* For a photo essay documenting the rally, see Pat Jarrett, "A Neo-Nazi Gathering in Kentucky—in Pictures," *The Guardian*, June 4, 2017. See also Bill Estep, "Hardly Peaceful, but No Violence as White Nationalists, Protesters Yell in Pikeville," *Lexington Herald-Leader*, April 29, 2017.

174 *"NO HATE IN MY HOLLER"* The T-shirts were designed by the Whitesburg-based artist Lacy Hale. www.lacyhale.com.

174 *He was doxxing* "White Nationalists, Counterprotesters Prepare for Kentucky Rally: Part 3," YouTube, posted by ABC News, August 19, 2017, www.youtube.com/watch?v=7DUfaorghFU.

174 *"sooner or later [become] your police officers"* See Estep, "Hardly Peaceful, but No Violence."

175 *Neo-Nazi Matthew Heimbach, Jeff Schoep* The Southern Poverty Law Center maintains profiles on prominent hate group leaders. For more information on Heimbach and Schoep, see SPLC's Extremist Files, https://www.splcenter.org/fighting-hate/extremist-files/individual.

175 *Among the neo-Nazis, a winsome* Jarrett, "A Neo-Nazi Gathering in Kentucky."

175 *a criminal summons* Canadian Press, "Man Charged with Harassment over Removal of Trump Protesters," Battlefords Now, May 1, 2017, www.battlefordsnow.com/2017/05/01/man-charged-with-harassment-over-removal-of-trump-protesters/.

177 *The tune originated* Civil rights activist Fannie Lou Hamer performed a version of this hymn, recounting that her mother would sing it in the fields as a sharecropper in Mississippi. See Fannie Lou Hamer, "I'm Gonna Land on the Shore," YouTube, posted by Fannie Lou Hamer—Topic, July 8, 2015, www.youtube.com/watch?v=TP2I_BYo8VY.

177 *Florence Reece* Florence Reece cites two different hymns as the source melody for "Which Side Are You On?" In a 1996 interview she remembers it as "Lay the Lily Low." There is no audio or written record of this specific hymn, which is not unusual in the folk genre. See Guy Carawan and Candie Carawan, *Voices from the Mountains: The People of Appalachia—Their Faces, Their Words, Their Songs* (Athens, GA: Brown Thrasher Books, 1996). In a prior 1978 interview, she cannot recall the name of the source hymn, but notes that it includes the lyrics "I'm gonna land on that shore / I'm gonna land on that shore / I'm gonna land on that shore and be saved forever more." See Florence Reece, "Lay the Lily Low," Digital Library of Appalachia, Appalachian College Association, 1978, audiocassette ww08406.mp3.

177 *The strike in which Reece's husband* John C. Hennen, "Introduction to the New Edition," *Harlan Miners Speak: Report on Terrorism in the Kentucky Coal Fields Prepared by Members of the National Committee for the*

Defense of Political Prisoners (Lexington: University Press of Kentucky, 2008).

178 *folk singer Ani DiFranco* Ani DiFranco, "¿Which Side Are You On?," MP3 audio, track 3 on *¿Which Side Are You On?*, 2012.

179 *rewritten by an alt-right songwriter* Paddy Tarleton, "Which Side Are You On," MP3 audio, track 2 on *Diversity Is Our Strength*, 2016. See also Brendan Joel Kelley, "The Alt-Right's New Soundtrack of Hate," Southern Poverty Law Center, October 9, 2017.

179 *Each set of lyrics reflected moments* Thanks to Kirstin Krusell for this idea about the emotional importance of music in social movements.

Chapter 12

181 *a chorus of five hundred* Roger Alford, "Hundreds of Singers Sign Up for 'Hope for the Mountains' Choir," *Kentucky Today*, October 17, 2018.

181 *Pikeville's first LGBTQ parade* Chris Kenning, "'Things Have Changed': Why More Kentucky Towns Are Embracing LGBTQ Pride Parades," *Courier Journal*, June 13, 2019. For the website of Pikeville's Pride events, see www.pikeville-pride.square.site/.

181 *In 2020, a Black Lives Matter parade* Emily Bennett, "Many Gather in Pikeville to Rally for 'Public Grief,'" *Mountain News WYMT*, June 1, 2020.

181 *organized a follow-up event* Cory Sanning, "Back the Blues Rally Aims to Spread Awareness for Law Enforcement," WKYT, September 5, 2020.

182 *its Gun and Knife Show* Gun Show Trader, "Pikeville Gun & Knife Show," www.gunshowtrader.com/gun-shows/pikeville-gun-show/."

182 *Things had changed in Matthew's political life* Michael Edison Hayden, Hannah Gais, Cassie Miller, Megan Squire, and Jason Wilson, "'Unite the Right' 5 Years Later: Where Are They Now?," Southern Poverty Law Center, August 11, 2022.

182 *Referring to it as a "car accident"* Laura Santhanam, "How White Nationalist Leader Matt Heimbach Defends Violence at Saturday's Rally in Charlottesville," *PBS NewsHour*, August 15, 2017.

184 *he had been banned from traveling* Rose Falvey, "White Nationalist Matthew Heimbach Banned from the United Kingdom," Southern Poverty Law Center, November 4, 2015.

186 *This was the first time* The one exception was his discussion of the Black Muslims with whom he had once agreed about racial separation.

188 *A movement for racial justice was on the rise* Larry Buchanan, Quoctrung

Bui, and Jugal K. Patel, "Black Lives Matter May Be the Largest Movement in US History," *New York Times*, July 3, 2020.

188 *Ninety-three percent of the 7,750* Sanya Mansoor, "93% of Black Lives Matter Protests Have Been Peaceful, New Report Finds," *Time*, September 5, 2020.

189 *Between 2015 and 2020, 405 attacks* Dan Glaun, "A Timeline of Domestic Extremism in the US, from Charlottesville to January 6," PBS, April 21, 2021.

189 *Inside the right* Meanwhile, Jeff Schoep was to pursue a course of action that set off a bizarre train of events, shifting the theater of violence from truth to fiction and back. Having stood proudly beside Matthew first in Pikeville and then in Charlottesville, Schoep now found himself sued for $25 million on behalf of nine victims for having planned the violence that led to their injuries. Schoep feared losing his house and more, and wanted to escape the lawsuit. For help, Schoep appealed to a Black California-based Baptist preacher and self-described civil rights activist, James Hart Stern. Born in Watts, California, Stern, an ordained minister and mediator, later found himself in a Mississippi jail for embezzlement. There Stern shared a cell with the notorious white racist Edgar Ray Killen, a KKK Grand Wizard jailed for the murder of three civil rights workers in Mississippi in 1964. To the astonishment of many, Stern and Killen struck up a highly unlikely prison friendship. When Killen was close to death, he deeded his land and power of attorney over his personal affairs to his Black cellmate, Stern. After Killen died and Stern was released from prison, Stern used this same power of attorney to disband the KKK chapter Killen had once led. When facing financial woes, Schoep also turned to Stern, filing paperwork with the Michigan Department of Licensing and Regulatory Affairs formally transferring the presidency of the NSM to James Stern. Here again Stern "flipped" the radical group. Newly in charge of NSM, Stern changed its plea from "innocent" to "guilty." He removed all antisemitic writing from the NSM website and posted a link to Steven Spielberg's anti-Nazi blockbuster *Schindler's List*, a film that portrays the Auschwitz gas chambers Matthew Heimbach still denied. In a later interview he gave to the *Washington Post*, Stern proudly described himself as the "race whisperer." Meanwhile, Schoep discovered that he remained liable for the Charlottesville-related financial charges and claimed Stern had deceived him. Schoep's appeal to antiracist James Stern resembled the Black hero of Spike Lee's *BlacKKKlansman*—and

that film ended with footage of actual marchers in Charlottesville, which Matthew Heimbach and Jeff Schoep had once proudly led. At age forty-seven Jeff Schoep renounced his racism in earnest and began his new career as a "former," publicly denouncing racism. "The liberals are using Jeff and he's making money as a sellout for the Simon Wiesenthal Center," Heimbach complained. See Katie Mettler, "The 'Race Whisperer,'" *Washington Post*, October 30, 2019.

189 *Representative Thomas Massie* See Aila Slisco, "Is Kentucky Republican Thomas Massie Making a Case for Secession?," *Newsweek*, December 17, 2021. U.S. Congresswoman Marjorie Taylor Greene has called for a national divorce and warned of a looming civil war. See Hall, "Marjorie Taylor Green Gets Sean Hannity On Board for National Divorce." And according to a March 2023 poll of 1,500 U.S. adults fielded by YouGov for *The Economist*, 23 percent of respondents "strongly agree" or "somewhat agree" that "We need a national divorce. We need to separate by red states and blue states." See https://docs.cdn.yougov.com/1i6zpqns9b/econtoplines.pdf.

189 *Representative Marjorie Taylor Greene* See Colby Hall, "Marjorie Taylor Green Gets Sean Hannity On Board for National Divorce—Then Warns of Looming Civil War," MSN, February 22, 2023.

189 *Senator Lindsey Graham* Kim Bellware, "There Will Be 'Riots in the Street' If Trump Is Prosecuted, Graham Says," *Washington Post*, August 29, 2022.

189 *"Churchill Downs"* For a description of the events that day, see Emily Shugerman and Gerry Seavo James, "Three Injured as Rival Armed Militias Converge on Louisville," *Daily Beast*, February 15, 2021. For a description of NFAC, see "Not Fucking Around Coalition," Wikipedia, last modified August 22, 2023.

Chapter 13

193 *80 percent of voters* See Commonwealth of Kentucky, State Board of Elections, "Official 2016 General Election Results," 2016, https://elect.ky.gov/results/2010-2019/Documents/2016%20General%20Election%20Results.pdf.

193 *Vehicle parades* Tommy Pool and Dakota Makres, "Eastern Kentuckians Participate in a President Trump Caravan," WYMT, November 1, 2020, www.wymt.com/2020/11/01/eastern-kentuckians-participate-in-a-president-trump-caravan/.

193 *Skydivers and a helicopter* Lucas Aulbach, "Hundreds of Boats Hit Kentucky Lake on Saturday for Pro-Trump Parade," *Courier Journal*, September 6, 2020.

194 *A national Barna survey* Barna, "U.S. Adults Believe Hate Speech Has Increased—Mainly Online," July 16, 2019, www.barna.com /research/hate-speech-increased/.

198 *Rose Montoya* Houston Keene, "Republicans Hammer Biden After Trans Activists Go Topless at White House event: 'Very Disgraceful,'" Fox News, June 13, 2023.

198 *1.03 percent of Americans* "What Percentage of the US Population Is Transgender?," USA Facts, August 3, 2023, https://usafacts.org/articles /what-percentage-of-the-us-population-is-transgender/.

198 *Back the Blues* Cory Sanning, "Back the Blues Rally Aims to Spread Awareness for Law Enforcement," WKYT, September 5, 2020.

199 *the* Appalachian News-Express *dismissed January 6* J. K. Coleman, "Opinion," *Appalachian News-Express*, January 12–14, 2021.

200 *Chevron, Shell, and Exxon* John Cassidy, "As Gas Prices Reach New Highs, Oil Companies Are Profiteering," *New Yorker*, May 11, 2022.

200 *widened the gap* Jacob Hacker and Paul Pierson, *Winner-Take-All Politics: How Washington Made the Rich Richer—and Turned Its Back on the Middle Class* (New York: Simon & Schuster, 2010).

202 *Roy Cohn* Michael Kruse, "The Final Lesson Donald Trump Never Learned from Roy Cohn," *Politico*, September 19, 2019, https://www.politico .com/magazine/story/2019/09/19/roy-cohn-donald-trump-documentary -228144/.

204 *Black Robe Regiment* See David Gilbert, "Meet the 'Black Robe Regiment' of Extremist Pastors Spreading Christian Nationalism," *Vice*, November 8, 2022. See also Jonathan Den Hartog, "What the Black Robe Regiment Misses About Revolutionary Pastors," *Christianity Today*, January 20, 2021.

205 *It removes judgment* More accurately, the deep story relocates judgment from a statement like "X is wrong and Y is right" to a statement like "this story expresses the truth, which itself implies judgement about the deservingness of those positioned as line waiter and line cutter."

205 *deep story* See Arlie Russell Hochschild, *Strangers in Their Own Land: Anger and Mourning on the American Right* (New York: The New Press, 2016), 135–151.

206 *Trump organization began selling digital trading cards* Michael C. Bender and Maggie Haberman, "Trump Sells a New Image as the Hero of $99 Trading Cards," *New York Times*, December 15, 2022.

207 *Starting in 2012, Donald Trump* Terrance Smith and Jessie DiMartino, "Trump Has Longstanding History of Calling Elections 'Rigged' If He Doesn't Like the Results," ABC News, November 11, 2020.

207 *The idea caught on* FiveThirtyEight, "60 Percent of Americans Will Have an Election Denier on the Ballot This Fall," November 8, 2022, https://www.projects.fivethirtyeight.com/republicans-trump-election-fraud/.

207 *By May 2023, CNN found* Philip Bump, "Six in 10 Republicans Still Think 2020 Was Illegitimate," *Washington Post*, May 24, 2023.

208 *Stop the Steal* See Charles Homans, "How 'Stop the Steal' Captured the American Right," *New York Times Magazine*, July 19, 2022.

208 *"termination" of the U.S. Constitution* Kristen Holmes, "Trump Calls for Termination of the Constitution in Truth Social Post," CNN, December 4, 2022.

208 *Quinnipiac University poll* Tim Malloy and Doug Schwartz, "Lowest Opinion of Trump Among Voters in Seven Years, Quinnipiac University National Poll Finds; Biden Approval Rating Climbs," Quinnipiac University poll, December 14, 2022, https://poll.qu.edu/poll-release?releaseid=3863.

208 *campaign confirmed the finding: not stolen* Steven Livingston, "An Exploration of Cognitive Science and Sociological Approaches to the Crisis of Democracy," Scripts Working Paper No. 31, Freie Universitat Berlin, Edwin-Redslob-Strabe 29, 14195, Berlin, Germany, p. 3.

209 *Trump's backers filed sixty-two lawsuits* Will Cummings, Joey Garrison, and Jim Sergent, "By the Numbers: President Donald Trump's Failed Efforts to Overturn the Election," *USA Today*, January 6, 2021.

209 *Wisconsin and Arizona* Brockton Booker, "Arizona and Wisconsin Certify Election Results, Affirming Biden Victories," NPR, November 30, 2020.

209 *Commentators on Fox News later admitted* Jared Gans, "Trump Won't Commit to Accepting 2024 Election Results," *The Hill*, May 10, 2024

210 *So why did Roger Ford* On his Facebook page he shared an open letter posted in "Flag Officers 4 America"—a group of 124 retired generals and admirals who questioned the legitimacy of the election, and called to counter "Socialism, Marxism and Progressivism." Many were two decades retired and there were no four-star generals, but Ford, a great fan of the military, posted it to affirm his own view, a view shared by most Republicans and a large minority of Americans.

210 *But Democrats, too, distrust* Pew Research Center, "Public Trust in Government: 1958–2022," June 6, 2022, www.pewresearch.org/politics/2022/06/06/public-trust-in-government-1958-2022/.

210 *In a highly revealing study* Michael H. Keller and David D. Kirkpatrick, "Their America Is Vanishing. Like Trump, They Insist They Were Cheated," *New York Times*, October 23, 2022.

210 *139 Republican House members* Congress held two separate votes dealing with Republican objections to the 2020 election. One centered on the vote count in Pennsylvania, and the other on the vote count in Arizona. In the House, 139 Representatives supported one or both objections, and 64 rejected both objections. For a breakdown of how every lawmaker voted on the objections, see Harry Stevens, Daniela Santamariña, Kate Rabinowitz, Kevin Uhrmacher, and John Muyskens, "How Members of Congress Voted on Counting the Electoral College Vote," *Washington Post*, January 7, 2020.

210 *Those in districts voting "stolen"* Keller and Kirkpatrick, "Their America Is Vanishing." See also Charles Homans, "How 'Stop the Steal' Captured the American Right."

210 *Of the twelve Republican districts* According to Keller and Kirkpatrick, in the 139 districts whose representatives believe the election was "stolen," the proportion of white residents dropped about 35 percent more over the last thirty years than in other Republican districts.

210 *Republicans who believed* Philip Bump, "Republicans Who Watch Fox News Are More Likely to Believe False Theories About Jan. 6," *Washington Post*, January 3, 2022.

212 *"Farewell Kentucky"* Roger Ford, "Farewell, Kentucky," *Appalachian News-Express*, January 9, 2018.

212 *nearly half of the nation's 2,050* David McGranahan, John Cromartie, and Tim Wojan, "The Two Faces of Rural Population Loss Through Outmigration," Economic Research Service, U.S. Department of Agriculture, December 1, 2010, www.ers.usda.gov/amber-waves/2010/december/the-two-faces-of-rural-population-loss-through-outmigration/.

212 *the working-age population* James C. Davis, Anil Rupasingha, John Cromartie, and Austin Sanders, "Rural America at a Glance: 2022 Edition," Economic Research Service, U.S. Department of Agriculture, Bulletin No. 246, November 2022, https://www.ers.usda.gov/webdocs/publications/105155/eib-246.pdf?v=1662.

214 *Nicholas Jacobs and Daniel Shea* Nicholas F. Jacobs and Daniel M. Shea,

The Rural Voter: The Politics of Place and the Disuniting of America (New York: Columbia University Press, 2023), 272–273.

214 *"None of them could come up with one"* "The Rise and Implications of the Rural Voter with Dan Shea," YouTube, posted by Rural Urban Bridge Initiative, March 2, 2023, www.youtube.com/watch?v=P3emb1r8zmI.

214 *What came to mind instead* Jacobs and Shea, *The Rural Voter*, 274–275.

214 *127 "reality shows"* Jacobs and Shea, *The Rural Voter*, 275–276. From there the dominant image moved to quirky, lovable dramas such as *Schitt's Creek*, which was set in rural Canada.

214 *When asked how often* Jacobs and Shea, *The Rural Voter*, 282.

215 *In this he closely resembled* Katherine J. Cramer, *The Politics of Resentment: Rural Consciousness in Wisconsin and the Rise of Scott Walker* (Chicago: University of Chicago, 2016).

215 *overpaid and represented by "greedy" unions* Cramer, *The Politics of Resentment*.

215 *"Our schools also integrated early and well"* For an account of school integration in Pikeville from 1956 to 1965, see Mark Sohn, "The Black Struggle for Education and Learning," *Appalachian Heritage* 15, no. 4 (1987): 35–42.

215 *"outliers"* Malcolm Gladwell, *Outliers: The Story of Success* (New York: Little, Brown, 2008).

215 *Blacks are vastly poorer* Heather Long and Andrew Van Dam, "The Black-White Economic Divide Is as Wide as It Was in 1968," *Washington Post*, June 4, 2020.

216 *earn lower wages than whites* Eduardo Porter, "Black Workers Stopped Making Progress on Pay. Is It Racism?," *New York Times*, June 28, 2021.

215 *Bette Midler* Lisa Respers France, "Bette Midler Apologizes to West Virginia Residents for 'Poor, Illiterate, Strung Out' Tweet," CNN, December 22, 2021.

217 *"[sit in their] high perches"* Roger Ford, "Tale of Two States," *Appalachian News-Express*, July 18, 2017.

218 *twelve thousand well-paid corporate lobbyists* Ford was referring to government workers he imagined as wealthy and living in Washington, DC. Note: not all twelve thousand lobbyists *registered* in Washington, DC, necessarily live there. See Tala Hadavi, "Lobbying in Q1 Topped a Record $938 Million, but Lobbyists Say Their Profession Is Misunderstood," CNBC, October 5, 2020.

218 *"In 2014, Obama passed national legislation"* Suzanne Goldenberg, "Obama

Unveils Historic Rules to Reduce Coal Pollution by 30%," *The Guardian*, June 2, 2014.

218 *they came to undersell coal* As a result of cost competition from natural gas and renewable resources, almost a quarter of the country's coal-fired plants are scheduled to close by the end of the decade. See M. Tyson Brown, "Nearly a Quarter of the Operating U.S. Coal-Fired Fleet to Retire by 2029," U.S. Energy Information Agency, November 7, 2022, https://www.eia.gov/todayinenergy/detail.php?id=54559.

218 *On average, the marginal cost* Oliver Milman, "US Renewable Energy Farms Outstrip 99% of Coal Plants Economically—Study," *The Guardian*, January 30, 2023. Additional research projects that half of the country's remaining coal-fired capacity is on track to close by 2030. See Seth Feaster, "U.S. on Track to Close Half of Coal Capacity by 2026," Institute for Energy Economics and Financial Analysis, April 1, 2023, www.ieefa.org/resources/us-track-close-half-coal-capacity-2026.

218 *"coal companies out of business"* Scott Horsley, "Fact Check: Hillary Clinton and Coal Jobs," NPR, May 3, 2016.

219 *$20 billion a year on direct* Environmental and Energy Study Institute, "Fossil Fuel Subsidies: A Closer Look at Tax Breaks and Societal Costs," July 29, 2019, www.eesi.org/papers/view/fact-sheet-fossil-fuel-subsidies-a-closer-look-at-tax-breaks-and-societal-costs.

219 *40 percent of Kentucky's state budget* During fiscal year 2019, prior to the pandemic, Kentucky received 39.8 percent of its state revenue from federal funds. Rebecca Thiess, Justin Theal, and Brakeyshia Samms, "2019 Federal Share of State Revenue Remains Stable," Pew Trusts, December 22, 2021. In fiscal year 2021, that figure reached 46.2 percent, driven in part by federal pandemic aid. Rebecca Thiess, Justin Theal, and Kate Watkins, "Pandemic Aid Lifts Federal Share of State Budgets to New Highs," Pew Trusts, August 28, 2023.

219 *22 percent of residents receive SNAP* As of May 2023, 20.6 percent of Pike County residents were receiving SNAP benefits. That's 11,591 residents, or 5,847 households. See Jessica Klein, "Tracking SNAP in Kentucky," Kentucky Center for Economic Policy, June 23, 2023, https://kypolicy.org/tracking-snap-in-kentucky/. And following dramatic increases in enrollment due to COVID-era policy changes, as of August 2023 46.6 percent of Pike County residents were enrolled in Medicaid. See "Monthly Medicaid Counts by County," Department for Medicaid Services, Kentucky Cabinet for Health and Family Services, https://www.chfs.ky.gov

/agencies/dms/dafm/Pages/statistics.aspx?View=2023%20Reports%20 by%20County&Title=Table%20Viewer%20Webpart.

220 *people "on the other side of New Jersey"* Glenn Kessler, "Trump's Outrageous Claim That 'Thousands' of New Jersey Muslims Celebrated the 9/11 Attacks," *Washington Post*, November 22, 2015.

220 *"Our great African-American president"* Sheryl Gay Stolberg, "Baltimore to Trump: You Lost Your Authority to Criticize," *New York Times*, July 29, 2019.

220 *"When Mexico sends its people"* Alexander Burns, "Choice Words from Donald Trump, Presidential Candidate," *New York Times*, June 16, 2015.

220 *"due to the recent derogatory statements"* Nathan Layne, "Macy's Cuts Ties with Trump, New York City Reviews Contracts," Reuters, July 1, 2015.

220 *Univision also announced* Layne, "Macy's Cuts Ties with Trump."

220 *New York City mayor Bill de Blasio* Layne, "Macy's Cuts Ties with Trump."

220 *Macy's announced* Layne, "Macy's Cuts Ties with Trump."

221 *Ana Maria Salazar* Sean Hannity later characterized Salazar's reaction as a typical example of how the "alt-left propaganda media" "mercilessly mocked" Trump. Sean Hannity, "Trump's Warning on Illegal Immigrants Proves Grimly Prophetic," Fox News, March 22, 2017.

221 *"If NBC is so weak"* Adam B. Lerner, "Sean Hannity: Trump's Remarks Not 'Racially Tinged,'" *Politico*, June 30, 2015.

221 *Trump sued Univision* Nick Gass, "Macy's Dumps Trump," *Politico*, July 1, 2015. Also see Joseph Ax, "Trump Sues Univision for $500 Million over Miss USA Cancellation," Reuters, June 30, 2015.

221 *"I will knock the hell out of ISIS"* David Keen, *Shame: The Politics and Power of an Emotion* (Princeton, NJ: Princeton University Press, 2023, p. 111).

221 *Trump broad-jumped to the claim* David Keen, *Shame: The Politics and Power of an Emotion* (Princeton, NJ: Princeton University Press, 2023, p. 111).

221 *the "founder" of ISIS* Sabrina Siddiqui, "Donald Trump calls Obama the 'founder of Isis,'" *The Guardian*, August 11, 2016.

222 *White House Correspondents' Association Dinner* Tom Kludt, "Trump to Snub White House Correspondents' Dinner for Third Year in a Row," CNN, April 5, 2019.

222 *"Why do I have to repent"* See Ray Nothstine, "Trump: 'Why Do I Have to Repent or Ask for Forgiveness if I Am Not Making Mistakes?,'" *Christian Post*, July 2015. For a video of the appearance, see C-SPAN, "Presidential Candidate Donald Trump at the Family Leadership Summit," July 18, 2015, www.c-span.org/video/?327045-5 /presidential-candidate-donald-trump-family-leadership-summit.

223 *He was the son* Mary L. Trump, *Too Much and Never Enough: How My Family Created the World's Most Dangerous Man* (New York: Simon & Schuster, 2022).

224 *"I was indicted for you"* Donald Trump speech, YouTube, https://www.you tube.com/watch?v=f9NNBQaHD9I, July 17, 2023.

224 *a quasi-religious figure of sacrifice* "Donald Trump, 'The Apprentice,' and Secular Rapture" *The Boston Globe*, September 6, 2017.

225 *the cultural space for the displaced* Geoffrey Gorer, *Death, Grief, and Mourning* (Garden City, NY: Doubleday-Anchor, 1967).

Chapter 14

227 *fell from 6,460 in 2016 to 3,911 in 2020* For coal mining employment figures from 2000 to present, see "Quarterly Coal Dashboard," Kentucky Energy and Environment Cabinet, https://eec.ky.gov/Energy/News-Publi cations/Pages/quarterly-coal-dashboard.aspx.

227 *"the fastest decline in coal-fuel capacity"* Eric Lipton, " 'The Coal Industry Is Back,' Trump Proclaimed. It Wasn't," *New York Times*, October 18, 2020.

228 *the number of the nation's coal jobs* For a chart illustrating coal mining employment between 1985 and 2023, see U.S. Bureau of Labor Statistics, "All Employees, Coal Mining [CES1021210001]," retrieved from FRED, Federal Reserve Bank of St. Louis, September 5, 2023, https://fred.st louisfed.org/series/CES1021210001. See also Will Wade, "US Coal Use Is Rebounding Under Biden Like It Never Did with Trump," Bloomberg, October 12, 2021.

228 *most workers (58 percent)* John Caplan, "America's Hourly Workers," *Forbes*, March 12, 2021.

228 *During this period, hourly workers' total compensation* David Salkever, "Real Pay Data Show Trump's 'Blue Collar Boom' Is More of a Bust for US Workers, in 3 Charts," *The Conversation*, February 7, 2020. Other wage calculations between 2016 and 2020 don't include benefits. BBC News, "US 2020 Election: The Economy Under Trump in Six Charts," November 3, 2020.

228 *the Dow Jones Industrial Average had grown* Moreover, the cumulative Gross Domestic Product (GDP)—the value of goods and services produced during a given period—rose higher (18 percent vs 7 percent) under Biden than Trump. Facts First, "Presidential Comparison: Biden vs Trump," last updated December 20, 2023, https://www.factsarefirst.com/comparison /joe-biden/donald-trump.

228 *thickened the wallets of CEOs and stock owners* Catherine Thorbecke, "A Look at Trump's Economic Legacy," ABC News, January 20, 2021.

228 *indeed rose in a frightening way under Biden* U.S. Bureau of Labor Statistics, "12-Month Percentage Change, Consumer Price Index, By Region and Division, All Items," October 2023, https://www.bls.gov/charts/consumer-price-index/consumer-price-index-by-region.htm.

228 *Working Families Tax Relief Act* U.S. Representative Rosa DeLauro, "DeLauro, DelBene, Torres Reintroduce Legislation to Expand and Improve Child Tax Credit," press release, June 7, 2023, https://delauro.house.gov/media-center/press-releases/delauro-delbene-torres-reintroduce-legislation-expand-and-improve-child.

229 *Four protesters and five police officers died* Chris Cameron, "These Are the People Who Died in Connection with the Capitol Riot," *New York Times*, January 5, 2022.

229 *called family members to say goodbye* Marin Pengelly, "Pence Secret Service Detail Feared for Their Lives During Capitol Riot," *The Guardian*, July 21, 2022.

229 *some 9,600 threats* Zachary Cohen and Whitney Wild, "Frustrated Lawmakers Want Protection for Their Families as Threats Increase," CNN, October 28, 2022.

229 *72 percent felt* Hannah Hartig, "In Their Own Words: How Americans Reacted to the Rioting at the US Capitol," Pew Research Center, January 15, 2021.

229 *Among those who broke in* Nick Niedzwiadek, "Capitol Police Officer Says Jan. 6 Rioters Used N-Word Against Him, Others," *Politico*, July 27, 2021.

229 *"one woman in a pink 'MAGA' shirt"* Aaron Morrison, "Racism of Rioters Takes Center Stage on Jan. 6 Hearing," Associated Press, July 28, 2021.

230 *the axe of public judgment* John Gramlich, "A Look Back at Americans' Reactions to the Jan. 6 Riot at the U.S. Capitol," Pew Research Center, January 4, 2022.

230 *they returned to their like-minded circle* David Keen, *Shame: The Power and Politics of Emotion* (Princeton, NJ: University of Princeton Press, 2023, p. 125).

231 *Robert Pape* Pape, "Deep, Divisive, Disturbing and Continuing." See also Lois Beckett, "Most Alleged Capitol Rioters Unconnected to Extremist Groups, Analysis Finds," *The Guardian*, March 4, 2021.

231   *less likely to embrace violence* Tyler Austin Harper, "An Utterly Misleading Book About Rural America," *The Atlantic*, April 4, 2024.

231   *Newsmax* Jeremy Barr, "Why These Fox News Loyalists Have Changed the Channel to Newsmax," *Washington Post*, December 27, 2020.

231   *a 2023 CNN/SSRC poll* Alison Durkee, "Republicans Increasingly Realize There's No Evidence of Election Fraud—But Most Still Think 2020 Election Was Stolen Anyway, Poll Finds," *Forbes*, March 14, 2023.

231   *Americans believed the election fair* Brittany Shepherd, "Majority of Americans Think Jan. 6 Attack Threatened Democracy: POLL," ABC News, January 2, 2022.

231   *Tucker Carlson, then at Fox News* Sarana Hale Spencer, Robert Farley, and D'Angelo Gore, "Explaining the Missing Context of Tucker Carlson's Jan. 6 Presentation," FactCheck.org, March 10, 2023.

232   *"crimes committed in the spirit of play"* Hannah Arendt, *The Origins of Totalitarianism* (New York: Harvest/Harcourts, 1951), 190. Cited in David Keen, *Shame: The Politics and Power of an Emotion*, 125.

233   *"there is a kind of instant escape"* Keen, *Shame: The Power and Politics of Emotion*, 125.

233   *the Department of Justice had indicted 1,265 people* U.S. Department of Justice, "Three Years Since the Jan. 6 Attack on the Capitol," press release, January 5, 2024, https://www.justice.gov/usao-dc/36-months-jan-6-attack-capitol-0.

233   *thirty were residents of Kentucky* Natalie Pasquinelli, my research assistant, used several databases, including LexisNexis, Westlaw, and Bloomberg, as well as PACER and Court Listener, to locate dockets of the cases, including "character letters" and "personal letters" for all the Kentucky defendants. For a searchable database of all federal criminal cases related to January 6, see NPR, "The Jan. 6 Attack: The Cases Behind the Biggest Criminal Investigation in U.S. History," last updated February 16, 2024, https://www.npr.org/2021/02/09/965472049/the-capitol-siege-the-arrested-and-their-stories.

234   *Gracyn Courtright* Samantha Hawkins, "Prison for University of Kentucky Student Who Stormed the Capitol," Courthouse News Service, December 17, 2021.

234   *Lori Vinson* Billy Kobin, "Kentucky Nurse, Air Force Veteran Sentenced for Their Roles in Jan. 6 Riot at US Capitol," *Courier-Journal*, October 22, 2021.

234   *"I'd do this all over again tomorrow"* Dan Cancian, "Lori Vinson, Nurse

Who Entered Capitol During Riot, Says She 'Would Do It Again,'" *Newsweek*, January 17, 2021.

234 *"In reflection, I regret"* Kobin, "Kentucky Nurse."

234 *Both Gracyn Courtright and Lori Vinson* Vinson was sentenced to five years of probation, a $5,000 fine, $500 in restitution, and 120 hours of community service. See Kobin, "Kentucky Nurse."

235 *In a recorded phone call, Trump said* "'I Need 11,000 Votes,' Trump Told Ga. Election Official | Jan. 6 hearings," YouTube, posted by PBS NewsHour, June 21, 2022, www.youtube.com/watch?v=AbFc9T7KXA0.

235 *posed for a memorable mugshot* "Trump Leaves Atlanta After Surrendering at Fulton County Jail," FOX 5 Atlanta, August 24, 203.

235 *The Trump scowl* Tara Suter, "Trump Unveils Digital Trading Cards 'MugShot Edition,'" *The Hill*, December 12, 2023.

235 *"Due to the great Excitement and Success"* See Collect Trump Cards, "Frequently Asked Questions," https://collecttrumpcards.com/#faqs.

236 *on sale for $99 each* See Collect Trump Cards, "Frequently Asked Questions," https://collecttrumpcards.com/#faqs.

238 *such words as "kill, destroy, fight"* Patrick Healy and Maggie Haberman, "95,000 Words, Many of Them Ominous, From Donald Trump's Tongue," *New York Times*, December 5, 2015.

239 *punched a Latino gas station attendant* Mike Levine, "'No Blame'? ABC News Finds 54 Cases Invoking 'Trump' in Connection with Violence, Threats, Alleged Assaults," ABC News, May 30, 2020.

239 *Trump predicted "death and destruction"* Maggie Haberman, Jonah E. Bromwich, and William K. Rashbaum, "Trump, Escalating Attacks, Raises Specter of Violence If He Is Charged," *New York Times*, April 4, 2023.

239 *"ALVIN: I AM GOING TO KILL YOU."* David French, "The Rule of Law Now Depends on Republicans," *New York Times*, March 31, 2023. The powder was later determined to be not harmful. We will "not tolerate attempts to intimidate our office or threaten the rule of law in New York," Bragg responded. Since that time, Trump has called Mr. Bragg, the first Black district attorney in Manhattan, an "animal" and posted on his Truth Social feed a large picture of himself holding a baseball bat, juxtaposed with an image of Mr. Bragg.

239 *He invited Kanye West* Maggie Haberman and Alan Feuer, "Trump's Latest Dinner Guest: Nick Fuentes, White Supremacist," *New York Times*, November 25, 2022. See also Jason Wilson, "Kanye's Antisemitic Hate

Speech Platformed by Enablers in Tech, Media, and Politics," Southern Poverty Law Center, December 7, 2022.

239 *Trump offered to help pay the legal defense fees* Bevan Hurley, "Trump Says He Is Financially Supporting Some Jan 6 Suspects and Plans to Pardon Them if Re-elected," Yahoo News, September 1, 2022.

239 *song called "Justice for All"* Marisa Dellatto, "Trump Hits No. 1 with 'Justice for All' Song Made with Jan. 6 Arrestees," *Forbes*, March 21, 2023.

Chapter 15

241 *"most police are bad people"* Arlie Hochschild, "The Republicans Are Disconnected from Reality? It's Even Worse About Liberals," *The Guardian*, July 21, 2019. For data on misperceptions about opposing political parties, see Douglas J. Ahler and Gaurav Sood, "The Parties in Our Heads: Misperceptions About Party Composition and Their Consequences," *Journal of Politics* 80, no. 3 (2018): 964–981, and Daniel Yudkin, Stephen Hawkins, and Tim Dixon, "The Perception Gap: How False Impressions are Pulling Americans Apart," More in Common, June 2019.

241 *cut off contact at first signs* Mark Jurkowitz and Amy Mitchell, "A Sore Subject: Almost Half of Americans Have Stopped Talking Politics with Someone," Pew Research Center, February 5, 2020.

241 *personal contact makes more of a difference* Christopher Garneau, "The Limits of Tolerance in Polarized Times" (paper presented at Building Bridges 2.0: Liberty, Justice & Equality Conference, University of Science & Arts of Oklahoma, Chickasha, Oklahoma, October 23, 2023). Also see Christopher R. H. Garneau and Philip Schwadel, "Examining the Influence of Political Affiliation and Orientation on Political Tolerance," *Socius* 8: 1–17.

242 *race has become key* See, for example, Marsha Blackburn, "Why Is Critical Race Theory Dangerous for Our Kids?" July 12, 2021, www.blackburn .senate.gov/2021/7/why-is-critical-race-theory-dangerous-for-our-kids.

242 *Since 2020, at least thirty-five states* Kiara Alfonseca, "Map: Where Anti-Critical Race Theory Efforts Have Reached," ABC News, March 24, 2022.

242 *"educators are indoctrinating students"* Alfonseca, "Map."

242 *"any classroom instruction or discussion"* "An Act Relating to Public Education and Declaring an Emergency," H.B. 14, Kentucky General Assembly, 2022 Regular Session (2021), https://apps.legislature.ky.gov/record/22rs /hb14.html.

242 *In 2022, the Kentucky state legislature* Peter Greene, "Teacher Anti-CRT Bills Coast to Coast: A State-by-State Guide," *Forbes*, February 16, 2022.

242 *"people of many different races and ethnicities"* Juliana Menasce Horowitz, Pew Research Center, "Americans See Advantages and Challenges in Country's Growing Racial and Ethnic Diversity," May 8, 2019. Also see Kim Parker, Juliana Menasce Horowitz, Anna Brown, Richard Fry, D'Vera Cohn, and Ruth Igielnik, "What Unites and Divides Urban, Suburban, and Rural Communities," May 22, 2018.

243 *Among rural white Americans, it was* Urban whites were far more sympathetic than were rural whites (62 percent agreement compared to 33 percent), and women slightly more than men (51 percent agreement compared to 49 percent). American National Election Studies, *ANES 2020 Time Series Study Full Release* [dataset and documentation], July 19, 2021, www.electionstudies.org.

245 *"They understand that a Minneapolis police officer"* Evan Hill, Ainara Tiefenthäler, Christiaan Triebert, et al., "How George Floyd Was Killed in Police Custody," *New York Times*, May 31, 2020.

248 *the 2020 American National Election Studies (ANES)* American National Election Studies, *ANES 2020 Time Series Study Full Release* (dataset and documentation), July 19, 2021, www.electionstudies.org.

Chapter 16

252 *Hatfield-McCoy Reconciliation Day* Rome Neal, "Official End of Legendary Feud," CBS News, June 13, 2003.

253 *The Hog Trail Cabin became a local voting center* Buddy Forbes, "Hatfield & McCoy cabin opens doors to politics for first time in 140 years," *WYMT*, November 8, 2022.

252 *if the McCoys and the Hatfields could settle* The GroundTruth Project, "An Appalachian Trail: Finding the Real McCoy," October 11, 2017, https://thegroundtruthproject.org/crossing-the-divide-kentucky/.

253 *each clan in the material and pride economies* See historian Altina L. Waller's commentary on the social and economic context of the feud in Kenneth Best, "Hatfield-McCoy Feud Carries Lessons for Today," *UConn Today*, University of Connecticut, September 10, 2019. See also Altina L. Waller, "Hatfield-McCoy: Economic Motives Fueled Fed That Tarred Region's Image," *Lexington Herald-Leader*, July 30, 2012.

253 *forced to work as hired hands on Hatfield land* Altina L. Waller, "The Hatfield-McCoy Feud," University of North Carolina Press (blog),

June 11, 2012. See also Altina L. Waller, *Feud: Hatfields, McCoys, and Social Change in Appalachia, 1860–1900* (Chapel Hill: University of North Carolina Press, 1988). See also Nadia Suleman, "The Causes of the Hatfield and McCoy Feud Ran Deeper Than You May Think, *Time Magazine*, September 10, 2019. As Suleman writes, "Many of the McCoy sons were working as hired hands. They weren't going to own their own homes. They were going to have to live in company homes. There's a lot of frustration."

253 *"a situation ripe for resentment, aggression and violence"* Altina L. Waller, "The Hatfield-McCoy Feud," University of North Carolina Press (blog), June 11, 2012.

254 *Of all the Civil War–based reenactments staged in 2023* LivingHistoryArchive, "Civil War Reenactment Events 2023—the Complete List," https://www.livinghistoryarchive.com/article/civil-war-events-in-america.

254 *dedicated to the losers than to the winners* Southern Poverty Law Center, *Whose Heritage? Public Symbols of the Confederacy*, 3rd edition, 2022, www.splcenter.org/sites/default/files/whose-heritage-report-third-edition.pdf.

254 *there exist far more Confederate monuments than Union ones* Wikipedia, "List of American Civil War monuments in Kentucky," last edited March 8, 2022.

254 *obelisk dedicated to Jefferson Davis* Historical Marker Database, "Memorialization of Jefferson Davis," www.hmdb.org/m.asp?m=81014.

254 *"nineteenth-century equivalent of the Third World"* Wolfgang Schivelbusch, *The Culture of Defeat: On National Trauma, Mourning, and Recovery*, trans. Jefferson Chase (New York: Metropolitan Books, 2004), 84.

254 *More powerful than the joy of victory* See Thomas Laqueur, "Lost Cause," review of *The Culture of Defeat: On National Trauma, Mourning, and Recovery*, by Wolfgang Schivelbusch, *The Nation*, November 24, 2003.

255 *a strong personality rose to power* Thomas Scheff, Reginald G. Daniel, and Joseph Sterphone, "Shame and a Theory of War and Violence," *Aggression and Violent Behavior* 39, 109–115.

255 *David Keen explores the underlying role of shame* Keen, *Shame: The Politics and Power of an Emotion* (Princeton, NJ: Princeton University, 2023)

255 *but always, Keen argues, there is shame* History has shown the disturbing rise of popular support for authoritarian leaders on both left and right. As I write in 2023, across the world such regimes are appearing more on the right—Marine Le Pen's National Front party in France, Ilias Kasidiaris's Golden Dawn party in Greece—the party whose members Matthew Heimbach befriended, Jair Bolsonaro's conservative Liberal Party in

Brazil, Narendra Modi's BJP (Bharatiya Janata Party). Around the world, right-tending politics often revolve around loss, humiliation, and the rhetorical journey from loss to stolen. But history offers counterexamples with the rise of the Bolsheviks in Russia and the Maoists in China. And in many such cases, we can detect the powerful appeal to pride—either the restoration of a yearned-for bygone past on the right or extending pride to groups formerly without sufficient pride on the left. Appeals to pride in nation have appeared on both the right and left.

256 *nation's GDP, employment rate, and personal incomes* Indeed, a plethora of federal boosts—the American Rescue Plan Act ($1.9 trillion), the Infrastructure Investment and Jobs Act ($1 trillion), the U.S. Chips and Science Act ($53 billion), the Inflation Reduction Act ($430 billion), and the Bipartisan Infrastructure Law ($350 billion) were helping incomes in red states more than blue states. Ben Winck, "Biden's economic scorecard touts fragile advantage," Reuters, November 9, 2023. U.S. Department of the Treasury, "New U.S. Department of the Treasury Analysis: Two Years In, Bipartisan Infrastructure Law Is Spurring Historic Surge in Infrastructure Investments, Especially in States with the Greatest Need," Press release, November 15, 2023, https://home.treasury.gov/news/press-releases/1909.

256 *twenty-seven billion dollars of new investment* WSON, "Gov. Beshear: $27.5 Billion in Investments Announced to Support Job Growth, Economic Development Across Kentucky," October 5, 2023, https://wson radio.com/2023/10/05/gov-beshear-27-5-billion-in-investments-announced-to-support-job-growth-economic-development-across-kentucky/.

256 *forty-eight thousand new in-state jobs* For example, Hitachi Astemo Americas, which makes electric vehicle parts, announced an expansion of its operations in Berea, three hours west of Pikeville, offering 167 full-time jobs with an average hourly wage of $26 including benefits. Envision AESC broke ground on an electric vehicle battery factory expected to create 2,000 full-time jobs in Bowling Green, half an hour west of Pikeville. And four hours northwest in Boone County, Matrix Pack North America is locating a new facility that will bring 144 full-time jobs manufacturing sustainable paper products, at an average hourly wage of $24. For press releases announcing these plant openings, see Kentucky Cabinet for Economic Development, "News Releases," https://ced.ky.gov/Newsroom/News_Releases.

256 *wished a factory job would follow him* This was in addition to the local job opportunities that already existed. Pike County's largest employer

was the Pikeville Medical Center. The town was also a growing center of tourism, elk spotting, ziplining at the nearby Breaks Interstate Park, and local concerts featuring Tayla Lynn and Tre Twitty singing songs by their famous grandparents—Loretta Lynn ("I'm a Coal Miner's Daughter") and Conway Twitty ("That's My Job")—as well as Jelly Roll, Tommy Ratliff's favorite musician, famous for his 2017 song, "Addiction Kills."

256 *The largest source of new jobs* Data USA, "Congressional District 5, KY," https://datausa.io/profile/geo/congressional-district-5-ky#economy.

256 *a new whiskey distillery* Shepherd Snyder, "Pike county distillery plans to repurpose underground coal mine to age Kentucky bourbon," WKMS, October 30, 2023.

256 *I met harvests local ginseng* "US Grown Wild-Crafted Botanicals," Appalachian Herbal Company, www.appalachianherbalcompany.com.

256 *mushrooms in an abandoned coal mine shaft* Nicole Ziege, "Pikeville Couple Grows Mushroom Farm," *Appalachian News-Express*, June 11, 2021.

256 *The largest solar farm in Kentucky* Michelle Lewis, "The Largest Solar farm in Kentucky Will Be Built on a Former Coal Mine," *Electrek*, December 29, 2021,

257 *the median household income had risen* Data USA, "Congressional District 5, KY," https://datausa.io/profile/geo/congressional-district-5-ky.

257 *gathered activists to plan a "Rural New Deal"* Anthony Flaccavento, "A Rural New Deal Could Help Progressives Win Rural America," *In These Times*, October 4, 2023.

257 *funds to strengthen border control* Carl Hulse, "On the Border, Republicans Set a Trap, Then Fell Into it," *New York Times*, February 6, 2024.

257 *half of Americans expected violence* Shauneen Miranda, "Poll: Many Americans Expect Election-Related Violence over Future Losses," *Axios*, Jan 7, 2024.

257 *advised taking Trump at his word* David Corn, "Trump 11: How Bad It Could Be?," *Mother Jones*, January 11, 2024.

257 *If NATO allies don't pay more* NBC News, "Trump Says He'd Let Russia Do 'Whatever the Hell They Want' to NATO Countries That Don't Pay Enough," NBC News, February 10, 2024.

257 *He's said that illegal immigrants are "animals"* David Corn, "Trump II: How Bad It Could Be," *Mother Jones*, January 11, 2024.

258 *Trump's lawyers have argued that* John Cassidy, "Trump's Fascistic Rhetoric Only Emphasizes the Stakes in 2024," *The New Yorker*, November 14, 2023.

258 *It would come in the front door* Dylan Riley, *The Civic Foundations of Fascism in Europe* (Baltimore: Johns Hopkins University, 2010). Also see "Enigmas of Fascism," *New Left Review* 30, November 1, 2024.

259 *fifty-two books at his desk in a cabin* Hope Reese, "A champion of the unplugged, earth-conscious life, Wendell Berry is still ahead of us," *Vox*, October 9, 2019.

260 *in both cases, from the land* Those in the country were migrating to cities. The rural sociologist Ben Winchester discovered a countertrend in Minnesota: city residents between age thirty and forty-nine were actually moving into rural areas, bringing with them a "brain gain." For these reverse migrants, cheaper housing, safety, and the rural ambiance loomed large, and some migrants' internet-based jobs allowed them to work remotely from their new rural homes. With the Internet, Winchester notes, increasingly we "live in the middle of everywhere." See Marc Perry, Luke Rogers, and Lindsay Spell, "Domestic Outmigration From Some Urban Counties Slowed, Smaller Gains in Rural Counties," US Census Bureau, March 30, 2023, https://www.census.gov/library/stories/2023/03/domes tic-migration-trends-shifted.html; Benjamin Winchester, "Continuing the Trend: The Brain Gain of the Newcomers. A Generational Analysis of Rural Minnesota Migration, 1990–2010," University of Minnesota Extension Center for Community Vitality, May 16, 2012; Benjamin Winchester, "Living in the middle of everywhere," University of Minnesota Extension, April 28, 2022; Meltem Odabas, "Concern about drug addiction has declined in U.S., even in areas where fatal overdoses have risen the most," Pew Research Center, May 31, 2022.

260 *Tons of soil and rock are then bulldozed* Gabriel Popkin, "The Green Miles," *Washington Post Magazine*, February 13, 2020.

Goodbyes

263 *Beshear won seventeen of its eighty-five* Tim Marema, "Rural Voters Shift Toward Democrat in Kentucky Governor's Race," *Hoptown Chronicle*, November 11, 2023, https://hoptownchronicle.org/rural -voters-shift-toward-democrat-in-kentucky-governors-race/.

263 *In nearby Corbin* Christina Ford, "Corbin: The Former Sundown Town Works Toward Diversity," LEX18, July 7, 2022, www.lex18.com/news /lex-in-depth/corbin-the-former-sundown-town-works-toward-diversity. For more information about the Sunup Initiative, see www.sunupcorbin .com. Also see Angela Turner, "Corbin Women, Racial Justice Initiative

Planning Event to Remember 100th Anniversary of Racial Cleansing," *Times-Tribune*, July 13, 2019.

263 *Meanwhile, one central Kentucky county banned* Jess Clark, "Kentucky School District Bans More Than 100 Books, Citing Anti-LGBTQ+ Law," Louisville Public Media, October 19, 2023. See also Andrew Lapin, "A New Version of the Famous Holocaust Diary Is Being Called 'Anne Frank Pornography' and Getting Banned From Schools," Jewish Community of Louisville, June 12, 2023, https://jewishlouisville.org/a-new-version-of -the-famous-holocaust-diary-is-being-called-anne-frank-pornography -and-getting-banned-from-schools/.

263 *"For the 'Libre Initiative'"* Russell Contreras, "Koch Group Targets Latinos with Anti-'Bidenomics' Campaign," Axios, August 3, 2023.

Appendix 1

271 *One district was urban, the other rural* Using 2010 census data, Bloomberg's CityLab developed a Congressional Density Index (CDI), which classifies every congressional district by the density of its neighborhoods. CityLab classified Khanna's congressional district, CA-17, as "pure urban" and Rogers's district, KY-5, as "pure rural." See David Montgomery, "City-Lab's Congressional Density Index," Bloomberg, November 18, 2018, www.bloomberg.com/news/articles/2018-11-20/citylab-s-congressional -density-index.

271 *The median household income in 2021* U.S. Census Bureau, American Community Survey (ACS), 1-Year Estimates, 2021.

271 *In 2018, I wrote an op-ed* Arlie Hochschild, "The Coders of Kentucky," *New York Times*, September 21, 2018.

Appendix 2

275 *We began by analyzing responses to the statement* In the ANES data, rural and urban white respondents differed in their empathy toward Black people by a 32-point margin (32 percent to 64 percent). Urban respondents were twice as likely to express empathy as their rural counterparts.

Bibliography

Abbot, Lisa. "Many Affected as Revelation Energy Files for Chapter 11 Bankruptcy." Kentuckians for the Commonwealth, July 9, 2019. https://archive.kftc.org/blog/many-affected-revelation-energy-files-chapter-11-bankruptcy.

ABC News. "White Nationalists, Counterprotesters Prepare for Kentucky rally: Part 3." YouTube. Posted August 19, 2017. www.youtube.com/watch?v=7DUfaorghFU.

Ahler, Douglas J., and Gaurav Sood. "The Parties in Our Heads: Misperceptions About Party Composition and Their Consequences." *Journal of Politics* 80, no. 3 (2018): 964–981.

Alexander, Michelle. *The New Jim Crow: Mass Incarceration in the Age of Colorblindness.* Rev. ed. New York: The New Press, 2012.

Alfonseca, Kira. "Map: Where Anti-Critical Race Theory Efforts Have Reached." ABC News, March 24, 2022.

Alford, Roger. "Hundreds of Singers Sign Up for 'Hope for the Mountains' Choir." *Kentucky Today*, October 17, 2018.

Alpert, Abby, William N. Evans, Ethan M. J. Lieber, and David Powell. "Origins of the Opioid Crisis and Its Enduring Impacts." *Quarterly Journal of Economics* 137, no. 2 (May 2022): 1139–1179.

American National Election Studies. ANES 2020 Time Series Study Full Release [dataset and documentation], July 19, 2021. www.electionstudies.org.

Anti-Defamation League. "Blood Drop Cross." Hate Symbols Database, accessed May 28, 2023. www.adl.org/resources/hate-symbol/blood-drop-cross.

Appalachian News-Express. "Staff Report," October 11–12, 2022.

Arendt, Hannah. *The Origins of Totalitarianism.* New York: Harvest/Harcourt, 1951.

Aulbach, Lucas. "Hundreds of Boats Hit Kentucky Lake on Saturday for Pro-Trump Parade." *Courier-Journal*, September 6, 2020.

Ax, Joseph. "Trump Sues Univision for $500 Million over Miss USA Cancellation." Reuters, June 30, 2015.

Barna. "U.S. Adults Believe Hate Speech Has Increased—Mainly Online." July 16, 2019. www.barna.com/research/hate-speech-increased/.

Barr, Jeremy. "Why These Fox News Loyalists Have Changed the Channel to Newsmax." *Washington Post*, December 27, 2020.

Basu, Zachary. "Trump's Words Turn Violent as Pressure on Him Builds." Axios, October 4, 2023.

BBC. "'Drug Dealers, Criminals, Rapists': What Trump Thinks of Mexicans." August 31, 2016. https://www.bbc.com/news/av/world-us-canada-3723 0916.

BBC. "US 2020 Election: The Economy Under Trump in Six Charts." November 3, 2020.

Beckett, Lois. "Is There a Neo-Nazi Storm Brewing in Trump Country?" *The Guardian*, June 4, 2017.

Beckett, Lois. "Most Alleged Capitol Rioters Unconnected to Extremist Groups, Analysis Finds." *The Guardian*, March 4, 2021.

Beckett, Lois. "Neo-Nazis and Anti-Fascist Protesters Leave Kentucky After Standoff." *The Guardian*, April 30, 2017.

Beebout, Christopher. "Effie Waller Smith," Explore KY History. www.ex plorekyhistory.ky.gov/items/show/880.

Belew, Kathleen. *Bringing the War Home: The White Power Movement and Paramilitary America*. Cambridge, MA: Harvard University Press, 2018.

Bellware, Kim. "There Will Be 'Riots in the Street' If Trump Is Prosecuted, Graham Says." *Washington Post*, August 29, 2022.

Bender, Michael C., and Maggie Haberman. "Trump Sells a New Image as the Hero of $99 Trading Cards." *New York Times*, December 15, 2022.

Bennett, Emily. "Many Gather in Pikeville to Rally for 'Public Grief.'" WYMT, June 1, 2020.

Beshear, Steven L., J. Michael Brown, and LaDonna Thompson. "2011 Annual Report." Department of Corrections, Commonwealth of Kentucky. www .corrections.ky.gov/About/researchandstats/Pages/default.aspx.

Best, Kenneth. "Hatfield-McCoy Feud Carries Lessons for Today." Uconn Today, University of Connecticut, September 10, 2019. https://today .uconn.edu/2019/09/hatfield-mccoy-feud-carries-lessons-today/.

Blackburn, Marsha. "Why Is Critical Race Theory Dangerous for Our Kids?" July 12, 2021. www.blackburn.senate.gov/2021/7/why-is-critical-race -theory-dangerous-for-our-kids.

Bogel-Burroughs, Nicholas, and James C. McKinley Jr. "Key Takeaways from the Trump Indictment in Georgia." *New York Times*, August 24, 2023.

Boissoneault, Lorraine. "The Coal Mining Massacre America Forgot." *Smithsonian Magazine*, April 25, 2017.

Bone, Greg. "Kentucky Coal Facts, 17th Edition." Energy and Environment Cabinet, Kentucky Department for Energy Development and Independence, 2017.

Booker, Brockton. "Arizona and Wisconsin Certify Election Results, Affirming Biden Victories." NPR, November 30, 2020.

Bowles, Nellie. "I Used to Make Fun of Silicon Valley Preppers. Then I Became One." *New York Times*, April 24, 2020.

Brennan, Geoffrey, and Philip Pettit. *The Economy of Esteem: An Essay on Civil and Political Society*. Oxford: Oxford University Press, 2004.

Breuilly, John. "Max Weber, Charisma and Nationalist Leadership." *Nations and Nationalism* 17, no. 3 (May 2011): 477–499.

British Medical Journal. "Widening Gap in Death Rates Between Democrat and Republican in the US." June 7, 2022. www.bmj.com/company/newsroom/study-finds-widening-gap-in-death-rates-between-us-areas-that-vote-for-democratic-rather-than-republican-party/.

Brown, Karida. *Gone Home: Race and Roots Through Appalachia*. Chapel Hill: University of North Carolina Press, 2018.

Brown, M. Tyson. "Nearly a Quarter of the Operating U.S. Coal-Fired Fleet to Retire by 2029." U.S. Energy Information Agency, November 7, 2022. https://www.eia.gov/todayinenergy/detail.php?id=54559.

Buchanan, Larry, Quoctrung Bui, and Jugal K. Patel. "Black Lives Matter May Be the Largest Movement in US History." *New York Times*, July 3, 2020.

Bullington, Jonathan. "How a College Student, a Felon and 90K Followers Turned Kentucky into a Gun Sanctuary." *Courier-Journal*, February 14, 2020.

Bump, Philip. "Republicans Who Watch Fox News Are More Likely to Believe False Theories About Jan. 6." *Washington Post*, January 3, 2022.

Bump, Philip. "Six in 10 Republicans Still Think 2020 Was Illegitimate." *Washington Post*, May 24, 2023.

Burns, Alexander. "Choice Words from Donald Trump, Presidential Candidate." *New York Times*, June 16, 2015.

Business Insider. "These Ex-Coal Miners Learned How to Code with the Help of a Tech Company in Rural Kentucky." YouTube. Posted November 3, 2022. www.youtube.com/watch?v=mSj_zNhS5l4.

Byman, Daniel L. "Assessing the Right-Wing Terror Threat in the United

States a Year After the January 6 Insurrection." Brookings Institution, January 5, 2022.

C-SPAN. "Presidential Candidate Donald Trump at the Family Leadership Summit." C-SPAN. July 18, 2015. www.c-span.org/video/?327045-5/presidential-candidate-donald-trump-family-leadership-summit.

Cameron, Chris. "These Are the People Who Died in Connection with the Capitol Riot." *New York Times*, January 5, 2022.

Campbell, Courtney. "Television's 'Rural Purge' Is the Reason So Many Classic '60s Sitcoms Were Canceled." Wide Open Country, July 1, 2021. www.wideopencountry.com/rural-purge/.

Canadian Press. "Man Charged with Harassment over Removal of Trump Protesters." Battlefords Now, May 1, 2017. www.battlefordsnow.com/2017/05/01/man-charged-with-harassment-over-removal-of-trump-protesters/.

Cancian, Dan. "Lori Vinson, Nurse Who Entered Capitol During Riot, Says She 'Would Do It Again.'" *Newsweek*, January 17, 2021.

Caplan, John. "America's Hourly Workers." *Forbes*, March 12, 2021.

Carawan, Guy, and Candie Carawan. *Voices from the Mountains: The People of Appalachia—Their Faces, Their Words, Their Songs*. Athens, GA: Brown Thrasher Books, 1996.

Case, Anne, and Angus Deaton. *Diseases of Despair and the Future of Capitalism*. Princeton, NJ: Princeton University Press, 2020.

Cassidy, John. "As Gas Prices Reach New Highs, Oil Companies Are Profiteering." *New Yorker*, May 11, 2022.

Catte, Elizabeth. "Liberal Shaming of Appalachia: Inside the Media Elite's Obsession with the 'Hillbilly Problem.'" *Salon*, March 21, 2017.

Catte, Elizabeth. *What You Are Getting Wrong About Appalachia*. Cleveland, OH: Belt, 2018.

Caudill, Harry M. *Night Comes to the Cumberlands: A Biography of a Depressed Area*. Boston: Little, Brown, 1962.

CBS News. "Minnesota Man Who Shot 5 Black Lives Matter Protestors Found Guilty." February 3, 2017.

Center for American Progress. "Drivers of Authoritarian Populism in the United States: A Primer." May 10, 2018. https://www.americanprogress.org/article/drivers-authoritarian-populism-united-states/.

Centers for Disease Control and Prevention. "Drug Overdose Deaths Remained High in 2021." August 2023. www.cdc.gov/drugoverdose/deaths/index.html.

Chakradhar, Shraddha, and Casey Ross. "The History of OxyContin, Told Through Unsealed Purdue documents." *STAT*, December 3, 2019.

Chambers, Cassie. *Hill Women: Finding Family and a Way Forward in the Appalachian Mountains.* New York: Ballantine Books, 2020.

City of Prestonsburg. "Vacant Foreclosed Property Registration." www.prestonsburgcity.org/wp-content/docs/CE_VacantForeclosedPropertyRegistration.pdf.

Clark, Jess. "Kentucky School District Bans More Than 100 Books, Citing Anti-LGBTQ+ Law." Louisville Public Media, October 19, 2023.

Clifford, Scott. "How Emotional Frames Moralize and Polarize Political Attitudes." *Political Psychology* 40, no. 1 (2019): 75–91.

Cline, Jerry. "Hatfield-McCoy Feud: The Truth About Perry Cline's Involvement in the Feud." Cline Family Association, 2013. www.clinefamilyassociation.com/hatfield_mccoy_feud.

CNN Politics. "Exit Polls." 2020. www.cnn.com/election/2020/exit-polls/president/national-results/46.

Coal Camp Documentary Project. Appalachian Center, University of Kentucky. https://appalachianprojects.as.uky.edu/coal-camps.

Cohen, Zachary, and Whitney Wild. "Frustrated Lawmakers Want Protection for Their Families as Threats Increase." CNN, October 28, 2022.

Cole, Brendan. "Marjorie Taylor Greene Asks If US Should Be Divided Between GOP and Democrats." *Newsweek*, October 12, 2021.

Commonwealth of Kentucky, State Board of Elections. "1996 Primary and General Election Results." https://elect.ky.gov/SiteCollectionDocuments/Election%20Results/1990-1999/1996/96Gen_president.txt.

Commonwealth of Kentucky, State Board of Elections. "Official 2016 General Election Results." https://elect.ky.gov/results/2010-2019/Documents/2016%20General%20Election%20Results.pdf.

Contreras, Russell. "Koch Group Targets Latinos with Anti-'Bidenomics' Campaign." Axios, August 3, 2023.

Cook Political Report. "The Cook Partisan Voting Index." www.cookpolitical.com/cook-pvi.

Cottom, Tressie McMillan. "Reading Hick-Hop: The Shotgun Marriage of Hip-Hop and Country Music." June 2015. https://tressiemc.com/wp-content/uploads/2015/06/cottom-reading-hick-hop.pdf.

Cramer, Katherine J. *The Politics of Resentment: Rural Consciousness in Wisconsin and the Rise of Scott Walker.* Chicago: University of Chicago Press, 2016.

Creamer, John, Emily A. Shrider, Kalee Burns, and Frances Chen. "Poverty in the United States: 2021." Report No. P60-277, U.S. Census Bureau,

September 2022. www.census.gov/library/publications/2022/demo/p60 -277.html.

Cross, Al. "Kentucky Has Very High Rate of Addicted Mothers; Rose by Double-Digit Percentages Early in Decade, Seemed to Level Off in 2015– 16." *Kentucky Health News*, September 3, 2018.

Cummings, Will, Joey Garrison, and Jim Sergent. "By the Numbers: President Donald Trump's Failed Efforts to Overturn the Election." *USA Today*, January 6, 2021.

Daniels, Jessie. "Why White Americans Love to Claim Native Ancestry." *Huffington Post*, October 16, 2018.

Data USA. "Comparison: Pike County, KY and Martin County, KY." Accessed December 5, 2023. www.datausa.io/profile/geo/pike-county-ky ?compare=martin-county-ky.

Data USA. "Congressional District 5, KY." Accessed December 5, 2023. https:// datausa.io/profile/geo/congressional-district-5-ky.

Data USA. "Poolesville, MD." Accessed February 16, 2024. www.datausa.io /profile/geo/poolesville-md.

Davis, Darren W., and David C. Wilson. *Racial Resentment in the Political Mind*. Chicago: University of Chicago Press, 2022.

Davis, James C., Anil Rupasingha, John Cromartie, and Austin Sanders. "Rural America at a Glance: 2022 Edition." Bulletin No. 246, Economic Research Service, U.S. Department of Agriculture, November 2022. https:// www.ers.usda.gov/webdocs/publications/105155/eib-246.pdf?v=1662.

Dellatto, Marisa. "Trump Hits No. 1 with 'Justice for All' Song Made with Jan. 6 Arrestees." *Forbes*, March 21, 2023.

Deruy, Emily, Thomas Peele, and David Debolt. "Milo Yiannopoulos' 15 Minutes in Berkeley Cost University $800,000." *Mercury News*, September 24, 2017.

Deskins, William David. *Ginseng, Coal Dust, Moving Mountains: A History of Pike County, Kentucky*. Paintsville, KY: East Kentucky Press, 2018.

Dias, Nicholas, and Yphtach Lelkes. "The Nature of Affective Polarization: Disentangling Policy Disagreement from Partisan Identity." *American Journal of Political Science* 66, no. 3 (2022): 775–790.

DiFranco, Ani. "¿Which Side Are You On?" MP3 audio, track 3 on *¿Which Side Are You On?* 2012.

Donahue, Arwen. *This Is Home Now: Kentucky's Holocaust Survivors Speak*. Lexington: University of Kentucky Press, 2009.

Donaldson, Rachel. "West Virginia Mine Wars." National Park Service.

Douglas, Harper. "Etymology of Proud." Online Etymology Dictionary. www
.etymonline.com/word/proud.

Douglas, Harper. "Etymology of Redneck." Online Etymology Dictionary.
www.etymonline.com/word/redneck.

Drutman, Lee, Larry Diamond, and Joe Goldman. "Follow the Leader: Exploring American Support for Democracy and Authoritarianism." Democracy Fund Voter Study Group, March 2018. www.voterstudygroup.org
/publication/follow-the-leader.

Dunn, Amina. "Partisans Are Divided over the Fairness of the US Economy—
and Why People Are Rich or Poor." Pew Research Center, October 4,
2018.

Durkee, Alison. "Republicans Increasingly Realize There's No Evidence of
Election Fraud—But Most Still Think 2020 Election Was Stolen Anyway,
Poll Finds." *Forbes*, March 14, 2023.

Durkin, Alanna, and Geoff Mulvhill. "Purdue Pharma Family Sought to Profit
Off Opioid Crisis, Filing Alleges." *PBSNewsHour*, February 1, 2019.

Duyvendak, Jan Willem, and Josip Kesic. *The Return of the Native: Can Liberalism Safeguard Us Against Nativism?* New York: Oxford University Press,
2022.

Edsall, Thomas B. "There Are Two Americas Now: One with a BA and One
Without." *New York Times*, October 5, 2022.

Educational Fund to Stop Gun Violence. "Kentucky Gun Deaths: 2019." www
.efsgv.org/state/kentucky/.

Eller, Ron D. *Miners, Millhands, and Mountaineers: Industrialization of the Appalachian South, 1880–1930*. Knoxville: University of Tennessee Press,
1982.

Elson, Martha. "Our History: LBJ Visits E. Kentucky in 1964." *Courier-Journal*,
April 17, 2015.

Ely, William. *The Big Sandy Valley: A History of the People and Country from
the Earliest Settlement to the Present Time*. Catlettsburg, KY: Central
Methodist, 1887.

Environmental and Energy Study Institute. "Fossil Fuel Subsidies: A Closer
Look at Tax Breaks and Societal Costs." July 29, 2019. www.eesi.org
/papers/view/fact-sheet-fossil-fuel-subsidies-a-closer-look-at-tax-breaks
-and-societal-costs.

Estep, Bill. "Hardly Peaceful, but No Violence as White Nationalists, Protesters Yell in Pikeville." *Lexington Herald-Leader*, April 29, 2017.

Facts First. "Presidential Comparison: Biden vs Trump." Last updated December 20, 2023. https://www.factsarefirst.com/comparison/joe-biden /donald-trump.

Falvey, Rose. "White Nationalist Matthew Heimbach Banned from the United Kingdom." *Southern Poverty Law Center*, November 4, 2015.

FARE Network. *Guide to Discriminatory Practices in European Football*, Version 6, June 2021. www.farenet.org/uploads/files/2021_Fare_guide_to _discriminatory_practices_UEFA_.pdf.

Feaster, Seth. "U.S. on Track to Close Half of Coal Capacity by 2026." Institute for Energy Economics and Financial Analysis, April 1, 2023. www.ieefa .org/resources/us-track-close-half-coal-capacity-2026.

Federal Election Commission. "Federal Elections 2020: Election Results for the US President, the US Senate and the US House of Representatives." October 2022. www.fec.gov/resources/cms-content/documents/federal elections2020.pdf.

Ferrara, Andreas, Patrick A. Testa, and Liyang Zhou. "New Area-and Population-Based Geographic Crosswalks for U.S. Counties and Congressional Districts, 1790–2020." Inter-university Consortium for Political and Social Research, Ann Arbor, MI, October 19, 2022. https://doi.org/10.3886/E1 50101V4.

Fessler, Pam. "Kentucky County That Gave War on Poverty a Face Still Struggles." *Morning Edition*, NPR, January 8, 2014.

Feuer, Alan. "As Right-Wing Rhetoric Escalates, So Do Threats and Violence." *New York Times*, August 13, 2022.

Finkel, Eli J., Christopher A. Bail, Mina Cikara, Peter H. Ditto, Shanto Iyengar, Samara Klar, Lilliana Mason, et al. "Political Sectarianism in America." *Science* 370, no. 6516 (2020): 533–536.

Finnegan, Michael, and Noah Bierman. "Trump's Endorsement of Violence Reaches New Level: He May Pay Legal Fees for Assault Suspect." *Los Angeles Times*, March 13, 2016.

Fischer, David Hackett. *Albion's Seed: Four British Folkways in America*. New York: Oxford University Press, 1989.

FiveThirtyEight. "60 Percent of Americans Will Have an Election Denier on the Ballot This Fall." November 8, 2022. https://www.projects.fivethirty eight.com/republicans-trump-election-fraud/.

Flaccavento, Anthony. "A Rural New Deal Could Help Progressives Win Rural America." *In These Times*, October 4, 2023. https://inthesetimes.com /article/a-rural-new-deal-could-help-win-rural-america.

Forbes, Buddy. "Hatfield & McCoy Cabin Opens Doors to Politics for First Time in 140 Years." WYMT, November 8, 2022.

Ford, Christina. "Corbin: The Former Sundown Town Works Toward Diversity." LEX18, July 7, 2022. www.lex18.com/news/lex-in-depth/corbin-the-former-sundown-town-works-toward-diversity.

Ford, Colt. "No Trash in My Trailer." MP3 audio, track 3 on *Ride Through the Country*, 2008.

Ford, Roger. "Farewell, Kentucky." *Appalachian News-Express*, January 9, 2018.

Ford, Roger. "Tale of Two States." *Appalachian News-Express*, July 18, 2017.

Formisano, Ron. "Addiction's Profit Stream Broad, Deep." *Lexington Herald-Leader*, November 19, 2017.

FOX 5 Atlanta. "Trump Leaves Atlanta After Surrendering at Fulton County Jail." August 24, 2023.

France, Lisa Respers. "Bette Midler Apologizes to West Virginia Residents for 'Poor, Illiterate, Strung Out' Tweet." CNN, December 22, 2021.

Frank, Thomas. *What's the Matter with Kansas? How Conservatives Won the Heart of America.* New York: Metropolitan Books, 2004.

Frank, Thomas. *Listen, Liberal.* New York: Metropolitan, 2016.

Fraser, Max. *Hillbilly Highway: The Transappalachian Migration and the Making of a White Working Class.* Princeton, NJ: Princeton University Press, 2023.

French, David. "The Rule of Law Now Depends on Republicans." *New York Times*, March 31, 2023.

Ganz, John. *When the Clock Broke: Con Men, Conspiracists, and How America Cracked Up in the Early 1990s,* New York: Farrar, Straus and Giroux, 2024.

Garneau, Christopher R. H. "The Limits of Tolerance in Polarized Times." Paper presented at the Building Bridges 2.0: Liberty, Justice and Equality Conference, University of Science and Arts of Oklahoma, Chickasha, OK, October 23, 2023.

Garneau, Christopher R. H., and Philip Schwadel. "Examining the Influence of Political Affiliation and Orientation on Political Tolerance." *Socius* 8 (2022): 1–17.

Gass, Nick. "Macy's Dumps Trump." *Politico*, July 1, 2015.

Gibson, Campbell, and Kay Jung. "Historical Census Statistics on Population Totals by Race, 1790–1990, and by Hispanic Origin, 1970–1990, for the United States, Regions, Divisions, States." Working Paper No. 56,

Population Division, U.S. Census Bureau, September 13, 2002. https://www.census.gov/library/working-papers/2002/demo/POP-twps0056.html.

Giffords Law Center to Prevent Gun Violence. "Firearm Prohibitions in Kentucky." Updated January 5, 2023. www.giffords.org/lawcenter/state-laws/firearm-prohibitions-in-kentucky/.

Giffords Law Center to Prevent Gun Violence. "Kentucky Gun Laws." Updated January 5, 2023. www.giffords.org/lawcenter/gun-laws/states/kentucky/.

Giffords Law Center to Prevent Gun Violence. "Stand Your Ground in Kentucky." Updated January 5, 2023. www.giffords.org/lawcenter/state-laws/stand-your-ground-in-kentucky/.

Gilbert, David. "Meet the 'Black Robe Regiment' of Extremist Pastors Spreading Christian Nationalism." *Vice*, November 8, 2022.

Gladwell, Malcolm. *Outliers: The Story of Success.* New York: Little, Brown, 2008.

Glaun, Dan. "A Timeline of Domestic Extremism in the US, from Charlottesville to January 6." PBS, April 21, 2021.

Goldenberg, Suzanne. "Obama Unveils Historic Rules to Reduce Coal Pollution by 30%." *The Guardian*, June 2, 2014.

Graham, Carol, and Sergio Pinto. "Unequal Hopes and Lives in the USA: Optimism, Race, Place, and Premature Mortality." *Journal of Population Economics* 32 (2019): 665–733.

Gramlich, John. "A Look Back at Americans' Reactions to the Jan. 6 Riot at the U.S. Capitol." Pew Research Center, January 4, 2022.

Greenberg, Jon. "Most Republicans Still Falsely Believe Trump's Stolen Election Claims." Politifact, June 14, 2022.

Greene, Peter. "Teacher Anti-CRT Bills Coast to Coast: A State-by-State Guide." *Forbes*, February 16, 2022.

Gregory, James N. "The Southern Diaspora and the Urban Dispossessed: Demonstrating the Census Public Use Microdata Samples." *Journal of American History* 82, no. 1 (June 1995): 112.

Griggs, Kristy Owens. "The Removal of Blacks from Corbin in 1919: Memory, Perspective, and the Legacy of Racism." *Register of the Kentucky Historical Society* 100, no. 3 (Summer 2002): 293–310.

Grossman, Matt, and David A. Hopkins. *Asymmetric Politics: Ideological Republicans and Group Interest Democrats.* Oxford: Oxford University Press, 2016.

GroundTruth Project. "An Appalachian Trail: Finding the Real McCoy."

October 11, 2017. https://thegroundtruthproject.org/crossing-the-divide -kentucky/.

Haberman, Maggie, Jonah E. Bromwich, and William K. Rashbaum. "Trump, Escalating Attacks, Raises Specter of Violence If He Is Charged." *New York Times*, April 4, 2023.

Haberman, Maggie, and Alan Feuer. "Trump's Latest Dinner Guest: Nick Fuentes, White Supremacist." *New York Times*, November 25, 2022.

Hacker, Jacob S., and Paul Pierson. *Winner-Take-All Politics: How Washington Made the Rich Richer—and Turned Its Back on the Middle Class.* New York: Simon & Schuster, 2010.

Hacker, Jacob S., and Paul Pierson. *Off Center: The Republican Revolution and the Erosion of American Democracy.* New Haven, CT: Yale University Press, 2006.

Hadavi, Tala. "Lobbying in Q1 Topped a Record $938 Million, but Lobbyists Say Their Profession Is Misunderstood." CNBC, October 5, 2020.

Hagley Museum and Library. "Home & Hell: Sundown Towns & the Great Migration in Appalachia with Matthew O'Neal." YouTube, posted January 23, 2022. www.youtube.com/watch?v=vKH74cgMph4.

Hakim, Danny, Roni Caryn Rabin, and William K. Rashbaum. "Lawsuits Lay Bare Sackler Family's Role in Opioid Crisis." *New York Times*, April 1, 2019.

Hall, Colby. "Marjorie Taylor Greene Gets Sean Hannity on Board for National Divorce—Then Warns of Looming Civil War." MSN, February 22, 2023.

Hamer, Fannie Lou. "I'm Gonna Land on The Shore." YouTube, posted July 8, 2015. www.youtube.com/watch?v=TP2I_BYo8VY.

Hannity, Sean. "Trump's Warning on Illegal Immigrants Proves Grimly Prophetic." Fox News, March 22, 2017.

Hansell, Tom. *After Coal: Stories of Survival in Appalachia and Wales.* Morgantown: West Virginia University Press, 2018.

Harkins, Anthony, and Meredith McCarroll (eds.). *Appalachian Reckoning: A Region Responds to* Hillbilly Elegy. Morgantown: West Virginia University Press, 2019.

Hartig, Hannah. "In Their Own Words: How Americans Reacted to the Rioting at the US Capitol." Pew Research Center, January 15, 2021.

Hartog, Jonathan Den. "What the Black Robe Regiment Misses About Revolutionary Pastors." *Christianity Today*, January 20, 2021.

Hawkins, Samantha. "Prison for University of Kentucky Student Who Stormed the Capitol." Courthouse News Service, December 17, 2021.

Hayden, Michael Edison, Hannah Gais, Cassie Miller, Megan Squire, and Jason Wilson. "'Unite the Right' 5 Years Later: Where Are They Now?" Southern Poverty Law Center, August 11, 2022.

Healy, Patrick, and Maggie Haberman. "95,000 Words, Many of Them Ominous, from Donald Trump's Tongue." *New York Times*, December 5, 2015.

Hedegaard, Holly, Arialdi M. Miniño, and Margaret Warner. "Drug Overdose Deaths in the United States, 1999–2019." Data Brief No. 394, National Center for Health Statistics, Centers for Disease Control and Prevention, December 2020. www.cdc.gov/nchs/products/databriefs/db394.htm.

Hennen, John C. "Introduction to the New Edition." *Harlan Miners Speak: Report on Terrorism in the Kentucky Coal Fields Prepared by Members of the National Committee for the Defense of Political Prisoners.* Lexington: University Press of Kentucky, 2008.

Henson, Robby, dir. *Trouble Behind: A Film About History and Forgetting.* Cicada Films, 1990.

Hill, Evan, Ainara Tiefenthäler, Christiaan Triebert, Drew Jordan, Haley Willis, and Robin Stein. "How George Floyd Was Killed in Police Custody." *New York Times*, May 31, 2020.

Hilleary, Cecily. "Going 'Native': Why Are Americans Hijacking Cherokee Identity?" Voice of America, July 23, 2018.

Hiltzik, Michael. "How the Supreme Court Could Kill a Wealth Tax Before It's Been Tried." *Los Angeles Times*, October 17, 2023.

Historical Marker Database. "Memorialization of Jefferson Davis." www.hmdb.org/m.asp?m=81014.

Historical Marker Database. "Pikeville Cut-Through." Updated January 4, 2023. www.hmdb.org/m.asp?m=212047.

Historical Marker Database. "The Dils Cemetery." Updated March 6, 2020. https://www.hmdb.org/m.asp?m=146196.

Hochschild, Adam. "Another Great Yesterday." Review of *Shadowlands: Fear and Freedom at the Oregon Standoff—A Western Tale of America in Crisis*, by Anthony McCann. *New York Review of Books*, December 19, 2019.

Hochschild, Adam. "The Proud Boys and the Long-Lived Anxieties of American Men." Review of *We Are Proud Boys: How a Right-Wing Street Gang Ushered in a New Era of American Extremism*, by Andy Campbell. *New York Times*, September 18, 2022.

Hochschild, Arlie Russell. "The Black and White Southerners Who Changed the North." Review of *Hillbilly Highway: The Transappalachian Migration and the Making of a White Working Class* by Max Fraser and *Black Folk: The Roots of the Black Working Class* by Blair L. M. Kelley. *New York Times*, September 27, 2023.

Hochschild, Arlie Russell. "The Coders of Kentucky." *New York Times*, September 21, 2018.

Hochschild, Arlie Russell. "The Republicans Are Disconnected from Reality? It's Even Worse About Liberals." *The Guardian*, July 21, 2019.

Hochschild, Arlie Russell. *Strangers in Their Own Land: Anger and Mourning on the American Right*. New York: The New Press, 2016.

Hofstadter, Richard. "The Paranoid Style in American Politics." *Harper's Magazine*, November 1964.

Holmes, Kristen. "Trump Calls for Termination of the Constitution in Truth Social Post." CNN, December 4, 2022.

Holohan, Meghan. "White Supremacists Recruit Teens by Making Them Feel Someone Cares." *Today*, August 21, 2017.

Homans, Charles. "How 'Stop the Steal' Captured the American Right." *New York Times Magazine*, July 19, 2022.

House, Silas, and Jason Howard. *Something's Rising: Appalachians Fighting Mountaintop Removal*. Lexington: University Press of Kentucky, 2009.

Huber, Patrick, and Kathleen Drowne. "Redneck: A New Discovery." *American Speech* 76, no. 4 (Winter 2001): 434–437.

Humphreys, Keith, and Ekow N. Yankah. "Prisons Are Getting Whiter. That's One Way Mass Incarceration Might End." *Washington Post*, February 26, 2021.

Hurley, Bevan. "Trump Says He Is Financially Supporting Some Jan. 6 Suspects and Plans to Pardon Them if Re-elected." Yahoo News, September 1, 2022.

Igielnik, Ruth, and Maggie Haberman. "More Republicans Say Trump Committed Crimes. But They Still Support Him." *New York Times*, August 1, 2023.

Illouz, Eva. *The Emotional Life of Populism: How Fear, Disgust, Resentment, and Love Undermine Democracy*. Hoboken, NJ: Polity Press, 2023.

Iyengar, Shanto, Yphtach Lelkes, Matthew Levendusky, Neil Malhotra, and Sean J. Westwood. "The Origins and Consequences of Affective Polarization in the United States." *Annual Review of Political Science* 22 (2019): 129–146.

Iyengar, Shanto, Gaurav Sood, and Yphtach Lelkes. "Affect, Not Ideology: A Social Identity Perspective on Polarization." *Public Opinion Quarterly* 76, no. 3 (2012): 405–431.

Iyengar, Shanto, and Sean J. Westwood. "Fear and Loathing Across Party Lines: New Evidence on Group Polarization." *American Journal of Political Science* 59, no. 3 (2015): 690–707.

Jabbour, Alan, and Kaen Singer Jabbour. *Decoration Day in the Mountains: Traditions of Cemetery Decoration in the Southern Appalachians.* Chapel Hill: University of North Carolina Press, 2010.

Jacobs, Nicholas F., and Daniel M. Shae. *The Rural Voter: The Politics of Place and the Disuniting of America.* New York: Columbia University Press, 2023.

Jardina, Ashley. *White Identity Politics.* Cambridge: Cambridge University Press, 2019.

Jarrett, Pat. "A Neo-Nazi Gathering in Kentucky—in Pictures." *The Guardian,* June 4, 2017.

Jaspin, Elliot. *Buried in the Bitter Waters: The Hidden History of Racial Cleansing in America.* New York: Basic Books, 2007.

Jayadev, Arjun, and Robert Johnson. "Tides and Prejudice: Racial Attitudes During Downturns in the United States 1979–2014." *Review of Black Political Economy* 44, no. 3–4 (2017): 379–392.

Jelly Roll. "The Bottom." MP3 audio, track 1 on *A Beautiful Disaster,* 2020.

Johnson, Eric M., and Justin Madden. "Clash at California Capitol Leaves at Least 10 Injured." Reuters, June 26, 2016.

Jones, Loval, and Billy Edd Wheeler. *Laughter in Appalachia: Southern Mountain Humor.* Atlanta: August House, 1987.

Judge, Liz. "Mountain Hero Gets Help from Author Wendell Berry." Earthjustice, June 25, 2012. https://earthjustice.org/article/mountain-hero -gets-help-from-author-wendell-berry.

Jurkowitz, Mark, and Amy Mitchell. "A Sore Subject: Almost Half of Americans Have Stopped Talking Politics with Someone." Pew Research Center, February 5, 2020.

Kane, Paul. "New Report Outlines Deep Political Polarization's Slow and Steady March." *Washington Post,* April 8, 2023.

Kang-Brown, Jacob, and Ram Subramanian. "Out of Sight: The Growth of Jails in Rural America." Vera Institute of Justice, June 2017. www.vera.org /publications/out-of-sight-growth-of-jails-rural-america.

Keefe, Patrick Radden. "The Family That Built an Empire of Pain." *The New Yorker,* October 23, 2017.

Keen, David. *Shame: The Politics and Power of an Emotion.* Princeton, NJ: Princeton University Press, 2023.

Keene, Houston. "Republicans Hammer Biden After Trans Activists Go Topless at White House Event: 'Very Disgraceful.'" Fox News, June 13, 2023.

Keller, Michael H., and David D. Kirkpatrick. "Their America Is Vanishing. Like Trump, They Insist They Were Cheated." *New York Times*, October 23, 2022.

Kelley, Blair L. M. *Black Folk: The Roots of the Black Working Class.* New York: Liveright, 2023.

Kelley, Brendan Joel. "The Alt-Right's New Soundtrack of Hate." Southern Poverty Law Center, October 9, 2017.

Kennedy, Rachel, and Cynthia Johnson. "The New Deal Builds: A Historic Context of the New Deal in East Kentucky, 1933–1943." Kentucky Heritage Council, State Historic Preservation Office, June 2005. https://heritage.ky.gov/Documents/NewDealBuilds.pdf.

Kenning, Chris. "'Things Have Changed': Why More Kentucky Towns Are Embracing LGBTQ Pride Parades." *Courier-Journal*, June 13, 2019.

Kenning, Chris. "Why Can't Kentucky Reduce Its Sky-High Prison Populations? Look to Lawmakers, Report Says." *Courier-Journal*, December 29, 2021.

Kentucky Cabinet for Health and Family Services. "Monthly Medicaid Counts by County, Department for Medicaid Services." https://www.chfs.ky.gov/agencies/dms/dafm/Pages/statistics.aspx?View=2023%20Reports%20by%20County&Title=Table%20Viewer%20Webpart.

Kentucky Coal and Energy Education Project. "Pike County, Kentucky Coal Camps." www.coaleducation.org/coalhistory/coaltowns/coalcamps/pike_county.htm.

Kentucky Department of Corrections. "Policies and Procedures, Chapter 15.2: Rule Violations and Penalties." August 12, 2016. https://corrections.ky.gov/About/cpp/Documents/15/CPP%2015.2%20-%20Effective%201-6-17.pdf.

Kentucky Energy and Environment Cabinet. "Quarterly Coal Dashboard." https://eec.ky.gov/Energy/News-Publications/Pages/quarterly-coal-dashboard.aspx.

Kentucky General Assembly. "An Act Relating to Public Education and Declaring an Emergency." H.B. 14, 2022 Regular Session. https://apps.legislature.ky.gov/record/22rs/hb14.html.

Kentucky Injury Prevention and Research Center. "Drug Overdose and Related Comorbidity County Profiles." University of Kentucky. https://kiprc.uky.edu/programs/overdose-data-action/county-profiles.

Kentucky to the World. "Coal to Coding Entrepreneur Rusty Justice on Going from Coal Miner to Tech Worker." YouTube, posted August 7, 2021, https://youtu.be/eAo973oULZ0?si=3IFHh5YuwjRBI57M.

Kessler, Glenn. "Trump's Outrageous Claim That 'Thousands' of New Jersey Muslims Celebrated the 9/11 Attacks." *Washington Post*, November 22, 2015.

Khanna, Ro. *Dignity in a Digital Age: Making Tech Work for All of Us*. New York: Simon & Schuster, 2022.

Kids Count Data Center. "Children Ages Birth to 17 Entering Foster Care in United States, 2021." Annie E. Casey Foundation. https://datacenter.aecf.org/data/tables/6268-children-ages-birth-to-17-entering-foster-care?loc=1&loct=2#detailed/2/2-53/true/2048/any/15620.

Kids Count Data Center. "Children in Kinship Care in United States, 2020–2022." Annie E. Casey Foundation. https://datacenter.aecf.org/data/tables/10455-children-in-kinship-care?loc=1&loct=2#ranking/2/any/true/2479/any/20161.

Kimmel, Michael. *Healing from Hate: How Young Men Get Into—and Out of—Violent Extremism*. Oakland: University of California Press, 2018.

Kingsolver, Barbara. *Demon Copperhead*. New York: HarperCollins, 2022.

Kingsolver, Barbara. *Flight Behavior*. New York: HarperCollins, 2012.

Kingsolver, Barbara. *The Bean Trees*. New York: Harper and Row, 1988.

Kirschman, Lauren. "Prescription Opioid Companies Increased Marketing After Purdue Pharma Lawsuit, UW Study Shows." UW News, University of Washington, October 9, 2023. www.washington.edu/news/2023/10/09/prescription-opioid-companies-increased-marketing-after-purdue-pharma-lawsuit-uw-study-shows/.

Klein, Jessica. "Tracking SNAP in Kentucky." Kentucky Center for Economic Policy, June 23, 2023. https://kypolicy.org/tracking-snap-in-kentucky/.

Kleinfeld, Rachel. "Polarization, Democracy, and Political Violence in the US: What the Research Says." Working Paper, Carnegie Endowment for International Peace, September 5, 2023. www.carnegieendowment.org/2023/09/05/polarization-democracy-and-political-violence-in-united-states-what-research-says-pub-90457.

Kludt, Tom. "Trump to Snub White House Correspondents' Dinner for Third Year in a Row." CNN, April 5, 2019.

Kobin, Billy. "Kentucky Nurse, Air Force Veteran Sentenced for Their Roles in Jan. 6 Riot at US Capitol." *Courier-Journal*, October 22, 2021.

Krosch, Amy R., and David M. Amodio. "Economic Scarcity Alters the Perception of Race." *PNAS* 111, no. 25 (June 2014): 9079–9084.

Krosch, Amy R., Tom R. Tyler, and David M. Amodio. "Race and Recession:

Effects of Economic Scarcity on Racial Discrimination." *Journal of Personal Social Psychology* 113, no. 6 (December 2017): 892–909.

Krusell, Kirstin. "Political Subjectivity in a Risk Society: A Comparative Ethnography of Left- and Right-Wing Doomsday Preppers." PhD diss. prospectus, Department of Sociology, University of California, Berkeley, January 4, 2023.

Kuttner, Robert. *Everything for Sale: The Virtues and Limits of Markets.* New York: Knopf, 1997.

Lapin, Andrew. "A New Version of the Famous Holocaust Diary Is Being Called 'Anne Frank Pornography' and Getting Banned from Schools." Jewish Community of Louisville, June 12, 2023. https://jewishlouisville .org/a-new-version-of-the-famous-holocaust-diary-is-being-called-anne -frank-pornography-and-getting-banned-from-schools/.

Laqueur, Thomas. "Lost Cause." Review of *The Culture of Defeat: On National Trauma, Mourning, and Recovery,* by Wolfgang Schivelbusch. *The Nation,* November 24, 2003. www.thenation.com/article/archive/lost-causes/.

Layne, Nathan. "Macy's Cuts Ties with Trump, New York City Reviews Contracts." Reuters, July 1, 2015.

Ledford, Katherine, Teressa Lloyd, and Rebecca Stephens (eds.). *Writing Appalachia: An Anthology.* Lexington: University Press of Kentucky, 2020.

Lerner, Adam B. "Sean Hannity: Trump's Remarks Not 'Racially Tinged.'" *Politico,* June 30, 2015.

Lerner, Kira. "'Anger and Radicalization': Rising Number of Americans Say Political Violence Is Justified." *The Guardian,* July 25, 2023.

Levine, Mike. "'No Blame'? ABC News Finds 54 Cases Invoking 'Trump' in Connection with Violence, Threats, Alleged Assaults." ABC News, May 30, 2020.

Lewis, Helen Block. *Shame and Guilt in Neurosis.* Madison, CT: International Universities Press, 1974.

Lewis, Michelle. "The Largest Solar Farm in Kentucky Will Be Built on a Former Coal Mine." Electrek, December 29, 2021. www.electrek.co/2021 /12/29/the-largest-solar-farm-in-kentucky-will-be-built-on-a-former-coal -mine/.

Lewis, Ronald L. *Black Coal Miners in America: Race, Class and Community Conflict 1780–1980.* Lexington: University Press of Kentucky, 1987.

Limke, Andrea. "This Tiny Kentucky Town Literally Moved a Mountain in One of the Largest Engineering Feats in the World." Only in Your State, July 13, 2023. www.onlyinyourstate.com/kentucky/pikeville-cut-through-ky/.

Lipton, Eric. "'The Coal Industry Is Back,' Trump Proclaimed. It Wasn't." *New York Times*, October 18, 2020.

Loewen, James. *Sundown Towns: A Hidden Dimension of American Racism.* New York: Simon & Schuster, 2006.

Long, Heather, and Andrew Van Dam. "The Black-White Economic Divide Is as Wide as It Was in 1968." *Washington Post*, June 4, 2020.

Long, Michael E. "Wrestlin' for a Livin' With King Coal." *National Geographic*, June 1983.

Lu, Yanqin, and Jae Kook Lee. "Partisan Information Sources and Affective Polarization: Panel Analysis of the Mediating Role of Anger and Fear." *Journalism and Mass Communication Quarterly* 96, no. 3 (2019): 767–783.

Lucas, Marion B. *A History of Blacks in Kentucky from Slavery to Segregation 1760–1891.* Frankfort: Kentucky Historical Society, 2023.

Lysy, Frank J. "Why Wages Have Stagnated While GDP Has Grown: The Proximate Factors." *An Economic Sense* (blog), February 13, 2015. www.an economicsense.org/2015/02/13/why-wages-have-stagnated-while-gdp-has -grown-the-proximate-factors/.

Macy, Beth. "America's Other Epidemic." *The Atlantic*, May 2020.

Malloy, Tim, and Doug Schwartz. "Lowest Opinion of Trump Among Voters in Seven Years, Quinnipiac University National Poll Finds; Biden Approval Rating Climbs." Quinnipiac University Poll, December 14, 2022. https:// poll.qu.edu/poll-release?releaseid=3863.

Manfield, Lucas, and Lauren Peace. "As Opioid Epidemic Raged, Drug Company Executives Made Fun of West Virginians." Mountain State Spotlight, May 13, 2021.

Mann, Michael. *Fascists.* Cambridge: Cambridge University Press, 2006.

Mansoor, Sanya. "93% of Black Lives Matter Protests Have Been Peaceful, New Report Finds." *Time*, September 5, 2020.

Marema, Tim. "Rural Voters Shift Toward Democrat in Kentucky Governor's Race." *Hoptown Chronicle*, November 11, 2023. https://hoptownchron icle.org/rural-voters-shift-toward-democrat-in-kentucky-governors-race/.

Martinez, Peter. "Hate Groups Hit New High, Up 30 Percent in Last 4 Years, Southern Poverty Law Center Says." CBS News, February 20, 2019.

Mason, Lilliana. *Uncivil Agreement: How Politics Became Our Identity.* Chicago: University of Chicago Press, 2018.

Mason, Lilliana, Julie Wronski, and John V. Kane. "Activating Animus: The

Uniquely Social Roots of Trump Support." *American Political Science Review* 115, no. 4 (2021): 1508–1516.

McArdle, Terence. "The Day 30,000 White Supremacists in KKK Robes Marched in the Nation's Capital." *Washington Post*, August 11, 2018.

McGranahan, David, John Cromartie, and Tim Wojan. "The Two Faces of Rural Population Loss Through Outmigration." Economic Research Service, U.S. Department of Agriculture, December 1, 2010. www.ers.usda .gov/amber-waves/2010/december/the-two-faces-of-rural-population-loss -through-outmigration/.

McGreal, Chris. "Big Pharma Executives Mocked 'Pillbillies' in Emails, West Virginia Opioid Trial Hears." *The Guardian*, May 16, 2021.

McGreal, Chris. "Why Were Millions of Opioid Pills Sent to a West Virginia Town of 3,000?" *The Guardian*, October 2, 2019.

McGreal, Chris. *American Overdose: The Opioid Tragedy in Three Acts*. New York: Public Affairs, 2018.

McNicholas, Celine, and Margaret Poydock. "The Trump Administration's Attacks on Workplace Union Voting Rights Forewarned of the Broader Threats to Voting Rights in the Upcoming Election." Economic Policy Institute, October 21, 2020.

McNicholas, Celine, Margaret Poydock, and Lynn Rhinehart. "Unprecedented: The Trump NLRB's Attack on Workers' Rights." Economic Policy Institute, October 16, 2019.

Merriam-Webster Dictionary. "Pride: The Word That Went from Vice to Strength." *Wordplay* (blog). www.merriam-webster.com/words-at-play /pride-meaning-word-history.

Mettler, Katie. "The 'Race Whisperer.'" *Washington Post*, October 30, 2019.

Miller, Claire Cain. "The Long-Term Jobs Killer Is Not China. It's Automation." *New York Times*, December 21, 2016.

Mills, Michael F. "Obamageddon: Fear, the Right, and the Rise of 'Doomsday' Prepping in Obama's America." *Journal of American Studies* 55, no. 2 (2019): 1–30.

Milman, Oliver. "US Renewable Energy Farms Outstrip 99% of Coal Plants Economically—Study." *The Guardian*, January 30, 2023.

Mistich, Dave. "'Surrender Under Protest': Another Take on Pikeville, Kentucky's White Supremacist Rally and Counter Protest." 100 Days in Appalachia, May 8, 2017.

Monnat, Shannon M. "Trends in US Working-Age Non-Hispanic White

Mortality: Rural-Urban and Within-Rural Differences." *Population Research and Policy Review* 39 (September 2020): 805–834.

Montanaro, Domenico. "Most Republicans Would Vote for Trump Even If He's Convicted of a Crime, Poll Finds." NPR, April 25, 2023.

Montgomery, Blake. "The Far Right and Left Confronted Each Other in a Small Kentucky Town but It Remained Mostly Peaceful." BuzzFeed News, April 29, 2017.

Montgomery, David. "CityLab's Congressional Density Index." Bloomberg, November 18, 2018. www.bloomberg.com/news/articles/2018-11-20/city lab-s-congressional-density-index.

Morrison, Aaron. "Racism of Rioters Takes Center Stage on Jan. 6 Hearing." Associated Press, July 28, 2021.

Morrison, Andrew P. *Shame: The Underside of Narcissism*. Hillsdale, NJ: Analytic Press, 1989.

Morrison, Andrew P. *The Culture of Shame*. New York: Ballantine Books, 1996.

Mosse, George L. *Nationalism and Sexuality: Respectability and Abnormal Sexuality in Modern Europe*. New York: Howard Fertig, 1985.

Mudde, Cas. *The Far Right Today*. Cambridge: Polity, 2020.

Muro, Mark, and Jacob Whiton. "America Has Two Economies—and They're Diverging Fast." Brookings Institution, September 19, 2019.

Mutz, Diana C. "Status Threat, Not Economic Hardship, Explains the 2016 Presidential Vote." *PNAS* 115, no. 19: E4330–E4339.

National Center for Health Statistics. "Drug Overdose Mortality by State." Centers for Disease Control and Prevention, 2021. www.cdc.gov/nchs /pressroom/sosmap/drug_poisoning_mortality/drug_poisoning.htm.

National Institute on Drug Abuse. "Criminal Justice DrugFacts." Updated June 2020. www.drugabuse.gov/publications/drugfacts/criminal -justice.

National Park Register of Historic Places Digital Archive on NPGallery (National Register ID 84001927). "National Register of Historic Places Inventory—Nomination Form for Multiple Resources of Pikeville, Huffman Avenue Historic District." August 8, 1984. https://npgallery.nps.gov /NRHP/AssetDetail?assetID=17acea18-d844-45d5-afe3-8b4068e6d010.

Neal, Rome. "Official End of Legendary Feud." CBS News, June 13, 2003.

Neel, Joe. "Is There Hope for the American Dream? What Americans Think About Income Inequality." NPR, January 9, 2020.

Newman, Lainey, and Theda Skocpol. *Rust Belt Union Blues*. New York: Columbia University Press, 2023.

Niedzwiadek, Nick. "Capitol Police Officer Says Jan. 6 Rioters Used N-Word Against Him, Others." *Politico*, July 27, 2021.

Noah, Timothy. "You'll Be Very Surprised Who's Benefiting Most from Bidenomics." *New Republic*, July 12, 2023.

Norberg-Hodge, Helena. *Ancient Futures*. 3rd ed. White River Junction, VT: Chelsea Green, 2016.

Norris, Pippa, and Ronald Inglehart. *Cultural Backlash: Trump, Brexit, and Authoritarian Populism*. Cambridge: Cambridge University Press, 2019.

Norton, Jack, and Judah Schept. "Keeping the Lights On: Incarcerating the Bluegrass State." Vera Institute of Justice, March 4, 2019. www.vera.org /in-our-backyards-stories/keeping-the-lights-on.

Notable Kentucky African Americans Database. "African American Schools in Pike County, KY." Updated January 16, 2023. https://nkaa.uky.edu/nkaa /items/show/2794.

Notable Kentucky African Americans Database. "Pike County (KY) Enslaved, Free Blacks, and Free Mulattoes, 1850–1870." Updated January 10, 2023. https://nkaa.uky.edu/nkaa/items/show/2528.

Notable Kentucky African Americans Database. "Smith, Effie Waller." Updated July 17, 2017. https://nkaa.uky.edu/nkaa/items/show/1033.

Nothstine, Ray. "Trump: 'Why Do I Have to Repent or Ask for Forgiveness if I Am Not Making Mistakes?'" *Christian Post*, July 2015.

NPR. "The Jan. 6 Attack: The Cases Behind the Biggest Criminal Investigations in U.S. History." Accessed February 16, 2024. www.npr.org/2021 /02/09/965472049/the-capitol-siege-the-arrested-and-their-stories.

Nwanguma et al. v. Trump. No. 17-6290 (6th Cir. 2018). https://www.opn.ca6 .uscourts.gov/opinions.pdf/18a0202p-06.pdf.

Nygaard, Egil, Kari Slinning, Vibeke Moe, and Kristine B. Walhovd. "Behavior and Attention Problems in Eight-Year-Old Children with Prenatal Opiate and Poly-Substance Exposure: A Longitudinal Study." *PloS One* 11, no. 6 (2016): e0158054.

Odabaş, Meltem. "Concern About Drug Addiction Has Declined in U.S., Even in Areas Where Fatal Overdoses Have Risen the Most." Pew Research Center, May 31, 2022.

O'Neil, Cathy. *The Shame Machine: Who Profits in the New Age of Humiliation*. New York: Crown Books, 2022.

Osnos, Evan. "Donald Trump and the Ku Klux Klan: A History." *New Yorker*, February 29, 2016.

Palmer, Tom G. "The Terrifying Rise of Authoritarian Populism." Cato Institute, July 24, 2019. https://www.cato.org/commentary/terrifying-rise-authoritarian-populism.

Pape, Robert A. "Dangers to Democracy: Tracking Deep Distrust of Democratic Institutions, Conspiracy Beliefs, and Support for Political Violence Among Americans." Chicago Project on Security and Threats, University of Chicago, July 10, 2023. https://cpost.uchicago.edu/publications/july_2023_survey_report_tracking_deep_distrust_of_democratic_institutions_conspiracy_beliefs_and_support_for_political_violence_among_americans/.

Pape, Robert A. "Deep, Divisive, Disturbing and Continuing: New Survey Shows Mainstream Support for Violence to Restore Trump Remains Strong." Chicago Project on Security Threats, University of Chicago, January 2, 2022. https://cpost.uchicago.edu/publications/deep_divisive_disturbing_and_continuing_new_survey_shows_maintream_support_for_violence_to_restore_trump_remains_strong/.

Parker, Christopher Sebastian. "Status Threat: Moving the Right Further to the Right?" *Daedalus* 150, no. 20 (Spring 2021): 56–75.

Parker, Kim, Juliana Menasce Horowitz, Anna Brown, Richard Fry, D'Vera Cohn, and Ruth Igielnik. "What Unites and Divides Urban, Suburban and Rural Communities." Pew Research Center, May 22, 2018.

Paxton, Robert. *The Anatomy of Fascism*. New York: Alfred A. Knopf, 2004.

PBS NewsHour. "'I Need 11,000 Votes,' Trump Told Ga. Election Official | Jan. 6 Hearings." YouTube, posted June 21, 2022. www.youtube.com/watch?v=AbFc9T7KXA0.

Peisner, David. "Rhymes from the Backwoods: The Rise of Country Rap." *Rolling Stone*, January 24, 2018.

Pengelly, Marin. "Pence Secret Service Detail Feared for Their Lives During Capitol Riot." *The Guardian*, July 21, 2022.

Perlstein, Rick. "American Fascism." *The American Prospect*, January 24, 2024.

Pew Research Center. "Americans' Views of Government: Decades of Distrust, Enduring Support for Its Role." June 6, 2022.

Pew Research Center. "The Partisan Divide on Political Values Grows Even Wider." October 5, 2017.

Pew Research Center. "Public Trust in Government: 1958–2022." June 6, 2022.

Picciolini, Christian. *White American Youth: My Descent into America's Most Violent Hate Movement—And How I Got Out.* New York: Hachette Books, 2017.

Pikeville Medical Center. "PMC Expands Black Lung Screening Services." June 22, 2018. www.pikevillehospital.org/pmc-expands-black-lung-screen ing-services/.

Pikeville-Pike County Visitor's Center. "Pikeville Cut-Through Project." www .tourpikecounty.com/things-to-see-do/outdoor_adventure/pikeville-cut -through-project/.

Pool, Tommy, and Dakota Makres. "Eastern Kentuckians Participate in a President Trump Caravan." WYMT, November 1, 2020.

Porter Square Books. "Paul Farmer with Ophelia Dahl: Fevers, Feuds and Diamonds." Recorded January 28, 2021. Facebook video. www.face book.com/Porter-Square-Books-112608362085830/videos/530717931 197122/?refsrc=deprecated&_rdr.

Porter, Eduardo. "Black Workers Stopped Making Progress on Pay. Is It Racism?" *New York Times*, June 28, 2021.

Prine, John. "Paradise." MP3 audio, track 5 on *John Prine*, 1971.

Prison Policy Initiative. "Kentucky Profile." www.prisonpolicy.org/profiles /KY.html.

PRRI. "The Persistence of Qanon in the Post-Trump Era: An Analysis of Who Believes the Conspiracies." February 24, 2022.

Radmacher, Dan. "Blackjewel's Catastrophic Bankruptcy and the Collapse of the Mine Cleanup System." *Appalachian Voices*, March 3, 2022. www .appvoices.org/2022/03/03/bankruptcy-mine-cleanup-collapse/.

Raju, Manu, Dan Merica, and Julia Horowitz. "Andrew Puzder Withdraws as a Labor Secretary Nominee." CNN, February 16, 2017.

Ramey, John. "New Statistics on Modern Prepper Demographics from FEMA and Cornell." Prepared, August 4, 2021. www.theprepared.com/blog /new-statistics-on-modern-prepper-demographics-from-fema-and-corn ell-university/.

Randolph, J. W. "Impacts of Coal 101: Mountaintop Removal = Job Removal." Appalachian Voices, January 21, 2011. www.appvoices.org/2011/01/21 /impacts-of-coal-101-mountaintop-removal-job-removal/.

Ray, Raka. "A Case of Internal Colonialism? Arlie Hochschild's *Strangers in Their Own Land.*" *British Journal of Sociology* 68, no. 1 (2017): 129–133.

Real Appalachia. "Christmas in Appalachia (1964)—Revisiting the CBS

Special Report by Charles Kuralt with Updates." YouTube, posted December 14, 2020. www.youtube.com/watch?v=4ECdhjJTHRc.

Recovery First Treatment Center. "The Dangers of Hiding Drugs in Body Cavities." December 20, 2022. www.recoveryfirst.org/blog/treatment/the-dangers-of-hiding-drugs-in-body-cavities/.

Reece, Florence. "Lay the Lily Low." Recorded 1978 [ww08406.mp3]. Digital Library of Appalachia. Appalachian College Association. https://dla.con tentdm.oclc.org/digital/collection/Warren/id/2200/rec/23.

Reese, Hope. "A Champion of the Unplugged, Earth-Conscious Life, Wendell Berry Is Still Ahead of Us." *Vox*, October 9, 2019.

Resnik, Judith, Jenny E. Carroll, Skylar Albertson, et al. "Legislative Regulation of Isolation in Prison: 2018–2021." University of Alabama Legal Studies Research Paper No. 3914942. SSRN (June 21, 2023).

Retzinger, Suzanne M. "Shame, Anger, and Conflict: Case Study of Emotional Violence." *Journal of Family Violence* 6, no. 1 (March 1991): 37–59.

Reuters. "Donald Trump: I Was '100% Right' About Muslims Cheering 9/11 Attacks." *The Guardian*, November 29, 2015.

Rich, Frank. "No Sympathy for the Hillbilly." *New York Magazine*, March 20, 2017.

Riley, Dylan. *The Civic Foundations of Fascism in Europe*. Baltimore: Johns Hopkins University, 2010.

Riley, Dylan. "Enigmas of Fascism." *New Left Review* 30 (November 1, 2024).

Rogers, Luke, Marc Perry, and Lindsay Spell. "Domestic Outmigration from Some Urban Counties Slowed, Smaller Gains in Rural Counties." U.S. Census Bureau, March 30, 2023. https://www.census.gov/library/stories/2023/03/domestic-migration-trends-shifted.html.

Rosenthal, Lawrence. *Empire of Resentment: How the Populist Revolt Shook America*. New York: The New Press, 2020.

Rouse, Stella. "Poll Reveals White Americans See an Increase in Discrimination Against Other White People and Less Against Other Racial Groups." *The Conversation*, July 1, 2022.

Rural Urban Bridge Initiative. "The Rise and Implications of the Rural Voter with Dan Shea." YouTube, posted March 2, 2023. www.youtube.com/watch?v=P3emb1r8zmI.

Ruther, Matt, Tom Sawyer, and Sarah Ehresman. "Projections of Population and Households: State of Kentucky, Kentucky Counties, and Area Development Districts 2015–2040." Kentucky State Data Center, University of

Louisville, 2016. http://ksdc.louisville.edu//wp-content/uploads/2016/10/projection-report-v16.pdf.

Salkever, David. "Real Pay Data Show Trump's 'Blue Collar Boom' Is More of a Bust for US Workers, in 3 Charts." *The Conversation*, February 7, 2020.

Samuels, Robert. "Americans in Search of a Better Life Are Moving from Blue States to Red States—but It Could Backfire Big Time." *Forbes*, May 25, 2023.

Sandel, Michael, J. *The Tyranny of Merit: What's Become of the Common Good?* New York: Farrar, Straus and Giroux, 2020.

Sanders, Linley, and Jill Colvin. "Trump's GOP Support Dips Slightly After His Indictment over Classified Documents, AP-NORC Poll Finds." AP News, June 28, 2023.

Sanning, Cory. "Back the Blues Rally Aims to Spread Awareness for Law Enforcement." WKYT, September 5, 2020.

Santhanam, Laura. "How White Nationalist Leader Matt Heimbach Defends Violence at Saturday's Rally in Charlottesville." *PBS NewsHour*, August 15, 2017.

Scerri, Andy. "Moralizing About Politics: The White Working-Class 'Problem' in Appalachia and Beyond." *Journal of Appalachian Studies* 25, no. 2 (October 1, 2019): 202–21.

Scheff, Thomas J. *Bloody Revenge: Emotions, Nationalism and War*. Boulder, CO: Westview, 1994.

Scheff, Thomas J. "The Shame-Rage Spiral: Case Study of an Interminable Quarrel." Essay. In *The Role of Shame in Symptom Formation*, 109–50. Hillsdale, NJ: Erlbaum, 1987.

Scheff, Thomas. "The Ubiquity of Hidden Shame in Modernity." *Cultural Sociology* 8, no. 2 (February 17, 2014): 129–41.

Scheff, Thomas, G. Reginald Daniel, and Joseph Sterphone. "Shame and a Theory of War and Violence." *Aggression and Violent Behavior* 39 (March 2018): 109–15.

Scheff, Thomas J., and Suzanne M. Retzinger. *Emotions and Violence: Shame and Rage in Destructive Conflicts*. Lexington, MA: Lexington Books, 1991.

Scheler, Max, and Manfred S. Frings. *Ressentiment*. Milwaukee, WI: Marquette University Press, 1994.

Schivelburch, Wolfgang. *The Culture of Defeat: On National Trauma, Mourning, and Recovery*. Translated by Jefferson Chase. New York: Metropolitan Books, 2004.

Schwartzman, Gabe. "Anti-Blackness, Black Geographies, and Racialized Depopulation in Coalfield Appalachia from 1940 to 2000." *Journal of Appalachian Studies* 28, no. 2 (October 1, 2022): 125–43.

Scott, Rebecca R. *Removing Mountains: Extracting Nature and Identity in the Appalachian Coalfields.* Minneapolis: University of Minnesota Press, 2010.

Sharone, Ofer. *Flawed System/Flawed Self: Job Searching and Unemployment Experiences.* Chicago: University of Chicago Press, 2013.

Shear, Michael D., and Julie Hirschfeld Davis. "Shoot Migrants' Legs, Build Alligator Moat: Behind Trump's Ideas for Border." *New York Times*, October 1, 2019.

Shugerman, Emily, and Gerry Seavo James. "Three Injured as Rival Armed Militias Converge on Louisville." *Daily Beast*, February 15, 2021.

Silva, Jennifer. *Coming Up Short: Working-Class Adulthood in an Age of Uncertainty.* New York: Oxford University Press, 2013.

Silva, Jennifer. *We're Still Here: Pain and Politics in the Heart of America.* Oxford: Oxford University Press, 2019.

Simi, Peter, Kathleen Blee, Matthew DeMichele, and Steven Windisch. "Addicted to Hate: Identity Residual Among Former White Supremacists." *American Sociological Review* 82, no. 6 (2017): 1167–1187.

Skocpol, Theda, and Vanessa Williamson. *The Tea Party and the Remaking of Republican Conservatism.* Oxford: Oxford University Press, 2012.

Slisco, Aila. "Is Kentucky Republican Thomas Massie Making a Case for Secession?" *Newsweek*, December 17, 2021.

Smith, Adam. *The Wealth of Nations: Books I–III.* London: Penguin Books, 1999 (1776).

Smith, Samantha. "Why People Are Rich and Poor: Republicans and Democrats Have Very Different Views." Pew Research Center, May 2, 2017.

Smith, Terrance, and Jessie DiMartino. "Trump Has Longstanding History of Calling Elections 'Rigged' If He Doesn't Like the Results." ABC News, November 11, 2020.

Smithers, Gregory D. "Why Do So Many Americans Think They Have Cherokee Blood?" *Slate*, October 1, 2015.

Snyder, Shepherd. "Pike County Distillery Plans to Repurpose Underground Coal Mine to Age Kentucky Bourbon." WKMS, October 30, 2023, www .wkms.org/business-economy/2023-10-31/pike-county-distillery-plans-to -repurpose-underground-coal-mine-to-age-kentucky-bourbon.

Snyder, Timothy. *On Tyranny: Twenty Lessons from the Twentieth Century.* New York: Penguin Books, 2007.

Social Security Agency. "OASDI Beneficiaries by State and Zip Code, 2021." https://www.ssa.gov/policy/docs/statcomps/oasdi_zip/.

Sohn, Mark. "The Black Struggle for Education and Learning." *Appalachian Heritage* 15, no. 4 (1987).

Southern Poverty Law Center. "Heimbach." Extremist Files Database. www.splcenter.org/fighting-hate/extremist-files/individual/matthew-heimbach.

Southern Poverty Law Center. "Ku Klux Klan." Updated 2021. www.splcenter.org/fighting-hate/extremist-files/ideology/ku-klux-klan.

Southern Poverty Law Center. "National Socialist Movement." Extremist Files Database.www.splcenter.org/fighting-hate/extremist-files/group/national-socialist-movement.

Southern Poverty Law Center. "Hate Map, 2000." www.splcenter.org/hate-map?year=2000.

Southern Poverty Law Center. "Hate Map: Kentucky, 2017." www.splcenter.org/hate-map?year=2017&state=KY.

Southern Poverty Law Center. "Whose Heritage? Public Symbols of the Confederacy," 3rd edition. 2022. www.splcenter.org/sites/default/files/whose-heritage-report-third-edition.pdf.

Spencer, Sarana Hale, Robert Farley, and D'Angelo Gore. "Explaining the Missing Context of Tucker Carlson's Jan. 6 Presentation." FactCheck.org, March 10, 2023.

Steele, Rachel, and Misti Jeffers. "The Future of Appalachian Identity in an Age of Polarization." *Journal of Appalachian Studies* 26, no. 1 (April 1, 2020): 57–75.

Stevens, Harry. "America Needs Clean Electricity. These States Show How to Do It." *Washington Post*, April 12, 2023.

Stevens, Harry, Daniela Santamariña, Kate Rabinowitz, Kevin Uhrmacher, and John Muyskens. "How Members of Congress Voted on Counting the Electoral College Vote." *Washington Post*, January 7, 2020.

Stolberg, Sheryl Gay. "Baltimore to Trump: You Lost Your Authority to Criticize." *New York Times*, July 29, 2019.

Stoll, Steven. *Ramp Hollow: The Ordeal of Appalachia.* New York: Hill and Wang, 2017.

Strategic Management Society. "New Study Shows Drug Manufacturers Actually Increased Opioid Marketing After Kentucky's Purdue Pharma Lawsuit." Medical Xpress, August 3, 2023. www.medicalxpress.com/news/2023-08-drug-opioid-kentucky-purdue-pharma.html.

Stuewig, Jeffrey, June P. Tangney, Caron Heigel, Laura Harty, and Laura

McCloskey. "Shaming, Blaming, and Maiming: Functional Links Among the Moral Emotions, Externalization of Blame, and Aggression." *Journal of Research in Personality* 44, no. 1 (February 2010): 91–102.

Suleman, Nadia. "The Causes of the Hatfield and McCoy Feud Ran Deeper Than You May Think." *Time*, September 10, 2019.

Sullivan, Andy, and Jason Lange. "Analysis: Despite Republican Opposition, Red States Fare Well in Biden's COVID-19 Bill." Reuters, March 10, 2021.

Sullivan, Kate. "Trump's Anti-Immigrant Comments Draw Rebuke." CNN, October 6, 2023.

Suter, Tara. "Trump Unveils Digital Trading Cards 'MugShot Edition.'" *The Hill*, December 12, 2023.

Swenson, Ali, and Michael Kunzelman. "Fears of Political Violence Are Growing as the 2024 Campaign Heats Up and Conspiracy Theories Evolve." AP News, November 18, 2023.

Tarleton, Paddy. "Which Side Are You On." MP3 audio, track 2 on *Diversity Is Our Strength*, 2016.

Tenold, Vegas. *Everything You Love Will Burn: Inside the Rebirth of White Nationalism in America*. New York: Nation Books, 2018.

Thiess, Rebecca, Justin Theal, and Brakeyshia Samms. "2019 Federal Share of State Revenue Remains Stable." Pew Trusts, December 22, 2021.

Thiess, Rebecca, Justin Theal, and Kate Watkins. "Pandemic Aid Lifts Federal Share of State Budgets to New Highs." Pew Trusts, August 28, 2023.

Thorbecke, Catherine. "A Look at Trump's Economic Legacy." ABC News, January 20, 2021.

Trump, Mary L. *Too Much and Never Enough: How My Family Created the World's Most Dangerous Man*. New York: Simon & Schuster, 2022.

Truscott, Lucian K., IV. "Slow Motion Civil War." *Salon*, November 17, 2018.

Tuğal, Cihan. "An Unmoving Wall or a Shifting One? The American Right's Deep Emotional Politics and Its Emaciated Counterpart." *British Journal of Sociology* 68, no. 1 (2017): 137–142.

Turner, Angela. "Corbin Woman, Racial Justice Initiative Planning Event to Remember 100th Anniversary of Racial Cleansing." *Times-Tribune*, July 13, 2019.

Turner, William H. *The Harlan Renaissance: Stories of Black Life in Appalachian Coal Towns*. Morgantown: West Virginia University Press, 2021.

U.S. Bureau of Economic Analysis. "Gross Domestic Product by State and Personal Income by State, 1st Quarter 2023." June 30, 2023. https://www

.bea.gov/news/2023/gross-domestic-product-state-and-personal-income -state-1st-quarter-2023.

U.S. Bureau of Labor Statistics. "12-Month Percentage Change, Consumer Price Index, by Region and Division, All Items." October 2023. https:// www.bls.gov/charts/consumer-price-index/consumer-price-index-by-re gion.htm.

U.S. Bureau of Labor Statistics. "All Employees, Coal Mining [CES1021210001]." Retrieved from FRED, Federal Reserve Bank of St. Louis. September 5, 2023. https://fred.stlouisfed.org/series/CES1021210001.

U.S. Bureau of Labor Statistics. "Nonunion Workers Had Weekly Earnings 81 Percent of Union Members in 2019." *The Economics Daily* (blog). U.S. Department of Labor, February 28, 2020. https://www.bls.gov/opub /ted/2020/nonunion-workers-had-weekly-earnings-81-percent-of-union -members-in-2019.htm.

U.S. Bureau of Labor Statistics. "State Unemployment Rates over the Last 10 Years, Seasonally Adjusted." December 2023. https://www.bls.gov/charts /state-employment-and-unemployment/state-unemployment-rates-ani mated.htm.

U.S. Bureau of Labor Statistics. "Table 7, Survival of Private Sector Establishments by Opening Year." March 2023. www.bls.gov/bdm/us_age _naics_00_table7.txt.

U.S. Census Bureau. American Community Survey 1-Year Estimates, 2021. https://data.census.gov/table.

U.S. Census Bureau. American Community Survey 1-Year Geographic Comparison Tables, 2021. www.census.gov/acs/www/data/data-tables-and-tools /geographic-comparison-tables/.

U.S. Census Bureau. American Community Survey 5-Year Estimates, 2017– 2021. https://data.census.gov/table.

U.S. Census Bureau. "Harlan County, Kentucky." QuickFacts. Accessed December 5, 2023. www.census.gov/quickfacts/fact/table/harlancountyken tucky/PST045222.

U.S. Census Bureau. "Pike County, Kentucky." QuickFacts. Accessed December 5, 2023. www.census.gov/quickfacts/fact/table/pikecountyken tucky,US/PST045222.

U.S. Department of Justice. "Three Years Since the Jan. 6 Attack on the Capitol." Press release, January 5, 2024. www.justice.gov/usao-dc/36 -months-jan-6-attack-capitol-0.

U.S. Department of the Treasury. "New U.S. Department of the Treasury Analysis: Two Years In, Bipartisan Infrastructure Law Is Spurring Historic Surge in Infrastructure Investments, Especially in States with the Greatest Need." Press release, November 15, 2023. https://home.treasury .gov/news/press-releases/jy1909.

U.S. Energy Information Administration. "Coal Explained: Where Our Coal Comes From." Updated October 19, 2022. https://www.eia.gov/energyex plained/coal/where-our-coal-comes-from.php.

U.S. Energy Information Administration. "Table 4.1. Count of Electric Power Industry Power Plants, by Sector, by Predominant Energy Sources Within Plant, 2011 Through 2021." https://www.eia.gov/electricity/annual/html /epa_04_01.html.

U.S. National Archives. "Civil Rights Act (1964)." Milestone Documents. Updated February 8, 2022. www.archives.gov/milestone-documents/civil -rights-act.

U.S. News & World Report. "Best States: Education." Accessed December 20, 2023. https://www.usnews.com/news/best-states/rankings/education.

U.S. Representative Rosa DeLauro. "DeLauro, DelBene, Torres Reintroduce Legislation to Expand and Improve Child Tax Credit." Press release, June 7, 2023. https://delauro.house.gov/media-center/press-releases/delauro -delbene-torres-reintroduce-legislation-expand-and-improve-child.

U.S. v. Farkas, et al. No. 7:20-CR-17-REW (E.D. Ky. September 3, 2020). https://www.justice.gov/opa/press-release/file/1327486/download.

USA Facts. "Our Changing Population: Kentucky." Updated July 2022. https:// usafacts.org/data/topics/people-society/population-and-demographics /our-changing-population/state/kentucky.

Van Zee, Art. "The Promotion and Marketing of OxyContin: Commercial Triumph, Public Health Tragedy." *American Journal of Public Health* 99, no. 2 (February 2009): 221–227.

Vance, J. D. *Hillbilly Elegy: A Memoir of a Family and Culture in Crisis.* New York: Harper, 2016.

Vera Institute of Justice. "Incarceration Trends." Updated February 14, 2023. www.trends.vera.org/.

Vice. "White Student Union (Documentary)." YouTube, posted June 4, 2013. www.youtube.com/watch?v=GJ_MHp8iqtQ.

Vito, Christopher, Amanda Admire, and Elizabeth Hughes. "Masculinity, Aggrieved Entitlement, and Violence: Considering the Isla Vista Mass Shooting." *International Journal for Masculinity Studies* 13, no. 2 (2018): 86–102.

Wade, Will. "US Coal Use Is Rebounding Under Biden Like It Never Did with Trump." Bloomberg, October 12, 2021.

Walker, Frank X. *Affrilachia: Poems by Frank X. Walker.* Athens: Ohio University Press, 2000.

Waller, Altina L. *Feud: Hatfields, McCoys, and Social Change in Appalachia, 1860–1900.* Chapel Hill: University of North Carolina Press, 1988.

Waller, Altina L. "Hatfield-McCoy: Economic Motives Fueled Feud That Tarred Region's Image." *Lexington Herald-Leader,* July 30, 2012.

Waller, Altina L. "The Hatfield-McCoy Feud." *University of North Carolina Press Blog,* June 11, 2012. https://uncpressblog.com/2012/06/11/altina-l-waller-the-hatfield-mccoy-feud/.

Wang, Hansi Lo. "Most Prisoners Can't Vote, but They're Still Counted in Voting Districts." NPR, September 26, 2021.

Ward, Ken, Jr., Alex Mierjeski, and Scott Pham. "In the Game of Musical Mines, Environmental Damage Takes a Back Seat." ProPublica, April 26, 2023.

Watt, Cecilia Saixue. "Redneck Revolt: The Armed Leftwing Group That Wants to Stamp Out Fascism." *The Guardian,* July 11, 2017.

Weber, Max. "The Sociology of Charismatic Authority." In *From Max Weber: Essays in Sociology,* edited by H. H. Gerth and C. Wright Mills, 245–252. New York: Oxford University Press, 1946.

Weber, Max. *The Protestant Ethic and the Spirit of Capitalism.* Translated by Talcott Parsons. New York: Charles Scribner's Sons, 1958.

Webster, Steven W., and Alan I. Abramowitz. "The Ideological Foundations of Affective Polarization in the U.S. Electorate." *American Politics Research* 45, no. 4 (2017): 621–47.

Webster, Steven W., and Bethany Albertson. "Emotion and Politics: Noncognitive Psychological Biases in Public Opinion." *Annual Review of Political Science* 25, no. 1 (2022): 401–418.

Weller, Jack E. *Yesterday's People: Life in Contemporary Appalachia.* Lexington: University Press of Kentucky, 1965.

White House. "Bipartisan Infrastructure Law Rural Playbook: A Roadmap for Delivering Opportunity and Investments in Rural America." April 2022. https://www.whitehouse.gov/build/resources/rural/.

Wickenden, Dorothy. "Wendell Berry's Advice for a Cataclysmic Age." *New Yorker,* February 28, 2022.

Widra, Emily, and Tiana Herring. "States of Incarceration: The Global Context 2021." Prison Policy Initiative, September 2021. www.prisonpolicy.org/global/2021.html.

Wike, Richard, Katie Simmons, Bruce Stokes, and Janell Fetterolf. "Globally, Broad Support for Representative and Direct Democracy." Pew Research Center, October 16, 2017.

Wikipedia. "List of American Civil War Monuments in Kentucky." Last modified March 8, 2022.

Wikipedia. "Not Fucking Around Coalition." Last modified August 22, 2023.

Wilkerson, Isabel. *Caste: The Origins of Our Discontents.* New York: Random House, 2020.

Williams, Kevin. "The Muslims of Appalachia: Kentucky Coal Country Embracing the Faithful." Al Jazeera America, February 21, 2016.

Wilson, Jason. "Kanye's Antisemitic Hate Speech Platformed by Enablers in Tech, Media, and Politics." Southern Poverty Law Center, December 7, 2022.

Wilson, Ryan. "Detroit Lions Disavow Use of Their Logo During Violent Rally in Charlottesville." CBS Sports, August 16, 2017.

Wilson, William Julius. *The Truly Disadvantaged: The Inner City, the Underclass, and Public Policy.* 2nd ed. Chicago: University of Chicago Press, 2012.

Wilson, William Julius. *When Work Disappears: The World of the New Urban Poor.* New York: Vintage Books, 1997.

Winchester, Benjamin. "Continuing the Trend: The Brain Gain of the Newcomers. A Generational Analysis of Rural Minnesota Migration, 1990–2010." University of Minnesota Extension Center for Community Vitality, May 16, 2012. https://conservancy.umn.edu/bitstream/handle/11299/171648/continuing-the-trend.pdf?sequence=1.

Winchester, Benjamin. "Living in the Middle of Everywhere." University of Minnesota Extension, April 28, 2022. www.extension.umn.edu/community-news-and-insights/living-middle-everywhere.

Winck, Ben. "Biden's Economic Scorecard Touts Fragile Advantage." Reuters, November 9, 2023.

Winetemute, Gary, Sonia Robinson, Andrew Crawford, Julia P. Schleimer, Amy Barnhorst, Vicka Chaplin, Daniel Tancredi, et al. "Views of American Democracy and Society and Support for Political Violence: First Report from a Nationwide Population-Representative Study." UC Davis Violence Prevention Research Program, July 2022. www.medrxiv.org/content/10.1101/2022.07.15.22277693v1.full.pdf.

WKYT. "Counter Rally Planned to Oppose White Nationalists Canceled for 'Safety Reasons.'" April 28, 2017.

WLKY. "Protester Pushed at 2016 Trump Rally." April 4, 2017. www.cnn.com

/videos/politics/2017/04/02/protester-pushed-trump-rally-louisville-kashi
ya-nwanguma-sot.wlky.

Wood, Daniel, and Geoff Brumfiel. "Pro-Trump Counties Continue to Suffer Far Higher COVID Death Tolls." NPR, May 19, 2022.

Woodall, Candy. "Trump Calls for Police to Shoot Shoplifters as They Leave the Store." *USA Today*, October 1, 2023.

Woodard, Benjamin. "How the Shooting at the UW Protest of Milo Yiannopoulos Unfolded." *Seattle Times*, January 23, 2017.

Woodard, Colin. *American Nations: A History of the Eleven Rival Regional Cultures of North America*. New York: Penguin Books, 2011.

World Economic Forum. "Global Social Mobility Index 2020: Why Economies Benefit from Fixing Inequality." January 2020, www.weforum.org /publications/global-social-mobility-index-2020-why-economies-bene fit-from-fixing-inequality.

Wright, George C. *Racial Violence in Kentucky 1865–1940: Lynchings, Mob Rule, and "Legal Lynchings."* Baton Rouge: Louisiana State University Press, 1990.

Wright, Will. "How This Jewish Attorney Escaped the Holocaust and Changed Eastern Kentucky Forever." *Lexington Herald-Leader*, April 23, 2019.

Wright, Will. "Kentucky Coal Communities Are Bracing for Financial Crisis." *The Messenger*, April 10, 2020. www.the-messenger.com/article _a104a5b7-29d4-5101-a21a-69130435e4dd.html.

WSON. "Gov. Beshear: $27.5 Billion in Investments Announced to Support Job Growth, Economic Development Across Kentucky." October 5, 2023.

Wuthnow, Robert. *The Left Behind: Decline and Rage in Rural America*. Princeton, NJ: Princeton University Press.

Yoakam, Dwight. "Readin', Rightin', Rt. 23." MP3 audio, track 5 on *Hillbilly Deluxe*, 1987.

YouGov. "*The Economist*/YouGov Poll." March 4–7, 2023. https://docs.cdn.you gov.com/1i6zpqns9b/econtoplines.pdf.

Youn, Soo. "Suboxone Maker Reckitt Benckiser to Pay $1.4 Billion in Largest Opioid Settlement in US History." ABC News, July 12, 2019.

Yudkin, Daniel, Stephen Hawkins, and Tim Dixon. "The Perception Gap: How False Impressions Are Pulling Americans Apart." More in Common, June 2019. https://perceptiongap.us/media/zaslaroc/perception-gap-re port-1-0-3.pdf.

Zeng, Zhen. "Jail Inmates in 2018." Bureau of Justice Statistics, U.S. Department of Justice. March 20200. www.bjs.ojp.gov/content/pub/pdf/ji18.pdf.

Zerubavel, Eviatar. *Don't Take It Personally: Personalness and Impersonality in Social Life*. Oxford: Oxford University Press, 2024.

Ziege, Nicole. "Pikeville Couple Grows Mushroom Farm." *Appalachian News-Express*, June 11, 2021.

Ziege, Nicole. "State Rep. Charles Booker Visits Pikeville, Discusses Candidacy." *Appalachian News-Express*, February 18, 2020.

Zito, Salena, and Brad Todd. *The Great Revolt: Inside the Populist Coalition Reshaping American Politics*. New York: Crown Forum, 2018.

Index

ABC News, 45, 173, 174
Abingdon, Virginia, 66
Adams, James Truslow, 29–30
African Americans: coal workers,
64–65, 68; Corbin expulsion (1919),
68–69, 163, 263, 296–97n; David
Maynard on, 116, 123–26, 162, 249;
film and television depictions of Black
history and family life, 139–40; Great
Migration, 64, 67–68, 87, 296n;
and Heimbach's white nationalist
march, 61–63, 78, 172, 176; "hood
and holler," 116, 123–26, 162, 249;
James Browning and, 162–63, 247–48;
Kentucky population during and
after the Civil War, 67–68; Kentucky
population during World War I, 68–69,
296–97n; mortality rates and drug
crisis of the 1970s-1980s, 165; parallels
to lives of poor whites, 116, 123–26,
162–63, 249; Pikeville population,
61–70; race and incarceration rates,
101–2; racial wealth gap, 125, 215–16;
Roger Ford on, 215–16; and segregated
Pikeville, 65–66, 69, 76; and sundown
towns, 68–69, 263, 296n; Tommy
Ratliff and, 139–40; University of
Pikeville students, 63, 176, 245–46;
and whites' education in Black history,
139–40, 162–63; whites' views of
government aid to, 249, 276–77;
whites' views of impact of slavery and
discrimination on, 242–43, 248–49,
275–77. *See also* Mullins, Ruth; racism
Akron, Ohio, 41
Albion's Seed (Fischer), 18
alcoholism, 7, 123, 165, 210; among
prisoners, 100; among white
nationalists, 184; pride hierarchy among
drinkers, 142; Tommy Ratliff and his
family, 140–43, 145
Alt-Right TV, 4
Amazon, 89, 132
American Dream, 29–34; alternative,
emotional, 128; belief in individual
responsibility and hard work as route to
success, 31–33, 89–90, 113, 135–36,
242–43; corporate, 33–34; "deep story"
and, 5, 205; Democrats and, 30–34,
242–43; pride paradox and, 29–34,
77–78, 127, 165, 219–20, 242, 258;
re-envisioning and equalizing access
to, 258, 261; Republicans and, 30–34,
242–43; standard of living embedded
in, 89; survivor's pride and, 128; Tommy
Ratliff on impossibility of achieving,
135–36, 155, 261
American Military University, 211
American National Election Studies
(2020), 17–18, 248, 275–77
American Rescue Plan Act, 326n
American Revolutionary War, 197
Americans for Prosperity, 263
AmerisourceBergen, 154

About the Author

Arlie Russell Hochschild is the author of many groundbreaking books, including *The Second Shift, The Managed Heart,* and *The Time Bind.* Her most recent book, *Strangers in Their Own Land* (The New Press), became an instant bestseller and was a finalist for a National Book Award. Hochschild is professor emerita of sociology at the University of California, Berkeley. She lives in Berkeley with her husband, the writer Adam Hochschild.

Publishing in the Public Interest

Thank you for reading this book published by The New Press. The New Press is a nonprofit, public interest publisher. New Press books and authors play a crucial role in sparking conversations about the key political and social issues of our day.

We hope you enjoyed this book and that you will stay in touch with The New Press. Here are a few ways to stay up to date with our books, events, and the issues we cover:

- Sign up at www.thenewpress.com/subscribe to receive updates on New Press authors and issues and to be notified about local events
- Like us on Facebook: www.facebook.com/newpressbooks
- Follow us on Twitter: www.twitter.com/thenewpress

Please consider buying New Press books for yourself; for friends and family; or to donate to schools, libraries, community centers, prison libraries, and other organizations involved with the issues our authors write about.

The New Press is a 501(c)(3) nonprofit organization. You can also support our work with a tax-deductible gift by visiting www.thenewpress.com/donate.